DATE			

© THE BAKER & TAYLOR CO.

INVESTMENT BANKING

A Tale of Three Cities

Samuel L. Hayes III
and
Philip M. Hubbard

Harvard Business School Press
Boston, Massachusetts

94 93 92 91 90   5 4 3 2

The paper used in this publication meets the
requirements of the American National Standard for
Permanence of Paper for Printed Library Materials Z39.49-1984.

Library of Congress Cataloging-in-Publication Data

Hayes, Samuel L.
   Investment banking: a tale of three cities / Samuel L. Hayes III
and Philip M. Hubbard.
      p.   cm.
   Includes bibliographical references.
   ISBN 0-87584-220-8 (alk. paper)
   1. Investment banking—New York (N.Y.) 2. Investment banking—
England—London.   3. Investment banking—Japan—Tokyo.   4. Banks
and banking. International.   I. Hubbard, Philip M., 1938–   .
II. Title.
HG4534.H39   1989
332.66—dc20   89-20019
                                                           CIP

To
Colette Devauvre Hubbard
and
Ann Barclay Hayes and Samuel L. Hayes, Jr.

Contents

ACKNOWLEDGMENTS

The research that produced this book involved the cooperation of many astute and helpful people as well as organizations in the United States, Europe, and the Far East. While it is impossible to list them all, we must nonetheless single out some for special mention.

Professor Joseph Auerbach has been an important resource throughout the process, as have been researchers William Allen, John Case, and Andrew Regan. In connection with the chapter on the history of the Japanese financial markets, we are also grateful to the Kodansha International Publishing Company for permission to utilize materials from writings by T. F. M. Adams and Iwao Hoshii.

Numerous financial firms, government and regulatory organizations, and their personnel contributed immensely to the research. In particular we want to mention Eugene Atkinson, Nicholas Downer, Frederick Fisher III, John Hennessy, Takuro Isoda, Ariyoshi Okumura, Michael Perry, Geoffrey Picard, and Robert Salomon. The New York Stock Exchange, the Securities Industry Association, and Securities Data Corporation were particularly valuable data sources.

A number of our colleagues at Harvard and elsewhere offered important feedback and suggestions. They include Ryoichi Mikitani, Hirokazu Sago, Michael Yoshino, and Dwight Crane, Director of the Division of Research at the Harvard Business School, which provided generous financial support for the entire project.

Our research assistants are, in many ways, the unsung heroines and heroes of the effort. They include Andrew Arends, Tomoya Aoki, Glen Earle, Barry Feldman, Sean Healey, Marnie Hoyle, Brian Imrie, Mindy Lee, Koichi Noda, Margarita Sweeney, Jun Tsusaka, and Kumiko Yokoi.

We received invaluable assistance and unfailing encouragement from our two editors at the Harvard Business School Press: Natalie Greenberg and Richard Luecke. Peggy McQueeney labored long and hard on the actual production of the manuscript, ably assisted by Duncan Bauer Todd.

While we received a wealth of material and assistance in our research, we are responsible for any shortcomings in the final product.

August 1989

Samuel L. Hayes III
Boston, Massachusetts

Philip M. Hubbard
London, England

INTRODUCTION

When the authors began their careers in finance, they prepared in a far simpler era of lower volatility, fewer options for investors and borrowers, and far less international activity. The post–World War II financial world was born out of a stable but highly compartmentalized framework created by the governments of a dozen countries in the aftermath of depression and war. Financial intermediaries with designations such as investment banks, merchant banks, clearing banks, commercial banks, city banks, stockbrokers, securities dealers, long-term credit banks, universal banks, discount houses, and private banks went about their appointed functions, generally competing within the confines of a single national capital market.

However, two powerful forces, the offspring of post–World War II politics and the technology of a shrinking world, breached these relatively closed financial systems:

Internationalization, which was seen as linking a plurality of friendly nations through free trade and cultural exchange, both as a substitute for old imperial rivalries and Soviet state socialism. This new economic order drew on the principle of comparative advantage for logic and saw trade rather than aid as an objective. One of its further manifestations was the European Economic Community, which, although a trading block, was relatively liberal, outward looking, and open to regular additions to its membership.

Deregulation, a trend that began gradually in a spirit of regulatory relaxation and later accelerated out of a rebirth of free enterprise economics. Deregulation had its roots in politics as well as economics and particularly in the perception that an unfettered private sector could improve upon rigorous systems of governmental control.

Although gradual and regularly redirected, the cumulative effect of these changes on the financing industry has been dramatic. For purposes of this volume, we have defined the financing industry to include managing public securities issues, corporate financial advisory and mergers-and-acquisitions services, and brokerage and market making in bonds and shares. We often refer to these activities collectively as investment banking and to the firms as vendors of investment banking services. Within roughly the past two decades,

1

such firms have grown from being nationally oriented businesses, sometimes employing less than a hundred people, to being international enterprises with twenty-five to fifty times as many staff located in multiple offices spread across Europe, North America, and Asia. Prior to 1970, many of the firms were privately owned and unfamiliar to the general public; since then, many have become publicly owned, and an even larger number have become high-profile organizations whose profits have multiplied accordingly.

As investment banking activity became more international, firms from Great Britain, Germany, the United States, France, Switzerland, Canada, and Japan began to encroach with greater frequency on each other's territory or into the freewheeling environment of the Euromarkets. The originally accepted logic was often the opportunity to follow an existing clientele overseas to service their international as well as domestic needs. The earliest to take advantage of these openings were often British, German, and U.S. firms, which undertook Euromarket expansions as early as the mid-1960s, while others followed in subsequent waves in the 1970s and 1980s. Some competitors, such as the German, French, and Swiss, came from universal banking traditions that encompassed both commercial and investment banking functions, while others were more focused stockbrokers or merchant banks. Widely dissimilar institutional orientations, varying national and firm cultural backgrounds, and differing emphasis on placing, origination, or trading gave these early jousts a unique flavor.

We began the research leading to this book because of our interest in the impressive growth of the offshore markets in public financings. The Euromarket, which represents the first truly "supranational" capital market, has grown exponentially for more than a decade to the point where, in 1986, it represented a larger volume of new financing than was completed in the corporate debt market in New York (excluding U.S. Treasury issues). This growth in the Euromarkets vis-à-vis the New York market seemed to us to be an important milestone along the road toward the "global market," which has been so widely discussed in the financial media in recent years. We set out to chronicle this development, to examine the strategies of several of the principal competitors and nations involved, and to consider the paths that further market integration might take.

What we found once we had gotten into the research was somewhat different. There was no doubt that this offshore market for money had grown dramatically in recent years and was now providing vigorous competition to the national markets (particularly in the United States), which had theretofore been the most important sources of fund raising and investing. There was also little question that there were powerful forces propelling the various national markets and firms toward more interaction, both with one another and with the London-based Euromarkets. Nevertheless, we also identified powerful independent forces that affect the pace and direction of that integration. Central among these are the important domestic capital markets around the world. These financing centers have evolved in unique ways over long periods of time in response to particular circumstances of culture and politics. They and their government overseers have not gone into eclipse in response to the international trends just discussed. On the contrary, they have continued to develop as discrete and unique capital-raising centers that must figure importantly in an understanding of the patterns of capital flows and competition in world financing.

Government attitudes toward globalization have been variable and oftentimes ambivalent. In earlier years, government administrations were preoccupied with the possibility of losing control over monetary and even fiscal policy. Through a financing-issue approval process centered around national currencies, as well as through exchange controls and licensing, governments first attempted to limit the flows of funds and the activities of competitors. Later, with the growth of deregulation, they became more accustomed to giving up selected ground to a range of progressively freer competition. Even today, the principal Group of Seven governments remain vitally interested in developments that touch their national debt management policies and are profoundly concerned by interest and exchange rate pressures, most of which now result from the heavy weight of capital rather than trade flows.

National regulation channeled the competitive struggles in the investment banking arena by determining the legal forms of the competitors and the products by which they could enter one another's territory. Universal banks grew accustomed to using the weight of their greater capital resources and captive placing power, while American firms saw corporate finance skills and secondary-market making as particular strengths. Thus, the interaction of governments with the financial markets and the process of globalization became an important focus of our study. The extended periods of time over which these interactions became apparent, and the importance that we attach to putting the national environments in proper context, have resulted in a considerable volume of historical research, which is reflected in this book.

The process of globalization occurs incrementally as borrowers and investors cross national borders to seize opportunities in foreign markets. As a result, the securities field has seen an internationalization of competition for the mandates of borrowers, not only between investment banking firms but also between individual capital markets. Cost and efficiency have usually been the most important determinants of success, and new-issue business has tended to gravitate to markets with lower levels of regulation, transaction costs, and interest rates. At the same time, the linkages between markets through arbitrage (assisted by interest-rate and currency swaps) have grown to the point where firms with global contacts and sophisticated techniques have often been able to mobilize lower-cost forms of finance by tapping a combination of markets. As a result, domestic investors have gained a more international perspective, and the assembly of diversified portfolios of multicurrency assets, often purchased through foreign intermediaries, has become an increasingly common occurrence. Again, history—in this case, a chronicle of landmark deals and trends that changed various markets—is the stuff of globalization.

In reacting to the changing currents of competition, many of them amplified by currency and interest rate volatility, individual investment banking firms have devised new and comprehensive strategies to position themselves globally. The contrasts among these strategies are sharp indeed. American, European, and Japanese firms are all approaching the task with different products, skills, and domestic firm histories. Thus, a principal mandate of this book is to examine the competitive strategies of some of the major players in light of both market-integrating forces and governmental intervention and to identify some of the factors likely to be key variables for the future. The three major geographic centers of that strategic positioning are, of course, London, New York, and Tokyo; hence our title, *Investment Banking: A Tale of Three Cities*.

In Chapter 1, we look back to some antecedents of present-day international finance. What becomes clear from this review is that there is ample precedent for upswings in international financial activity such as we have seen in the past twenty years. To be sure, most of the historical examples stemmed from government-related needs, often having to do with major wars. And these cross-border financings were strictly of a national-market-to-national-market nature.

The distinct departure in the history of the Euromarkets (discussed in Chapter 2) was that this did not represent country-to-country transactions, but rather transactions outside the constraints of national regulation. In a sense, the capital being tapped in the Euromarkets was like the debris from earth satellites shot into space. It circled the globe outside the normal reach of individual countries and was available for the borrowing by a needy capital user on what-ever terms the user and the investors could agree upon, regardless of the rules that would ordinarily apply if the funds were being raised in the host country's own national capital market.

Chapter 2 and Chapter 3, which deal with the contemporary Euromarket environment, demonstrate that, in the absence of regula-tory constraints, price competition and innovation are encouraged. These chapters also reveal, however, that this extraordinary market-place is not the free-trade nirvana it is sometimes claimed to be. The currencies utilized there are "free" only to the extent that the coun-tries of issue wish them to be. Most of the countries have from time to time shown ambivalence in this area, although recent trends, heavily influenced by the politics of deregulation, are positive. In addition, some vendors have recently drawn back (at least temporarily) toward their own national markets after a giddy period of growth in commit-ment to the Euromarkets.

Following a review of competition in the Euromarkets, we exam-ine several of the most important national financial markets, since these still constitute the bulk of the total worldwide financing volume and appear to continue to be the principal building blocks on which vendors base their overall strategy. We chose, therefore, to look at the domestic investment banking environments in the United States, Japan, and the United Kingdom. Obviously, we are far from all-inclusive, since we did not examine in detail such important national markets as Switzerland, West Germany, or France. Nonetheless, it was our hope that an analysis of these markets would show the factors at the national level that influence the ways in which the national governments and vendors would participate at the suprana-tional level and also give some clues about how principal markets might evolve in the future.

Chapter 4 is an historical perspective of the U.S. securities mar-kets. Following the text's parallel organization structure, Chapter 5 looks at the recent operations of the investment banking industry in the United States and the quality of competition there. One is struck by the extent to which the U.S. investment banking industry has become both more concentrated and bipolar in recent years, and by the persistent informal barriers to entry that relegate foreign securi-ties firms to a relatively minor role in that marketplace.

We then turn to Japan, which has become a huge source of ex-portable capital for the world. Chapter 6 takes an historical look at the country's public financial markets since the Meiji Restoration and provides a vivid contrast to the United States in national purpose and the role of government leadership. In the United States, both centralized government supervision and large, powerful private-sector institutions have long been feared. In Japan, the public perception of external threat to the country produced a profoundly different attitude toward government intervention and the power of individual private-sector companies. As a result, institutional arrangements were put in place that, despite the efforts of the U.S. occupation forces after World War II to remold them, have yielded financial services competitors and a pattern of doing business (discussed in Chapter 7) markedly different from that of the United States. A common outcome, however, is that the barriers to entry for foreign securities firms in both markets are formidable, thereby reinforcing our conviction that the process of market integration is far from complete.

Next, we examine the British national capital-market evolution, which has greatly influenced the development of other markets. Chapter 8 looks at the laissez-faire environment within which the classic British merchant banks (on which the U.S. wholesale investment banks are modeled) operated during the Empire and thereafter. With a long history of international commercial and financial operations, the United Kingdom was receptive to financial market innovation, a trait that was to serve it well in capturing for London the largest part of the Euromarket activity. Later, the U.K. government engineered the deregulatory "Big Bang" and the Financial Services Act 1986, which imposed additional rules and regulations on both domestic public financing and London-based Euromarket activities. Chapter 9 provides a snapshot of the contemporary British domestic-public financial markets.

Because our study is focused as much on the strategy of individual firms as on the characteristics of the marketplaces themselves, we uncovered considerable data on how such firms have fared both in their home markets and ventures abroad. To illustrate specific evolutions as well as strategies and tactics for international expansion, we have profiled three distinctly different vendors. Salomon Brothers (Chapter 10) is an American wholesale investment bank that has pursued a global strategy with particular targets on Tokyo and London. Nomura Securities (Chapter 11) is the largest Japanese securities firm, a leading retail broker, and, in the late 1980s, one of the most profitable private-sector corporations in the world. It, too, has articulated a global strategy, prioritizing the U.S. market in New York and London for special attention. Credit Suisse First Boston (Chapter 12) is a joint venture between one of the classic European "universal banks" and a leading U.S. wholesale investment bank. Its unique success in the Euromarket setting is worthy of careful study for clues as to how vendors might band together to compete effectively in a future marketplace that will be even more closely integrated globally.

Chapter 13 draws together the common threads relating to individual firm strategy: its formulation, its critical elements, its national bias, and its limitations in helping individual firms deal with the problems of planning in a rapidly changing environment. Finally, Chapter 14 summarizes our conclusions with respect to government and the markets, the process of globalization, and the competitive behavior of individual firms.

For readers interested in the more detailed securities industry data on which our study drew, Appendices A, B, and C include vendor statistics on the Euromarkets, the domestic U.S. markets, and the domestic Japanese markets, respectively.

CHAPTER 1

THE ORIGINS OF INTERNATIONAL BANKING

The business of international investment banking has been shaped by history. The chronicle of the growth of this business and of the securities marketplace is essentially the story of episodic needs for capital that outgrew the capacity of conventional (and usually domestic) private banking.

In earlier periods, instances of outsized financing crises were typically precipitated by governments and often involved dramatic political events, wars being the most notable. As colonial expansion and industrial development gathered steam, first in Europe and later in other parts of the world, large business-related financing needs arose that challenged and stimulated the public financing markets.

As the scale of government and private capital needs expanded, the role of what we know today as the investment bankers—the financing intermediaries—has been key. In earlier periods, these bankers worked alone in their efforts to stitch together large financing arrangements. The infrastructure of modern-day finance just did not exist. Securities exchanges were either absent or extremely primitive. Credit-rating facilities and much of the basic data upon which to base credit assessment were nonexistent. Correspondent and interbanking relationships were also primitive, and because of both the paucity of hard information and its slow transmission, vendors in each geographic center of finance and commerce had to act either alone or, if collaborating with partners in other locations, move with sometimes fatal caution and slowness. Yet despite these difficulties, the eighteenth and nineteenth centuries saw the formation of nascent "syndicates" of bankers to share both the burden of distribution and the accompanying capital exposures, an arrangement that would grow dramatically in the twentieth century.

The Church, Usury, and Bills of Exchange

Following the dictums of the Catholic Church against the practice of usury, early banking suppressed the lending function and drove it underground. The condemnation of lending in exchange for a fixed profit, which was reiterated at the Council of Reims in 1049 and at various other times in the Middle Ages, did not, however, extend to currency exchanges. Pope Gregory the Great felt free to avail himself of such services as early as A.D. 600 while reproving usury, that is, interest charges.[1]

The Catholic prohibition on usury undoubtedly delayed the introduction of debt securities into European commerce and also led certain non-Catholic groups, notably Jews, and later Protestants, to specialize in the money-lending business. It also permitted the development of Bills of Exchange, which were negotiable contracts allowing the holder to exchange one currency for another at a future date. These flourished during the Renaissance because the central focus of most such bills was an exchange transaction. They were generally considered legal by church scholars, but in their several varieties, a number undoubtedly contained elements of interest compensation built into the future foreign exchange quotation. Such bills therefore could be used as de facto borrowing or credit instruments. The debate about interest did not, of course, extend to equity ownership shares or parts of an enterprise, since the church's focus was on the usurious receipt of a *certain* profit as part of a contractual undertaking. The receipt of profits from an *uncertain* venture, which might either succeed or fail, was regarded as acceptable, much as Islamic law today treats loans and interest.

During the Renaissance, the weakening of church restrictions on commerce allowed the banking industry to take on relatively greater importance, and distinctive vendors with brand images began to emerge. While most such banks remained local in character, the largest ones developed branches or alliances in other European countries. The Medici bank, which dealt in a number of Bills of Exchange that were actually camouflaged loans, had its headquarters in Florence and branches in Venice, Rome, Milan, Bruges, Avignon, London, and Geneva by the mid-fifteenth century. London, at that time, was regarded as something of a frontier town.[2] Thus, despite the ambivalence of the church and the general public, banking prospered and, with the introduction of foreign branches, became international not only in its principal product but also its geographic reach. Individual branches of the Medici bank were separately capitalized, with the

1. For a more detailed discussion of banking and usury see, Center for Medieval and Renaissance Studies, UCLA, *The Dawn of Modern Banking* (New Haven: Yale University Press, 1979), pp. 3–52; and Francis A. Lees and Maximo Eng, *International Financial Markets* (New York: Praeger, 1975), pp. 3–4.
2. Raymond de Roover, *The Medici Bank: Its Organization, Management, Operations and Decline* (New York: New York University Press, 1948).

central partnership in Florence retaining a majority of the capital but with local managers having a minority ownership stake and a somewhat larger share in branch profits, as is true in some of today's investment banking profit-sharing arrangements.

But just as some banking institutions in the twentieth century have risen to prominence only to subsequently fade from the scene, the same pattern afflicted notable earlier bankers. By the late fifteenth century, the Medici bank had fallen into difficulty, especially after the death in 1464 of its key leader, Cosimo de Medici. His successor, Lorenzo de Medici, was more interested in politics and the arts than banking, and the profitability of the lending and bills business consequently declined substantially.[3] By 1478, the bank's London branch, which had made loans to King Edward IV, had to be closed with substantial write-offs. In 1494, even the Medici bank's home office in Florence, which had made a number of imprudent loans to local princes, was closed because it had insufficient assets to meet the claims of its depositors. This was not the last time that a bank or borrower of formerly unchallengeable standing would fall into insolvency.

By the seventeenth and eighteenth centuries, northern and western European prejudices against lending for profit had diminished. Economic prosperity had advanced to the point where both surplus savings and new types of financing needs began to appear, which portended the growth of public securities and bankers to deal in them. First among these were merchant venturing needs, often linked to the colonial powers' overseas expansion in exploration and trade. Individual shipping ventures, as well as such enterprises as the Dutch East India Company, were normally financed by equity interests privately distributed among wealthy government personages or merchants from the sponsoring countries. Similarly, early mining ventures were routinely funded by the issue and sale of shares or participations. The second type of need was the financing of governments, ranging from major European countries to smaller princely states, often for the purpose of pursuing military campaigns. Since such wars obviously did not lend themselves to being financed through equity participations, their funding commonly took the form of "loan contracting."

Loan Contracting and Securities Syndication

Loan contracting flourished in several western European countries in the late eighteenth century, especially in Holland and England.

---

3. Those who value the art of the Renaissance, of which Lorenzo "The Magnificent" was a leading patron, will forgive his shortcomings as a banker.

Lenders would make a written contract with either a king or a government. Loans were frequently secured: in the seventeenth century, specific assets were pledged,[4] but, by the eighteenth century, liens on streams of revenue from customs duties or other sources became the more common form, much like the municipal revenue bonds so common in the United States today. These loans were originally taken almost entirely by the lenders for their own investment accounts but subsequently came to be shared through syndication with other merchants and wealthy individuals. It was through this syndication process that a contracting bank could broaden and enlarge its distribution of a debt financing to a proprietary list of investors and thereby both strengthen its bargaining power with the borrower and diversify its own assets and those of its in-house clients.[5] That syndication technique was a cornerstone that was to evolve into the modern-day risk-sharing and securities distribution process we now know as *securities underwriting*.

Initially, such loans were mostly transnational, involving a borrower from one country and lenders from another, and often developed into continuing relationships. For example, the leading Amsterdam firm of Hope and Company (now known as Mees & Hope) floated ten loans for the Kingdom of Sweden between 1767 and 1787 and eighteen loans for Russia from 1788 to 1793. In such instances, the loan contractor generally assumed responsibility for retailing the bonds to investors not only on the Amsterdam stock exchange but also elsewhere in Europe. Thus the financing business was, even in some of its earliest manifestations, essentially interna-

---

4. C. K. Hobson in *The Export of Capital* (London: Constable and Company, 1914) describes how Charles I of England borrowed £300,000 in 1625 from the States-General of the Netherlands to carry on the war against Spain by pledging the crown jewels and certain gold vessels.
5. Fritz Redlich in *The Molding of American Banking: Men and Ideas* makes the point that the practice of loan contracting became "investment banking" when banks began purchasing loans entirely for distribution (syndication) and when final investors were no longer in competition with such intermediaries for the mandates of borrowers (pp. 320, 326). However, our research indicates that the practice of syndication was well established by the late eighteenth century and that the individual generally referred to as the most important loan contractor of his time, Walter Boyd, was adept at both syndication and distribution in the 1790s. (See S. R. Cope, *Walter Boyd: A Merchant Banker in the Age of Napoleon* [Gloucester, England: A. Sutton, 1983], pp. 24, 58–59, 159–160, and 162.) In general, syndication appears to have been adapted to the needs and opportunities of a particular financing. The term "investment banker" was rarely employed in the U.S. securities industry before the late 1880s, although it was used in England as early as the 1840s by traveling salesmen. (Vincent P. Carosso, *Investment Banking in America: A History* [Cambridge, Mass.: Harvard University Press, 1970], p. ix.)

tional and characterized by the "relationship banking" that so preoccupies the present-day investment banking community.

During the 1790s, the most important loan contractor in the London market was undoubtedly Walter Boyd, who headed the firm of Boyd, Benfield and Co. Working with the encouragement of William Pitt, then Britain's prime minister, in 1794 Boyd completed the placement of a large loan of £6 million for the Imperial Government of Austria, placed principally in the British market.[6] At the time, the Austrians were allies of Britain against the new French Republic, which had declared war on a number of the European powers. Boyd had obtained an introduction to the Austrian government through the firm of Veuve Nettine et Fils, which was prominent in the Austrian sector of what is now Belgium and with whom Boyd had a long working relationship. Following this important operation, Boyd successfully obtained the mandate for a financing of £18 million for the British government itself. This, in turn, led to other large operations.

Financial Markets as Government Policy Instruments

The records of Boyd's discussions with Pitt and the Bank of England make it clear that the government believed that favorable conditions in the London capital market were important to its national policy objectives, a sentiment that carries forward to contemporary financial markets and governments. The British national debt had grown from £16 million in 1702 to £128 million by 1775, to £249 million by 1783, and to £520 million by 1802. City of London capital was fundamental to the government's continued successful refunding. Furthermore, making financing available on reasonable terms to Britain's allies and denying it to belligerent France was seen as astute management of wartime relationships. Thus, the level of interest rates and the volume of new securities issues on the financial market were then, as now, a constant preoccupation of both the government and Britain's private sector.

Despite its successes, Boyd's firm in London suffered the fate of innumerable bankers before and since: it became overextended after 1798 and was forced to close (although it was ultimately able to repay all creditors). The turbulent era of the French Revolution and the wars among France, Holland, England, Austria, and smaller states that erupted in its wake not only produced substantial borrowing requirements but also caused significant disruptions in the financial markets. While these conditions led to difficulties at many firms such as

6. Cope, *Walter Boyd*, p. 24.

Boyd's, they also contributed to the rise of new merchant bankers such as the Rothschilds.[7]

After having dealt in cloth and coinage, Meyer Amschel Rothschild became active in Frankfurt in the middle of the eighteenth century in money changing and discounting bills for the local ruler, the Landgrave of Hesse-Kassel.[8] Rothschild later sent his five sons to the financial capitals of Europe—Paris, Vienna, Naples, London, and Frankfurt—thereby laying the foundation for an important family-run international banking house operating under the sign of "The Five Arrows." One of the sons, Nathan Meyer Rothschild, arrived in Manchester, England, in 1797, and moved to London in 1806. There he became involved in transmitting subsidies on behalf of the government to Britain's European allies and later in raising funds for them. It was their understanding of the interaction of international politics and finance and the reputation for reliability in meeting their end of the bargain that placed firms like Rothschilds and Baring Brothers ahead of purely domestic firms and the local stock exchange community.

In addition to pioneering the technique of syndicating risk and distribution responsibilities, the loan contractors of the late eighteenth and early nineteenth centuries also used a form of fixed-price underwriting in which they, together with others in the syndicate, purchased securities from the issuer at a fixed price before distributing the securities in the marketplace. In return for the opportunity to earn an underwriting commission, they accepted the risk of being able to resell the securities above their cost price. Absorbing this underwriting risk, a hallmark of the securities industry even today, obviously required an understanding of financial conditions. And one of the principal skills of the international loan business from the beginning was the assessment of markets and the taking of soundings,

7. The term "merchant banker" is mainly of English origin and was often seen in its earliest form as "merchants and bankers." Generally, it describes a firm that began as merchants or traders and then extended its activities by offering credit to its clients. Such credits were sometimes retained by the merchant banker as principal but were often sold as Bills of Exchange or acceptances. By the early twentieth century most such firms had ceased to act as goods merchants and were concentrated in trade finance, securities, investment management, and venture capital; however, the original term is still used. In the United States the term "securities dealer" or "investment banker" was the more common form, although in the 1980s certain U.S. investment banks began to refer to leveraged buyout and corporate restructuring activities where they invest funds as principal as "merchant banking."
8. Karl Erich Born, *International Banking in the 19th and 20th Centuries* (New York: St. Martin's, 1983), pp. 25–26, 52–58.

all leading to a judgment as to what terms were appropriate for a particular borrower. William Pitt's conversations with Walter Boyd were riddled with discussions as to appropriate terms and conditions.[9]

Pax Britannica and the Rise of London

With the defeat of Napoleon at Waterloo in 1815, a period of greater political stability ensued. With Britain triumphant, the world's financial center of gravity—which had shifted since the Middle Ages from Northern Italy to Spain and Portugal for a brief period, then to France and to Amsterdam—came to rest in London. There it would remain for one hundred years until yet another war (World War I) forced that market's temporary closing and subsequent decline. New York would then take its turn on center stage.

The end of the Napoleonic Wars found English merchants and aristocracy with substantial surplus funds to invest. In 1818, Prussia was able to float a £5-million issue through Rothschild, and there followed a whole series of international financing originating in London. During the continuing prosperity of the early 1820s, such strong demand developed for foreign issues that Spain, Chile, Peru, Mexico, Brazil, and Colombia each came to the London market at least twice. Many of these financings fell into default within a few years, and investigations revealed that some had originally been undertaken in scandalous circumstances.

For instance, during the insurrection of the Greeks against the Turks beginning in 1821, Greece formed a committee (of which the British poet Lord Byron was a member) to float bond issues in the London market. The first loan in 1824 for £800,000 was successful, and a second financing of £2 million was undertaken in 1825 by the loan contracting firm of J & S Ricardo.[10] At a point when British government bonds were yielding 4 percent, these bonds required a current yield of almost 10 percent and an even higher yield to maturity. When the Greek government subsequently defaulted on the bonds, a committee of bondholders was formed in late 1826 to find out what had happened to the funds. The committee learned that a large portion of the financing had never reached Greece but had, instead, been paid to various agents, middlemen, and hangers-on. Such unsavory practices, together with defaults, led the London

9. Cope, *Walter Boyd*, pp. 75, 89.
10. See C. K. Hobson, *The Export of Capital* (London: Constable, 1914), p. 101; and Mark Tapley, *International Portfolio Management* (London: Euromoney, 1986), pp. 2–3.

Stock Exchange to subsequently adopt the practice of refusing quotation to a new issue if any of the borrower's outstanding bonds were in default.

Growth in U.S. Financings

During the 1830s, a number of British railways managed to maintain and even increase their dividends during the recession and panic of 1837. This, in turn, gave rise to a favorable market for railway securities in London. During the 1840s and 1850s, a large number of bond issues for British and foreign railways from the United States, China, France, and other countries were undertaken, further developing the public securities markets in London. The profitability and frequency of U.S. railway financings, as well as issues for individual U.S. state governments, encouraged European banking firms to forge alliances with American securities firms or to establish their own branches in the United States as conduits for such new business.

In 1828, London's Baring Brothers added an American partner, Joshua Bates; two years later the firm established Thomas Ward as its resident American agent.[11] At the same time, the firm increased its alliances with other American banking and securities firms. In 1837, the Frankfurt and Paris Rothschild firms sent a young German-born executive, August Belmont, to New York to investigate conditions. Following the bankruptcy of Rothschild's existing American agent in 1837, Belmont established a new firm in his own name and became the Rothschild agent in New York. A few years later, in the 1840s, George Peabody, an American citizen, moved to London and established an investment business that initially sold bonds of the state of Maryland to British investors. In 1854, he took into his partnership another American, Junius Spencer Morgan; when Peabody retired in 1864, the firm was renamed J.S. Morgan & Co. While its principal offices were in London, it operated a significant business in the United States under the name of Junius's son, J. Pierpont Morgan.[12] Leading the pack in U.S. railway financing in the 1850s was Winslow, Lanier & Co., which had established ties with American railways for the negotiation of railway securities and which had alliances with the Rothschild banks in London and Paris as well as Hope and Company in Amsterdam.

As the nineteenth century wore on, the mixture of financing began to change, reflecting the development of private-sector corporate financing needs. In aggregate terms, government loans were still very important and in 1870 represented approximately 60 percent of

11. Carosso, *Investment Banking in America*, pp. 9–10.
12. Ibid., pp. 20–21.

British foreign investment. By 1914, however, their total share of British foreign investment had dropped to less than a third, while investments in railway securities had increased to 37 percent of the total. The remaining shares of British foreign investments were spread among mines, public utility companies, industrial enterprises, and other interests. Nevertheless, sovereign government finance remained extremely important, and when N.M. Rothschild & Sons celebrated its one-hundredth anniversary in 1904, a catalog of public issues covering the previous century was published. This catalog showed total loans raised on behalf of European governments of £1,300 million (the equivalent of more than U.S. $7 billion at the time).[13]

The international and entrepreneurial nature of the securities business in the United States as it developed in the nineteenth century is illustrated by the story of Joseph Seligman, a Jewish native of Bavaria who arrived in America in 1837 at the age of seventeen with resources of less than one hundred dollars. Seligman's first job was as a store clerk in a small Pennsylvania town. Within twelve months, he had left his job to become a traveling peddler, and within five years he was joined by his seven brothers, who dealt in a variety of domestic and imported goods. By the outbreak of the Civil War in 1860, the Seligman brothers had established outlets for goods in New York, St. Louis, and San Francisco and were importing and exporting regularly to London. Profits from the clothing business were substantial and led the family to establish the New York banking firm J. & W. Seligman & Co. During the Civil War, when U.S. government financing requirements grew dramatically, Seligman distributed some $200 million of U.S. government bonds in Germany, where the company had opened a Frankfurt office in 1862. By 1864, J. & W. Seligman & Co. had established another branch in London; others in Paris, Amsterdam, Berlin, and San Francisco followed. In 1869, the immensely prosperous James Seligman purchased a seat on the New York Stock Exchange.[14]

Effective communication was central to the operation of the far-flung Seligman branches, and, as it was with the Rothschilds, the network of contacts within the family was vital. The parallel to modern investment banks as vendors of information is obvious since they

13. Born, *International Banking*, p. 56.
14. As Carosso states in *Investment Banking*, "What distinguished these firms, such as Drexel, Morgan & Co. and J. & W. Seligman & Co., was their ability to recruit foreign capital. Some houses did this through branches of their own in Europe; others like Kidder, Peabody & Co. maintained close ties with a prominent London bank, in this case Baring Brothers" (p. 30).

too nourish highly developed internal communications systems and the selective transmission of important information to their clients.

The nineteenth-century application of international public-security-issue techniques to the U.S. corporate securities sector is illustrated by the 1879 sale of 250,000 shares of New York Central common stock by railroad magnate William H. Vanderbilt. Vanderbilt needed to dispose of shares to reduce his stake in the railroad, but he realized that such a large offering in the New York market would not only depress share prices but raise questions about his own motives in selling. He therefore consulted J. P. Morgan in New York, and they agreed to market the shares in England through a syndicate headed by Philadelphia-based Drexel, Morgan & Co.—which had a London office—and by Morgan's father's firm, J. S. Morgan & Co. The syndicate purchased Vanderbilt's shares for $120 per share ($30 million) and resold them for $130 per share ($32.5 million). As an added inducement, investors were guaranteed an 8 percent dividend for the following five years and assured that their investment would be protected by J. P. Morgan joining the board of directors of the New York Central. When the skillfully orchestrated operation became public knowledge in America, J. P. Morgan, then forty years old, was acclaimed by the press as the leading railroad banker in the United States.[15] Once again, the imprimatur of the investment banking intermediary implied a credit-screening process and a presumption of quality that carried the day. And both the celebrity and franchise value of the House of Morgan were further embellished.

Syndication and Sales

It was during the nineteenth century that issue procedures and techniques began to harden and become more uniform on both sides of the Atlantic. While in England it had been the custom to underwrite issues at fixed prices by having banks enter into purchase contracts with issuers, thereby assuming the market risk of success or failure, this procedure began to be fully accepted in the United States only after 1870. The first such issue in the United States was one undertaken by Jay Cooke & Co. for the Pennsylvania Railroad in the amount of $2 million in 1870 (for more on Cooke, see Chapter 4). Lists of banks participating in the syndicates for particular issuers became more traditional and did not change from financing to financing as frequently after 1870. It is not surprising that banks were particularly attentive to the positions they were accorded within such

15. Ibid., p. 37.

more-or-less static syndicates, and that "apex" firms—firms that were most active in originating issues for distribution by themselves and others—came to exercise great power in the choice of participating firms and the development of syndicate lists. The advantage of apex firms in such situations stemmed not only from their relative positions of leadership within the industry and their traditional closeness to the most prolific borrowers, but also from the financing commission structure. Although the total commission or gross spread for an issue often ranged between 3 and 5 percent, the lead manager of the financing, in return for its efforts in origination and documentation, generally took a management commission of ½–1 percent of the total principal amount of the issue off the top; it divided the remaining fees among itself and the other firms depending on their underwriting and selling responsibilities.

Although syndication was desirable from the standpoint of distribution and risk sharing, it cut against the natural competitive feelings of the principal banking firms. In 1865, for example, while competing for a financing by the Austrian government, Baron Nathaniel Rothschild wrote to his colleagues in London regarding the need for syndication: "I think you will not only require your friend Baring, but likewise some of the joint-stock banks to unite with you, and however disagreeable it may be to have such partners, if it is the means of making the affair go down, you ought not to mind it."[16]

During the eighteenth and nineteenth centuries, the quality of bank sponsorship was generally felt to be one of the most important elements in international financings. Having a major financier or bank lead manage and thereby sponsor an issue gave the financing a definite edge in attracting investors, banking firms often refused to participate in the syndication of issues they felt to be of questionable credit standing. Our sources do not record what happened to J & S Ricardo following their leadership of the scandalous Greek financings in England in the 1820s, but we can surmise that one reason for their lack of continuing success was the disclosure in October 1826 regarding that Greek loan. A default in an outstanding financing not only had an adverse impact on the sponsoring bank's reputation but also often reduced the value of the bank's trading inventories in such securities. Defaults obviously also hurt the fortunes of investors and friends of the bank who had subscribed to the issue at its original offering. The 5 percent Greek issue of 1825, which was originally offered at 56½, was quoted as low as 14½ in the 1826–1827 period.

16. Stanley Chapman, *The Rise of Merchant Banking* (London: Allen & Unwin, 1984), p. 156, for reference to the records and archives of N. M. Rothschild & Sons, London.

The merchant banks that had led the financing of previous issues were expected by clients and syndicate members to follow the borrower's affairs on an ongoing basis. Should default occur, such banks were expected to negotiate with the issuer regarding early resumption of debt-service payments or exchange of old securities for new bonds. Such refinancings occurred frequently in the nineteenth and early twentieth centuries, with major government borrowers from Latin America, Asia, and even individual American states going into default and then re-emerging after a period of time. A present-day parallel can be found in the efforts of investment bankers such as Drexel Burnham to refinance "junk bond" financings whose issuers are unable to meet the payment expectations built into the original financing contract.

Collateral and Currency

Although collateral was sometimes involved as security for certain government loans and more frequently for railroad bonds, foreclosing on such property and reselling it for the benefit of the bondholders in the event of default was often fraught with procedural land mines. However, collateral did provide a bargaining tool in the event of default by allowing bondholders' representatives a stronger position in negotiations, or a ranking superior to that of other creditors in the subsequent restructuring of debt.

Of course, the instantaneous international bank transfers and communications that are now daily routine in moving funds and information from one country to another did not exist in the nineteenth century. Thus, both the development of financing proposals and the formulation of distribution plans moved much more slowly. Although some financings involved parties from several countries, the typical pattern was for a borrower in one country, such as a U.S. railroad, to offer an issue of securities in another country, such as Great Britain, over a period of several months. In such a financing, the bonds typically would be denominated in the currency of the lenders (in this case pounds sterling), and the form of the securities, including the law under which the contract was drawn, would be that pertaining in the lenders' country (in this case, English law). Although the currency of denomination was generally the currency of the lenders, occasionally this arrangement was modified if a lender wanted to receive payment in a second currency, or in gold. Obviously, this type of option was more frequent in cases where there were doubts about the long-term value of the original currency and concern about the effect of inflation on the bondholders' prospective payment stream. The development in recent years of a broad variety of derivative securities is a similar response by investment bankers and issuers to the need to create securities that enhance opportunities or reduce costs for either or both parties to the financing transaction.

International issues such as those just described came to be called "foreign bonds," and the London Stock Exchange even set up a separate section for foreign securities in its quotation sheet. Foreign bond issues were, of course, most frequently offered in countries where there were savings and balance-of-payment surpluses, especially Britain, Holland, and France in the nineteenth century. While demand in the lender's own country represented the largest subscriptions to such issues, references in the literature regularly allude to investors from third countries maintaining accounts in, for example, London and purchasing foreign bonds offered there or subscribing to such issues through non-British banks. Thus, by the late nineteenth century, London had developed a significant entrepôt activity selling sterling-denominated securities of non-British borrowers to non-British investors and collecting fees for placement, custody, and paying-agency services.

Broader Distribution

Although the distribution of public bond issues during the nineteenth century was generally completed in large blocks to major individual and institutional purchasers, small investors became increasingly important after 1860. The Philadelphia firm of Jay Cooke & Co. was the single most active firm in opening up this channel of distribution in America. In the mid-1860s, as we will discuss in the next chapter, Cooke employed advertising and individual salesmen to attract buying interest in U.S. government securities from small investors and was a substantial factor in funding operations in the northern states during the Civil War. This process of packaging debt arrangements into marketable securities for sale throughout England, France, and the United States (known today as "securitization") led to significant growth in the business of investment banking during the years leading up to World War I. Such securitization both increased the numbers of issues completed during that time to well beyond twenty financings per year for most major securities firms and expanded the total amounts raised in each subsequent financing.

The Far East

The active market in securities on both sides of the Atlantic was not replicated in the Pacific Basin, and Tokyo remained very much a local financial marketplace. As Chapter 6 details, until 1868 the Shoguns reigned over a semifeudal economy, consciously endeavoring to limit international influences. Even following the restoration of the Meiji emperor in that year, modernization did not come easily. When, in 1881, government officials suggested that foreign loans should be floated to bolster the country's external reserves, a cabinet debate over the advisability of involvement with western capitalists had to be personally resolved by the emperor. After considering the matter, he decided against such a financing, quoting advice he had received earlier from U.S. President Ulysses S. Grant. "Look at Egypt, Spain and Turkey," Grant had counseled on a visit to Japan, "and consider their pitiable condition. . . . Some nations like to lend money to poor nations very much. By this means they flaunt their authority and cajole the poor nation. The purpose of lending money is to get political power for themselves."[17] By the early twentieth century, however, a stronger and more confident Japan had become a regular borrower in foreign markets, but there was little two-way commerce in securities until the 1980s, when Japan became a major international investor (see Chapter 7).

The linkages in the nineteenth century between the growth in international commerce and the supply of financial resources were inescapable. As the great colonial powers Britain and France, later joined by Germany, vied for success elsewhere in the world, the availability of equity and bond financing in their capital markets (often for railway development) became a significant factor in their geographic expansion. In the Ottoman Empire, it was the efforts of Germany acting through the Deutsche Bank to complete the Berlin to Baghdad railway; in Canada, it was the completion of the Canadian Pacific Railway; and in South Africa, it was the building of railway lines north from the Cape of Good Hope. All were alliances between colonialist ambitions and international financing activities. Similarly, France's purchases of significant amounts of Russian Czarist bonds followed the rapprochement between those two countries after the signing of the Franco-Russian Military Convention in August 1892. Financing railway expansion in China became a means by which the great powers hoped to expand their influence in that country.[18] In addition to public financings, such arrangements often involved the purchase of materials and supplies on a tied-in basis from the colonial power. Thus, such countries, by means of their financing infrastruc-

---

17. Kamekichi Takahashi, *The Rise and Development of Japan's Modern Economy* (Tokyo, Jiji, 1969), quoted in *Japan: 1853–1881*, Harvard Business School Technical Note #9-375-347.
18. Born, *International Banking*, pp. 146–155.

ture, in effect were often exporting capital equipment and construction services on a deferred-payment basis.

The Tilt toward New York

World War I ushered in a new era in international investment banking. Following a general mobilization of Russia on July 30, 1914, which was proclaimed on the 31st, all the principal stock exchanges in Europe were closed in fear of financial panic. The New York Stock Exchange, however, remained open. Although prices declined initially, America benefited from being the only principal market to continue trading. The U.S. dollar was also the only currency that remained convertible into gold.[19] During the years, between August 1914 and April 1917, of America's official neutrality, the United States (like Japan) enjoyed a substantial increase in economic activity fueled by demand from Europe for wartime goods. A high rate of domestic savings, together with the fact that the New York market remained open, encouraged substantial amounts of international financing to be directed from Europe to the U.S. market. Despite the official neutrality of the American government, U.S. investment banking firms increased new-issue activity dramatically, especially for British and French interests. Indeed, the $500 million Anglo-French loan of October 1915 was the largest bond offering ever undertaken in the U.S. market to that date. It was lead managed by J. P. Morgan & Co., which headed a substantial distribution syndicate. The Morgan bank also acted as purchasing agent for the British and French governments and assisted the Russian government with certain purchases of arms and other equipment.

These public financing efforts were seen as a means of providing war matériel to the friendly powers on an extended-term basis. While Germany undertook several financing operations in the United States during this same period, they were relatively modest by comparison and generally of short duration. A compilation of foreign loans during the period August 1914 to April 1917 shows Britain as the largest borrower at $1,250 million, France with $640 million, Russia with $107 million, and the central powers, Germany and Austria, raising only $35 million.[20] In addition, U.S. investment bankers arranged for the resale to American investors of more than $3 billion of American securities previously held in Europe; some of them offered voluntarily and others acquired by European governments on a compulsory basis to obtain much-needed foreign exchange. Financial operations

19. Lees and Eng, *International Financial Markets.*
20. Carosso, *Investment Banking in America*, pp. 193–223.

linked to these international war-related developments were the principal source of business for American investment bankers during this period and resulted in the transformation of the United States from a debtor nation to a creditor nation. They also effectively succeeded in transferring the financial capital of the world from London to New York.

After the entry of the United States into the war in April 1917, the burden of investment banking shifted to financing the U.S. government's requirements, as Chapter 3 chronicles. During the period 1917–1919, four Liberty Loans of U.S. Treasury bonds totaling $17 billion were offered, together with a victory loan of $4.5 billion in April 1919. To raise such comparatively large sums, the entire distribution system of the U.S. investment and commercial banking industries was mobilized and succeeded in attracting the interest of small individual savers as well as large investors. This increased interest, once stimulated, solidified and thus created fertile ground for the U.S. public's much broader and more active interest in securities during the 1920s.

The decade of the 1920s was a prolific period for the issuance of foreign, as well as domestic, securities in the United States. Such operations were generally denominated in U.S. dollars and consisted of debt instruments rather than shares. They were offered not only for the established countries of Europe, endeavoring to rebuild their economies after World War I, but also for countries in Latin America and eastern Europe. Foreign issues often carried interest rates well in excess of U.S. Treasury obligations and, while regarded as speculative, were distributed to American investors without great difficulty.

In 1921, then-Secretary of Commerce Herbert Hoover persuaded President Harding to call a White House conference to consider what Hoover regarded as the danger of speculative foreign loans and to try to put into place methods for controlling access to the U.S. capital market.[21] His proposal was generally resisted by Treasury Secretary Andrew Mellon, Secretary of State Charles Evans Hughes, and former Secretary of the Treasury Carter Glass, then a U.S. senator (and the co-author of the 1933 Glass-Steagall Act, which separated investment banking from commercial banking). Actual controls never developed, and America, newly ascendant to financial primacy, was doomed to repeat the mistakes of English investors in unsound cred-

---

21. In 1918, an informal capital issues committee was formed under the aegis of the Federal Reserve Board and composed of Reserve Board members and representatives of commercial and investment banking firms. Its purpose was to control the offering of new financings in the United States during the period of hostilities to ensure that their purposes were consistent with the war effort.

its of a hundred years before. The 1920s also saw a modernization of securities issue origination and distribution procedures; with the increased availability of telephone and telegraph services, such operations could be completed with substantially greater speed than in earlier years.

Depression and War

The crash of 1929 and the depression of the 1930s dealt a crippling blow to international financing by undermining confidence in bond issuers and credit institutions. During the 1930s, virtually all of the previous bond issues by sovereign governments of Latin America and eastern Europe fell into default and, with the intervention of the Second World War, many such issues could not be restructured or reorganized until the late 1940s. The 1930s were also a period of heavy reregulation in certain countries (such as the United States) and of exchange controls to attempt to stem foreign purchasers and capital flight; the heretofore relatively free movement of international capital was thus curbed. Even borrowers who could pay and intermediaries who might have facilitated were prohibited from doing so by government fiat. The Smoot-Hawley tariffs and similar acts by other countries were symptomatic of rising barriers to international commerce and the preoccupation with domestic concerns that permeated those years. With international private financing almost totally closed, bilateral government efforts to assist friendly allies before, during, and after World War II accounted for the bulk of international funding for an entire decade.

Out of this calamitous situation came a postwar system in which smaller investment firms and more highly regulated and compartmentalized securities industries emerged in a number of countries, operating almost entirely on a national basis. International financing was limited by both continuing exchange controls (Europe did not achieve free convertibility until the late 1950s) and lack of investor confidence. In such a climate, it was not surprising that government-sponsored forms of finance were called upon to fill the void. Specific programs and institutions such as the Marshall Plan, the World Bank (International Bank for Reconstruction and Development), and the International Monetary Fund were created to deal with such needs.

Thus, by the 1950s, a less international financing environment existed. While occasional foreign bond issues were undertaken in New York by some Western European nations and Japan, the other principal financing markets that had been active in nineteenth- and twentieth-century Europe were generally closed by exchange controls or stifled by the absence of investor interest. The U.S. dollar was the pre-eminent international currency, and public-sector institutions in Washington, together with private-sector commercial and investment banks in New York, dominated a quieter international financing scene.

Conclusion

Reviewing the history of investment banking, it is striking to note the extent to which this entrepreneurial sector has been shaped by the political tone of the times. Whether in medieval Europe, Renaissance Italy, Napoleonic France, or colonial Britain, the means of finance was closely related to political circumstances and the requirements of rulers and governments. Indeed, the success of a government has regularly been linked to its ability to marshal financial as well as popular support. Public attitudes toward international borrowing and lending have also shaped the flows of funds; whether the transactions were Bills of Exchange, colonial empire projects, or contemporary OPEC investments, differing views about debt have colored the eventual likelihood of repayment.

Successful investment bankers have therefore needed to combine traditional values of constancy and the sanctity of contracts, so endearing to investors, with the flexibility and imagination needed to deal with governments and other borrowers. Projecting the nuances of such situations internationally has made communications critical and allowed us to see investment bankers in their central role as vendors of information. Culturally, a high sense of firm loyalty and even separateness from other groups undoubtedly helped in achieving the necessary teamwork.

During the last thirty years, as world economic prosperity has broadened and financial deregulation has occurred, international capital movements have grown dramatically. Investment bankers have seized upon such transfers and the availability of more efficient data communication to create the foundation for an eventually integrated global capital market. An entirely new forum—the Eurobond market—rather than any of the individual national capital markets, was the spur to that integration.

CHAPTER 2

A HISTORY OF EUROBONDS:
THE SHAPING OF A GLOBAL MARKETPLACE

The post–World War II development of the international debt capital, or Eurobond, market represented an important further step toward internationalization and integration of the world's public financing activities. The Eurobond market was a product of the several centuries of international financing described in Chapter 1 and specific developments after the 1939–1945 world war. It was, essentially, the first marketplace without a home base. It was a financing medium without a specific political or regulatory infrastructure to shape and mold it, perhaps because most sovereign governments chose to ignore it during its first ten years of existence. It was to become the world's first supranational capital market, and its growth and developing sophistication were to have an important impact on public securities markets around the world and on the pace of global-market integration.

Market Beginnings

The birth of the Eurobond market in 1963 owes much to several factors that had been developing in the international monetary sphere during the preceding decade. First, there was a relatively stable international economic climate; interest rates were low and currency parities were fixed in terms of gold and U.S. dollars. Big power political relationships had stabilized since the 1940s and were viewed as likely to remain so; transnational portfolio and direct investments, particularly from the United States toward Europe, were expanding rapidly. Most of the developed countries of the world enjoyed relative prosperity.

By the early 1960s, following sterling crises in 1955 and 1957, the U.S. dollar had largely replaced the British pound as the principal vehicle for international trade financing. In December 1958, the major European countries adopted policies of external convertibility, which allowed nonresidents to acquire their currencies, thus raising the level of confidence in the international payments system. At the same time, those countries relaxed restrictions on the purchase of foreign

27

Table 2-1
U.S. Balance of Payments
(U.S.$ millions)

	Balance	
Year	Liquidity Basis	Official Reserve Transactions Basis
1950	$−3,489	a
1951	−8	a
1952	−1,206	a
1953	−2,184	a
1954	−1,541	a
1955	−1,242	a
1956	−973	a
1957	578	a
1958	−3,365	a
1959	−3,870	a
1960	−3,676	$−3,403
1961	−2,521	−1,348
1962	−2,864	−2,650
1963	−2,713	−1,934
1964	−2,695	−1,534
1965	−2,477	−1,289
1966	−2,151	219
1967	−4,683	−3,418
1968	−1,610	1,641
1969	−6,122	2,702
1970	−3,851	−9,839
1971	−22,002	−29,765

a. No officially published figures on this basis are available prior to 1960.
Source: U.S. Senate Finance Committee Report on the Interest Equalization Tax, 1973.

securities by their residents, while retaining rigid controls over access to their domestic capital markets.

After modest U.S. balance-of-payments deficits in the early 1950s, which were welcomed as enhancing international liquidity and investment, America experienced more worrisome annual deficits of $2.5 billion to $3.8 billion during 1958–1962 (see Table 2-1). This, in turn, fostered a short-term money market in foreign currencies, principally U.S. dollars, established in Europe and centered in London in the late 1950s. This so-called "Eurodollar" market consisted of dollar deposits held at banks outside the United States and loaned out or redeposited by such banks, frequently to borrowers in other countries. The Bank of England encouraged the development of this market as a means of financing international trade following the restrictions placed on the use of sterling in external transactions in 1957.

The growth of the Eurodollar market was also stimulated by the presence of Federal Reserve Board Regulation Q, which limited the interest rates U.S. banks could pay on domestic U.S. dollar deposits. This ceiling, for example, was an unrealistic 2½ percent on three- to six-month deposits during the 1957–1961 period. Eurodollars were generally deposited and onlent for periods of one, three, or six months and carried interest rates slightly higher than those prevailing in the U.S. domestic money market. The depositors, who dealt with banks in a "telephone market" rather than on an exchange floor, included a variety of multinational corporations investing cash balances, as well as central banks and public authorities of various Western European, Eastern European, and Asian nations with dollar reserves in excess of their immediate requirements. Banks in London, again with the encouragement of the Bank of England, were quick to seize the opportunity presented by this emerging market. Their specialized personnel utilized existing clerical and communications infrastructure and the relative freedom from regulation traditionally present in Britain to help develop the market's potential.

In 1963, the Eurodollar money market (including currencies other than the dollar) was estimated by the Bank for International Settlements to total $12.4 billion, of which $9.3 billion were in U.S. dollars. The growth of the Eurodollar market assisted the subsequent Eurobond market by facilitating currency-matched funding of dealer inventory positions in the short-term money market and providing benchmark interest rates for the repricing of later issues of floating-rate notes. More important, to European financial institutions, this money market represented an obvious instance in which a philosophy of free and open international competition had led to the successful establishment of a marketplace that involved firms from different geographic centers participating outside the exchange control and restrictive regulatory mechanisms of individual nation-states. In other words, there was, for the first time, a truly supranational marketplace.

U.S. Policy Creates Opening for London

As the U.S. balance-of-trade surpluses narrowed in the 1950s and the balance-of-payments deficits deepened beyond $2 billion, the U.S. government, especially during the administration of President Kennedy, became uncomfortable with the American role as a capital exporter to Europe. The Treasury Department prepared studies of the

European capital markets, and in February 1962, Secretary of the Treasury Douglas Dillon gave a speech in Paris encouraging the European financial authorities to develop their own capital markets and to raise at home, rather than in the New York market, the capital required for economic expansion. These suggestions were well received by certain authorities in Europe—particularly in Great Britain—and on October 3, 1962, Lord Cromer, governor of the Bank of England, in his annual speech to the Lord Mayor's dinner stated:

> The time has now come when the City once again might provide an international capital market where the foreigner cannot only borrow long-term capital but where, equally important, he will once again wish to place his long-term investment capital. This entrepôt business in capital would not only serve this country well, but would fill a vital and vacant role in Europe in mobilising foreign capital for world economic development.

These words of encouragement, together with natural investor and borrower interest, gave rise to a climate of experimentation with foreign currency issues offered outside home jurisdictions in the early 1960s. In 1961 and 1962, Kredietbank in Brussels offered issues, principally in the Benelux countries, denominated in European units of account, a composite currency unit made up of the seventeen currencies of the original European Payments Union. In May 1963, the merchant banking firm of Samuel Montagu completed a $20-million, three-year private placement for the Kingdom of Belgium offered principally through the London market.

In June 1963, the most important of these experiments resulted in what is generally regarded as the first genuine Eurobond issue. Autostrade, an Italian state highway authority guaranteed by Istituto per la Ricostruzione Industriale, issued $15 million of 5½ percent bearer (i.e., unregistered) bonds due in fifteen years. The financing was lead managed by the British merchant banking firm of S.G. Warburg & Co. Ltd., with Banque de Bruxelles in Belgium, Deutsche Bank in Germany, and Rotterdamsche Bank of the Netherlands as comanagers, and was listed on the London and Luxembourg stock exchanges. This financing, which required significant effort on the part of the sponsors, their counsel, and the Bank of England to obtain relief from the British stamp tax, was signed in London on July 1, 1963. Definitive bearer certificates were delivered to purchasers at Banque Internationale in Luxembourg following payment on July 17.

Since 1950, the U.S. dollar-bond market in New York for foreign issuers had undergone a significant expansion. Public issues there by the Commonwealth of Australia (thirteen offerings), the Kingdom of Belgium (four financings), the Japan Development Bank (three issues), the Kingdom of Norway (five issues), the European Coal and Steel Community (four issues), the Kingdom of Denmark (two issues), the government of New Zealand (three issues), and entities of the French and Italian governments, as well as a broad range of foreign corporate borrowers, resulted in a total of $500 million to $1 billion of financing in each of the years leading up to 1963. Investment banks such as First Boston, Kuhn Loeb, Lazard Frères, and Morgan Stanley were active as lead managers.

Foreign bond issues in New York were usually of $20 million to $50 million in size, carrying maturities of five to twenty years with interest rates in the range of 4½–6 percent. Commissions were generally at the level of 2½ percent of the principal amount, compared with ⅞ of 1 percent for similar issues in New York by American borrowers. Selling-group members generally earned between 1¼ and 1½ percent of the 2½ percent total commission. These Securities and Exchange Commission-registered issues were sold to a growing number of U.S. domestic investing institutions but also enjoyed substantial subscription abroad. Non-U.S. investors generally absorbed between 25 and 75 percent of these issues. In some instances, foreign investors accounted for 80–90 percent of the sales. Distribution outside the United States was generally carried out by European banks, which were invited to participate as selling-group members in the New York syndicates.

Thus, despite the fact that such issues were underwritten and listed in New York, their principal markets were often in Europe, where investors were attracted by the U.S. dollar-denominated obligations of well-known and substantial European borrowers. It was these non-U.S. distribution channels for U.S. dollar-denominated securities that the early Eurobond issues, managed out of London or Brussels, attempted to tap. In addition to the public issues offered in the New York market, a substantial number of private placements were also made in the 1958–1963 period, generally in the range of $15 million to $50 million. These private issues were easier to document than public offerings, especially for corporations, because they did not involve the extensive accounting adjustments and disclosure statements required by the SEC under the Securities Act of 1933 in public-offering prospectuses.

New York was the largest of the postwar national capital markets and handled the largest volume of international financing, but it was

Table 2-2
Foreign Bond Issues, 1955–1962

	U.S.$ Equivalent (millions)
Belgium	$393
Italy	72
Netherlands	298
Switzerland	882
United Kingdom	1,064
United States	4,171
West Germany	163

Source: Jean Mensbrugghe, "Foreign Issues in Europe," *IMF Staff Papers,* July 1964, p. 329.

not the only player. Table 2-2 shows the total amounts of foreign bond issues offered in the principal European countries and the United States during the 1955–1962 period.

U.S. Capital Controls

While foreign financing in New York yielded substantial commissions to the U.S. investment banks, the U.S. balance-of-payments deficit and capital exports by mid-1963 were increasing to such an extent that the American government decided to take action. On July 18, 1963, in a speech before Congress regarding the balance of payments, President Kennedy announced the imposition of an interest equalization tax (IET) to be effective from that day for a period of two years. The tax was on the purchase by U.S. residents of all non-U.S. securities with maturities of longer than three years (excluding securities from less developed countries, Canada, and public institutions such as the World Bank). At the time, it was calculated that American interest rates were lower by approximately 1 percent than several European rates, and so the rate of the new tax was determined by increasing the cost of borrowing to European issuers by approximately 1 percent above nominal U.S. interest-rate levels.

The IET was enacted in 1964 despite arguments from some U.S. investment banks in favor of modifications that would have allowed European issue activity to continue in New York on a limited basis, thus helping to preserve New York's pre-eminence in international financing. Instead, on February 10, 1965, President Johnson actually broadened the tax to include bank loans with maturities of one year or longer. The IET was extended by congressional action in 1965, 1967, 1969, and finally in 1971. The 1967 extension raised the tax to rates that increased the annual incremental borrowing costs from 1 percent to 1½ percent, and in 1969 the president was given authority to vary the effective annual tax rate from zero to 1½ percent. (In January 1974, following a period of U.S. balance-of-payments strength, the tax was removed and the legislation allowed to expire in June 1974.)

The IET was criticized by some as failing to aid the U.S. balance of payments significantly, while at the same time injuring New York's competitive position in world finance. It undoubtedly did reduce certain types of issuance activity in New York. The U.S. Treasury Department indicated that sales of new foreign securities to U.S. residents fell from a total of $1 billion in the first half of 1963 to $250 million in the second half of that year (the $250 million represented securities that were exempt from the tax either because the purchase commitments had been entered into prior to the IET announcement or because the issues originated in less developed countries or Canada).

In 1965, the U.S. capital controls program was further buttressed by the Federal Reserve announcement of guidelines for banks and nonbank financial institutions limiting their purchases of foreign securities and credit extensions under a voluntary foreign credit-restraint program. In addition, on January 1, 1968, President Johnson announced a new balance-of-payments program that created the Office of Foreign Direct Investments (OFDI) within the U.S. Treasury Department to supervise the overseas capital movements of U.S. corporations. In general, the OFDI required that foreign investments by large corporations above a base level be financed by borrowings outside the United States. This encouraged a substantial expansion in Euromarket borrowings by American companies during 1968 and 1969 in the form of issues, loans, and private placements. The OFDI program was eventually eliminated in 1974 along with the IET. Again, there were extensive criticisms of the program and its effect on U.S. companies and their international operations. Questions were also raised about whether the balance of payments was favorably affected by these controls, which many observers believed adversely affected the longer-term position of New York as an international financing center.

The Supranational Market Takes Root

The closing of the American capital market to most developed-country borrowers and the ongoing interest of European banks in placing international securities in their countries enhanced the opportunity for issuers such as Autostrade to utilize the established European distribution system for what was essentially a new type of international security. These instruments, labeled Eurobonds, were generally offered outside the borrower's country of residence, denominated in an international currency (often not the currency of the borrower), and placed by a multinational underwriting syndicate of financial institutions. Given the role of the U.S. dollar as the world's principal reserve and trading currency, the U.S. government did not place any limitations on the use of its currency for the denomination of such issues. This laissez-faire attitude was an essential ingredient in the rooting and subsequent development of the Euromarkets.

The Eurobond market thus became a supranational market. Because it dealt in intangible obligations that could be produced, bought, sold, and transported virtually anywhere, the market was elevated out of the traditional pattern of regulated national capital markets; it thus found a shape of its own that was congruent with a free-market philosophy and with the needs of investors, borrowers, and intermediaries. Eurobond financings have generally lacked a single-country locus and have been offered by borrowers from virtually every major country, through a broad range of lead managing and co-managing banks. These issues are normally not registered with the securities commission or central banking authorities of any single country and are usually, from a legal standpoint, classified as being outside national regulatory jurisdictions.

The word "Eurodollar" originally appeared in the early 1960s in the writings of Dr. Paul Einzig, a prominent British financial writer and journalist. The term "Eurobond" was developed later to describe the longer-term instrument discussed above; it is in direct contrast to the term "foreign bond," which described the traditional local currency-denominated instruments offered by domestic bank syndicates in, say, New York or London and denominated in U.S. dollars or sterling on behalf of foreign obligors. Sometimes the term "Eurodollar bond" or "EuroDeutsche mark bond" is used to describe Eurobonds denominated in those particular currencies; similarly, "foreign dollar bonds" was often used to describe bonds offered in the U.S. market for foreign obligors prior to 1963. Such foreign dollar bonds were, however, rechristened "Yankee bonds" in the mid-1970s with the revival of activity that followed the removal of the IET. Similarly, foreign bonds in sterling and Japanese yen were called "bulldog bonds" and "samurai bonds," respectively, in the 1980s. Generally, the term "international bonds" is used to encompass both foreign bonds and Eurobonds.

Obviously, the term "Eurobonds" is no longer entirely descriptive, because the market for such instruments has broadened substantially beyond the European continent. By the end of the 1980s, the term "global capital market" was used to denote a market broader than the original Eurobond market and encompassing various national and international capital markets in a single interlinked entity. The term "globalization," when applied to the capital markets, generally relates to the process by which a market or product spreads beyond its original geographic locus to approach worldwide usage.

Early Competition in the Supranational Market

Following the launch of the Autostrade issue in July 1963, the Eurobond market expanded rapidly (see Table 2-3) while continuing to experiment with new forms. The most frequent lead managers of new Eurobond issues during the last half of 1963 and all of 1964 are shown in Table 2-4.

Merchant banking firms based in the United Kingdom rapidly achieved leadership in issuing Eurobonds, and the largest issue during this period was a $30-million financing undertaken in November 1964 by S.G. Warburg for the European Coal and Steel Community. Many of the issuers were Scandinavian government borrowers, which had previously offered foreign dollar bonds in the New York market.

The element of experimentation that characterized the market during this early period was evident in the different forms of issues that were launched, as well as in the syndication methods used. In December 1963, for instance, the first equity convertible Eurobond issue in the amount of $5 million was launched for Canon Camera by M. Samuel & Co. Ltd., later Hill Samuel & Co. Limited. In October 1964, S.G. Warburg launched a dual-currency issue for the city of Turin denominated in pounds sterling with an option for the bondholder to receive interest or principal payments in Deutsche marks. Other experimental issues included the first issue, in June 1964, of debt with equity warrants attached and the first issue, in June 1965, of bonds by a U.S. multinational corporation, Mobil Oil. In July 1965, ENEL, the Italian state electric energy authority, undertook a financing under the Abs Plan (named for Herman Abs of Deutsche Bank AG), with six simultaneous issues denominated in the currencies of the six European Economic Community countries and offered in those countries.

Experimentation with various syndication methods included varying the length of the selling period from one to three weeks, linking the underwriting to, or separating it from, the selling function, and using different numbers of underwriters in a syndicate, ranging

Table 2-3
Eurobond New Issues Volume, 1963–1987

Year	Fixed Rate U.S.$ millions	%	Floating-Rate Notes U.S.$ millions	%	Equity Convertible and Warrants U.S.$ millions	%	Total U.S.$ millions
1963	$128	86.5	—	—	$20	13.5	$148
1964	623	91.5	—	—	58	8.5	681
1965	750	92.6	—	—	60	7.4	810
1966	1,146	85.3	—	—	197	14.7	1,343
1967	1,547	87.2	—	—	227	12.8	1,774
1968	1,366	44.3	—	—	1,719	55.7	3,085
1969	2,042	71.0	—	—	834	29.0	2,876
1970	2,273	82.3	$300	10.9	189	6.8	2,762
1971	3,044	92.6	—	—	245	7.4	3,289
1972	4,397	79.8	60	1.1	1,051	19.1	5,508
1973	3,199	86.2	40	1.1	470	12.7	3,709
1974	1,707	88.1	145	7.5	85	4.4	1,937
1975	6,987	95.9	215	3.0	80	1.1	7,282
1976	11,021	85.3	1,100	8.5	794	6.2	12,915
1977	13,254	84.2	1,595	10.1	893	5.7	15,742
1978	8,910	72.7	2,300	18.8	1,044	8.5	12,254
1979	9,244	63.8	4,058	28.0	1,185	8.2	14,487
1980	12,224	64.9	4,129	21.9	2,475	13.2	18,828
1981	16,761	64.3	6,700	25.7	2,623	10.0	26,084
1982	34,770	73.6	11,197	23.7	1,299	2.7	47,266
1983	30,492	64.5	14,960	31.7	1,799	3.8	47,251
1984	43,579	54.9	31,684	39.9	4,161	5.2	79,424
1985	72,460	53.4	55,460	40.8	7,840	5.8	135,760
1986	107,371	61.0	46,879	26.7	21,696	12.3	175,946
1987	90,143	63.1	15,716	11.0	36,920	25.9	142,779

Sources: Euromoney magazine (1963–1986); *International Financing Review* (1987).

from a handful of managers to twenty or thirty underwriters in various countries. By the late 1960s, these efforts had produced more standardized practices among the principal lead managers, including a selling period of approximately two weeks, the use of a group of perhaps twenty-five to forty underwriters assisted by a selling group of fifty to seventy-five firms, and the separation of the underwriting and selling functions in commission arrangements.

U.S. Investment Banking Initiatives

The American firms that had operated so successfully in the old foreign dollar-bond market in New York were in a quandary as to how to

Table 2-4
Lead Managers, Eurobonds, 1963–1964

	U.S.$ Equivalent (millions)[a]	Number of Issues
S.G. Warburg & Co. Ltd.	$137	9
Hambros Bank Ltd.	131	9
Deutsche Bank AG	91	4
Hill Samuel & Co. Limited	40	3
Kuhn Loeb & Co.	38	2
S.C.S. Banque Lambert	29	3
Kredietbank S.A. Luxembourgeoise	27	3
White Weld & Co. Ltd.	20	2
Baring Brothers	20	1
N.M. Rothschild & Sons	18	2

a. Full credit to book-running lead manager.

approach this new offshore market. They entertained hopes that the IET would be modified or allowed to lapse, thus directing financing activity back to New York. Several of the U.S. firms did not have offices in Europe and relied on traditional alliances with European firms for their principal relationships in London and on the Continent. Nevertheless, a number of them saw in the emerging Eurobond market not just a threat but also an imperative that they follow their New York market clients abroad and play an active role in this new international market. Gradually, from 1964 to 1967, leading U.S. investment banks such as Morgan Stanley, First Boston, Smith Barney, Kuhn Loeb, and Lehman Brothers established offices in Europe, and White Weld expanded its existing operations in London and Zurich. These efforts by American firms to establish themselves in the new Eurobond market ultimately proved successful, as is evident in the "league" tables (i.e., the annual tabulations of vendor shares of total industry financing volumes) for lead managements of Eurobond issues during 1965, 1966, and 1967 (see Table 2-5).

As Table 2-5 indicates, by 1967 the competitive race had turned largely into an Anglo-American merchant investment banking contest, with banks from other countries also establishing strong positions based primarily on currency concentration, such as the Deutsche Bank in Deutsche marks, or on specialized placing capability, such as Banca Commerciale Italiana's access to large international bond investors.

By early 1968, a handful of American investment banks and German universal banks were well positioned to take advantage of a larger flow of new borrowing in the Eurobond marketplace. This

Table 2-5
Lead Managers, Eurobond Issues, 1965–1967

	U.S.$ Equivalent (millions)[a]	Number of Issues
Morgan Stanley	$385	14
Kuhn Loeb	311	16
Deutsche Bank	291	12
S.G. Warburg	265	17
N.M. Rothschild	218	8
Hambros Bank	215	14
White Weld	215	12
Banca Commerciale Italiana	213	10
First Boston	135	6
Lehman Brothers	120	5
Kredietbank S.A. Luxembourgeoise	119	11

a. Full credit to book-running lead manager.

occurred in 1968 and 1969 in the form of a substantial increase in the amount of U.S. dollar financing, largely as a result of equity convertible issues by American companies, and an increase in Deutsche mark financing. The annual amount of new Eurobond issues approximately doubled to $3 billion per year in 1968 and 1969, from the substantially lower totals in 1965–1967. In 1968 and 1969, large convertible issues by Philips Gloeilampenfabrieken of $100 million, by Texaco of $75 million, and by others substantially increased the average size of issues to $25 million in each of those two years, compared to an average of approximately $15 million per issue during the previous periods. Equity-convertible Eurobonds totaled approximately 40 percent of all new issues in 1968 and 1969 combined. Total issues by various lead managers in 1968 are shown in Table 2-6, in which the improved competitive positions of the U.S. and German banks are evident.

Issue Placement

Although the origination and lead management of Eurobond issues had become concentrated in American, British, and German investment banks, actual placement was often completed by underwriters and dealers in other countries, thus adding to the overall perception of a market that was becoming more and more integrated internationally. Retail investors in Switzerland and the Benelux countries in particular (the "Belgian dentist," who has long been the prototype individual investor in Eurobonds) were able to invest relatively free of exchange controls and represented a substantial proportion of

Table 2-6
Lead Managers, Eurobonds, 1968

	U.S.$ Equivalent (millions)[a]	Number of Issues
Morgan Stanley	$355	10
Lehman Brothers	297	11
Deutsche Bank	259	10
S.G. Warburg	241	11
White Weld	194	9
Kuhn Loeb	169	6
Goldman, Sachs	141	4
Dresdner Bank	140	5
First Boston	135	5
Commerzbank	133	6
N.M. Rothschild	126	2

a. Full credit to book-running lead manager.

Eurobond investor demand. It has been estimated that Swiss banks alone accounted for the placement of 50–80 percent of Eurobond issues at certain points in these early years. Investors through Swiss banks in turn were often residents of other countries. Patterns of final investor demand shifted over time, however, and during periods when domestic interest rates in particular countries were high. Similarly, when some countries enjoyed heavy balance-of-payments surpluses, such as the oil-producing countries in the 1970s, these nations represented a more significant portion of Eurobond investor demand.

Conversely, when countries had significant balance-of-payments deficits, there was a tendency for their financial authorities to encourage their borrowers to use the Eurobond market as a means of acquiring foreign currency, which subsequently could be added to the reserves of the central bank. Thus, Scandinavian countries in the mid-1960s, U.S. corporations in 1968, 1969, and 1972, and the French government in 1969, 1974–1976, and 1982–1983 were substantial users of the Eurobond market as borrowers. Central banks and finance ministries of various countries closely monitored this supranational market and from time to time directed their country borrowers or investors toward the market either explicitly or implicitly through such means as the strengthening or relaxation of exchange controls or the rationing of access to the domestic capital market.

The use of the international capital-market borrowing and lending process in managing governmental payments imbalances has changed radically. In the 1950s and 1960s, most such phenomena could be dealt with by drawing down reserves or by using inter-

governmental borrowing or International Monetary Fund accommodation. Later, especially following the oil price increases of 1973–
1974, the amounts involved escalated and participants in the private
capital market were able to play an increasing role in recycling balances. Although public securities issues and the expanded Eurobond
sales networks were important in this process, the role of private
placements of whole issues of securities or loans was significant in
exporting surpluses from Italy in 1966, from Germany in 1968, from
Japan in 1972, and from certain Arab countries in 1974–1977.

A variation on this process, which was actively used after 1975,
was the "targeted issue." In a targeted issue, a public offering of
securities was arranged in the Eurobond market, but the maturity and
other product features were designed to appeal to specific investors
in a surplus country. With the addition of a management group designed to encourage placement in the surplus country, a substantial
targeted placement could be achieved. During the period of Japanese
surpluses in the 1980s, so-called "sushi" issues were structured to be
of specific interest to Japanese investors.

As indicated, Swiss banks were important placers of new Eurobond issues, even though they did not appear in the lead manager's
league tables of new Eurobond issues during the 1963–1970 period.
Their absence was due largely to restrictions in Switzerland that
required new-issue underwriting participations by Swiss banks to
be subject to the Swiss issue tax, then 1½ percent of the principal
amount of issues so underwritten. This tax, apparently originally
instituted as a revenue generator, made it expensive for Swiss banks
to participate directly as underwriters in most Eurobond issues. Initially, the banks attempted to overcome this problem by forming a
syndicate similar in composition to the group that underwrote Swiss-
franc foreign issues. The syndicate was prepared to participate in new
Eurobond issues, provided the Swiss issue tax was paid to the federal
tax authorities in Berne. Occasionally, it was possible, on the strength
of concentrated Swiss placing power, to modify the offering terms of
a proposed issue to accommodate the cost without raising the issuers'
cost of borrowing.

Although a half-dozen issues were launched in the 1960s with
the participation of the Swiss syndicate (following an initial financing
for N.V. Philips in September 1966), the syndicate was not successful
in establishing itself as a permanent feature in the marketplace. Subsequently, in the late 1960s and early 1970s, the three principal Swiss
banks established foreign subsidiaries in London and other centers
outside Switzerland to participate as underwriters, co-managers, and
lead managers of new Eurobond issues. By the mid-1970s, these sub-

sidiaries, backed by their parents' placing power, had become a significant force in Eurobond lead-management activities.

Commissions

As mentioned earlier, the sponsors of the first Eurobond issues endeavored to utilize channels of distribution that had been established in Europe for U.S. dollar-denominated foreign bond issues listed and offered in New York. In attempting to stimulate such distribution, lead managers found it helpful to offer the same commission incentives that had prevailed in foreign bond issues in New York, namely a total commission of 2½ percent to be allocated as follows: ½ percent to the lead manager as a management fee, ½ percent to the underwriters as an underwriting commission, and 1½ percent to the members of the selling group as selling commission. This structure was generally used in most early Eurobond issues and facilitated the transfer of such business to Europe. This commission structure was higher than that prevailing in the U.S. domestic-capital market and provided a strong incentive for securities firms to expand their placing capacity.

During the 1960s and 1970s, European universal banks with large branch systems developed their internal placing capacity through expanded branches, most notably in Belgium, Germany, Luxembourg, the Netherlands, and Switzerland. The lucrative commission structure also encouraged the sale of bonds to institutions such as insurance companies and pension funds across national boundaries by international sales personnel.

Once the institutional market for Eurobonds had developed greater size and sophistication, and the sophisticated investors came to realize just how lucrative the commission structure was to the placing banks, investors began to pressure the banks for price discounts. Beginning in the late 1960s, such discounts, or "reallowances," were regularly granted to large institutional investors. By the early 1970s, reallowances by London-based bond salesmen were offered to large institutions with such increasing aggressiveness that, for slow-moving issues, the reallowance began to approach the full amount of the selling and underwriting commissions. The original commission structures were preserved, however, by most Swiss and other continental European banks with substantial retail-distribution systems. The structures were rationalized as necessary because of the cost of servicing smaller retail investors. Even today, Eurobonds are often sold either in modest amounts at par across the counters of universal banks or in large blocks with substantial reallowances to institutional investors. Thus, the relatively large commission spread allows both types of investors to be serviced with different re-allowance arrangements. This is in sharp contrast to commission arrangements on high-grade, fixed-income securities in the United States, for example, in which the total fee paid is too low to permit sales to small investors through branch offices on a profitable basis. Thus, various commentators on the Eurobond market have observed that Eurobonds are generally sold rather than bought, meaning that heavy selling efforts are often necessary to complete a distribution. The strong emphasis on sales also indicates the importance attached to distribution abilities as a competitive weapon in the Eurobond marketplace. It also partially explains the disparities that develop between the yields of selected Eurobond issues with substantial retail participation and the yields on comparable instruments in other countries. Such disparities are consistent with the pattern that would be expected in a marketplace that is distribution driven and where sales occur over a wide geographic area to heterogeneous groups of retail investors.

During the late 1960s and 1970s, lead managers in competitive issuer solicitation situations made several efforts to reduce commissions below the prevailing level of 2½ percent. These efforts did gradually achieve reductions to 2 percent on ten-year issues and to 1⅞ percent for five- and seven-year issues. But reductions have not proceeded further toward domestic U.S. levels because of substantial resistance by many continental European banks that support the higher commissions as a means of compensating their branch distribution systems. Various low-commission issues were effectively boycotted by such banks, and by the late 1980s, the level of commissions appears to have settled at 1⅞ percent for medium-term issues and at 2–2¼ percent for longer-term financings.

Although nominal commission levels have been generally maintained by market participants in the 1970s and 1980s, the focus of price competition among investment banks has shifted toward *net effective cost* of borrowing, that is, the relationship among commissions, coupons, and issue price. As this competition has intensified in various sectors, the practice has grown among lead managers of pricing issues to sell in the institutional and intradealer markets at initial trading levels below the nominal issue prices. Thus, an issue that is priced at 100 percent with a commission of 2 percent and that begins trading at 98½ percent may represent, under certain circumstances, a satisfactory flotation from the point of view of the underwriting banks. Institutional investors purchase the bonds at 98½ percent, while individual investors being serviced through the branch distribution systems of continental banks may pay up to 100 percent, thus allowing at least a portion of the financing to be placed on a profitable basis. Clearly, the borrower in such a circumstance is interested in the effective cost of borrowing. If a financing with a market-price discount is able to carry an interest rate of, say, 9 percent rather than 9⅛ percent, the final cost of borrowing will be lower by the ⅛ percent coupon differential. Thus, the practice has developed of pricing new issues to sell in the institutional market at discounts from issue price, while encouraging placement in selected retail markets at higher levels.

As participants in a placement-oriented market, Eurobond investment banks devote substantial effort to determining the types of investments that appeal to segments of the investor community. Firms pay significant attention to the types of issues, by currency, maturity, and special features that attract most investor interest at a particular time in various geographic markets. This attention to changes in investor sentiment has contributed to the continuing elaboration and development of the market. It has also allowed the market to direct its attention to the interests of new investor groups, such as OPEC investors in the 1970s and Japanese investors in the mid-1980s. Thus, the sales executives of investment banking firms have become increasingly helpful in developing new products for borrowers.

Central Bank Interventions

As shown in Table 2-1, the U.S. balance of payments, after being contained at modest deficit levels in the mid-1960s by the capital controls program, substantially increased after 1966 and reached a high in 1971, by which time the U.S. trade surplus had also slipped into deficit. International payments difficulties, together with an increase in the price of gold following 1967 and the sterling devaluation of 1968, raised concerns about the future of the once stable U.S. dollar. These concerns resulted in an increase in the amount of non-U.S. dollar financing in the Eurobond market, as investors sought to currency-diversify their portfolios. In 1968 and 1969, substantial increases in Deutsche mark-Eurobond financing resulted, and the Dutch guilder-note-issue market opened to investors in 1970.

Activity in the EuroDeutsche mark market did not, however, reflect the same open competition among international investment banks that had been present in the U.S. dollar sector. Following a substantial increase in Deutsche mark-issue activity during early 1968, a subcommittee for EuroDeutsche mark bonds was formed in November of that year with representatives of six leading German banks

Table 2-7
Lead Managers, Eurobonds, 1972

	U.S.$ Equivalent (millions)[a]	Number of Issues
Deutsche Bank	$513	17
White Weld	451	21
Morgan Stanley	406	12
N.M. Rothschild	284	9
Kuhn Loeb	270	9
Westdeutsche Landesbank Girozentrale	241	8
Dresdner Bank	234	8
Amsterdam-Rotterdam Bank	203	12
Kredietbank S.A. Luxembourgeoise	200	8
S.G. Warburg	185	7

a. Full credit to book-running lead manager.

meeting together to schedule issues under the auspices of the German central bank. In addition to its scheduling function, the subcommittee established with the German authorities a number of guidelines for EuroDeutsche mark issues that limited their size, form, and maturities. The committee also reaffirmed the preference of the Bundesbank that all Deutsche mark issues be lead managed by German banks. Thus, the rise of the Deutsche mark as a more active Euromarket currency in the late 1960s and early 1970s was accompanied by a further increase in the position of German banks in the lead management of issues, as shown in Table 2-7. The prohibition of non-German banks acting as lead manager was justified by the Deutsche Bundesbank on the basis that the restriction allowed the Bundesbank a greater measure of control over the German currency and avoided conflicts in the scheduling of such financings in relation to domestic government-bond issues. But to the extent that these controls were exercised, they reflected a reversion to the old foreign-bond markets that had been prevalent prior to the founding of the Euromarket.

The leading manager of EuroDeutsche mark issues was the Deutsche Bank, with Westdeutsche Landesbank, Dresdner Bank, and Commerzbank as significant competitors. With a smaller number of competitors than in the U.S. dollar sector, this market enjoyed a relatively lower level of commission reallowances, and scheduling of issues by the subcommittee for EuroDeutsche mark bonds resulted in a greater spacing of issues during periods of market congestion. These market conditions resulted, however, in less innovation and placement development in the Deutsche mark sector than was the case in the more open currencies.

Certainly, the desire of German central bankers to maintain controls over their own currency was not unique. The process by which certain other central banks asserted their authority with respect to the use of their currencies in Euromarket transactions is exemplified by a financing of 60 million Swiss francs in October 1963 by the city of Copenhagen under the lead management of Morgan Grenfell & Co., a London merchant bank. This was a fifteen-year Eurobond issue publicly offered with a 5 percent coupon rate and listed in London and Luxembourg, as had been the Autostrade U.S.-dollar issue three months earlier. Although it was denominated in Swiss francs, the Swiss National Bank was not notified in advance of the financing, which was organized in London. Although the issue was allowed to be completed, the Swiss National Bank protested the financing to the Bank of England. The Swiss National Bank felt strongly that it wished to control access to its currency as a means of limiting flows of funds into Swiss francs during periods of currency speculation. As a result, Morgan Grenfell was reprimanded by the Bank of England, and other British banks were notified that certain central banks took an extra-territorial view of the use of their currencies even where the nexus of borrower, management, and listing was outside their national borders.

The Swiss franc sector of the international capital market continued to develop, but entirely as a foreign bond market in Switzerland rather than as a Euromarket sector, and such issues were managed, underwritten, and placed within Switzerland. Of the various market sectors in the 1970s, the U.S. dollar sector, as well as the sectors involving the Australian dollar, the Canadian dollar, the European unit of account, and the European currency unit (ECU), were open to full and free competition. In contrast, the Deutsche mark, the French franc, the Dutch guilder, the sterling, and the yen sectors became heavily regulated beginning in the 1960s and then were significantly liberalized in the 1980s (see Table 2-8).

Secondary-Market Trading

Just as procedures in the new-issue market of the 1960s were being shaped by a combination of consensus, initiative, and occasional central bank interventions, so the secondary market, or aftermarket, in Eurobonds was undergoing significant change. The most active firms in the Eurobond secondary market were often different from those already identified as frequent lead managers of new issues. Secondary-market trading firms included Bank of London and South America (Bolsa), Bondtrade, Deltec, Dominion Securities, Strauss Turnbull, and Weedon, all of which had no significant new-issue

Table 2-8
Degree of Major Currencies' Recent Liberalization

The attitudes of the monetary authorities of the principal nations determined the ability of potential lead managers to use a particular currency as the denomination of Eurobond issues. The attitudes of the relevant national authorities of various currency sectors can be summarized as follows:

- *Australian dollar*—Initially, the Reserve Bank of Australia required that it be notified in advance of potential borrowings in the Euromarkets denominated in EuroAustralian dollars. This requirement was eliminated in the mid-1980s.
- *Canadian dollar*—The Canadian authorities follow the U.S. pattern and do not require any notification or place any limitations on use of the Canadian dollar as a currency of denomination.
- *Deutsche mark*—Until the 1980s, the German central bank required that a capital market subcommittee be notified of all EuroDeutsche mark issues and that the lead manager of such issues be a German bank. Beginning in 1985, the central bank had to be notified directly, and the lead manager could be a German-incorporated intermediary of either German or non-German parentage.
- *European unit of account*—Because the European unit of account is a composite currency unit involving seventeen European currencies with no one currency representing a majority, there is no requirement that any central bank be notified or give prior approval for such issues.
- *European currency units (ECU)*—The ECU is a composite currency unit of the Common Market currencies, and no prior notification or approval from any central authority is required.
- *French franc*—The French authorities require that all EuroFrench franc issues be scheduled by a committee that includes banks and representatives of the Ministry of Finance and also that the lead manager of all such financings be a French bank.
- *Dutch guilder*—The Dutch central bank originally required that all guilder issues meet its guidelines with respect to limitations on maturity and size of issue and also be subject to its guidance with respect to timing. Dutch guilder note issues could not be lead managed by non-Dutch banks. However, in 1986 the central bank announced a program of liberalization intended to permit foreign-owned banks with affiliates in the Netherlands to participate more actively in the management of international guilder issues.
- *Pound sterling*—The Bank of England requires that it be notified of all sterling-denominated issues prior to announcement and be lead managed by either a British bank or a bank located in a country that extends reciprocity to British banks that want to establish themselves in the investment banking business in such countries. This allows the British government to use the potential leadership of sterling issues in negotiations with other countries regarding reciprocal treatment.

- *Swiss franc*—The Swiss National Bank has adopted the most rigid requirements of any central bank and does not permit Swiss franc issues to be offered outside Switzerland or lead managed or co-managed by non-Swiss banks. However, it does allow such issues to be lead managed by Swiss subsidiaries of foreign banks operating within Switzerland. Such issues were, until recently, also subject to limitations with respect to the amount of each issue and maturity.
- *Japanese yen*—At the time of the opening of the Euroyen market in the 1970s, the Japanese authorities required that all such issues meet rigid requirements prior to approval and be lead managed by a Japanese securities firm. In 1985, following pressure for liberalization from foreign banks and governments, the procedures for issue approval by the Japanese Ministry of Finance were simplified, and non-Japanese firms were permitted to lead manage yen issues.
- *U.S. dollar*—No meaningful restrictions.

---

operations, as well as several firms, such as Kidder, Peabody, First Boston, Deutsche Bank, and White Weld, that were important factors in the new-issue market. Trading firms began to experience substantial difficulties in the settlement of secondary-market transactions in the late 1960s as a result of the rudimentary clearing arrangements in use at that time. These difficulties included physical delivery of U.S. dollar-denominated bonds in New York or Luxembourg and entirely different procedures for Deutsche mark-denominated Eurobonds. In addition, methods used in calculating accrued interest and yields were far from uniform, and trading practices sometimes differed between firms located in various national jurisdictions.

In an effort to standardize secondary-market dealing practices, the Association of International Bond Dealers (AIBD) was formed in 1969 and held its first annual meeting in London in October of that year. Subcommittees on settlements, liaison with issuing houses, and standard market practices were formed. Perhaps the group's most important contributions were the development of buy-in procedures in cases where one firm could not complete the delivery of securities it had sold and the development of standard tables so that bond prices could be expressed in terms of yields on a common basis. A counterpart to the AIBD in the primary market was formed in the 1980s with the organization of the International Primary Market Association (IPMA). The IPMA endeavored to set standards of information disclosure and practice with respect to new-issue activity.

In 1968 and 1969, in the face of heavy trading volume on the New York Stock Exchange and significant increases in the volume of

Eurobond transactions, the secondary-market clearing mechanisms began to break down. Clearing requirements provided for payment against physical delivery of U.S. dollar-denominated bonds in New York, which gave rise to a substantial number of failed-to-deliver transactions in which one or both parties to a secondary-market bargain were unable, through their banks, to deliver the securities or make payment. As a result, a number of leading Eurobond houses, their back offices choked with error telexes from New York banks, began to consider the development of a truly European clearing system.

In December 1968, Morgan Guaranty Trust Company of New York announced that it had formed a clearing system, to be called Euroclear, that would keep bonds in a number of depositories in various countries. Rather than through physical delivery, however, transactions would be cleared by bookkeeping entry and funds transfers, with the bonds never physically leaving the Euroclear system as long as delivery was between clearing-system members. This fungible-bond clearing system was strikingly successful, and following initial acceptance by 50 participants, the system grew rapidly to a total of 150 participants in 1973 and to approximately 1,450 participants by the mid-1980s. Euroclear proved substantially more efficient and less expensive than the previous physical delivery system in New York, but it caused some concern on the part of market participants because it was owned by a single American institution. As a result, a competitive system called Cedel S.A. was formed in September 1970 and headquartered in Luxembourg. Cedel operated a nonfungible system under which individually numbered bonds were specifically assigned to participants but did not leave the depository banks. Cedel's operation also grew rapidly, and the competition between the two systems is generally considered to have resulted in lowering system-usage fees.

Market Foundations Completed

By the end of 1972, the Eurobond market had expanded substantially, and a total of $5.6 billion of new issues was placed that year. During its first nine years of operation, the market had passed through periods of experimentation with various currencies and types of issues and had roughed out the lines of demarcation between what borrowers, investors, and intermediaries would accept and what the monetary authorities of the various European countries would permit. The market had refined its syndication system into an effective modus vivendi between originating firms and placers. The commission structure, the exemption of interest payments from withholding taxes, and the anonymity provided by bearer bonds were powerful incentives to placers and investors and resulted in large segments of the market being effectively insulated from the competition of the principal national capital markets.

At the same time, specialist executives working together on syndications and within committees of the AIBD had established networks of personal relationships that linked the Eurobond departments of a broadening array of national firms. Most such executives shared a free-market antiregulatory bias, which was based on the success achieved by the market thus far and on suspicions of the consequences of government intervention in the capital-raising process. Also, a clearing system had been created de novo which was regarded as more modern and less costly than most of the national clearing systems.

The Post–1972 Period

During 1973 and 1974, the market underwent a series of difficulties that resulted in a decline in new-issue volume from $5.6 billion in 1972 to $3.7 billion in 1973 and to $1.9 billion in 1974. These difficulties derived principally from the decline of the U.S. dollar in the early part of this period as well as a general increase in interest rates and precious metals prices. By late 1974, the market for new issues had almost dried up, and secondary-market dealers, including major firms, were reporting substantial losses in the market values of their inventories. In some firms, difficulties or opportunities appeared in other segments of their business that distracted attention and support from the quieter Eurobond operations.

Often, international securities activities were little understood by the managements of firms engaged in businesses of which Eurobonds were only a small part. Some banks significantly reduced their commitment to the Eurobond market during this period, and certain firms that had been significant new-issue lead managers or secondary-market dealers left the business or reduced their scale of operations. Thus, the competitive environment following the 1973–1974 difficulties was materially altered. Among the Eurobond lead managers who surrendered their prominent standings were Hill Samuel, Kredietbank, Kuhn Loeb, Lehman Brothers, and N.M. Rothschild & Sons.

Fortunately, the years 1975 and 1976 saw a substantial improvement in bond market conditions. Interest rates declined and the OPEC surpluses, which exceeded $50 billion in each of those years, swelled the flow of funds entering the international bond markets. At the same time, many industrialized countries were running oil-related balance-of-payments deficits that had to be financed. This increase in both supply and demand resulted in a substantially higher level of borrowing activity. Thus, as Table 2-3 shows, Eurobond new issues rose dramatically between 1974 and 1977. Many of these new issues were directed specifically at OPEC investors, and the presence of Arab securities firm co-managers became a regular feature of Eurobond issues. Less developed countries without oil reserves also became substantial borrowers in the international capital markets to cover their balance-of-payments deficits. Most such borrowings were channeled into the floating-rate Eurocurrency credit market, but a number of the higher-income developing countries such as Mexico, Venezuela, and Malaysia offered Eurobond issues at fixed rates of interest denominated principally in U.S. dollars or Deutsche marks.

New York's Bid for International Activity

In addition to the surge in Eurobond issue activity, the New York market for U.S. dollar-denominated foreign bond issues expanded rapidly following the expiration of the IET in 1974. The total volume of new issues by non-U.S. borrowers in this market increased from approximately $1.0 billion in 1973 to $3.3 billion in 1974, $6.4 billion in 1975, and $10.6 billion in 1976, before declining to $7.4 billion in 1977 and smaller figures in 1978 and 1979. This time, the expansion in foreign issue activity in New York came on the heels of a period of U.S. dollar strength in 1974 and 1975.

American investment banks were understandably pleased by the reopening of the New York marketplace, and significant efforts were devoted to the establishment of placing and trading markets for so-called Yankee issues in the United States. Issues by the governments of France, Norway, Sweden, and the United Kingdom, as well as the European Investment Bank and other sovereign and corporate borrowers again became regular features of the New York capital market. Indeed, in each of four years—1974, 1975, 1976, and 1978—the volume of U.S. dollar-issues by foreign obligors offered in the U.S. capital market exceeded the amount of U.S. dollar Eurobond issues. This led to some hopes that the U.S. dollar-bond market might permanently return to the United States, but it was not to be. European placing capabilities and distribution channels were by this point strongly entrenched, and when the New York market faltered in 1979 and 1980 in the wake of higher domestic interest rates, the activity in Eurobond U.S.-dollar new issues in London doubled and then tripled the amount of issues offered in the Yankee bond market on an annual basis.

From Relationship to Price Banking

With the revival of capital market activity following the recession of 1974, the competitive environment in the Eurobond market changed yet again. In general, the origination of new-issue mandates became more transactional and less relationship-oriented, and certain big issuers were the subject of intense competitive bidding for mandates on a least-cost-of-borrowing basis. In this new environment and with U.S. securities firms temporarily focusing more attention on the New York marketplace, European banks pushed themselves forward in the lead-management league tables. Table 2-9 shows the lead-management leaders for the years 1976–1978. At the same time, offering sizes got larger. The market began to see occasional issues of $100 million to $500 million, and the average size per issue increased from $25 million in the early 1970s to just below $50 million for the years 1976–1978. Issue activity became increasingly concentrated in sovereign borrowers covering their balance-of-payments deficits; corporations represented a smaller portion of the total.

Product Innovation

From its earliest years, the Eurobond market demonstrated a strong tendency toward innovation, both in product development and distribution methods. In the early years, new securities forms were often tools for establishing the boundaries between the supranational Eurobond market and the existing national capital markets; others were experiments with types of securities that were commonplace in the principal national capital markets but whose acceptance in the Eurobond context had not been tested. Thus, the late 1960s saw

Table 2-9
Lead Managers, Eurobonds, 1976–1978

	U.S.$ Equivalent (millions)[a]	Number of Issues
Deutsche Bank	$7,003	84
Westdeutsche Landesbank Girozentrale	2,942	70
Credit Suisse First Boston	2,876	64
S.G. Warburg	2,340	57
Morgan Stanley	2,008	42
Union Bank of Switzerland	1,970	23
Dresdner Bank	1,944	61
Commerzbank	1,228	27
Orion Royal Bank	1,044	27
Hambros Bank	832	18

a. Full credit to book-running lead manager.

the first fixed-rate Eurobond issue with warrants attached, the first Dutch-guilder Euronote issue, the first dual-currency issues, the first French franc-denominated Eurobond issue, as well as experimentation with concepts such as delayed delivery of a portion of an issue.

By the 1970s, with the boundaries of the market generally established and the basic offering and clearing systems in place, the Eurobond market began a series of innovations that would allow it to broaden its product range significantly and attract business away from the national capital markets. These innovations included three major new techniques and a series of lesser improvements to existing products.

The first innovation was the *floating-rate note,* developed for the issue, launched in April 1970 for Ente Nazionale per L'Energia Elettrica (ENEL) and lead managed by Bankers Trust International and S.G. Warburg. Offered during a period of high short-term interest rates in which the fixed-rate U.S. dollar-bond market was experiencing some difficulties, the $125 million ten-year issue was indexed to pay interest at ¾ percent above the six-month LIBOR. (LIBOR is the acronym for the London interbank offered rate for deposits, a short-term interest rate benchmark.) This followed the pattern of previous syndicated loans with interest rates commonly related to LIBOR, but it was in the form of a securities issue, thus representing one of the earliest instances in the modern era of "securitization" of banking assets (discussed in more detail in Chapters 4 and 5). With investors duly nervous over the volatility of rates, the issue was well received and was followed a few months later by a similar financing in the amount of $75 million for Pepsico. By the late 1970s, the floating-rate note had become a significant feature of the Eurobond market and accounted for 20–30 percent of all new-issue activity. It was a product for its time. The concept appealed to borrowers as representing an alternative source of funds to the floating-rate credit markets at a somewhat lower cost; it attracted investors, at least in part, because of the ready marketability of the securities instrument.

The second major innovation of the 1970s was the use of *fixed-price* and *firm-bid issue* techniques beginning in 1975–1977. Until that time, virtually all Eurobond issues had been offered to the public during a two-week selling period with the final terms fixed only at the end, depending on sales response and market conditions. This approach subjected issuers to the risk of changes in market price during the selling period and did not permit them to know the final cost of borrowing until the last minute. The firm-bid technique, commonly used in U.S. negotiated-debt underwritings, consisted of a lead manager fixing the terms of the issue prior to its announcement and communicating those terms to the potential co-managers and under-writers in the course of syndication. It shifted the risk of changes in market conditions from the borrower to the lead manager and thus provided a competitive tool for the aggressive lead manager prepared to assume such risks (with attendant enhancement).

The first prepriced issue in which a group of managers agreed to fix the price of a financing prior to announcement occurred in October 1975 with the launch of a $50-million financing for the government of New Zealand, lead managed by Kidder, Peabody. The first firm-bid issue where a single bank purchased an entire financing for subse-quent reoffering (known in the United States as a "bought" deal) was undertaken for Mobil Oil Corporation in a $200-million issue under-written by Union Bank of Switzerland (Securities) Ltd. in January 1977. Interestingly, the latter financing was intended for ultimate syndication to underwriters, but because of adverse changes in mar-ket conditions, it could not be successfully syndicated and was taken and placed entirely by the lead manager. Such firm-bid deals became, in the late 1970s and early 1980s, a customary method of fixing the terms of Eurobond issues. This was in sharp contrast to the practices used in a number of domestic markets prior to the 1980s, in which underwriters assumed the risk of market price change only after the bonds were effectively placed.

Fixed-price and firm-bid financings proved a potent competitive weapon in broadening the Eurobond market by encroaching on vari-ous domestic capital markets. This factor was particularly evident in the market for Yankee issues to the detriment of the New York mar-ket in the late 1970s. The fixed-price technique also allowed easier linkage of such issues with swaps or other financial market products, since the terms of the financing could be agreed on in advance of launch. Initially, fixed-price issues were used principally with larger and better-known borrowers whose securities were well accepted by the investing public, but the practice rapidly spread to virtually all sectors.

The third principal innovation that allowed a significant expan-sion in Euromarket activity was the development of the *swap* market in the late 1970s and early 1980s. A *capital market swap* is a contract that provides for an exchange of liabilities, possibly in different curren-cies, between two or more entities and stretching several years into the future. Swaps can be used not only to exchange currency liabili-ties but also to convert interest rates from fixed to floating and vice versa. The first currency-swapped Eurobond issue was a financing of 60 million Deutsche marks at 6¾ percent for five years for the Royal Bank of Canada, undertaken in September 1979, in which the borrower's liability was swapped into a combination of U.S. and Canadian dollars. The first interest-rate swapped issue was undertaken in 1981. Currency and interest-rate swaps allowed issues to be undertaken in one market sector and swapped into another currency or sector. Thus, borrowers whose credit was especially favored by investors in one sector could borrow in that currency (perhaps at unusually favorable rates) and obtain an obligation denominated in another currency to match their liabilities to their preferred exposures. Swaps allowed arbitrage to occur between different sectors of the market and between the national capital markets and the Euromarkets. They represented important linkages between markets and permitted a more effective liability-management policy on the part of issuers. Typically, interest-rate and currency swaps resulted in lower costs of borrowing because the concerned parties could borrow in the most advantageous sectors from the standpoint of their own credit acceptance. In the broadest context, the proliferation of the swap technique in the early 1980s pushed the capital markets a quantum leap toward globalization.

In addition to the three major innovations, a number of lesser ones were made in the Eurobond market during the 1970s and early 1980s. Perhaps the first of these was the *adjustable-coupon rectractable Eurobond* issue offered for certain Canadian borrowers beginning in 1974. In an adjustable-coupon retractable issue, the maturity is generally long, say, fifteen years, but the interest rate is refixed every three or five years at the issuer's discretion; bondholders have the option to retain or sell the bond back to the borrower if the refixed interest rate is not attractive. Another innovation that occurred in 1977 was the development of the *multiple tranche*, or *tap stock* issue. The first financing of this kind was undertaken for the Österreichische Kontrollbank, guaranteed by the Republic of Austria. It provided for the authorization of a total principal amount of $200 million of bonds, of which only $100 million was offered initially. The remainder was to be purchased from the issuer and later placed with investors as market conditions permitted and at prices to be fixed by negotiation between the issuer and the lead manager at the time. A multiple tranche therefore allowed delayed drawdown of funds, although not at a known cost.

A third innovation, also undertaken in 1977, was the development of the first *floating-rate certificate of deposit* issue for Japan's Daiichi Kangyo Bank and lead managed by Credit Suisse First Boston. Still another Euromarket innovation was the launch in August 1980 of the first partly paid Eurobond issue for Alcoa of Australia, Ltd. The offering provided for an initial payment of 25 percent of the principal amount of each bond on September 4, 1980, with final payment of the remaining 75 percent on January 15, 1981. This feature produced a leverage effect that allowed investors to benefit from not having to put up the remainder of the principal amount for a further four months. As a result, the financing could be completed on slightly more favorable terms to the issuer than would otherwise have been possible.

In December 1980, the Euromarkets saw another innovation in the first issue of warrants to purchase new debt securities with a fixed rate of interest. Such issues became increasingly popular in 1981 and 1982 and allowed investors to employ certain hedging and leverage strategies in fixed-income portfolio management.

The 1979–1981 period saw greater market volatility than had previously occurred. Higher interest rates spawned a number of financial innovations designed to appeal to segments of the Eurobond investing public. There was also a re-emergence of corporate borrowing in significant volumes and a rebalancing of the competitive picture away from German and Swiss underwriters. Table 2-10 sets forth the lead manager list for the years 1979–1981. This list includes banks from France and shows a return to significant participation by American firms. It also represents a larger number of firms than in previous periods. By 1981, the fortieth bank on the lead-management list had managed five issues totaling $170 million, a record that during most of the 1970s would have earned a position in the top twenty firms. Thus, the number of effective competitors in the Euromarket had increased substantially.

Table 2-10
Lead Managers, Eurobonds, 1979–1981

	U.S.$ Equivalent (millions)[a]	Number of Issues
Credit Suisse First Boston	$7,163	135
Deutsche Bank	5,040	83
Morgan Stanley	3,640	60
S.G. Warburg	2,955	66
Société Génerale	1,816	55
Salomon Brothers	1,690	35
Merrill Lynch	1,572	49
Goldman, Sachs	1,550	23
Credit Commercial de France	1,508	32
Westdeutsche Landesbank Girozentrale	1,449	34
Orion Royal Bank	1,436	34
Dresdner Bank	1,409	30

a. Full credit to book-running lead manager.

Following 1981, the period of volatile economic conditions, high inflation, and unprecedented interest rates gradually gave way to a decline in rates, lower inflation, and more settled development in most Western economies. These factors led to a substantial increase in the volume of total Eurobond financing in the 1982–1986 period (see Table 2-3). Part of this increased activity resulted from refinancing operations as borrowers either converted floating-rate, medium-term obligations into fixed-rate bond issues or exercised call options on existing high-rate bond issues and replaced them with lower interest rate obligations.

Information Technology

The 1980s ushered in an era of striking increases in the speed and quantity of information disseminated about the Eurobond and other capital markets. Information is, of course, integral to the development of any capital market. The schedule in Table 2-11 chronicles significant developments in the availability of Eurobond information.

The progressive availability of more and timelier information about the Eurobond market has not only demystified it but has also diminished the advantage enjoyed by the small group of investment firms at the center by allowing access by new competitors and investors. During the 1980s, transatlantic use of common economic and quotation data and the abandonment of U.S. withholding taxes on publicly traded debt securities (in 1984) resulted in greater integration of the New York and Eurodollar bond markets. Not only did securities move more easily between the two, but Eurodollar bonds were often quoted in the traditional New York convention of basis points of yield (each basis point being equal to 1/100 of 1 percent above or below benchmark U.S. Treasury securities).

Modern telecommunications also changed significantly the way investment bankers and potential borrowing clients communicated with one another. In the 1960s, borrowers typically received information about the Eurobond market through memoranda prepared by leading investment bankers and infrequent articles in the international press. Investment bankers would follow up their written communications with personal visits at borrowers' offices and settle details of financings in face-to-face, sometimes week-long, meetings with senior management.

By the mid-1970s, communications between borrowers and investment bankers were more frequent and included not only general market intelligence, but details of one or more financing alternatives involving innovations that the investment banker wished to introduce.

Table 2-11
Significant Developments in the Availability of Information about the Eurobond Market

Date	Development
April 1969	First meeting of the Association of International Bond Dealers (AIBD) in London.
June 1969	First edition of *Euromoney* magazine.
June 16, 1969	First regular weekly newspaper column covering developments in the Eurobond market appears in the *International Herald Tribune* (Paris).
June 1970	First edition of the *Financial Times Euromarket Newsletter*, a weekly publication.
Early 1972	First edition of the *International Insider*, a weekly printed market newsletter.
November 1973	First AIBD training program in Montreux, Switzerland; 106 trainee participants.
1973	Introduction of Reuters Monitor electronic screen service with later dissemination of Eurobond price quotations.
October 1974	First issue of the *Agefi Newsletter*, since renamed *International Financing Review*, a weekly newsletter.
April 1976	First issue of the international edition of *Institutional Investor*, a monthly magazine.
March 1978	AIBD begins publishing official monthly quotation list of all Eurobonds. Prices transmitted to AIBD at the end of the month; printed price lists available ten days later.
February 1979	Ross & Partners (Securities) Limited begins listing gray market (pre-offering) prices of new issues on the Reuters Monitor service. New-issue syndication techniques are significantly affected.
1980	Telerate electronic screen service becomes generally available in Europe with improved real-time data regarding the U.S. capital markets and the foreign exchange markets.
May 1983	*International Insider* begins real-time transmission of new-issue announcements and other market news over Reuters Monitor electronic screen service.
June 1983	AIBD quotation list published weekly rather than monthly. Prices transmitted to AIBD on Friday; printed price lists available the following Monday.
September 1985	Vigil Information Service, containing real-time data on new issues and market developments and published by *International Financing Review*, becomes available on Telerate.
January 1987	AIBD-reporting dealers transmit to AIBD computers daily closing-price data on issues in which they make markets. Daily price data available in electronic or printed form by the following morning.

Communications were generally by telephone or telex, and document preparation was frequently completed in three to four days.

By the late-1980s, communications rarely included general descriptions of the Eurobond market. Instead, the dialogue focused on several product ideas that offered advantages to the borrower at that specific time. Communications were commonly by telephone, telex, or facsimile transmission equipment. Many borrowers by now subscribed directly to Reuters or Telerate electronic screen services, from which they derived daily market information. The "sense of the market," the commodity that had for so long made the investment banker invaluable to princes, prime ministers, and corporate moguls, was being let out of the bag. To retain or develop an information advantage, investment bankers employed specialized capital-market research personnel to prepare reports on narrow facets of the market for dissemination to selected borrowers and investors. Financing decisions were often made at a lower level in the corporate hierarchy than in the 1970s, and junior management staff commonly completed issue documentation over a period of two to four days after the launch of a financing.

Technological developments leading to the use of advanced data-processing equipment in trading rooms, in back offices, and at the clearing systems facilitated and lowered the cost of processing a growing volume of primary- and secondary-market transactions. In an ancillary vein, faster planes and more integrated air transportation made international travel and package delivery easier.

The increased new-issue volume during the 1982–1986 period was due not only to more frequent financing and refinancing activity but also to a preponderance of larger borrowings, including issues of $1 billion or more for the European Economic Community in 1983 and for Texaco in 1984. The combined lead-management league list for the years 1982–1986 is shown in Table 2-12. The competitive environment in the 1984–1986 period was characterized not only by investment banks' willingness to submit firm bids for large issues denominated in U.S. dollars, but also by a rise in importance of other currencies. This was especially true after 1984, with the general weakening of the U.S. dollar, the growth of swapped transactions, and the liberalization of certain other currency sectors.

Credit Suisse First Boston was far and away the leading underwriter during this period, and its leadership was spread among all the major currencies then represented in the Euromarkets. Deutsche Bank, the most powerful of the European universal banks, held a commanding second position. It was followed by the U.S. commer-

Table 2-12
Lead Managers, Eurobonds, 1982–1986

	U.S.\$ Equivalent (millions)[a]	Number of Issues
Credit Suisse First Boston	\$59,912	642
Deutsche Bank	35,639	468
Morgan Guaranty	26,994	379
Merrill Lynch International	23,048	296
Morgan Stanley	22,595	395
Salomon Brothers	22,123	361
Nomura Securities	21,685	346
S.G. Warburg	13,213	234
Daiwa Securities	13,191	260
Union Bank of Switzerland	11,850	208
Banque Paribas	11,773	228
Goldman, Sachs	11,175	190

a. Full credit to book-running lead manager.

cial bank Morgan Guaranty, which was implementing a policy decision to move into the public securities area in any market from which it was not specifically barred by the Glass-Steagall Act.

The presence of such an impressive group of U.S. investment banks was a testament to their increasing push into the international financing arena and the particularly large capital and personnel commitments they were making specifically to the London markets. The presence of Nomura and Daiwa, the two largest Japanese securities firms, was a portent of the drive they and other Japanese financial institutions were making to obtain leadership positions in the offshore markets. One of the market areas to emerge was the antipodean currencies, specifically the Australian and New Zealand dollars, as significant currencies of denomination, especially beginning in 1985. In addition, the ECU sector of the market, based on several European Common Market currencies, was particularly active after 1982 with placement concentrated in the continental European, especially the Benelux, countries. Finally, the Euroyen market, after a relatively slow start in the late 1970s, underwent successive waves of liberalization and currency strength in 1985–1988, resulting in a broadening market. Competition within the individual currency and product sectors became an important feature of the Eurobond market; by the latter 1980s, many firms specialized in one or more sectors of particular interest to their home country borrowers or swap counterparties.

Reinforcement of London's Position

One might have expected advances in communications to make a vendor's physical location almost irrelevant. But by the mid-1980s, the principal Eurobond origination activities of the leading firms had become centralized in London. Although some firms did keep their top managements, distribution executives, and home-country currency origination teams located in their country capitals, all the corporate finance, syndicate, and trading personnel for Eurodollar issues and most nondollar offerings were typically concentrated in London; IPMA had its operations there, as did the largest of the AIBD regional groupings. This centralization, which had occurred gradually over the previous ten years, was the product of several factors. The most important was London's attitude toward regulation of international securities issuance and trading. In contrast to U.K. banking and to securities activities in other OECD countries, where there were still barriers to entry and effective operation, the international securities business in Britain had remained relatively free. The London market also offered a growing pool of banking and clerical staff as well as an infrastructure of printers, lawyers, and other services; the presence of English law and language was also a significant asset. Although it is not possible to accurately gauge the contribution of the Euromarket activity to the overall U.K. economy, it undoubtedly has been important. The country's balance-of-payments data showed aggregate foreign-currency income from insurance, banking, commodity trading, and brokerage activities (excluding interest) of £6–8 billion per annum in the mid-1980s.

Although the British authorities gave a high priority to the retention of this activity in London, they were nonetheless drafting new legislation that would formalize and reregulate domestic financial services and, inevitably, also affect the Euromarkets (see Chapter 8). This process had begun in the 1970s following the secondary-banking crisis and had been accelerated in 1983 by the proposals for reform of the London Stock Exchange, which included the elimination of fixed commissions and the introduction of outside ownership of stock exchange members.

In 1986, the enactment of the Financial Services Act, discussed in detail in Chapter 8, created the Securities and Investments Board and established requirements for the authorization of firms carrying on investment business in the United Kingdom. Euromarket firms were not exempted from the legislation, but great efforts were made in drafting the bill to accommodate their concerns and requirements. The resulting regulatory statutes would prove to be relatively benign, although sometimes cumbersome. At the same time, opening up London Stock Exchange firms to foreign ownership during a period of buoyant equity prices created opportunities for Eurobond firms to broaden their base of activities into the British domestic market and to place a greater business emphasis on equity securities (see Chapter 9). In the months following passage of the act, there were several substantial acquisitions of London Stock Exchange firms by foreign and domestic banks and the entry of many of the same banks into dealing in British government securities (gilts).

Other Products and Services

Perhaps responding to the industry's maxim of risk reduction through diversification, many Eurobond firms endeavored during the mid-1980s to broaden their international investment banking product lines to include other services. One of the most popular related services was the placement of short-term paper in the form of Eurocommercial paper, or Euronotes. These instruments, generally denominated in U.S. dollars and having maturities of one, three, or six months, were often used to refund bank lines of credit. Later, such standby arrangements frequently were negotiated separately from Eurocommercial paper programs that were undertaken on a stand-alone basis with a series of appointed placing dealers. Citicorp, Swiss Bank Corporation, Merrill Lynch, and Credit Suisse First Boston were among the leading commercial paper dealers in 1986. Some banks were particularly active in placing paper with final investors, whereas others maintained the secondary-trading markets. Banks acting for their own accounts were frequent consumers of such notes, seeking short term liquidity at rates slightly above LIBOR. Smaller investors were also interested in such paper.

Another activity complementary to the product ranges of Eurobond investment banks was mergers and acquisitions. Transnational acquisitions were a natural extension for Euromarket banks. The banks could utilize their specialized knowledge of one or two particular countries to represent sellers or buyers from those countries seeking to complete transactions in other countries. Advice was not limited to mergers and acquisitions but extended to venture capital situations, corporate restructuring, and leveraged buyouts. The most frequent geographic axes for such activity were United Kingdom–United States, United Kingdom–Middle East, and continental Europe–United States.

A third activity frequently added to the product range was the investment management of fixed-income or equity-securities portfolios. Such services, of course, had been conducted alongside Eurobond activities since the market's origins and were an important field for Swiss and other continental banks, as well as for London merchant banks. In recent years, however, international investment management of a substantial and sophisticated nature has been added by both American commercial and investment banks as well as other firms active in the Eurobond market. To limit potential conflicts of interest, which abound in firms with this mix of services, safeguards were created to separate the investment-management decision functions from those of sales and trading departments. These safeguards were intended to preserve the autonomy and independence of the money managers.

A fourth area where certain international investment banks added substantially to product lines in 1986 and 1987 was in Euroequities. This addition coincided with a trend toward increased trading in domestic shares by international investors, frequently in offshore markets in different time zones. One of the London Stock Exchange's principal reasons for its 1986 merger with the International Securities Regulatory Organization was an interest in playing a more significant market-making role in international shares (see Chapter 7). London already had the largest market in the world for international shares and, following the liberalization of the procedures for ownership of London Stock Exchange firms, experienced a substantial expansion of market-making activities. Indications are that 1987 trading volumes of non-U.K. shares in London was greater than the combined trading in non-U.S. shares on the New York Stock Exchange and in the U.S. over-the-counter markets. It appeared that the London market, with its lower costs and taxes, had attracted business that might otherwise have been transacted on national stock exchanges elsewhere in the world.

Prior to the October 1987 crash, the Euroequity underwriting business underwent a substantial increase, with international distributions through underwriting syndicates of equity totaling $11.3 billion in 1986 for new issues alone. Such offerings have, in some cases, included privatization flotations involving government enterprises in Britain, France, Canada, and the United States. During the twelve months ending March 1987, the leading managers of new Euroequity issues were Credit Suisse First Boston, Merrill Lynch, Swiss Bank Corporation, and Morgan Stanley. Deutsche Bank managed fewer issues than the others but had the distinction of leading the first $1 billion Euroequity financing (Fiat). Within investment banking organizations, the newer Euroequity activities are often closely coordinated with the banks' existing trading and placement of equity convertible Eurobonds and Eurobonds with equity warrants attached.

The Contraction of 1987

Beginning in late 1986 with the decline of the perpetual floating-rate note market and continuing in 1987 with rises in interest rates and the equity crash of October, Eurobond secondary- and primary-market activity declined sharply. This resulted in a substantial reorientation by many firms after the earlier period of heavy expansion. The causes and results of these developments are discussed later in the book.

Conclusions

A number of generalizations about the manner in which the development of the market shaped the competitive environment are evident. First, the growth of the Eurobond new-issue market, which averaged 25 percent per annum during the past twenty years, was based significantly on a lack of international regulation—in sharp contrast to the often highly regulated national capital markets. This feature allowed the market and individual firms to compete with the principal national capital markets in both the mobilization and allocation of savings.

Second, despite the internationalism inherent in the Eurobond market, individual competitors frequently retained strong national identities, often specializing in national currency sectors or assisting clients with a base of operations in their home countries. Following clients overseas or developing home-country currency markets tended to be the predominant competitive thrust of most firms. Although several firms have taken steps beyond this—toward becoming global competitors—these initiatives are still in their early stages and often have been accomplished through extensions of existing home country or Eurobond services.

Third, a substantial broadening in the dissemination of information about the Eurobond market (and the related national markets) has raised the level of sophistication among investors and increased access to the market by new competitors from other financial services industries, especially commercial banking.

The rapid growth of the market and ease of entry have caused a large number of firms to set up Eurobond investment banking units. Whereas approximately 30 firms lead managed at least one issue ten years ago, more than 110 firms lead managed at least one issue in 1988. Although faced with an increasing array of competitors, the marketplace did not evidence a significant decrease in the concentration of mandates won by the few leading firms.

An analysis of the principal lead managers of Eurobond issues shows that the leading firms changed rapidly, with less than 50 percent of the firms that were prominent in the mid-1980s having been significant lead managers of issues in the 1960s and 1970s. The changes in lead-manager patterns resulted from changes of emphasis on Euromarket activities at the individual firms and from changes in the role of the various currencies and other securities products with which individual firms were particularly identified.

Last, it is apparent from the market's history (and from information set forth in the next chapter) that an increasing transactional orientation among issuers led to a partial breakdown of long-standing borrower-investment bank relationships and a rise in competitive bidding, often on a price basis for new mandates. This factor, together with an expansion in the number of qualified competitors, resulted in a significant increase in the intensity of interfirm competition.

CHAPTER 3

GLOBALIZATION AND SEGMENTATION: EUROBOND MARKET COMPETITION IN 1989

By the end of the 1980s, the Euromarkets had evolved and matured to become a large financing bazaar with a group of well-established players representing the major industrial powers of the Free World. Euromarket competitors can be classified into four separate groups: continental European banks; clearing banks; merchant banks; and investment banks, including securities dealers. Each group comes from a different business culture and approaches the competitive challenge with different objectives and strategies that often reflect their national characters.

Continental European Banks

Included in this category are the principal commercial banks in Belgium, France, Germany, Holland, Italy, and Switzerland, about twenty major entrants in all.[1] These are generally large national units with a long universal banking tradition of both lending activity and securities business in their home country markets. Even before the founding of the Euromarkets in 1963, these banks had many years of experience in distributing both domestic and international securities over the counters of their extensive branch office networks. In the Euromarket context, these banks have often been closely linked with issues denominated in the currencies of their home countries. As in the case of Germany, their national governments have often required that issues denominated in their currencies be lead managed by home country banks.

Continental European banks have been active in both the domestic equity and bond markets in their countries. Within their organizations, such securities activities are regarded as part of the mainstream of each firm's business, with representatives of both commercial banking and securities activities in the top management group. Despite their long experience in the securities business, continental

---

1. D. F. Lomax and P. T. G. Gutman in *The Euromarkets and International Financial Policies* (New York: John Wiley, 1981) describe the relationship of financial policies of each of these countries to the Euromarkets.

European banks demonstrate a relatively cautious approach to securities trading. As institutions of major importance in their own countries, they have close relationships with their central banking and monetary authorities, reflect a domestic orientation, and embody a financial conservatism that has held them back from pioneering in innovative Euromarket types of transactions.

The continental bankers favor operating from offices located in their home countries rather than in London; alternatively, they have in some cases utilized London-based subsidiaries that were closely controlled by the securities part of the parent bank's senior management. In practice, this organizational approach has been effective, because the individuals responsible for securities business in the parent bank understand the international securities industry and the potential problems of the Euromarket subsidiary. Salary and compensation levels of executives involved in Euromarket activities at continental European banks reflect the overall salary policies of their parent organizations and are on a lower scale than those of their most important competitors, the investment banks.

Clearing Banks

Another category of competitors is the clearing bank. This group includes U.S. commercial banks, Japanese city and long-term credit banks, Canadian chartered banks, and British and Australian clearing banks—in all, about twenty-five major players. These banks are large, national entities with numerous branch offices that prior to the 1970s specialized almost entirely in deposit taking and commercial lending. Until ten years ago, when there was a dramatic reversal of field, they were generally not involved in investment banking, stockbroking, or investment advisory services in their home-country securities markets, and with few exceptions, they did not distribute or sell securities through their branches. Often, the only working knowledge of securities business within the bank organization was in the treasurer's department, where the financing of the bank was carried out as a matter of liability management, or in clerical areas, where securities-custody functions were sometimes undertaken.

As important commercial lenders, clearing banks have had a long tradition of international banking and are accustomed to running both domestic and international branch systems across geographic time zones. Their London operations usually include Eurodollar deposit taking and lending functions, making them knowledgeable about international financial operations closely related to the securities business. The culture of these large organizations is typically one in which the senior individuals have significant prestige in their own countries; in some cases, the institution formerly had a disdain for the securities business in the home country, which was often undertaken by sales-oriented organizations lacking in the capital, prestige, and name recognition of the commercial banking tradition. Beginning in the 1970s, however, the clearing banks became interested in the securities business as a potential diversification into a profitable adjacent field. Although local law or tradition often barred their expansion into the domestic securities industry, many clearing banks were able to set up affiliates in London and elsewhere to participate directly in the Eurobond markets. Later, in the 1980s, following regulatory changes, clearing banks were able to enter discount brokering in the United States, securities dealing in Canada, and stockbrokering in Britain.

The Eurobond subsidiary of a major clearing bank generally reports to the international department, the world corporate banking department, or the treasury department of the parent bank. The individuals to whom the subsidiary reports, and who often control the board of directors of the merchant banking subsidiary, often have lacked practical experience in the securities industry. This has led in some instances to more difficult relationships between the Eurobond affiliates and the parent bank than is the case in the Eurobond operations of the continental European banks.

In most cases, the Eurobond or other securities market subsidiaries of the clearing banks are small in relation to the parent institution. In the past, the subsidiaries' profits or losses were not viewed as significant in the total organizational context; in some cases, profits were less important to the clearing bank than having a toehold in the international securities business. Such activities were regarded by bank managements in the 1970s and early 1980s as desirable in view of trends toward securitization and globalization, as well as representing a beachhead in seeking changes to domestic laws restricting securities activities.

In most clearing bank countries, the central bank either did not attempt to control the use of their currency as a currency of denomination in Eurobond issues, or, in the case of Japan, it exercised that control in favor of the nation's securities firms over the subsidiaries of the commercial banks. By the end of the 1980s, however, that view had darkened and retrenchment was the order of the day.

Merchant Banks

In this category are the traditional London merchant banks such as Hambros, Morgan Grenfell, and S.G. Warburg, as well as firms such as Banque Paribas and Lazard Frères in Paris, Mees & Hope and Pearson Heldring in Amsterdam, and Trinkaus and Richard Daus in

Germany. Although many national and consortium institutions are also in this category, only about five can claim to be significant Eurobond competitors. Usually, the merchant banks are smaller than the clearing or commercial banks in their home countries, both in terms of capital staff and branch offices. They have, however, traditionally engaged in entrepreneurial activities, including venture capital and securities issue business as well as trade-related financing. The merchant banks therefore share some common roots with their clearing bank counterparts and the investment banks.

As firms that are often family owned, merchant banks enjoy the relatively short and speedy lines of communication characteristic of smaller enterprises. Although merchant banks have been active in the Eurobond market since its earliest days, they have been influenced by a generally conservative operating philosophy and a limited capital base. In the 1980s, several have responded to sharper Eurobond price competition and higher operating costs by retreating to a largely domestic mix of business. Some have been overtaken in international securities business by larger banks from their own countries with greater capital resources and international reach. Their long securities tradition has allowed them to continue to be active in distribution and trading functions, but their placing capabilities tend to be with larger institutional accounts and wealthy individuals because they customarily have not had extensive retail branch-office systems like some of the investment banks. Merchant banks' greatest strength, however, lies in the origination of new Eurobond financings, where their intimate knowledge of the market and the ability to act quickly on that intelligence gives them a lead in dealing with potential Eurobond issuers.

Merchant banks are often close to the central banking and monetary authorities in their countries and have benefited from an understanding of government policy with respect to interest rates and use of the currency in international transactions. In some cases, this has provided merchant banks with useful intelligence in respect to new Euromarket products, which they can offer to borrowers worldwide. Several U.K. merchant banks, as well as Paribas and Banque Indosuez in France, have added other capital market functions to their activities in recent years and have become financial conglomerates both in their own markets and internationally.

Investment Banks and Securities Dealers

This category of firms generally encompasses securities dealers in the United States, Canada, and Japan and numbers about ten major entities. Their personnel often come from securities sales or trading backgrounds and are adept at managing securities inventories and exposures as well as providing investment banking services in their home markets to a variety of corporate and governmental borrowers. In character, they are generally entrepreneurial organizations and are considerably smaller than the commercial banks in their home markets. In some instances, they operate large-scale branch networks of securities salespeople and have had sales and trading branches in London and other international financial centers for many years. Investment banks and securities dealers have grown significantly in terms of capital and staff since the 1960s and have experienced high margins and substantial profit growth in their respective domestic markets. In some cases, this growth has been by fixed commissions on securities transactions as well as the substantial growth of home market securitization of financial assets and liabilities. Individual compensation scales in investment banks and securities dealers are substantially higher than in their banking counterparts and often include a contingent element based on individual or firm performance, as well as eventual share ownership or partnership. Historically, these firms have been separately owned rather than operated as parts of larger conglomerate firms. In recent years, however, investment dealers have added activities that significantly broadened their product lines, and they have developed more elaborate management systems for coping with the pressures and problems of individual units within the group.

Sales and distribution teams of investment banking firms and securities dealers are adept at servicing both retail and institutional accounts and tend to be commission driven in perspective, but with an increasing securities research orientation. Although national in original character, investment banks and securities dealers were one of the first groups to develop an expertise about the Eurobond market. Since the 1960s, they have been active in exploiting financing opportunities by originating issues, often of an imaginative character, for home country borrowers and international investors. In recent years, these firms have been able to broaden their client base beyond home country borrowers and investors, and several have now taken significant steps toward becoming truly global dealers. In contrast to their clearing bank competitors, most investment banks and securities dealers have top managements with lifetime experience in the securities business and have been able to staff overseas affiliates with skilled home-country nationals, thereby maintaining links between geographic units through interpersonal relationships.

Euromarket Strategies

The Eurobond market is thus characterized by a multiplicity of competitors who approach this market from very different national and institutional backgrounds and with a range of business cultures. These sharp differences have caused various firms to emphasize different strengths and qualities in the struggle for competitive advantage.

The old-line *merchant banks* of Europe have tried to approach the Eurobond market with a detachment and a perspective worthy of their long experience and traditions. They have built up their investment management departments as purchasers of attractively priced international securities and have continued to develop transnational merger-and-acquisition activities. They work from a solid base of profitable domestic and some international investment banking business and are able to exploit market niches in, or closely related to, the Euromarkets. They have generally steered clear of aggressively priced Eurobond deals, and few would be characterized as leaders in Eurobond trading. Some merchant banks, including Hill Samuel, Lazard, and N.M. Rothschild, had been prominent participants in the Euromarkets of the 1960s and 1970s, but more recently they have retained only small groups of Euromarket specialists. Some of these firms have de-emphasized Eurobond business relative to the significant efforts necessary to develop new domestic activities, often in liberalized marketplaces featuring substantial opportunities in the privatization of government-owned enterprises or stock exchange business. In the United Kingdom, only S.G. Warburg has endeavored to develop both a broad-based U.K. financial services conglomerate and a major international capital-markets unit with significant operations in London, New York, and Tokyo.

By the late 1980s, *continental European banks*, with a few notable exceptions, had also relegated Eurobond business to a lower priority in their multifaceted activities. Euromarket business is, for many, often part of a broader international department. In some countries, the national banks continue to benefit from, and be active in, protected Euromarket niches, often related to Euroissues denominated in the national currency or national currency swaps. Such opportunities are actively exploited by teams of executives working from the home-country national headquarters, and specialization in home country currency, for example, does not limit their ability to offer other opportunities to clients during visits. Few of these institutions have established separate units in London or have engaged in general competition for U.S. dollar-denominated issues, where bidding is fierce and syndicate losses are frequent. Thus, while they continue to lead manage issues regularly for home country borrowers, continental banks have not been surprised to lose mandates for Eurobond issues denominated in open currencies, or Eurocommercial paper or

Euroequity financings, to their global London-based competitors. The principal exceptions to this general pattern are Deutsche Bank AG and the three largest Swiss banks, which, because of their historic importance and placing power, have adopted a global strategy based on operations in London, New York, and Tokyo, as well as in the home country, and have successfully developed capabilities in several Eurocurrency sectors.

Investment banks and securities dealers from the United States, Japan, and, to a lesser extent, Canada have been the principal beneficiaries of the Euromarket territory won from the merchant banks and the continental European banks since the 1970s. They gained this market penetration through a combination of aggressive trading and origination practices in the traditional Eurobond sectors and emphasis on new product areas such as swaps, Eurocommercial paper, and Euroequities. The investment banks and securities dealers approached the Euromarket in the 1980s with state-of-the-art trading skills. The Americans brought substantial financial-engineering capabilities and impressive placing power, and the Japanese brought significant borrowing clients. Both have been significant beneficiaries of the trend toward world trade in securities and the erosion of national barriers to securities investment, as well as the more rapid dissemination and entrepreneurial utilization of information. More than many of their commercial banking competitors, these securities firms have been adept at rapidly capitalizing on changing market conditions. Interestingly, American and Japanese firms approach their individual staffing and compensation policies in diametrically opposite ways: the Americans feature high salaries and uncertain tenure, the Japanese relatively modest compensation and lifetime employment.[2] Yet both manage to obtain an intensity of effort and a coordination across geographic time zones, which give them a significant edge in capturing many mandates even outside their own countries. By 1988, U.S. investment banks and Japanese securities dealers or their affiliates had gained seven out of the first ten places in the Eurobond lead-managers league table.

Subsidiaries of clearing banks from Australia, Canada, Japan, the United Kingdom, and the United States have experienced difficulty in establishing themselves as top Eurobond lead managers. With their international roots in Eurocurrency lending and foreign exchange,

2. For a discussion of compensation and cultural differences in various firms, see J. Hakim, *The International Investment Banking Revolution* (London: The Economist Publications Limited, 1986), pp. 49–54.

they have the global reach, but their administrative and organizational policies have been more bureaucratic than either their merchant or investment banking competitors, and they have not found it easy to recruit and retain top international securities staff. Lacking senior clearing bank personnel versed in the securities business, they generally have approached the risk-taking aspects of becoming major dealers in marketable securities with caution. Although some clearing banks have been successful in carving out market niches related to the home country currency, the niches often have not been as well protected by government intervention as the currency niches of their continental European counterparts. During the declines in market activity in 1987 and early 1988, many clearing banks incurred significant losses on Eurobond operations and consequently reoriented or reduced staffing levels and abandoned expansion programs. Because most clearing banks were precluded from owning brokerage or investment banking firms in their home markets, senior managements often regarded their Eurobond affiliates as providing only a diversification from their core activities rather than a business central to their future strategy. But there are important exceptions.

For example, Morgan Guaranty, while naturally categorized with the U.S. money-center banks, has long exhibited the skills in investments, mergers and acquisitions, and currency banking characteristic of a U.S. investment bank or a British merchant bank. Banque Paribas, while often classed as a French merchant bank, has the larger balance sheet and staff resources common to many continental European commercial banks. And, very important, the Japanese commercial banks have been making a strong push into the Euromarkets to escape the regulation of Article 65, which constrains their securities-related activities in Japan. Industrial Bank of Japan, in particular, has used this route to reassert the premier investment banking credentials it had enjoyed prior to World War II.

As mentioned previously, international securities activity accounts for only a modest proportion of the total revenues and capital of most of the banks. Thus, most Eurobond units of these banks approach that market from a national perspective and are often constrained by the business cultures of their parent organizations. Many of the services supplied by these Euromarket subsidiary units are directed toward home country borrowers or investors. The international strategies of the parent banks tend to be slow to change. Accordingly, while the Euromarket is characterized by relative ease of entry and tactical movement between certain niches, the strategies of a number of competing vendors have not tended to adjust as might be expected. It is readily observable that a number of small Eurobond affiliates have been prisoners of their parents' overarching strategies and deeply ingrained cultures and could not change in response to new market circumstances as rapidly as, for instance, a Credit Suisse First Boston or a Morgan Stanley.

The Role of Capital

In any financial institution, risk capital (equity and subordinated debt) serves as a cushion to protect other more senior creditors and depositors against losses and to generally ensure that the firm will be able to meet all its obligations on a timely basis. Recently, much attention has been focused on commercial banks because of loan losses and concern that the banks' risk capital and reserves are insufficient to protect other creditors against principal losses; thus, there is the possibility of default or—more likely—the forced interposition of government bailout funds. Increasingly, these banks have been subject to complex capital ratios imposed by home country authorities as well as international regulatory advisories such as the Bank for International Settlements in Basel, Switzerland.

In the case of merchant and investment banks, however, capital was seen, at least until the 1970s, as being of secondary importance to product skills and market judgment; capital was understated by the presence of hidden reserves or partnership payout arrangements.

Beginning in the 1970s, significant capital and the ability to lend and book foreign exchange and swaps have been seen as a competitive advantage for most European and North American commercial banks. The parent banks' superior capital position gives their investment banking subsidiaries an edge over the subsidiaries of most securities dealers and merchant banks. The individual capital of the securities operating unit is, of course, necessary for underwriting and market making, but clients usually assume there is also a "deep pocket" backing the subsidiary. From inside the operating unit, however, capital is sometimes an issue between the parent and the subsidiary that relates to the autonomy and the decision-making authority of the operating unit. These questions are generally not critical, since the parent normally provides to meet the subsidiary's needs as long as the subsidiary achieves the parent's operating objectives. Within commercial banks and investment banks, however, the allocation of capital to specific subsidiaries is usually viewed as a rationing process, given the managements' preference for capital mobility controlled from the center.

In the classical investment bank, capital is seen as both a cushion against underwriting risks and the means for carrying substantial

inventories of tradable securities. Capital needs at most U.S. investment banks broadened significantly in the 1980s as these firms expanded domestically and internationally into product and service
areas adjacent to their traditional fields, notably into retail brokerage
and merchant banking. In some instances, particularly involving
overseas subsidiaries, stock-exchange or government-mandated insistence on local capital provisions further amplified the need.

Increased capital needs were also based on the investment banks'
perception that future growth possibilities would require even greater
capital. This prospect was related both to the rapid expansion of
trading activities and, in the case of the United States and Japan, to
possible deregulation that would eliminate barriers between investment banking and commercial banking. Additional capital was also
seen by senior management of investment banking firms as a statement to their personnel of their commitment to strategies of growth
that would yield attractive opportunities to people in the organization.

As discussed in more detail in Chapter 4, the trend of the 1970s
and 1980s toward public ownership of U.S. securities firms, which
had been private partnerships for decades, was spurred by at least
two important considerations. First was the desire to lock in capital so
that it would not have to be replaced as partners inevitably retired.
Second, public ownership facilitated access to additional capital. So
long as the equities of major investment banks, assisted by strong
earnings growth, remained well regarded, such equity could be sold
to raise cash or used in acquisitions or staff incentive plans at advantageous multiples of book value.

In a similar fashion, many British stockbrokers sought outside
capital in the mid-1980s. The potential for expanded market making
in the wake of Big Bang necessitated greater permanent capital. In
this instance, however, most capital was supplied by other financial
institutions, which acquired major U.K. stockbrokers. As detailed in
Chapter 7, Japanese securities firms have also been able to access
large amounts of capital via the public markets on very attractive
terms.

U.K. and European merchant banks generally operated with limited capital resources. Although many earned substantial returns in
the 1980s, their aspirations were, with few exceptions, more modest
than those of the U.S. and Japanese securities dealers. Most increased
their capital during this period, but their concentration on their relatively small domestic markets made capital a less critical factor in the
expansion process.

Use of Multiple Lead Managers

Earlier reference has been made to competitive bidding for Eurobond lead managements and to the trend toward the use of multiple managers.[3] Indeed, this became a feature of several principal domestic capital markets. To understand better the phenomenon, we examined data regarding the financing programs of frequent international borrowers, including three U.S. corporations—General Electric, Philip Morris, and RJR Nabisco. For these corporations, the periods in 1985, 1986, and 1987 immediately following their multibillion-dollar acquisitions of RCA, General Foods, and Nabisco Brands, respectively, have been reviewed. Such acquisitions generally give rise to large external financing programs that require significant use of the capital markets during the years that immediately follow.

The results of the review are set forth in Table 3-1.

All three borrowers tended to use lead managers with credible records in the various market sectors being tapped. Not surprisingly given their geographic locus, each borrower used a preponderance of American lead managers, sometimes even for their entry into Swiss franc and Deutsche mark-issue markets. On several occasions, they also used firms such as Daiwa Securities, Long-Term Credit Bank of Japan, and Union Bank of Switzerland for their U.S. dollar-denominated Eurofinancings. In only three instances was a manager used by a company in its international financing that also had lead managed a domestic issue for the corporation.

Discussions with borrowers and investment bankers, together with the evidence of the use of multiple lead managers, indicate that there was a substantial decline in borrower loyalty and relationship banking. Competitive bidding on a price basis was frequent and suggests a significant shift in favor of borrowers looking for external capital during the 1970s and 1980s. Regular borrowers among corporations, governments, and banks have developed in-house staffs of liability-management specialists, which have become more sophisticated and aggressive in seeking out optimal funding opportunities. Such staffs are adept in developing data resources on market developments—formerly the bailiwick of the financier—and in juggling the competitive initiatives of international investment banks to obtain relatively tighter issue terms. In addition, the general decline in

3. C. L. Courtadon in "The Competitive Structure of the Eurobond Underwriting Industry," unpublished master's thesis, New York University Graduate School of Business Administration, 1985, also finds a decline in the importance of historical ties in the selection of Eurobond lead managers.

Table 3-1
Sample Company Financing Programs

	General Electric		Philip Morris	RJR Nabisco
	13 financings in 10 months in 1986	20 financings in 16 months in 1985–1987	15 financings in 21 months in 1985–1987	15 financings in 21 months in 1985–1987
U.S. Domestic Financings				
Total	6	7	7	7
Number of different lead managers used	5	4	4	4
International Financings				
Total	7 (2 currencies)	13 (7 currencies)	8 (5 currencies)	8 (5 currencies)
Number of different lead managers used	7	9	4	4

interest rates during the 1982–1986 period allowed regular opportunities for refinancing of existing obligations at progressively lower costs, so that the finance function was seen by other groups in the borrower's hierarchy as making a significant contribution to the reduction of overall costs. In short, borrowers had gotten into the driver's seat and were shopping around.

The Competitive Pyramid

Although the Eurobond market in recent years has undergone a process of segmentation in which increasing emphasis has been given to niche strategies, success in the overall Eurobond market (see Appendix Table A-1) is still regarded by most major competitors as highly important. The ability to undertake issues in segments outside a firm's obvious niches is a hallmark of versatility and progress toward global capability. Such skills are important, given the currency and interest-rate swap process that links segments of the market in day-to-day business. Thus, certain specialties, such as U.S. dollar interest-rate swaps and U.S. dollar-Eurobond underwritings, are regarded as desirable building blocks in assembling swap-related financing packages for clients, even though these parts of the business are very competitive and not always profitable.

One measure of the intensity of competition within the Eurobond hierarchical structure is the number of firms that are active in lead managing new financings. Table 3-2 shows the numbers of firms that lead managed issues in all currencies in recent years. Although Table 3-2 partly reflects the overall growth of the market, it also illustrates the rapid rate at which new competitors have entered the field and achieved managing underwriter status.

A review of the Eurobond lead managers indicates that leader-

Table 3-2
Number of Investment Banks Lead Managing, 1980–1987

	At Least 1 Issue	At Least 5 Issues	At Least 10 Issues	At Least 20 Issues
1980	76	24	4	2
1981	76	27	13	2
1982	83	33	19	6
1983	75	35	15	4
1984	81	42	25	11
1985	94	57	35	20
1986	112	54	38	24
1987	117	60	39	18

ship of Eurobond issues has revolved among a limited number of vendor firms, but with rapid swings in year-to-year standing. On a longer-term basis, banks such as N.M. Rothschild, Westdeutsche Landesbank, and Kredietbank, which were prominent in the 1960s and 1970s, have receded, while others like Nomura, Nikko, and Morgan Guaranty have risen into the top ranks. Firms such as Credit Suisse First Boston, Deutsche Bank, Morgan Stanley, Paribas, S.G. Warburg, and their antecedents have been leaders in all three decades. Such shifts in position contrast with the principal national capital markets (see Chapters 5, 7, and 9), where status is more or less constant from year to year and where a small number of persistently leading firms underwrite most issues. Rapid change in leadership position is, of course, a product not only of changes in the popularity of different currency and product sectors and of the entry by new competitors, but also of the use of multiple lead managers by borrowers.

Market Share Concentration

In a market of increasing and vigorous competition, one would expect the concentration of market share in the hands of leading firms to decline over time. To examine this hypothesis, we undertook a statistical analysis to determine the leadership concentration during selected earlier years of the market and in each year in the 1980s.

In 1963–1964, with fewer firms participating in the new market, the leading firms showed a relatively high concentration of lead-manager positions; the foremost of these garnered 20–25 percent of total issues. However, from the mid-1960s through the mid-1980s, despite the growth in numbers of competitors in the overall Eurobond market, the top firm has generally achieved 10–20 percent of total Eurobond market volume with a further two to six firms each generating market shares of 5–10 percent; the remaining 50–60 percent of issues is divided among a growing number of firms, including the many new entrants.[4] Table 3-3 shows the market shares of various groups of lead managers in the total Eurobond market during the 1980s. While market shares of the most active managers have shown significant year-to-year swings, based principally on changes in individual sectors, the overall level of leadership concentration on a longer-term basis has been relatively consistent.

As mentioned, turnover within the group of leading firms has

4. Courtadon in "The Competitive Structure of the Eurobond Underwriting Industry" found an increase in concentration during the period from 1979 to 1984, but attributed it principally to developments in the floating-rate note sector.

Table 3-3
Market Shares of Total Eurobond Issues, 1980–1987

	Of 1st Lead Manager	Of Lead Managers in 2d–6th Positions	Of All Other Lead Managers	Total
1980	11.7%	29.8%	58.5%	100%
1981	13.6	28.4	58.0	100
1982	15.3	33.0	51.7	100
1983	21.6	30.7	47.7	100
1984	16.6	32.8	50.6	100
1985	14.3	28.6	57.1	100
1986	11.4	31.2	57.4	100
1987	13.0	29.0	58.0	100

been high. Of the ten most active managers in each of the years 1984–1987, four firms or their antecedents had been prominent lead managers in the late 1960s and the 1970s, while the other six firms represented new entrants principally from the United States and Japan that had come to significant prominence in the Eurobond market only in the 1980s. Leadership turnover in the 1980s (as illustrated in Appendix Table A-1) was not great until 1987.

Entry and Exit

The open environment of the 1980s made establishing a Eurobond affiliate in London with a reasonable staff complement an easy step for a large commercial bank with existing international and domestic networks. Such operations could be used to meet a variety of objectives, including the generation of securitized assets or syndications and the undertaking of a few prestige transactions each year to enhance the perceived international reach and versatility of the parent institution. Some leading Eurobond institutions, however, aimed at becoming serious broad-scaled competitors in worldwide investment banking. Their more ambitious objective involved heavy expenditures for trading facilities, personnel, and implantations in the principal domestic national marketplaces. That objective called for the coordination of enlarged businesses across time zones and multiple cross-selling and execution opportunities. Not surprisingly, only a limited number of the vendors in the Euromarketplace have succeeded in this objective.

While barriers to entry have been low, so have been barriers to exit. Although many institutions were proud to have an operating unit in London as a symbol of their strategic commitment to international investment banking, Euromarket difficulties in the 1986–1988 period caused a number to reconsider their positions. For some, operations were substantially reduced or, in several cases, shut down.

Currency and Country

The currency of denomination, the country of the borrower, and the type of security chosen for a Eurobond are all critical in the competitive struggle to lead manage a financing. Table 2-3 chronicled the evolution of three principal types of issues in the Eurobond market during the past twenty-five years. In the 1980–1987 period, the U.S. dollar was the overall leader by a substantial margin, but the denomination of new issues appears closely related to perceived trends in currency strength (see Appendix Table A-2). International investors have a well-established preference for securities denominated in strengthening currencies. The weakness of the U.S. dollar in 1980 and again in 1986–1987 accounted for subsequent declines in the percentage of dollar issues in Euromarket totals. Similarly, French franc-denominated issues were influenced by the fact that the franc was firm in 1980, declined in 1982 and 1983, and then rallied in 1986 and 1987. The strength of the Japanese yen and the Deutsche mark in 1986 and 1987 boosted the totals of issues in those currencies, too. Thus investment bankers with specializations in particular currencies find their levels of activity affected by the fortunes of those currencies.

Borrowers have shown a tendency to use investment banks from their own countries as lead managers in new Eurobond offerings because of a close relationship, because the national government encourages this, or both. Statistics showing the country of borrower of all Eurobond issues during the years 1980–1987 verify this predisposition (see Appendix Table A-3). While type-of-issue specialization, currency, home-country borrower relationships, or governmental intervention cannot guarantee an investment bank a mandate, a *perception* that a particular bank may have a competitive edge may deter other firms from competing quite as aggressively for the business. The result can be ad hoc barriers to entry in certain market sectors.

Market Niches

A market niche is a currency or product specialization in the Euromarket. Investment banks find it advantageous to develop strengths in certain niches to enhance their attractiveness to potential borrowers. Table 3-4 lists the principal issue-related market niches at the end of 1986 and 1987 and the leading firms within those niches.

In addition, a number of niches not directly related to new Eurobond issues exist, including those involving trading and arbitrage in various sectors, transnational mergers and acquisitions, international real estate, futures and options-related trading, and Euroequities.

Appendix Tables A-4 through A-12 set forth the league tables for lead managers and market share ranks in the nine principal currency sectors during the years 1982–1987. Tables A-13, A-14, and A-15 show the league tables for fixed-rate U.S. dollar issues, U.S. dollar floating-rate notes, as well as equity convertible and warrant issues during the same period. Some sectors evidence a large number of competitors and frequent changes in ranking, while others demonstrate a relatively consistent picture over time. For investment banking management, establishing and maintaining leadership in profitable niches is a central preoccupation.

Strength in a particular niche may derive from a variety of strategic skills. For example, in the Australian dollar-Eurobond sector, a high proportion of all new issues is swapped into floating-rate U.S. dollar obligations. For this reason, a capability in Australian dollar-currency swaps and U.S. dollar interest-rate swaps is important in achieving a strong niche specialization. In addition, Australian dollar-Eurobond issues in 1985 and 1986 were particularly attractive to investors in the German-speaking countries of Europe. Consequently, German, Swiss, and Austrian banks with syndication and distribution capabilities in those countries figured prominently in lead managing and co-managing these issues.

Each niche requires a different mix of vendor qualities to develop a successful specialization. Some, such as French franc Eurobonds, have significant regulatory aspects that restrict the use of that currency and involve direct government intervention in the financing process. Other niches involve different product life cycles or different skills for adding value in the issue formulation, marketing, execution, and distribution stages. The critical value-added elements at each stage may either change rapidly or remain constant over a long period of time.

In assessing its strategy for exploiting a particular niche, the investment bank must determine if it can bring together the particular skills that will allow it to achieve initial credibility or to penetrate further into an existing field. If expansion or initial entry is targeted, the critical elements must be assembled and possibly strengthened, often through the recruitment of specialized personnel in various locations and the negotiation of working-team relationships. Assuming the firm has brought together the right mix of people, products,

Table 3-4
Leading Firms in Principal Euromarket Niches, 1986–1987

Niches	1986	1987
U.S. dollar fixed-rate issues for large sovereign borrowers	Deutsche Bank AG Credit Suisse First Boston	Deutsche Bank AG Credit Suisse First Boston
U.S. dollar floating-rate notes	Credit Suisse First Boston Morgan Guaranty Salomon Brothers	Salomon Brothers Nikko Securities
Japanese equity warrant and convertible issues	Nomura Securities Daiwa Securities	Nomura Securities Nikko Securities
American convertible issues	Credit Suisse First Boston Morgan Stanley	Credit Suisse First Boston Morgan Stanley
Deutsche mark issues	Deutsche Bank AG Westdeutsche Landesbank Commerzbank AG Dresdner Bank AG	Deutsche Bank AG Commerzbank AG Dresdner Bank AG Westdeutsche Landesbank
Japanese yen issues	Nomura Securities Daiwa Securities Yamaichi Securities Nikko Securities	Nomura Securities Daiwa Securities Industrial Bank of Japan Nikko Securities

Pounds sterling issues	Samuel Montagu Morgan Grenfell Baring Brothers	Credit Suisse First Boston S.G. Warburg Baring Brothers
European currency unit issues	Banque Paribas	Banque Paribas
Canadian dollar issues	Wood Gundy & Co. Orion Royal Bank Limited Union Bank of Switzerland	Wood Gundy & Co. Union Bank of Switzerland Morgan Guaranty
Australian dollar issues	Orion Royal Bank Limited Morgan Stanley Salomon Brothers	Hambros Bank Deutsche Bank AG Credit Suisse First Boston
French franc issues	Credit Commercial de France	Credit Commercial de France
Dutch guilder issues	Amsterdam-Rotterdam Bank Algemene Bank Nederland	Algemene Bank Nederland Amsterdam-Rotterdam Bank
U.S. dollar interest-rate swaps	Bankers Trust Morgan Guaranty	Bankers Trust Morgan Guaranty
Currency swaps	Morgan Guaranty, and a variety of others	Different firms in various sectors
Eurocommercial paper	Citicorp Swiss Bank Corporation Merrill Lynch Shearson Lehman	Swiss Bank Corporation Shearson Lehman Citicorp Morgan Guaranty

market position, and prestige for the targeted niche, it may be able to become a serious contender for leadership within a relatively short period of one to three years.

A second management issue, after an initial niche position has been established, is whether the position can be expanded to a role of sector leadership or dominance. Sector dominance has the effect of diffusing competition; some issuers wishing to finance in a particular sector contact the market leader without consulting competitors for alternative bids. In addition, some issuers will accept the pricing view of a recognized market leader, even though doing so may involve a higher cost of borrowing than that offered by competing managers; to them, the market leader's view is more credible and offers a greater likelihood of success. Despite issuers' preoccupation with obtaining the least costly capital in each financing, most of them also value deal executions, which are well received by investors and which avoid the bad aftertaste of undistributed securities languishing in the hands of inexperienced lead managers.

Market dominance can place an investment banker in a position where borrowers will approach his or her firm initially to seek its market views. Even if such an initiative does not ultimately lead to a financing, the market intelligence derived by the vendor from the contact can be valuable. Knowledge of the potential backlog of forth-coming sector issuers can assist a sector's dominant manager in scheduling new issues at a time when the market is most receptive, and in moving quickly to bring new issues into market windows ahead of competing deals. Accurate backlog information can also allow a lead manager that is a secondary-market maker to better manage its trading positions. All of these aspects of market dominance translate into better firm margins.

Thus, maximum profitability in a market niche is achieved more readily from a position of dominance rather than mere significant specialization. The way in which such dominance can be best developed and defended depends on the particulars of the niche and the role of regulatory and competitive factors in limiting the entry of other firms. Some niches have been relatively enduring over time; often they have been currency or regulatory related or have involved the presence of low-cost producers in a foreign exchange or money market-related product such as a currency swap. Other niches have been transitory, representing in some cases only extensions of existing products in which the shortness of product life and the ease of duplication often preclude real competitive advantage or profitability beyond the initial series.

A principal task of investment banking management is the choice of suitable market specializations and the development of a firm's competitive strategy for achieving important market standing. In this context, an understanding by management of the critical strengths of the firm, perhaps within the context of a larger parent organization, is crucial. Also important are judgments relating to staffing strengths and the amount of time and investment necessary to assemble the critical elements in the structuring, origination, execution, distribution, and secondary-market trading aspects of a particular product.

Some of these critical strengths may be closely related to domestic capital-market skills, while others may depend entirely on the vendor's facility in operating in the Euromarkets. Examples of the former would be Salomon Brothers' importance in the mortgage-backed Eurobond-issue sector (paralleling its domestic leadership in that market) and the U.S. commercial banks' strength in U.S. dollar-denominated interest-rate swaps, an important profit center in their home office operations. Others are related to central bank regulation of currency of denomination, such as the importance of Credit Commercial de France in the French franc sector. In still other market niches, prestige, trading, and distribution skills appear to be the critical elements.

Nationality of Manager in Apex Firms

The most successful Euromarket vendors come from a surprisingly small number of home countries (see Table 3-5). Firms from four countries have accounted for 70–80 percent of all issues in recent years, with a further two countries representing another 15–18 percent.

In considering these data in conjunction with Appendix Table A-16, there is a definite impression that the weight of national financial importance is a factor in Eurobond leadership. Indeed, as indicated by studies of the U.S. investment banking industry,[5] there are, within the competitive pyramid, "apex firms," which combine not only qualities of leadership in the overall Eurobond market and specific market niches, but also elements of prestige and weight that give them special advantages in competing for mandates. Prestige in the Euromarket sense is often associated with the types of issuers with which a firm is identified; large, frequent borrowers of sovereign or AAA-corporate stature are preferred. Since the size of issuers is an important criterion, the elements of prestige are reflected to a

5. See especially Samuel L. Hayes III, A. Michael Spence, and David Van Praag Marks, *Competition in the Investment Banking Industry* (Cambridge, Mass.: Harvard University Press, 1983).

Table 3-5
Percentage of Euromarket Vendors by Country, 1980, 1984, 1987

Rank	1980		1984		1987	
	Country	Percentage	Country	Percentage	Country	Percentage
1	United States	24.8	United States	36.1	Japan	32.2
2	West Germany	18.6	Switzerland	18.8	United States	18.6
3	United Kingdom	14.7	West Germany	12.5	West Germany	14.6
4	Switzerland	13.5	United Kingdom	9.6	Switzerland	13.3
5	France	12.8	Japan	8.9	United Kingdom	8.0
6	Japan	6.0	France	7.5	France	6.5
7	Canada	3.8	Canada	2.5	Netherlands	2.1
8	Netherlands	2.7	Netherlands	1.4	Canada	1.8
9	Kuwait	1.3	Belgium	1.4	Italy	.7
10	Norway	0.5	Norway	0.3	Australia	.5
	Others	1.3	Others	1.0	Others	1.7

significant extent in the league-table positions already discussed, and the leaders tend to be those firms that handle the larger issues for the more prestigious borrowers.

Only a few firms have succeeded in establishing themselves as sustaining apex firms. Within this group, one would certainly place Deutsche Bank, Credit Suisse First Boston, Nomura Securities, Morgan Guaranty, Morgan Stanley, Salomon Brothers, S.G. Warburg, and Paribas. These vendors usually occupy dominant or leading positions in their home country markets. Achieving that recognition is important, since it not only offers advantage in getting new business but also yields privilege in syndicate relationships and in the allotment of particularly attractive or scarce securities. It also allows greater niche mobility than would be the case for most Euromarket firms, because banks with great acknowledged strength are more easily accepted by borrowers and other competitors in new areas where they may have had little previous experience. These Euromarket apex firms are also important in the domestic investment banking markets of the principal Western nations and in several cases represent significant capital-exporting or -importing countries.

Recent Developments

After several years of almost uninterrupted growth, the Eurobond market began a major contraction in late 1986 and 1987. While total issue volume during 1987 decreased only 20 percent from the 1986 period, to $142 billion, the amount of U.S. dollar financing dropped from 48 percent to only 42 percent of total Eurobonds, the lowest dollar proportion of the 1980s. At the same time, Euroyen issues rose 23 percent and Nomura Securities was the most active lead manager of both nondollar and U.S. dollar financings. These changes and related developments in interest and exchange rates had a number of effects on the competitive environment. First, the intensity of competition in the U.S. dollar fixed-rate sector in 1986, 1987, and 1988 reached the point where most observers agreed that the average transaction had become unprofitable to the managing underwriters. Second, the U.S. dollar floating-rate note market, formerly the second largest, contracted sharply in late 1986 and again in early 1988 both in secondary-market making and in new issues—becoming almost a second tier. Third, the currency instability of 1986 and 1987 and, particularly, the weakness of the U.S. dollar, together with the related increase in dollar interest rates in early 1987, had unsettled fixed-income investors and produced losses in inventory values to certain secondary-market makers. Finally, the rise in Euromarket staff salary costs and the number of new and relatively untrained recruits had begun to exert strong negative cost pressures on individual firm profitability.[6]

One result of the pressures has been selective retrenchment and rationalization in the operations of a number of Eurobond firms. In most cases, this amounted to much more than the previously-experienced review of trading limits and a trimming of bond inventories; at many firms, secondary-market making was selectively suspended in certain sectors such as floating-rate notes and fixed-rate dollar bonds. Perhaps the most significant early development was the announcement in June 1987 that Lloyds Bank had decided to terminate its market-making activities involving about 100 people in Eurobonds and U.K. gilts. Withdrawal from the latter sector was especially surprising since gilts are a home currency sector for this institution, which had become a primary dealer with the approval of the Bank of England in 1986. Lloyds Bank had lead managed nine Eurobond issues in 1985, seven issues in 1986, and one issue in the first half of 1987. In September 1987, Shearson Lehman announced that it was scaling down its market-making activities in international equities in London and reduced its staff by 150 people or approximately 10 percent of the London total. In October 1987, Orion Royal Bank, like Lloyds Bank, announced that it was suspending Eurobond underwriting and market making and closing its U.K. gilts dealership. Orion had been a leading factor in Eurobond new-issue business, especially in Australian and Canadian dollars. And in July 1988, a Citicorp affiliate announced its decision to leave the gilts market.

The downscaling followed a period of unparalleled expansion by Euromarket firms through additions to their traditional business lines and through new services, often more closely linked to a number of national capital markets than those of the past. Financial market liberalization by the authorities of most OECD countries had reduced tax and exchange-control barriers to international capital flows and facilitated access to the principal national capital markets by international borrowers. Thus, in some instances, the practical distinctions between the Euromarkets and the national markets became blurred, while in others the national markets regained ground against Euromarket competition. Euroequity trading, Eurocommercial paper, and swaps served to integrate classical Eurobond business more closely with national stock exchanges and money and capital mar-

---

6. For further elaboration, see The Economist, "A Survey of the Euromarkets," May 16, 1987; and P. M. Hubbard, "The Euromarkets Reshaped," Creditweek, February 29, 1988.

kets. At the same time, regulatory initiatives in the United Kingdom succeeded in bringing some facets of the market within the British legal orbit (see Chapter 9). The simplicity of the Euromarket's separate existence and limited product line thus gave way to a more complex environment.

The outcome of these trends on the competitive struggle depends on many factors, none of which is likely to be decisive. Nonetheless, it now appears that a weeding out of competitors is underway and that the staying power of those with announced commitments to the market is being tested.

Conclusions

Operating relatively free of regulation, the Euromarkets grew dramatically during the 1980s and attracted, by late in the decade, more than 100 isssue-managing participants, including almost 40 who were active enough to have managed ten or more issues per year. The ease of entry into the field and the competition for financing mandates, together with a decline in relationship banking, produced an intensity of competition that virtually eliminated margins of profit in many product lines. Following a slowing of growth and sharp decline in some subsectors (related to international economic tensions in 1987), the inevitable shakeout of firms and personnel occurred. Although new-issue volumes recovered somewhat in 1988, the rationalization mode that replaced expansion is likely to continue for some time.

Despite the general pattern of intense and dynamic interfirm competition, the market is a complex collection of currency and specialized product niches. Each area has unique origination, underwriting, and distribution characteristics. By developing competitive skills or special strengths in regulatory or borrower relationships, some firms have been able to develop enviable product-niche positions. Economic flows can alter product attractiveness; when combined with deregulation, the competitive situation in most product niches is likely to shift regularly, creating problems or opportunities for the firms involved.

CHAPTER 4

THE DEVELOPMENT OF THE U.S. SECURITIES MARKETPLACE

The firms competing in the Euromarket setting discussed in Chapters 2 and 3 come from distinct backgrounds and home market environments. One of the most important competitor groups is the U.S. group of vendors, which has a momentum and contemporary home market operating environment heavily influenced by its history. In this chapter, we trace the roots of the U.S. public securities vendor group.

Early History

The U.S.-based securities firms that have played such an important role in the international securities markets are rooted both in the European tradition of the British and continental merchant banks (see Chapter 7) and in the special circumstances of U.S. business and finance practices. Until the beginning of intensive railroad building in the mid-1800s, financial services had been provided by auctioneers and speculators, merchants like Stephen Girard and John Jacob Astor, brokers of every description, and incorporated commercial banks. By the 1840s, some had evolved into private bankers dealing in securities transactions. Some had originally been foreign exchange brokers; others had been merchants and shippers.

From the country's inception, America's need for capital had lured representatives of European houses like the Barings, the Rothschilds, and the Speyers. Alexander Baring came over in person to work out the arrangements for Jefferson's Louisiana Purchase in 1803. August Belmont, who quickly established his own banking operation, was initially an agent of the Rothschilds; he retained close ties with them for many years, which in practice meant privileged access to their financial backing.

Soon thereafter, a number of German-Jewish immigrants with commercial, if not directly financial family backgrounds—most notably the Seligmans, the Lehmans, Abraham Kahn, Solomon Loeb, and Marcus Goldman—moved from assorted mercantile activities into private banking. Like the Yankee houses of Lee, Higginson, and the several Morgan establishments in New York, London, and Philadelphia, the Jewish firms prospered because of their privileged access to European capital. Unlike the Yankee houses, however, they enjoyed the business advantages of extensive family ties in different geographic locations.

By the time of the great financial panic of 1873, the securities industry gave clear promise of its later development. Even though foreign buyers and large domestic institutions still absorbed the lion's share of new flotations, Philadelphia financier Jay Cooke's imaginative approach to selling government paper to recalcitrant farmers during the Civil War showed the value of aggressive sales tactics and a nationwide distribution system. It also identified the small individual investor as a new and potentially important dimension of the securities market (although Cooke's postwar bankruptcy suggests he was still ahead of his time). The concept of mass retailing had a distinctly American flavor. Public loan subscriptions had enjoyed some success in Europe, but aggressive retailing found its greater acceptance in America.

It was Cooke's genius to tap this universe of potential investors through a nationwide, centrally controlled network of distribution agents supported by mass advertising. His appeals to patriotism during the Civil War helped, but earlier patriotic appeals without Cooke's retailing expertise had utterly failed. Cooke's unique ability to reach middle-class investors and his willingness to support the price of securities in the aftermarket defined the mix of salesmanship and deal management characteristic of post–Civil War syndicates.

Relationship Banking

By the 1870s, the market for financial services was changing in important ways. More bankers were actively influencing the policies of client companies, through membership on corporate boards and finance committees. They were providing technical assistance with new issues and supplying a wide array of financial advice and support services such as sponsorship of their securities in the secondary-trading markets. As these involvements became more varied and extensive, longer-term loyalties between banker and client quite naturally emerged. These relationships became highly enough prized so that the client companies gradually encouraged long-term alliances with selected investment houses—their "principal bankers."

For bankers, relationships ensured a substantial and ongoing income, which was necessary to attract and motivate the talented people who serviced the clients. The importance of talented people has been a constant throughout the history of investment banking. Without the people who could recognize and adapt to changing circumstances, even established houses—like the Seligmans—could fall on hard times.

Leading houses like Morgan worked to reinforce their ties to the important companies of the time (e.g., Standard Oil Company and Carnegie Steel), but smaller establishments like N.W. Halsey & Co. nonetheless found their own lucrative niches, as did commercial banks outside the Eastern capital centers. Local and regional issues often attracted the second- and third-tier securities firms, many of which also had a relatively open field in distribution operations. The flotations of utility companies typically did not appeal to the major houses at this time largely because of their uncertain credit quality, just as a generation or two later, the flotations of retailers like Sears and of consumer-oriented light industries would not generate much interest for the majors. Imperial Kuhn Loeb & Co., for example, had little use for anything but railroad issues until the end of the nineteenth century.

Railroad Financing

Railroad development in the United States was on a scale unlike that experienced anywhere else in the world up to that time. The agricultural bounty of the mid-continent and cattle raising in the west created an unquenchable demand for freight transport. The discovery of gold in California at mid-century encouraged the dream of unimaginable riches for any owner of boots and a tin plate. And the road to those riches was over ties and rails. After the Civil War years, the move across the country via competitive railroads took on proportions that defied earlier predictions. A continent rich in natural resources and economic opportunity was there for development as fast as the railroads could open its gates. Railroads were quickly designed for several routes from the banks of the Mississippi to the Pacific. Northern, central, and southern routes were begun, as were north-south routes from the Plains to the Gulf of Mexico. More than a hundred railroads of various lengths were built in the westward move, with construction continuing until just before World War I.

At the dawn of the American railroad age, the role of the merchant banker was to supply a steady stream of capital. As the full century of railroad construction came to a close, railroad finance entered a new era; the merchant bankers then became active in consolidating and rationalizing rail lines. (Decades later, in the 1980s, merchant bankers had to rationalize the conglomerate merger frenzy of the 1960s.) This required new capital refinancing and the restructuring of old capital issues. Rail mortgages, many with 99-year maturities (and some with 999-year lives), needed refunding, and new equipment had to be financed. The federal government had granted extensive rights of way, complete with surface and mineral rights, to the railroad barons, and the development of these rich holdings required large amounts of capital.

Railroads were the seed corn of American industrialization. As railroad financing and construction were peaking at the end of the nineteenth century, the other sectors of the new industrial economy were coming into fruition. In the decade 1870–1880, the annual percentage rate of growth in industrial production in the United States was 5.8 percent; in the overlapping decade of 1875–1885 it was an even more impressive 6.3 percent.[1] Coal, steel, and other manufactured primary metals were in growing demand in part because of the railroad construction.

Early Regulation

The structures of business regulation were practically nonexistent during this period. Not until the establishment of the Interstate Commerce Commission (ICC) in 1887 to regulate the railroad industry's excesses, prevent public exploitation, and secure competition were the practices of the transportation moguls constrained.

The American character embodied a basic populist distaste for large, autocratic institutions; indeed, many had fled from Europe to avoid them. This spirit spawned the remarkably durable Sherman Antitrust Act in 1890. The Sherman Act intended not to regulate specific industries, in the manner of the Interstate Commerce Act, but to establish a public policy under which all industry would be monitored by the executive branch through the Attorney General. The passage of the Clayton Act in 1914 enlarged the scope of the initial antitrust initiative and established an administrative agency with quasi-judicial powers—the Federal Trade Commission—as a regulatory agency. Analogous in many respects to the ICC, particularly in its combined administrative-judicial purpose, the FTC was more concerned with creating standards than with resolving disputes between adversaries. The new spirit of reform and regulation was to have dramatic impacts on the American investment banking industry.

---

1. U.S. Bureau of the Census, *Historical Statistics of the United States, Colonial Times to 1970* (Washington, D.C.: 1976), vol. 2, p. 667.

Merger Movement of 1898–1902

An important wave of horizontal mergers arose at the turn of the century. The prime mover of this wave was the quest for larger market shares within industries where the transportation revolution had created competitive national markets.[2] The merger movement lasted less than a decade. In manufacturing, for instance, the number of business combinations jumped to sixteen in 1889 and to sixty-three a year later; the number then dropped to twenty-one in 1900, to nineteen in 1901, and to seventeen in 1902, returning thereafter to pre-1898 levels of about five.[3]

This was a period of accelerating activity for the fast-developing U.S. investment banking industry. In 1897, just before the merger movement commenced, four cash issues were sold to the public. In the 1898–1902 merger period, the total jumped to an astounding 360 issues, and then fell back to 28 in the 1903–1907 period. Similarly, the issuance of securities in exchange for other securities or assets totaled 62 in 1897, 3,026 in 1898–1902, and 285 in 1903–1907. This latter group of "recapitalization" moves was, of course, also part-and-parcel of the great consolidation movement, which, overall, created a bonanza for U.S. investment bankers.[4]

U.S. Capitalism Matures

At the turn of the century, the governmental sector was also generating substantial demand for funds in the public marketplace. The United States had been a net importer of capital prior to 1900, but by the end of World War I, the country had become a capital exporter. A number of foreign governments, as well as large offshore private-sector projects, successfully sought financing in New York, often at the bidding and encouragement of the U.S. State Department, which saw the accommodation of foreign borrowers as a useful instrument of foreign policy.

The size and composition of the domestic U.S. investor community were changing and expanding. Prior to World War I, wealthy individuals had been the most important source of both debt and

---

2. The Sherman Act forbade restraints of trade and monopolization but did not bar either horizontal or vertical mergers; the Clayton Act provided for public interest appraisals of the consequences of lessened competition in affected markets because of mergers, but it did not become law until 1914.

3. Hans B. Thorelli, *Federal Antitrust Policy* (Stockholm, 1954), pp. 294–303.

4. Ralph Nelson, *Merger Movements in American Industry, 1895–1956* (Princeton: Princeton University Press, 1959), pp. 33–34.

equity capital, but subsequent events and trends (particularly in the area of personal income taxation) drove them into other forms of investment. Coincidentally, the individual investor of more modest means was emerging into the public marketplace. It is likely that the Liberty Bond campaigns during World War I helped make these people comfortable with trading their cash for IOUs, much as Jay Cooke's efforts had a generation earlier.[5] In any case, the growing American middle class became a sizable fount of capital. Because wealthy individuals were reluctant to invest during the period after World War I, corporations actively solicited customers and employees to buy their equity securities. By the late 1920s, individual investors' holdings constituted the overwhelming majority of publicly held equity securities and about 50 percent of public debt securities.

Fragmented Regulatory Oversight

Government attempts to protect securities investors were hit-and-miss. There was virtually no regulation of securities market activities at the federal level, and the individual states each took a different tack to controlling securities activities within their borders.

In an effort to protect local investors from shady operators, various state legislatures followed the example of Kansas, which in 1911 had passed a measure regulating the in-state sale of securities by out-of-state issuers. Under the federal system, each state could protect its residents, but no state could extend its legislation to residents of another state. Support for local protective regulation came from in-state dealers and businessmen who wanted to shield themselves from potential competition for clients and investment dollars. In general, these "blue sky" laws were a perfectly understandable response to a long list of abuses and public cries for protection. Despite the soundness of its motives, the blue sky method of regulation proved inconsistent, inadequate, and impossible to administer.

Some states attacked the problem by regulating the process by which out-of-state securities were approved for sale—a form of registration procedure. Other forms of investor protection appeared: regulation of the dealers who sold securities; determination of the investment value of the securities themselves; disclosure of information about the solvency and business prospects of the issuer; insistence on guarantees that the investment would retain its value; and a

5. Samuel L. Hayes III, Michael Spence, and David Van Praag Marks, *Competition in the Investment Banking Industry* (Cambridge, Mass.: Harvard University Press, 1983), p. 11.

definition of fraud based on misrepresentation of fact. In practice, each blue sky state developed an idiosyncratic mix of approaches. Some states, considering themselves more important centers of finance, aspired to greater sophistication. To a major corporation (and its investment banker) seeking funds on a national basis, the crazy quilt of laws and regulations represented procedural quicksand. To an investor, it meant that even certain high-grade securities might be unavailable for purchase or available only through subterfuge. Incoherent public policy and unworkable laws create fertile fields for a variety of scoundrels, as unscrupulous securities operators discovered in this period.

The Early Investment Bankers

Among the principal financial intermediaries in the securities markets that operated after 1900, the historically dominant private banks are particularly noteworthy. Like their antecedent British and continental merchant banks, they were empowered to engage in a broad array of financing and investment activities. Typically, however, they chose to focus on the financing needs of substantial private corporations and foreign governments, and on the banking requirements of wealthy individuals. The other important group of financing intermediaries were the commercial banks. They had traditionally focused on taking deposits and extending loans. But with no federal regulations to bar them, many of these banks actively joined the booming securities business of the 1920s.

Although both traditional commercial as well as private banks could pursue similar lines of business, the securities industry in the period after World War I was far from homogeneous and egalitarian. It was characterized by a hierarchical structure characteristic of European merchant banking firms since at least the 1780s. At the apex were a few private banking houses that had figured prominently in private- and public-sector financing from immediately after the Civil War until World War I. This group included J.P. Morgan, Drexel & Co. (the Philadelphia affiliate of Morgan but not the forerunner of present-day Drexel Burnham Lambert), and Kuhn Loeb and Co. under the leadership of the legendary Jacob Schiff. Other securities firms with origins in Boston (the locus of an important early concentration of investable capital), Philadelphia, and Baltimore, as well as New York, also participated in this market. A second segment of the securities-issuance competitor group was composed of commercial banks that had begun to develop their corporate and investor activities; these included the National City Bank, the Chase National Bank, and The First National Bank of Boston.[6]

The traditionally dominant private banks enjoyed the bulk of the originating business in the early post–World War I period. It was only as the 1920s wore on that commercial bank managerships (and participations) picked up to a point where they rivaled those of the private banks in total volume. This did not imply a major shift of client loyalty away from the private banks; rather, it reflected the commercial banks' successful efforts to carve out a different market of issuers. Typically, these issuers were new to the public market, and their quality (or prodigious capital appetites) made them less attractive to the private banks.

Even as total banking assets grew impressively during the 1920s, the number of commercial banks actually declined, mirroring the industrial consolidations at the turn of the century. Further, an increased proportion of banking resources found its way into the hands of financial institutions based in the larger cities of the Eastern seaboard. And commercial banks were channeling more of their assets into the public securities sector. These factors undoubtedly nourished populist sentiment around the country. The vision of the flow of capital away from towns and villages throughout America into the vaults of pinstriped Eastern nabobs is a perennial red flag in the American psyche.

During this time, the use of syndicates of underwriters to accomplish public offerings was expanded and refined. Historically, the leading securities firms typically had bought entire offerings of securities and then either subcontracted their sale or sold them directly over a considerable period, often running into months. When activity in the public securities market increased during the 1920s, there was an acceleration in the use of syndicates to sell larger volumes of securities more quickly than previously had been possible. But with the rapid growth came a certain sloppiness and relaxation in credit analysis and investigation of the issuing businesses, which would subsequently come back to haunt the securities vendors.

Dawn of the Era of Regulation

The stock market crash in 1929 and the severe depression that followed brought cries of recrimination from politicians and feelings of betrayal from the U.S. public. Their ire was directed principally to-

---

6. See, for instance, Sheridan A. Logan, *George F. Baker and His Bank, 1840–1955* (Lunenberg, Vt.: The Stinehour Press, 1981), p. 156.

ward the bankers and financial institutions that were perceived to have orchestrated the debacle. As a consequence, Congress produced a series of far-reaching laws destined to change the face and conduct of the securities industry. The new system would persist for almost forty years without substantive change and would fundamentally alter the form of U.S. financial institutions and shape the character of the vendor group in the newly coined designation "investment banking."

During the period 1933–1940, a populist administration and Congress produced the Glass-Steagall Act, the Securities Act of 1933, the Securities Exchange Act of 1934 (which included creation of the Securities and Exchange Commission), the Public Utility Holding Company Act of 1935, the Trust Indenture Act of 1939, the Investment Company Act of 1940, and the Investment Advisers Act of 1940. Common to all these laws was the disclosure of information for the purpose of "letting in the light" to reveal the true facts of issuers' affairs and their overall business health.[7]

The Glass-Steagall Act (1933)

Although it was never established that the bank failures of the years prior to 1933 were a consequence of bank participation in securities underwriting, ownership of securities, or affiliation with investment bankers, public perceptions were enough to spur action in a reformist government.

The objective of the Glass-Steagall law[8] as generally interpreted for several decades was to separate the deposit-taking and loan-making ("commercial") banker from the underwriter or dealer ("investment") banker; thus was born the name "investment banker" to refer to a securities industry vendor. The commercial banker was prohibited from participating in risk taking with regard to all corporate securities and all governmental securities except those of the United States or general obligations of other select political entities. Underlying the new law was the assumption that functional separation of capital-supplying vendors (each of which at the time did about half of the securities underwriting) would promote the soundness of commercial banks and prevent conflicts of interest.

As a consequence, commercial banks had to divest or terminate all of their underwriting business that involved private issuers. J.P. Morgan chose to remain a commercial banker, but a few partners and staff left to form an investment bank, Morgan Stanley. Other

---

7. Franklin D. Roosevelt, *Public Papers* (New York: Random House, 1938), vol. I, p. 653.
8. 47 Stat. 56 Feb. 27, 1932; 48 Stat. 162 June 16, 1933; 49 Stat. 684 Aug. 23, 1935.

prominent investment banks, such as First Boston Corporation, were created. Some private bankers who had carried on depository functions and investment banking of the nature well known among English and European merchant bankers were forced to elect one function and, in the cases of such firms as Lehman Brothers and Dillon, Read, they chose to throw in their lot with the securities business.

Whether this abrupt separation of securities underwriting from lending has had the salutory effect on the stewardship of depositors' savings has been endlessly debated. There is little doubt, however, that the bifurcation had a profound impact on the subsequent development of the public securities sector in the United States and, by way of the U.S. occupation, in Japan.

Securities Act of 1933

This law became the foundation of Congress's attempt to restore and sustain public confidence in the financial system.[9] It did not try to cure the activities of scoundrels but to ensure that the public could identify those scoundrels for what they were. For example, congressional hearings revealed that "stock watering" and "preferred" customer lists had become common in the 1920s. Watering stock is simply a matter of baselessly writing up the valuation of assets to rationalize an increase in the number of outstanding equity shares. The approach of the 1933 Act to stock watering was not to forbid it or attach criminal penalties for having done it (leaving aside accounting regulation), but to require disclosing it. The failure to *disclose* is unlawful and carries possible criminal consequences.

Preferred-customer lists were not banned, but the issuer and the underwriter were required to disclose differences in offering prices to the public and to insiders. If the public purchaser is willing to pay $10 per share for what promoters and underwriters have just bought for $1, there is no offense under the 1933 Act as long as the facts and the investment consequences are revealed.

In making a securities trade, the disclosure requirement shifts the common law burden of "buyer beware" from the purchaser to the vendor. If the vendor fails to disclose the material facts that a prudent investor would need in making an objective investment decision, the transaction may be voided, the purchaser's money refunded, and the vendor subjected to penalties.

Under the 1933 Act, a public offering of securities may not be

9. 48 Stat. 74, 15 U.S. Code, pp. 77a–77aa.

made without a registration, which requires specific information relating to all aspects of the issuer's business, as well as the terms, purposes, and intended use of the proposed financing. A false prospectus leads to civil liabilities. The issuer is always liable, unconditionally, for a material misstatement or omission. The securities underwriters are always conditionally liable unless they can show they had conducted a "reasonable investigation" of the data, which must appear in the registration statement. The process of reasonable investigation is commonly referred to as "due diligence." It is important to note, however, that the government performs no *quality* test (i.e., assessment of the riskiness of the investment) under the 1933 Act, contrary to the conceptual approach of a number of state blue sky laws. Under the federal statute, the only quality appraisal comes from the purchaser's acceptance of the prospectus's content for making an investment and his or her reliance on the underwriter as having performed a reasonable investigation. The diligence requirement as a defense against liability, together with the legal requirement of full disclosure, has provided a regulatory structure that, in one sense, is *self-regulatory*, but that more realistically makes the investment banker the regulator at peril. The diligence requirement also provided a powerful boost to the public accounting profession in the United States. Someone had to generate the financial information called for under the new legislation, and the Scottish and other accountants who had originally emigrated to the United States to keep watch over European investments in America picked up on this legislatively mandated opportunity. The role of the "Big Eight" (now six) U.S. accounting firms in the generation of uniform public information on private-sector companies around the world is a matter of record.

Securities and Exchange Act of 1934

The 1933 Securities Act established a national policy on the public issuance of securities within the United States, leaving only a narrow window for offerings so private that the policy would not be applied. In the Securities and Exchange Act of 1934, Congress addressed the remaining area of public interest: securities trading in the public arena.[10]

Here, populism shone forth. The first policy reference in the statute is aimed at rascality. To regulate and control securities transactions "as commonly conducted upon securities exchanges and over-the-counter markets," the statute states that it is necessary to subject

10. 48 Stat. 881, 15 U.S. Code, pp. 78a–78jj.

to law "transactions by officers, directors, and principal security holders, [and] to require appropriate reports."

After determining that securities transactions had an impact on interstate commerce because of their scope and significance and because their prices affected taxes and bank loans, Congress addressed what it believed to be the nub of the issue:

> Frequently the prices of securities on such exchanges and markets are susceptible to manipulation and control, and the dissemination of such prices gives rise to excessive speculation, resulting in sudden and unreasonable fluctuations in price. . . .[11]

Following the 1929 market crash, the popular assumption was that *someone* had to be responsible; someone had been manipulating a system that was otherwise "pure." And those someones had to be company insiders who traded their company's securities and who controlled trading through membership in the exclusive club of the stock exchanges. Full-information disclosure required by the 1933 Act was important but insufficient; *conduct* also had to be regulated. A federal agency not only had to oversee disclosure requirements but also had to establish rules of conduct and act as a quasi-judicial administrator of compliance. In conception, like the self-regulation in assigning responsibility for disclosure, self-regulation could be the method of assigning responsibility for observing the rules.

The difference between the two types of self-regulation lay in their subject matter. A failure to disclose under the 1933 Act could be redressed by an action brought by an injured investor. Government intervention would be required only rarely, for example, to stop a public sale of securities or to bring a criminal action. In contrast, under the 1934 Act, trading in securities, whether on or off the stock exchanges, demanded *active* regulation to prevent "manipulation and control."

The 1934 Act required a highly specialized body of experts in the securities industry whose sophistication would regulate but not frustrate the efficiency of securities trading. The Securities and Exchange Commission (SEC) was created by the 1934 Act to fill this role. Understanding the relationships of raising capital through issuance of securities and the importance of free market trading of those securities, Congress assigned administration of the 1933 Act to the new agency.

The Investment Company Act of 1940

The study that led Congress to the 1934 Act made it aware of investment companies, pooled funds of individual savers managed by

---

11. 15 U.S.C. §786 (1976). Although enacted in 1934, the reference to codification of the 1934 Act (as well as the 1933 Act) is 1976.

professional portfolio managers, which had become important investment vehicles in the 1920s. Investment companies had emulated the
"unit trusts" so popular in Scotland, England, and Japan in developing their uniquely American vehicle: the "open-end trust." In an
open-end trust, the investor could redeem shares of the trust at net
asset value. These open-end companies were the forerunners of the
multibillion-dollar mutual fund industry of today. The basic Scottish
unit trust, by contrast, was "closed-end," i.e., the shares were not
redeemable at net asset value, but were freely transferable like other
shares on the open market at prices that might or might not reflect a
premium or discount from their real asset value.

During the 1920s, the American form of closed-end investment
funds became a popular way by which investors could focus on a
particular industry sector, such as public utilities (much as there are a
host of specialized mutual funds today). Unfortunately, because both
funds were allowed to use unlimited leverage (e.g., borrowed funds),
a number of these investment companies went bankrupt following
the 1929 market crash.

Looking at the investment company sector as a whole, Congress
concluded that investors had inadequate information, that many investments benefited management or advisers rather than investors,
that concentration of control and terms in securities were inequitable,
that resources and earnings statements were misleading, and that
leverage was excessive and reserves inadequate. Under the 1940 Investment Company statute, these matters were addressed, in some
instances, differently for open-end and closed-end fund companies.
While the latter were permitted specified maximums of leverage and
preferred stock, most open-end companies were prohibited from using borrowed funds. While neither kind of company was barred from
having an investment advisory contract with a third person, to prevent possible conflicts, an independent majority of the board of directors was required to determine whether the contract should be
approved.

The Post–Glass-Steagall Period

The 1930s' reform legislation, specifically the Glass-Steagall Act, fundamentally recast the organization of the financial intermediary community. Financial services vendors had to choose between taking
deposits and making loans, on the one hand, and selling and trading
corporate securities, on the other. In most cases, vendors chose to
stick with what was dubbed "commercial banking," with its much
larger volume of ongoing business and day-to-day interaction with

corporate customers, and to spin off their securities activities. These newly spun-off and independent securities firms had very small capitalizations, only a handful of employees, and a paucity of business. The environment for both underwriting and trading was dismal. Economic malaise persisted until World War II.

The extraordinary war years interrupted the evolution of these separated businesses. Immediately after the war, moreover, the securities industry was thrown on the defensive by a U.S. Justice Department's antitrust action against seventeen leading securities firms. The firms were charged with conspiring to divide up available underwriting business through a pattern of reciprocal business sharing of one another's clients' financings. The suit, a major preoccupation of the investment banks for several years, was ultimately dismissed.

Despite the fact that the government failed to prove its antitrust case against these seventeen industry leaders, underwriting and other corporate business were, for the most part, closely controlled by a relatively small number of securities firms, successors to the powerful banking houses that had dominated the nation's financing business before the depression.

By the 1950s, the extended postwar economic expansion began, which was to have a profound impact on developments within the securities industry, including patterns of underwriting new securities. This decade was characterized by robust secular growth, low inflation, a strong dollar, and a favorable American balance of payments. Securities firms as a group enjoyed relatively high prosperity during this period, in part because of tight cost controls inherited from the earlier lean years, which included a general hiatus on hiring new employees during the 1930s and 1940s. Although active hiring resumed as the U.S. economy gathered momentum during the 1950s, the individual leadership at the time of the 1930s legislation was largely still in place at the beginning of the 1960s.

It is important to note that, in contrast to the situation in Japan, U.S. securities firms—and not commercial bankers—emerged in the post–World War II period as the principal counselors to the U.S. corporate sector. Why the investment banks should have prevailed in that pre-eminent strategic counseling role is a matter of conjecture, but most investment banks were direct descendants of the nineteenth-century private banks that had forged long-term links with many leading U.S. companies. Significantly, the prewar and prereform Japanese securities firms had *not* been a part of the national banking fraternity, which traditionally counseled, financed, and partially owned the core of Japanese industry. After the war, the Japanese national banks, barred from direct participation in those public markets, did nothing to speed their development. In the United States, by controlling the flow of new securities, the investment banking firms could also exercise substantial influence over the smaller and more fragmented retail-securities distribution firms, whose heavier overhead costs made them more dependent on the selling commissions that resulted from the issue of new-securities product.[12]

This state of affairs arose in large part as a consequence of the Glass-Steagall Act. By separating the two financial-vendor groups with what looked to be an impermeable Chinese Wall, Congress had created for the investment bankers a protected industry, safe from effective challenge by the only vendor group that could have mounted a viable rivalry—commercial banks. The cartel-like division of the available public securities business within that enclave was reinforced by the failure of the government's antitrust action.

That division of business was publicly in evidence in the organization and hierarchical structure of the underwriting syndicates. The firms with the most impressive (and financially active) client lists were in the driver's seat and regularly accorded the most favored positions in Wall Street underwriting syndicates. Four firms— Morgan Stanley, First Boston, Dillon, Read, and Kuhn Loeb—had emerged from the difficult period of the 1930s as the most powerful and prestigious public-financings organizations. They were accorded the honor of inclusion in a "special" underwriting bracket (or category) that appeared at the top of a tombstone even if they were not a manager of the underwriting. Behind them followed a group of about eighteen firms considered to be major forces in generating new financing business; they were routinely carried (alphabetically) in a "major" bracket on Wall Street deals. Then came successively more junior brackets of national and regional firms who "knew their place" and generally acceded to this arrangement as the price for sharing the available business they needed to help cover their relatively higher overhead.[13]

The New Interfirm Competition

While the commercial banks were effectively excluded from vying for business in the public securities markets, developments in the late 1950s and the 1960s were introducing new elements and dimensions of competition into the securities business. Consolidations among the retail-oriented firms continued and somewhat increased their com-

12. Samuel L. Hayes III, "Investment Banking: Power Structure in Flux," *Harvard Business Review*, March–April 1971, p. 138ff.
13. Ibid.

petitive clout. Further, during the uninterrupted economic expansion of the 1960s, the operating profits of a wide variety of firms reached post-depression highs;[14] concurrently, a new, relatively young group of investment bankers began moving into senior partner positions. The new leadership of some of the aspiring retail firms used this sustained period of prosperity to challenge the firms that had dominated the apex positions in the industry structure ever since the banking reorganization of the 1930s. At the same time, the institutional investor emerged as a powerful new marketing focus for a number of securities firms.

Several firms were successful in challenging the traditional leadership structure. Merrill Lynch obtained the necessary leverage by creating an internally efficient organization to profitably service the needs of individual investors. Salomon Brothers built its competitive bargaining power by recognizing that institutional investors would need a deep-pocketed market-making supplement to the New York Stock Exchange specialists if their purchases and sales of securities were to be made without serious disruptions of the markets. Upstart Donaldson Lufkin & Jenrette (DLJ), founded in 1959, built a major position by perceiving that institutional investors would require a more sophisticated research product than that routinely produced for individual investors.

The first major postwar shakeout and realignment of securities firms came at the end of the long economic expansion of the 1960s. In 1969–1970, a number of firms were overwhelmed by the large increase in trading volume during the last heady months of the 1960s bull market. Some disappeared as independent entities when their back offices proved incapable of handling the volume;[15] others sought to strengthen their competitive positions by selling their own equity securities to the public to raise permanent capital. In doing this, they broke the prohibition of the New York Stock Exchange that barred exchange member firms from being publicly owned.[16] According to some, this move to raise public capital was justified by the firms' desire to lock in funds to better service the growing institutional sector and to cushion themselves from the consequences of volatile earning swings. Other observers held that public financing was a convenient bailout for those aging senior partners with substantial equity investments in their firms who were alarmed by what they viewed as adverse market and industry developments. Younger part-

14. Ibid.
15. "Funds Set Aside by Hayden Stone," *New York Times,* January 15, 1969, p. 59.
16. "Big Board Defied by Member Firm," *New York Times,* May 23, 1969, p. 1.

ners, however, often welcomed the removal of a threatened reduction in the firm's capital whenever a retiring or deceased partner's capital had to be redeemed.[17]

The alteration in the competitive hierarchy could be read directly from the tombstones in the financial press. By 1971, Salomon Brothers and Merrill Lynch had been elevated to the special bracket of leading underwriters and Dillon, Read and Kuhn Loeb were demoted to major-bracket status. DLJ was elevated from the submajor to the major bracket in 1976.

Because of recent reverses in their investment holdings, in 1970–1971 institutional investors adopted a much more defensive stance toward the public securities markets. This stance temporarily increased the competitive leverage of retail brokers that could deliver the buying power of their individual investor customers to corporate issuers eager to convert volatile short-term bank financing into longer-term, fixed-rate debt. Nevertheless, the growing importance of institutional investors to securities marketing had been recognized, so that leading wholesale firms made impressive new commitments of capital and personnel to the trading and institutional services areas. Morgan Stanley's realignment in that direction was considered a watershed in Wall Street's postwar evolution; in the hidebound world of high finance, it was a favorable indication of a leading firm's capacity and willingness to recognize change and exploit it aggressively. The ability to quickly adapt to new circumstances was very much in the tradition of European investment and merchant banks, which had successfully implemented such competitive responses over several centuries.[18]

Despite the markets' revival in 1971 and 1972, economic and organizational pressures pushed the fortunes of the securities industry to one of its lowest points since World War II.[19] Many of these problems were rooted in rising inflation. Purchasing-power erosion, which had been modest during much of the postwar period, gathered force during the late 1960s. The United States pursued the dual policy of guns and butter, sustaining a high level of civilian consumption while prosecuting an expensive war in Indochina. The consequent demand-pull inflation caused labor compensation to fall further behind in real purchasing power. Even after economic expansion stopped during the first quarter of 1969, intense pressure for wage

17. "Bache & Co. Posts a Three-Month Profit," *New York Times*, December 18, 1970, p. 59.
18. Hayes et al., *Competition in the Investment Banking Industry*, p. 6.
19. Ibid., p. 28.

increases continued unabated, leading to a new wave of cost-push inflation. By the summer of 1971, the dollar was under substantial pressure, and with a growing trade deficit, President Nixon floated the dollar in August of that year. The relevance of these developments to the U.S. securities industry was that they gave additional impetus to the growth of the Euromarkets and set the stage for larger-volume sales of U.S. issuers' securities in those markets in the decade ahead; they also precipitated a further—and international—realignment of U.S. investment banking, which is detailed elsewhere in this book.

Simultaneous expansion in the economies of the United States and other industrialized Western nations during 1972 and 1973 caused critical shortages in a number of raw materials. These were sufficient to set off a new round of commodity-based inflation, which was further exacerbated by a fourfold increase in the price of oil in the winter of 1973–1974. Interest rates soared in the United States, causing both bond and stock prices to plummet. As both institutional and individual investors withdrew from the market in disarray, securities firms were hit with both barrels: trading and underwriting volume dried up, while the costs of operating in a personnel- and systems-intensive business rose sharply, particularly for the retail-oriented firms. The stock market's disillusionment with publicly owned securities firms reached such proportions that at one point in November 1974 the shares of retail broker E.F. Hutton & Co. sold for barely $4 per share, less than either the sum of cash on hand or its projected earnings for one year of good trading volumes.[20] Wholesale securities firms fared better during this lean period, owing both to their lower overhead and continuing corporate fee-based business.[21]

The 1970s also marked the beginning of a general national disaffection with regulation as a means of allocating resources. Regulations and trade practices were challenged in industry after industry, including the securities business. Although volume discounts for large (mainly institutional) trades had existed for a number of years, academic researchers argued that fixed commissions had pegged total transaction fees at an artificially high level, thereby protecting inefficient securities brokers and reaping a windfall for the efficient vendors[22] (a charge now being made about the contemporary Japanese market). The SEC moved to abolish fixed brokerage commissions on

20. E.F. Hutton & Co., *Annual Report*, 1974.
21. Samuel L. Hayes III, "The Transformation of Investment Banking," *Harvard Business Review*, January–February 1979, p. 154.
22. Irwin Friend and Marshall Blum, "Competitive Commissions on the New York Stock Exchange," *Journal of Finance*, September 1973, pp. 795–819.

May 1, 1975 (thereafter colloquially referred to as "May Day"). Immediately after May Day, commissions fell to between 40 and 50 percent of the earlier fixed-rate levels.[23] This situation brought severe pressure on firms specializing in security analyses—the research boutique firms—that had depended largely on so-called "soft" commission dollars. These firms had given away their valuable research to institutions that gave them commission-rich chunks of their trading business in return. Another wave of consolidations followed, as a number of research boutique firms, like Mitchell Hutchins and H.W. Wainwright, were unable to cover their overhead expenses and were either liquidated or absorbed through merger.

There were parallel developments in the corporate services sector. Greater sophistication among corporate finance officers and other top-level managers accelerated product innovation and the range of new services in the investment banking community. Corporate clients continually sought more efficient and less costly ways to obtain Wall Street services; in certain instances, they brought financing-related activities in-house rather than rely on securities firm vendors. Notwithstanding solid resistance among securities-originating firms to any compromise on the traditional 7/8 of 1 percent gross spread on investment-grade public bond issues, de facto price cutting already existed through various indirect means, including "overtrading" on swaps of old bonds for new ones. In this sense, the underwriting market was experiencing pressures for margin reduction similar to those that had hit the institutional brokerage business in the period leading up to May 1975.

Meanwhile, on the retail side, the rise in interest rates that accompanied the accelerated inflation in 1973–1974 spawned an important new phenomenon: the money-market mutual fund. During the earlier period of high interest rates in 1970, retail brokerage firms had been able to channel much of their customers' cash balances into corporate clients' long-term, fixed-rate debt instruments; this, however, was no longer possible. The declines in securities values and the consequent losses investors sustained made investors much less willing to make longer-term, fixed-rate bond investments. They sought instead short-term debt arrangements, which gave them greater protection against capital loss, and they found those investments in the money-market mutual fund.

The money-market mutual funds established in response to this demand were subject to regulation under the Investment Company

<hr>

23. Securities and Exchange Commission, Directorate of Economic and Policy Analysis, *The Securities Industry in 1979* (Washington, D.C., September 1980), p. 9.

Act of 1940, administered by the SEC. Managers of money-market mutual funds confine their investments to short-term corporate and government notes and bank certificates of deposit (CDs). Being both open-end and "no-load" (free of commissions), the money market funds permitted investors to invest or redeem at will at a fixed price of one dollar per share. The fund investment fluctuates only in yield and not in terms of changes in asset value.

In an era of high, volatile interest rates, the funds quickly became phenomenally popular because they gave the investing public what it wanted: more interest on savings than banks were permitted to pay and safety of principal. With rates in excess of 10 percent, who needed stocks or bonds? By the end of the 1980s, total money-market fund assets had grown to more than $300 billion. Implicit in this growth was a fundamental shift in consumers' habits of handling their "safe money" (e.g., cash and interest-producing deposits). This shift was to have a large impact on most of the financial services sector, including commercial banks, savings and loans associations, credit unions, and insurance companies operating primarily on the deposit-taking side of the Glass-Steagall Chinese Wall. Retail securities firms on the other side of that wall raided the passbook-customer base of deposit institutions with great relish and success. At the same time, they moved to protect their customers' free-credit balances from encroachment by offering, at first, interest on selective customer cash deposits and later their own captive money-market mutual funds. Merrill Lynch's introduction of the cash management account in 1977 was a landmark event that was to change permanently the options available to, and the patterns of savings utilized by, investors.

The atmosphere of deregulation and high inflation upset the informal live-and-let-live compact within the financial industry. In the expanding postwar U.S. economy, financial institutions on both sides of the Glass-Steagall wall had been largely content to pursue business that, while overlapping in some instances, minimized head-to-head competition. But the slowdown in economic growth and changing savings and investing patterns strained the informal pact, at the same time that the government was adopting an attitude of benign neglect toward a number of areas of banker/broker competitive conflict.

In the immediate wake of the unfixing of securities commissions in 1975, a few discount brokerage houses sprang up to service individual investors. Their share of the market was small, however, and they were not seen as a significant threat to the full-service retail firms. But as commercial banks and insurance companies watched money-market mutual funds erode their savings bases and cheaper financing arrangements such as commercial paper erode relationships with blue chip clients, they pushed with increasing urgency into new services for these important constituencies. In addition, the commercial banks stepped up their campaign for relief from the constraints first imposed on them fifty years earlier by the Glass-Steagall Act.

The consequences of deregulation of financial services continued. The commissions (gross spreads) on conventional debt offerings came under increasing pressure by corporate issuers. A considerable volume of the business found its way offshore to the Euromarkets, beyond the reach of the U.S. securities legislation, with its accompanying time delays and expense. The SEC therefore began preparing for a more streamlined form of U.S. offering—"shelf registration"—which would hopefully make domestic U.S. issuance more cost effective and time efficient. Shelf offerings did produce cost savings but at the expense of the kind of diligent investigation that had been a principal objective of the 1933 Securities Act. Further, the shelf-underwriting business introduced what was in many cases a de facto competitive bidding; this in turn had an important impact on the league-table standings of the major securities firms. In particular, Salomon Brothers, which had made its early mark in the competitive-bid area, gained considerable ground at the expense of long-time underwriting leaders like Morgan Stanley.

But Morgan Stanley and several other leading wholesale securities firms benefited from a concurrent renewal of merger-and-acquisition activity. Beginning during the period of rapidly accelerating inflation in the mid-1970s, the stock prices of a number of publicly owned U.S. companies were selling at levels substantially below either their plant and equipment replacement cost or their break-up value (if sold off in pieces). This state of affairs spurred an initial wave of acquisitions by other cash- and credit-rich companies. The wholesale securities firms served as the financial advisers and strategists in effecting takeovers, some of which were regarded as hostile by the targeted companies' managements.

The takeover game played a large role in the "junk bond" phenomenon of the 1980s. Debt issuers with noninvestment-grade ratings had generally relied on private placements, only occasionally going to the public markets. But the rejuvenated securities firm of Drexel Burnham Lambert fine-tuned the procedure of selling such lower-quality bonds to public investors and, almost single-handedly, developed it into the major public-debt market sector it is today.

Because of its excellent record for delivering on its promises of successfully underwriting such bond financings, Drexel enabled a whole new round of merger activity featuring a cast of thinly capitalized and little-known entrepreneurs. With junk bond resources as a back-up, these entrepreneurs could launch credible bids for billion-

or even multibillion-dollar companies. Thus, the volume and variety of merger activity were much enhanced during the late 1970s and the 1980s.

Junk bond financing and commercial bank and institutional private-placement credit fueled still another dimension of the merger movement: the leveraged buyout (LBO). This financing technique, which typically involved taking a public company "private," had begun by the mid-1980s to recast the role of the securities firms: they were not just the facilitators of changes of corporate control, they became *principals* in the activity. This was a substantial departure from previous practice but harkened back to the activities of J.P. Morgan, Jacob Schiff, George Baker, and other bankers of a century before, who also had directly participated in the buying, reorganizing, and selling of companies.

In sum, well-meaning reforms introduced in the 1930s to remedy blatant excesses and misconduct at the time produced results in the competitive arena that were clearly not intended by the framers. By artificially separating the public and private segments of the U.S. financial services industry, the reforms substantially reduced the possibilities for effective competition among vendors. The government's loss of the *United States* v. *Morgan* antitrust case in 1953 further entrenched the cartel-like practices within the industry. Relationship banking was at its peak and price competition at its nadir.

It was not until the shift in economic circumstances during the 1960s and 1970s that the industry status quo began to unravel. The shift was abetted by an alteration in public and political sentiment toward deregulation. As a consequence, the 1970s and 1980s saw vigorous competition among conventional U.S. securities firms and incursions by nonconventional U.S. vendors and by firms from abroad.

Thus, by the end of the 1980s, successive assaults on the status quo had substantially altered the impact of the 1930s reform legislation. The Glass-Steagall wall separating commercial and investment banking had been substantially eroded by vendor responses to changes in the competitive marketplace. An effort by Senator William Proxmire to codify through legislation these de facto changes was beaten back in 1988 by a variety of aggrieved trade lobbying groups, most notably the Securities Industry Association. But in 1989, the Federal Reserve appeared to have broken the legislative gridlock by administratively granting some of the largest U.S. banks the right to establish separately incorporated securities affiliates authorized, for the first time in more than a half a century, to underwrite and trade in corporate securities.

CHAPTER 5

THE CONTEMPORARY U.S. SECURITIES MARKETPLACE

At the end of the 1980s, the basic structure of financial vendors in the domestic U.S. market was still being defined by the 1930s reform legislation, particularly the Glass-Steagall Act. On one side of the wall created by that act were almost 14,000 commercial banks, led by the "money center" banks, the "superregional" banks, and a host of regional and local banks and savings institutions, which, as a result of more recent legislation, had assumed a broader array of commercial banking powers.

On the other side of the wall were the securities firms. In 1989, 6,308 firms were members of the National Association of Securities Dealers (NASD), while membership in the New York Stock Exchange totaled 1,444. At the national level, the group of players was much smaller, dividing itself imprecisely into wholesale firms, which catered mainly to institutional investors and corporate and municipal clients, and retail firms, whose principal marketing thrust was toward individual investors. In addition, there was a substantial contingent of foreign securities firms with principal offices in New York and branch offices in other parts of the country.

In part because of the shift of savings and business toward the institutional sector and in part because of the lucrative fees derived from servicing the corporate sector, the wholesale securities firms were the pacesetters. Of the approximately seven dominant U.S. securities firms at the end of the 1980s, five were wholesale oriented. This competitive grouping was also the consequence of a substantial industry consolidation that had taken place since the early 1970s, when there were some twenty to twenty-five major securities firms that shared the available business. In the course of that shakeout and consolidation, the growth in scope, size, and operating results of the prevailing securities firms was impressive.

As noted in Chapter 4, the securities firms had diversified their products and services. The wholesale firms' earlier reliance on underwriting income was now reduced significantly. Similarly, the reliance of historically retail-oriented brokerage firms on commissions was now diminished. Both groups had turned to trading and various permutations of the merger-and-acquisition business for a larger share of their revenue.

Balance sheet assets of wholesale firms grew from a typical $100 million at the beginning of the 1970s to $30 billion by 1989. The equity capital component of the balance sheets grew from a typical $10 million to about $1 billion over the same period. Representative returns on equity numbers for the leading wholesale firms during this period were in the 25–40 percent range, and most of these profits were retained in the business. Although most of these firms went public during the intervening period as a means of financing growth, a larger part of their growth in equity capital came from retained earnings.

By contrast, the big U.S. money-center commercial banks had a much less favorable story to tell. Serious loan losses sapped their profits and capital reserves; revenues suffered as corporate treasurers did more shopping in the public securities markets; and new competition for savers' deposits diminished access to low-cost lendable funds. Profitability suffered accordingly, with typical returns on assets in the .6–.7 percent range (compared to 1.2 percent for the best-managed banks) and returns on equity at a substandard 10 percent.

A number of money center banks made strenuous efforts to move themselves into the more promising investment banking side of the business, but for most the results were disappointing. Part of the problem was the Glass-Steagall constraints. But another part of the problem related to the acquisition of skills and attitudes toward nonconventional lines of business and risk taking.

Nonetheless, the big banks were not giving up the effort, since they felt that they had no choice but to recapture their traditional corporate constituency. Several of the money center banks—Bankers Trust, Morgan Guaranty, and Citibank, for instance—had already made heavy commitments to the transformation process. Morgan Guaranty had gone so far as to publicly declare its intention of giving up its commercial banking license in favor of investment banking if regulatory barriers were not removed.

There was a clear perception that the tide of events in financial markets was moving in the direction of the wholesale investment banks. They had positioned themselves with the skills, resources, and geographic presence to exploit the rich opportunities of the expansive 1980s.

The recent revenue mix gives an idea of both the size and the range of the industry's contemporary activities. Table 5-1 indicates that these activities can be separated roughly into underwriting, secondary-market operations, money management, and corporate finance-related activities.

Table 5-1
Sources of Gross Revenue for NYSE Member Firms
(Percentage by Category)

	1972	1977	1982	1987*
Securities commissions	53%	42%	26%	18%
Trading and investments	15	19	28	25
Interest on debit balances	9	11	9	6
Underwriting	13	11	10	10
Mutual fund sales	2	1	1	3
Commodity revenues	2	4	3	3
Other income, securities related	6	10	19	30
Other income, securities unrelated		2	4	5
Total	100	100	100	100

* January–September. Latest NYSE data available at press time.
Sources: NYSE Fact Books.

Securities Underwriting

While by the end of the 1980s classic underwriting was no longer the dominant business focus for contemporary U.S. investment banks, it nonetheless had grown enormously in volume and diversity of specially tailored instruments. In 1988, some $222 billion of debt funds were publicly and privately raised on behalf of all private-sector businesses (compared to $43 billion in 1977), and an additional $42 billion of new equity was raised (as compared to $12 billion in 1977). Seventy-five billion dollars was raised for municipal and nonprofit units (compared to $36 billion in 1977). And the forms of the instruments were now much more numerous. A long-time chronicler of trends in financial securities identified more than 253 distinct financial instruments in use in the United States in the late 1980s, compared to barely 62 in 1982. While this proliferation makes a detailed review impractical, a close look at several large segments of the market are instructive as to the activities of the industry in general.

Conventional Negotiated Debt

The "plain vanilla," longer-term debt that had long been the financing mainstay of U.S. corporations remained an important part of the total underwriting. But behind these figures was a pattern of developments that considerably altered the way public financing business was conducted. For many years the gross spread (the bankers' commission) on investment-grade debt offerings had remained stable at approximately ⅞ of 1 percent (that is, $8.75 for each $1,000 bond

Table 5-2
Rankings of Lead Managers in Negotiated Corporate Debt Offerings
(Full Credit to Lead Managers)

	Rank			
	1980	1984	1986	1988
Goldman, Sachs	4	5	6	1
Merrill Lynch	6	4	5	2
Salomon Brothers	2	1	1	3
First Boston	3	3	2	4
Morgan Stanley	1	6	4	5
Shearson Lehman Brothers	5*	7	7	6
Drexel Burnham Lambert	12	2	3	7

* Lehman Brothers alone.
Sources: Corporate Sweepstakes, Institutional Investor publication, various issues.

sold). But this commission had been steadily eroded in recent years by domestic and foreign competitive pressures—including the alternative of the Eurobond markets, as discussed in Chapters 2 and 3.

The narrowing of the commission margins was further advanced by the introduction of domestic U.S. shelf registrations in 1982. Under this streamlined and accelerated procedure, qualifying corporate issuers could register with the SEC their intent to sell securities as much as two years in advance of the actual transaction. The securities were held "on the shelf" until an attractive selling opportunity presented itself, then sold swiftly through one or more securities firms with only brief advance notification to Washington regulators.

Since 1982, this modified offering form has captured more than half the total volume of corporate debt securities offerings. And, because in many cases the issuer shopped among securities firms for the cheapest issuing cost, shelf-registered underwritings have introduced a de facto competitive-bid format into the fund-raising process. Shelf registration has significantly influenced the industry standings of competing investment banking vendors (see Table 5-2).

Salomon Brothers increased its penetration of the debt market at the expense of several other firms, including Morgan Stanley, up through 1987 and then stumbled (see Chapter 10). Equally noteworthy, the composition of the top rank of securities firms in this market niche has remained remarkably stable. It is mainly the positions within this handful of securities firms that have shifted somewhat. Equally notable is the nominal position of foreign securities vendors in this bread-and-butter sector of the U.S. corporate-financing business. Although some foreign securities firms and banking houses

Table 5-3
Lead Underwriters of High-Yield Corporate Debt Offerings

	Percentage of Total			
	1982 (Total annual volume $3 billion)	1984 (Total annual volume $15 billion)	1986 (Total annual volume $34 billion)	1988 (Total annual volume $28 billion)
Drexel Burnham Lambert	55%	69%	46%	43%
First Boston	—	3	5	14
Morgan Stanley	—	2	8	11
Merrill Lynch	25	3	11	8
Salomon Brothers	—	6	8	6
Prudential-Bache	1	6	1	4
Goldman, Sachs	—	1	4	3
Others	19	9	17	11
	100	100	100	100

Sources: Institutional Investor, various issues; IDD Information Services, Inc.

have been a part of the U.S. domestic-financing scene for a number of years, their impact has been minimal.

High-Yield Corporate Debt

The emergence of a market for the public debt securities of smaller or lower-quality issuers (typically BB or lower in credit rating) has been an important recent development. This market sector, an outgrowth of the larger securitization of financial assets and liabilities discussed in Chapter 4, is in one sense the publicly traded version of conventional bank (or insurance company) term loans, which were the financing mainstay of many U.S. companies in the past. Total underwritings grew from a nominal amount in the early 1970s to more than $28 billion in 1988. A substantial part of this total has been used in the restructuring of companies that have either been taken private in leveraged buyouts or undergone major capital structure adjustments, often to prevent a raid. But contrary to public perception, the larger part of junk bond issues have been initiated by companies to finance internal growth, not acquisitions.

Drexel Burnham Lambert almost single-handedly created this financing sector and, as Table 5-3 indicates, persistently maintained its leadership through the end of 1988.

Once other firms recognized the gold in junk, Drexel has been

Table 5-4
Rankings of Lead Managers in Mortgage-Backed Securities Offerings
(Full Credit to Lead Manager)

	Rank				
	1984	1985	1986	1987	1988
Goldman, Sachs	—	—	7	4	1
Salomon Brothers	1	1	1	1	2
Merrill Lynch	4	4	3	3	3
First Boston	2	2	2	2	4
Shearson Lehman Brothers	3	3	4	5	5
Morgan Stanley	—	—	5	6	6
Bear, Stearns	6	—	—	—	7
Kidder, Peabody	—	—	6	7	—
Drexel Burnham Lambert	—	5	—	—	—
PaineWebber	—	7	—	—	—
Dean Witter Reynolds	5	6	—	—	—
Wheat, First Securities	7	—	—	—	—

Sources: Corporate Financing Week, Institutional Investor publication, various issues.

pressed by a number of new competitors. Table 5-3 indicates that leading firms such as First Boston, Merrill Lynch, and Morgan Stanley, have all moved into this market and obtained significant shares. Commercial banks are statutorily excluded, of course, and foreign firms have not been a significant factor, although there has been some foreign investor interest in the securities.

Asset-Backed Debt

Another important new market sector is asset-backed securities. These publicly traded securities represent formerly illiquid loans made by financial institutions to households on such durable assets as homes and autos. Like the high-yield sector's antecedent bank and institutional term loans, the asset-backed debt sector is an example of the securitization of formerly illiquid financial assets and liabilities that has become such an important phenomenon over the course of the 1980s.

The mortgage-backed securities market has grown dramatically over a relatively short period of time, climbing from approximately $12 billion in 1984 to $93 billion in 1988. As Table 5-4 shows, the vendor leadership in this area has shifted somewhat. And while these securitized mortgages constituted the great bulk of asset-backed debt, a growing volume of car loans and other durable IOUs was packaged and sold to investors. Even such nondurable IOUs as credit-card balances were securitized and marketed to investors hungry for high-yield debt. In the asset-backed financing sector, it has been Salomon Brothers and First Boston that have obtained the largest market shares, although the profit potential in this high-volume business segment has attracted a number of other vendors. Particularly grating to the commercial banks and thrifts, which have generated the bulk of the raw product, was that until a recent proposed change in U.S. regulations, they were not permitted to underwrite and distribute securitized products of their own balance sheets, even though they are permitted to trade the new securities once they are issued.

Municipal Debt

Typically, the term "municipal debt" has generically referred to debt whose interest is exempt from tax at the federal level. It is separable into a number of subcategories, the most important of which are general obligation (GO) bonds of states, cities, and towns; revenue bonds, which, unlike the GOs, have a specific income source dedicated to servicing their interest and principal payments (such as a turnpike authority bond); and bonds of a variety of nonprofit organizations, such as hospitals, educational institutions, and other entities that enjoy tax-exempt status.

Almost all of the larger U.S. securities firms have long-established (and separate) municipal finance departments to deal with the special needs of this client group. A few, such as Morgan Stanley and Dillon, Read, have been more recent entrants spurred most likely by the longer-term profit prospects as well as a conviction about the strategic importance of having a presence in the market. On the other hand, one firm generally regarded as having one of the strongest franchises in the sector, Salomon Brothers, abruptly announced its total withdrawal from municipal finance in late 1987, citing the expected greater competition from commercial banks when the restrictions of the Glass-Steagall Act on their participation in the revenue bond segment of the market were liberalized (see Chapter 10).

The market for municipal debt historically has been very large, reaching an all-time high of approximately $200 billion in 1985, just prior to the passage of the Tax Reform Act of 1986, which significantly restricted the granting of tax-exempt status to certain financing categories. Although total volume plummeted to less than $70 billion in 1988, many observers believe that annual volume will range upward of $90 billion during the decade of the 1990s.

Table 5-5
Rankings of Lead Managers in Municipal Debt Offerings
(Full Credit to Lead Manager)

	Rank				
	1980	1982	1984	1987	1988
Merrill Lynch	4	1	1	1	1
Goldman, Sachs	1	3	6	2	2
Shearson Lehman	—	—	7	7	3
First Boston	—	7	—	5	4
Smith Barney	7	6	4	3	5
PaineWebber	3	4	—	6	6
Salomon Brothers	6	5	3	4	—
E.F. Hutton	2	2	2	—	—
Kidder, Peabody	5	—	5	—	—
Prudential-Bache	—	—	—	—	7

Sources: Institutional Investor, various issues.

Table 5-5 shows the market shares of investment banking inter-mediaries in the municipal debt sector over the past decade.

As can be noted from Table 5-5, the leadership in the area has been relatively stable over time and, among the intermediaries, has tended to represent the same group of underwriters that also consti-tutes the leaders in the taxable debt markets. Foreign firms are nota-bly absent from the group, because their distribution outlets abroad are not usually able to take advantage of the U.S. tax deduction fea-ture. U.S. commercial banks, on the other hand, have been aggres-sive competitors in the GO part of the business, where they can legally compete and are expected to be vigorous competitors in any additional sectors that open up to them through future modification or repeal of Glass-Steagall.

U.S. Government Securities

The U.S. government-securities market dwarfs all others in the world. In 1987 alone, the U.S. Treasury issued some $1.2 trillion worth of securities.[1] The daily secondary market in these bills, bonds, and notes totaled $100 billion.[2] In contrast to offerings of the corpo-rate securities, all U.S. government securities are auctioned off in competitive bidding. While the market for capital in general is evolv-ing toward globalization, with the same products still being sold around

1. *BusinessWeek*, January 11, 1988, p. 60.
2. Ibid.

the world and at uniform prices, it can be argued that the U.S. government-bond market has already reached that status.

A select group of approximately 43 banking intermediaries, designated "primary dealers," are the only vendors permitted to bid directly to the U.S. Treasury for newly issued obligations. They also enjoy an insiders secondary market with more favorable terms than are available to the rest of the more than 300 vendors designated as dealers in the U.S. government-bond market. Among this wide group of participating vendors are U.S. commercial banks and a variety of foreign financial institutions.

Generally, U.S financial intermediaries able and willing to meet the specified capital and trading requirements are granted designation as primary dealers if they apply. A somewhat expanded set of considerations applies to foreign bank and securities firm applicants. U.S. regulators and policymakers exercise a special sensitivity to the reciprocal treatment accorded U.S. banking institutions in the home market of the foreign vendor seeking primary-dealer status. In the case of Japan, in particular, there is a de facto quid pro quo arrangement. At times, Japanese financial institutions' applications for primary-dealer status have been put on hold because of the perception that they have blocked U.S. dealers' access in Tokyo.

Appendix Table B-5 presents statistics on the volume of government and agency debt floated in recent years and the composition of the group of primary dealers who have bought and distributed it. Gross spreads on this debt have been very small, no more than $\frac{1}{16}$ of 1 percent on average, thus qualifying it as the ultimate commodity-type money market. Nonetheless, sheer volume and the robust foreign demand for this paper, along with opportunities for secondary market dealings, have made it an increasingly important sector of the U.S.—and international—securities business.

Corporate Equity Securities

Although the volume of new equities securities underwritten over the years has been small relative to the size of the corporate debt market, its importance in the competitive dynamics of the securities industry should not be minimized. This is partly because of the much higher gross spreads (commissions) involved and partly because equity underwritings are presumed to give the vendor a foot in the issuer's door. Equity business has been viewed as a way to establish a relationship with the issuer and an inside track for any subsequent financings. Thus, investment banks as well as their clients closely study equity league tables such as those presented in Table 5-6.

Table 5-6

Rankings of Lead Managers in Volume of Negotiated Corporate Equity Offerings (Full Credit to Lead Manager)

	Rank				
	1982	1984	1986	1987	1988
Merrill Lynch	2	3	4	2	1
Shearson Lehman	—	5	6	5	2
Prudential-Bache	—	—	—	—	3
Goldman, Sachs	3	1	1	1	4
PaineWebber	7	—	—	—	5
Wheat, First Securities	—	—	—	—	6
Drexel Burnham Lambert	—	—	3	6	7
First Boston	6	—	7	4	—
Salomon Brothers	5	4	2	7	—
Kidder, Peabody	4	7	—	—	—
Morgan Stanley	1	2	5	3	—

Sources: Institutional Investor, various issues.

Table 5-7 shows the league tables for a subset of equity financings: initial public offerings (IPOs). While several of the investment banks dominant in other market sectors are also prominent here, several other firms such as Hambrecht and Quist (San Francisco) and Alex. Brown (Baltimore) have operated historically as regional securities firms. Their special expertise and contacts with some of the fastest-growing U.S. industries and their successful record in both researching and bringing such companies public have given their standings in the Wall Street community a powerful boost. Both firms have won coveted admission to major-bracket status in the mainstream of Wall Street financings as a consequence of their IPO performance.

The more detailed Appendix Table B-6 demonstrates a relatively flat distribution of equity market shares (in contrast to a number of other financing sectors already discussed). The tables also show that all the important competitors are U.S. securities firms. Foreign vendors operating in the United States are only nominal participants, typically joining as syndicate participants and content to receive their sale allocations for placement with their clients in their home markets. One trend of note, however, is the use of foreign tranches (allocations) in equity offerings, with European and Asian firms as underwriters and distributors for a part of the issue. This trend reflects the increasingly international perspective of many U.S. corpo-

Table 5-7
Rankings of Lead Managers in Equity IPOs
(Full Credit to Lead Managers)

	Rank			
	1984	1986	1987	1988
Merrill Lynch	2	1	2	1
Shearson Lehman Brothers	6	6	5	2
Prudential-Bache	—	3	—	3
PaineWebber	—	—	3	4
Wheat, First Securities	—	—	4	5
Goldman, Sachs	4	4	1	6
Salomon Brothers	—	—	6	7
Alex. Brown	7	—	—	—
Drexel Burnham Lambert	5	2	7	—
First Boston	3	5	—	—
Lazard Frères	—	7	—	—
E.F. Hutton	—	—	—	—
Rothschild Unterberg Towbin	—	—	—	—
Morgan Stanley	1	—	—	—

Sources: Corporate Financing, Underwriting Totals publication, various issues.

rate issuers. A few private U.S. corporations have even forsaken the U.S. market altogether and made their initial public offerings in London under the auspices of a European investment bank. While the number of such instances is small thus far, it may have a growing influence on the IPO market in the future and further promote the globalization of corporate financing.

Secondary-Market Business

Commissions

What was once the largest part of the revenue stream for retail and institutional research boutique firms has declined dramatically since May Day 1975, when commissions were unfixed. A look at Table 5-1, will show that the proportion of the revenue dollar coming from brokerage commissions for NYSE member firms has dropped from 53 percent in 1975 to 18 percent in 1988. In absolute dollars, on the other hand, it has tripled during approximately the same period.

That figure masks a great deal of roiling within both the institutional and the retail parts of the brokerage business. Overall, the typical turnover ratio (total annual transactions divided by total market capitalization) of stocks almost doubled between 1982 and 1987. Institutional brokerage dollars, after the post–May Day freefall, rose from $860 million in 1980 to $1.8 billion in 1987.[3] At the end of the 1980s, however, institutional brokerage dollars accounted for only 14 percent of firm revenues among large investment banks, compared to 29 percent in 1980.[4]

Foreign brokerage firms have been increasingly important factors in the secondary-equity markets, reflecting the substantial interest of their home country investors in U.S. equity investments.

Trading

The sharp increase in the annual turnover of securities in the secondary markets, impelled in part by more active management of institutional portfolios, has certainly been one of the most important shifts in the public securities markets over the past 25 years. In 1977, for instance, 7.9 billion shares were traded on the combined NYSE, Amex, and NASDAQ markets (an average of 31 million per trading day). By 1987, that annual total had grown to 89.2 billion shares (an average of 353 million shares per day). Further, the importance of the organized exchanges has declined relative to the NASDAQ over-the-counter share of the total, which grew from 24.6 percent to 42.5 percent between 1977 and 1988.[5] A similar picture emerges with bond trading, which has benefited in recent years not only from more active management of bond portfolios, but also from the proliferation of new types of securities and the securitization of assets and liabilities.

The increase in trading activities has had a dramatic impact on the operations of securities firms. As shown in Table 5-1, the revenues of U.S. securities firms in recent years have shifted markedly toward increased reliance on secondary-market trading activity. This is in large part a response to the securities liquidity demands of important institutional clients. But another motivation has almost certainly been perceived opportunities to use the firms' own capital to make trading profits.

Like manufacturers who begin dealing in commodity markets to hedge supply prices but who subsequently catch the alluring scent of speculative profits, securities firms have turned their trading operations into major profit (and loss) centers, speculating on projected movements in that "commodity." It is true, of course, that the market intelligence gained through active trading can be put to profitable use in managing a firm's own securities-trading portfolio and in advising

---

3. Securities Industry Association.
4. Ibid.
5. Ibid.

clients. But in the 1980s, the quest for trading profits became an end in itself. Table 5-8 shows how these activities have driven the securities firms' balance sheets in recent years. Not only did the proportion of industry assets tied up in trading inventories increase from 51 percent to 73 percent between 1977 and 1988, but the total amount of assets themselves grew more than tenfold during the same period.

Like the categories of underwriting activity just discussed, the secondary markets are dominated by a relatively small group of U.S. investment banks that see their market positions as integral to their overall strength in the public securities marketplace. But a material amount of secondary-market equity trading is now being initiated by European and Japanese securities affiliates, acting both on behalf of offshore investors and, increasingly, for domestic U.S. institutional investors who exchange U.S. equity execution business for the foreign vendors' view of their home investors' appetite for U.S. securities.

Research

U.S. savings have flowed increasingly into institutionalized pools of capital. As the professional managers of these funds demanded more and better services, securities firms have been pushed to increase their commitment to trading and to provide more and better research. In the 1960s and early 1970s, an important group of vendors rode the wave of institutional research in exchange for "soft-dollar" commissions (i.e., directed brokerage payments) until negotiated commission rates were introduced on May 1, 1975. Prominent among these were Donaldson Lufkin & Jenrette (DLJ) and Mitchell Hutchins. Once brokerage commissions were drastically cut, the viability of firms specializing in research was deeply undercut. Some disappeared entirely or were absorbed by other firms. DLJ fortunately had undertaken a diversification of its business earlier, so it remained independent. Mitchell Hutchins merged with retailer PaineWebber; Donald Marron, CEO of Mitchell Hutchins, eventually surfaced as head of the new, consolidated PaineWebber. Research did not cease to be important after 1975, but it was an expense center. To carry the heavy burden of a first-class research department, a vendor had to have a large and efficient trading operation, spreading the fixed cost of research over a large volume of trades.

The number of research analysts in the United States has continued to grow, although not at the rate of the pre-1975 period. Research analysts are rated by the institutional investors in the annual *Institutional Investor's* "All-American" Investment Research Team statistics. An example is set forth in Table 5-9.

Table 5-8
Year-End Assets of NYSE Member Firms

Asset	1972		1977		1982		1988*	
	Amount ($ million)	Percentage of Total	Amount ($ million)	Percentage of Total	Amount ($ million)	Percentage of Total	Amount ($ million)	Percentage of Total
Cash	$803	2.8%	$797	1.8%	$3,947	2.3%	$8,472	1.5%
Accounts receivable: broker	3,674	12.6	4,982	11.4	20,255	11.8	57,261	12.6
Accounts receivable: customers/partners	12,541	43.0	13,768	31.6	24,503	14.2	39,657	9.6
Long position in securities	10,217	35.0	22,106	50.8	116,647	67.8	339,338	73.0
Other	1,939	6.6	1,968	4.4	6,789	3.9	20,288	3.3
Total assets	29,174	100.0	43,621	100.0	172,141	100.0	465,066	100.0

Year-End Liabilities and Capital of NYSE Member Firms

Liability	1972		1977		1982		1988*	
	Amount ($ million)	Percentage of Total	Amount ($ million)	Percentage of Total	Amount ($ million)	Percentage of Total	Amount ($ million)	Percentage of Total
Money borrowed	$12,955	44.4%	$21,879	50.2%	$84,350	49.0%	$248,198	53.4%
Payable to others: brokers and dealers	3,867	13.3	4,891	11.2	19,028	11.1	40,428	8.7
Payable to customers and partners	4,779	16.4	5,216	12.0	16,593	9.6	35,090	7.5
Short position: securities and commodities	1,383	4.7	3,980	9.1	28,771	16.7	72,731	15.6
Other accruals and accounts payable	1,800	6.2	3,722	8.5	12,620	7.3	30,462	6.6
Total liabilities	24,784	85.0	39,688	91.0	161,362	93.7	426,909	91.8
Total capital	4,390	15.0	3,933	9.0	10,779	6.3	38,157	8.2
Total liabilities and capital	29,174	100.0	43,621	100.0	172,141	100.0	465,066	100.0

* As of September 30.
Sources: NYSE Fact Books.

Table 5-9
Ranking of All-American Investment Research Teams

	Rank			
	1985	1986	1987	1988
Goldman, Sachs	2	3	3	1
First Boston	2	2	1	2
Drexel Burnham Lambert	8	5	4	3
Merrill Lynch	1	1	2	4
PaineWebber	5	4	5	5
Donaldson Lufkin & Jenrette	7	6	6	6
Prudential-Bache	—	11	8	7
Smith Barney	11	9	7	8
Shearson Lehman Hutton	15	—	15	9
Salomon Brothers	6	7	8	10
Kidder, Peabody	4	8	10	11
Dean Witter Reynolds	8	12	12	12
Cowen	13	14	—	13
Morgan Stanley	10	10	11	14
Wertheim Schroder	12	12	13	15
E.F. Hutton	—	15	14	—
Oppenheimer	14	—	—	—

Using a weighted count: a 4 rating to first teams, down to a 1 assigned to runners-up.
Sources: Institutional Investor, Wall Street Letter, various issues.

Analysts, like many professionals, are more loyal to their craft than to their firm. They move frequently from one firm to another in response to more lucrative offers. Thus, it is possible for a securities firm to buy visibility in research more easily than almost any other market dimension. Appendix Table B-13 presents recent rankings of the securities firms in terms of research depth and stature, measured by the number of analysts elected to the *Institutional Investor*'s All-American Investment Research Team. While some of the generally dominant securities firms are also prominent here, other firms are in evidence, including historically research-oriented DLJ and PaineWebber.

Money Management

Several securities firms have had a long tradition of money management. Lehman Brothers, for instance, managed several publicly traded closed-end mutual funds in the 1920s. But for most securities firms, large-scale management of investment funds (including money market funds) has been a recent phenomenon. Part of the earlier reticence to become portfolio managers may have been a fear of antagonizing important institutional-investor clients; no one likes doing business with potential competitors. Additionally, securities firms typically were not staffed to take on the activity on a large scale.

As the complexion of the business changed, however, and the attractiveness of traditional businesses like underwriting declined, securities firms searched for other activities that could feed off their central core of information generation and analysis. Money management fit that criterion. Not only did it make use of ongoing securities research, it provided the cyclical pattern of a number of other activities. It offset a more stable line of business that tended both to be more "captive" than many other businesses and to offer important economies of scale.

Some of the retail-oriented securities firms have gotten heavily involved in the portfolio management and distribution of open-end mutual funds as a natural adjunct to their dominant retail-distribution networks. Others have focused on managing large private pools of capital. Morgan Stanley, for instance, initially broke into the money management business by taking the Kuwaiti government's $4-billion equity account away from Citibank. A Citibank secretary, apparently disgruntled with her employers, leaked the complete list of the Kuwaitis' securities holdings to *The Wall Street Journal*. Kuwait considered the details of its investment portfolios to be highly confidential, since the press was full of unfavorable stories about the havoc OPEC price hikes were having on the economies of the United States and other consuming nations. The furious Kuwaitis yanked the account away from Citibank and gave it to Morgan Stanley, which has increased its money management activities to more than $20 billion in 1989.

Mention should be made of the money-market fund component of these managed pools of capital. As noted in Chapter 4, money market funds were started in the early 1970s during the upsurge in short-term interest rates. While initially a diversion of customer funds from what had been free-credit balances, the money funds grew to be very large, multibillion-dollar liquidity pools with attractive annual management fees for the securities firms that sponsored them.

Corporate Finance Activities

Traditional Corporate Finance versus Mergers and Acquisitions

Corporate financial counseling has long been a mainstay of the leading U.S. securities firms. Dating from the 1930s, when they were

separated from their commercial banking compatriots, these investment banks have dispensed advice on issues of capital structure,
dividend policy, acquisitions, and longer-term financial strategy. In
sharp contrast to practices in Japan—which we will analyze later—
U.S. securities firms have, over the post–World War II years, generally assumed the role of primary financial counselors to U.S.
corporations. During the 1950s and 1960s, advice and service were
relatively uncomplicated and straightforward. Investment bankers
would counsel CFOs on the appropriate mix of debt and equity and
would undertake the due diligence investigation of corporate affairs
required in conventional public issues of new securities. Investment
banks undertook financial structure and strategy studies typically
without charge, in the confident expectation of attractive management and distribution fees on future offerings in which they would be
lead underwriter.

In the turbulent economy of the 1970s, however, U.S. clients
increasingly sought less conventional and more innovative financing
solutions. And they displayed more and more willingness to talk to
securities firms with interesting ideas, even if they had no ongoing
relationship with those firms. The heightened level of competition
combined with new opportunities opened up by the M&A movement
pushed the wholesale securities firms into major expansions of their
corporate finance capabilities and the development of new in-house
skills and greater sophistication along a number of dimensions. These
dimensions included the valuation of companies and capabilities to
engineer new, esoteric financial instruments targeted at specific client
needs.

It has become fashionable in recent years to maintain that relationship banking is dead and that U.S. corporate business is up for
grabs. While the old bonds between corporations and certain investment banks have weakened, many corporations need a reliable and
loyal source of Wall Street assistance, and investment banks have
responded. A recent study by Eccles and Crane suggests that investment banks work hard to hold onto their stables of clients in the face
of a barrage of proposals from other securities firms offering competing services and products.[6] The authors also conclude that the more
diversified U.S. securities firms have had the most success in attracting and holding the most financially active U.S. corporations as
clients.

The once-dominant generalist, the "white shoe" gentleman

6. Robert G. Eccles and Dwight B. Crane, *Doing Deals* (Boston: Harvard Business
   School Press, 1988).

Table 5-10
Volume of U.S. Mergers

Year	($ Billion)
1970	$16.4
1975	11.8
1980	44.3
1985	179.8
1987	163.7
1988	247.6

Source: W. T. Grimm, Federal Reserve Board.

banker of tradition, has become an endangered species as securities firms turn to specialization and segmentation of their corporate finance activities. There are private placement specialists, pollution control specialists, utility industry specialists, real estate specialists, and so forth. Each represents a business niche under the broad corporate finance umbrella. Overall, as Appendix Table B-12 points out, the wholesale investment banks have drastically increased their staffing and, concurrently, the levels of both employee compensation and overall overhead.

One of the most important developments in U.S. investment banking in the last two decades has been the growing army of M&A specialists. M&A revenues and profits have grown rapidly; the M&A tail now wags the investment banking dog. The steady and persistent growth in volume of merger-related business has thus far defied the prognosticators' warnings of its imminent cyclical downturn (see Table 5-10). Instead, the M&A business has evolved through several phases. The original flurry in the mid-1970s was heavily dominated by U.S. corporations buying other domestic firms at perceived bargain prices. This phase was succeeded by a period of leveraged buyouts by entrepreneurial groups and foreign interests, as well as by self-directed public debt restructurings, usually in response to the threat of a raid. At the end of the 1980s, still a third phase appeared. Here, the investment banks abandoned the role of arm's-length counselors; instead, many now acted both as surrogate commercial banks and as principal equity investors in companies, some of which they had served as counselors in the past. No longer content to being coaches, they had joined the players.

These banks, attempting to consummate deals involving private (and management) investors, have often been called upon to line up all or part of the financing required. This has been at least part of the

Table 5-11
Investment Banking Merger Activity:
Market Shares During 1984–1986

	Representing Acquirer	Representing Target Company
Goldman, Sachs	7.4%	11.0%
Morgan Stanley	7.4	5.3
Salomon Brothers	6.5	6.2
Merrill Lynch	6.5	5.3
First Boston	6.1	6.9
Shearson Lehman	5.5	7.5
Drexel Burnham Lambert	5.1	5.0
Kidder, Peabody	4.4	7.1
Bear, Stearns	2.8	3.0
Lazard Frères	2.7	2.8
Prudential-Bache	2.5	2.1
PaineWebber	2.3	3.0
Dillon, Read	2.1	2.4
Smith Barney	1.7	1.8
Donaldson Lufkin & Jenrette	1.7	1.6
Alex. Brown	1.4	2.9
E.F. Hutton	1.0	1.3
Dean Witter Reynolds	0.6	0.7
L.F. Rothschild	0.4	0.5
Other	31.8	23.3
	100.0	100.0

Source: Adapted from Eccles and Crane, *Doing Deals*, p. 233.

motivation for developing the in-house, high-yield bond capabilities discussed earlier. It has also led to the commitment of the securities firms' own funds in bridge loans to ensure that deals can be consummated.

Perhaps even more important, there have been instances where securities firms have felt compelled to provide part or all of the *equity* funds needed to facilitate closure on an LBO. In some cases, this has meant the commitment of the firm's own equity funds. In other instances, the securities firms have mobilized large pools of institutional capital under the firm's management for investment as the equity in these LBOs. Returns earned on these investment pools over the past decade have made the job of attracting capital easy. And a number of the firms have aggressively committed their own capital in pursuit of the same proffered returns.

Table 5-11 presents a ranking of the major participants in the U.S.

M&A market. Once again, it is essentially the same group of U.S. firms that dominate a number of other sectors in the U.S. securities business. It is also important to note the minor roles of both U.S. commercial banks and offshore vendors in this lucrative, high-value-added marketplace.

It should be re-emphasized that the pattern of capital investing in M&A-related activity represents a fundamental shift in the role of the U.S. securities firms vis-à-vis their corporate (and institutional) clients. No longer the priest-confessors to corporations and institutional investors, they now sit at the table with the other players—and they have their own stack of chips. The potential for conflicts of interest, always a touchy subject for investment banks, has been magnified in the contemporary environment.

Venture Capital

Although several securities firms, such as DLJ, have had significant venture capital operations for a considerable period of time, for most other securities firms these operations represent an incremental activity added only recently. Although sometimes viewed as a way to "grow your future clients" for the high-margin IPOs, this trend appears also to be propelled by a desire to emulate the often impressive returns historically earned by the leading specialized venture-capital firms.

Real Estate

Securities firms' involvement in real estate is somewhat better established than venture capital operations, but it is nonetheless a phenomenon of the last two decades. A number of leading firms originally acquired real estate capabilities in response to perceived corporate and institutional clients' needs. For instance, Morgan Stanley purchased Brooks Harvey, and Goldman, Sachs acquired a mortgage banking firm and hired the necessary expertise to build its own real estate department. As many firms have moved more heavily into mortgage-backed securities as well as into principal investing in real properties, real estate activity has taken on increased significance.

Conclusions

The leading U.S. securities firms have forged for themselves a market position in the domestic arena that is the envy of other financial services vendors, domestic and foreign. Their broad range of activities has given them more stability than in the old single-product days of the 1950s and 1960s. A half-dozen or so firms with exclusive or substantial wholesale characteristics dominate the marketplace in most important categories. Their underwriting, trading, and corporate finance-related skills are at the leading edge, and the interrelated system of products and services they field is one that domestic commercial banks and foreign securities vendors alike strive to copy. In fact, the term "investment banking," which was coined in the United States to distinguish the newly spun-off securities operations from their former parents' commercial banking operations, is now the descriptive title that other domestic and foreign vendors use for their own securities-related operations.

The efforts of other vendors to replicate the U.S. wholesale investment banks' skills have not been very successful thus far. Even the retail U.S. securities firms have not, by and large, been able to challenge successfully the market grip of the wholesale U.S. firms in the underwriting and lucrative corporate finance end of the business. Most U.S. commercial banks have also failed to make significant progress in this business. And foreign securities vendors have had similar difficulties, except in those sectors where they have a distinct home-market advantage. It would appear that there are important and subtle barriers to entry in this high-value-added sector of U.S. business. Acquiring the skill and a recognized franchise to compete head-to-head with wholesale U.S. investment banks is easier said than done. It is not just a matter of hiring people but of imparting an accumulation of experience and a culture distinctly separate from other sectors of the financial services marketplace.

Still, there is recent evidence that even these U.S. wholesalers have their achilles' heels. They have grown so large and so fast that their leadership has been called upon to demonstrate unprecedented management skills as well as deal making. Some are running into serious internal control problems, as Chapters 10 and 12 chronicle. And their constituencies' demands that they provide services and access in other national and international market settings have created pressures and tensions that are likely to continue.

CHAPTER 6

JAPAN: A CENTURY OF CHANGE

The history of Japan's financial markets is both interesting and remarkable. To Western readers, it is interesting because Japan's markets evolved from institutions and cultural traditions vastly different from their own. And it is remarkable that this history of change and development was compressed into little over a century. Within that century, Japan emerged from feudal isolation to imperial eminence challenging the powers of the West; it endured a disastrous war and foreign occupation only to rebuild itself as the most dynamic economy in the Orient, if not the world.

At the close of the 1980s, the earning power of Japanese industries—and the propensity of its citizens to save—was piling up capital at a rate that makes the small island-nation awash with funds. Its pool of cash and the growing strength of its currency add to the global importance of its financial markets and institutions, making Japan a force to be reckoned with as we approach the twenty-first century.

As in the case of both London and New York, the key to understanding the competitive environment within the Japanese public securities markets is to first understand their historical evolution.

Several important forces have shaped the competitive environment in Japan: 1) a pervasive national concern with external perils, 2) society's acceptance of a major role for government in the financial markets, 3) openness to adapting the practices of Western financial institutions to its own needs, and 4) the particularly Japanese structure of industrial organization—the "zaibatsu."

The zaibatsu were business groups, the evolutionary result of Japan's business traditions and the influences of the Meiji era. They were giant conglomerates of companies in crucial industries; at the heart of each conglomerate, like the sun to its planets, was a holding company with a major private bank attached. The bank nourished the companies in its zaibatsu with the necessary financing. Collectively, the zaibatsu came to dominate the nation's economy and had a profound impact on the evolution of financial intermediaries, including securities firms, in modern Japan.

The Mobilizing External Threat

Under the rule of the Shoguns of the Tokugawa family, Japan existed in a self-imposed state of feudal isolation.[1] Foreigners were viewed with great suspicion, and it was government policy to insulate the country from contaminating foreign influences. Pressures from foreign powers began to be felt in the early and mid-1800s, however. First the Russian, and then American, British, French, and Dutch expeditionary forces demanded commercial trade and political concessions.

Japan, long isolated from the larger world, was ill-equipped to resist the intrusions. There was no modern industry, no financial infrastructure to channel savings,[2] and no shipping capability for moving goods. During the rule of the Shoguns, merchants had been relegated to the bottom of the official and social hierarchies. There was, to be sure, lively commerce, particularly in the Osaka area, and business and financial skills were being honed, but the merchant class was regarded as a threat to stability. The country's leadership worked hard "to keep the love of wealth and pleasures from affecting the samurai, the traditional warrior class."[3] Although the population paid tribute to the samurai, by the mid-1800s, this hereditary group was disintegrating and unable to provide any kind of effective protection against foreign incursions.

As a result, the Japanese had to accede to foreigners' demands for concessions relating to trade with Western countries' commercial firms. At the same time, there was a national sense of outrage at this violation of the nation's sovereignty and demands for remedial action. Given its failure to expel the foreigners, the sad state of the economy, widespread poverty, and the moral bankruptcy of the samurai, it was inevitable that, in 1868, the Tokugawa Shoguns would be deposed and the emperor, who had been only a figurehead during the Shogunate, restored to full power.

1. Japan's national product in the 1860s is estimated at ¥300 million, or roughly ¥10 per capita (or $10 per capita at the rate of exchange in the early 1870s). This compares with a per capita national product of $165 for the United States and $60 for Italy during the same period. See Raymond W. Goldsmith, *The Financial Development of Japan, 1868–1977* (New Haven: Yale University Press, 1983), p. 4.
2. The Japanese financial system was medieval at that point. It could be compared to the infrastructure that existed in Italy in the fifteenth century or in Germany in the sixteenth century: a feudalistic system with the object of financing the deficits of aristocratic and rural overspenders (Goldsmith, p. 7).
3. George C. Lodge and Ezra F. Vogel, eds., *Ideology and National Competitiveness* (Boston: Harvard Business School Press, 1987), p. 144.

The Early Meiji Restoration Period

The new government's policy was to make minimal concessions to the foreign powers, to reorganize the country, and to build up its strength economically, industrially, and militarily. The objective was "a rich country and a strong army,"[4] so that Japan could one day be on equal terms with other world powers and ultimately rid itself of the unequal status it had been forced to accept. Japan put itself on the fast track of economic and military development.

To accomplish this, Emperor Mutsuhito's new advisers turned to the West for guidance, example, and technology; emissaries were sent to various European countries and the United States to gather information. Their reports described these Western countries' essential reliance on private enterprise for industrial development. Japan had no comparable entrepreneurial class or developed financing infrastructure, so the government had to step in as initiator in the first stages of the country's development in the 1870s and 1880s.

The primary emphasis was on the transport, mining, and engineering industries, where military needs were greatest. The government built a model shipyard, cement and brick kilns, a glass factory, and silk and cotton spinning mills; it operated the most important mines, importing foreign machinery and hiring foreign engineers to run them. Experimental factories were set up for sugar, beer, chemicals, and a variety of Western-type goods. The techniques thus acquired became the foundation for the later development of Japan's industry.

In 1869, to establish a source of financing for these new enterprises, the government also authorized "exchange" firms ("exchange" was the Japanese expression for "bank"),[5] whose business consisted of taking deposits; issuing bank notes, loans, and exchange; and purchasing and selling gold and silver. The exchange firms were the first institutions in Japan that legitimately could be considered banks. They were, however, a short-lived solution and were soon

---

4. G. B. Sansom, *The Western World and Japan* (New York: Alfred A. Knopf, 1950), p. 441.
5. The English word "bank" derives from "bench." The process of banking in Europe grew from exchange business carried on by merchants from benches in the streets of Florence, Italy. When the Florentine merchants failed, they broke up their benches in the street, which gave rise to the word "bankruptcy," or "broken bench." (Oland D. Russell, *House of Mitsui* [reprint of 1939 ed., Westport, Conn.: Greenwood], p. 172.)

superseded by chartered national banks, modeled after American banks.[6]

In providing for the capitalization of many of these new national banks, the government relieved another problem: compensating the families of the old samurai class. During the long rule of the Shoguns, warrior families had received regular tribute (usually rice) from those living in the areas under their influence. In establishing a national system of taxation to provide its revenue, the national government wanted to eliminate these tributes and the feudal system they represented.[7] At the same time, it also wanted to avoid alienating this important stratum of Japanese society so as not to risk derailing the modernization effort. Therefore, the government instituted a system of pension payments to the samurai families in place of the old tributes. But because these payments proved a heavy financial burden for the new government, the pensions were subsequently converted into negotiable (and potentially liquid), capitalized pension bonds. These bonds paid an annual interest coupon but were much less valuable than the pensions that had been promised.

Many of the samurai families found that they could not live on the interest from the new bonds and therefore had to either attempt to sell them or use them as a source of capital to enter some form of private enterprise. When the government decreed that the bonds could be used as the capital infusion required to set up a bank, many warrior-class families set up small banks around the country, using their pension bonds as seed capital. Thus, many samurai traded their swords and armor for pinstripes.

Other important applicants for national bank charters were currency dealers. The Mitsui clan, for instance, was one of the oldest financial families in the country. For 200 years, the family had been engaged in textiles and money exchange; it acted as the exclusive provisioner of clothing to the Shogunate as well as adviser on its financial interests. The clan bankrolled the restoration of the emperor and eventually spun off its clothing and dry goods retail business[8] in favor of the financing business. Initially, the Mitsuis served as a de facto ministry of finance and central bank for the new government, but after the government set up its own internal treasury in 1880 and asked the family to cooperate with another group in establishing the First National Bank of Japan, the Mitsui family founded its own vehi-

---

6. Russell, *The House of Mitsui*, p. 168.
7. Lodge and Vogel, *Ideology and National Competitiveness*, p. 146.
8. This now constitutes the Mitsukoshi department store chain. "Koshi" is the Japanese word for store.

cle in 1876, the Mitsui Bank, which was the first private, non-national bank.[9] The Mitsuis subsequently went on to establish the powerful Mitsui zaibatsu.

Early Regulatory Attitudes

The government's regulatory policy in the economic and financial spheres during the early years of the Meiji Restoration often seemed to back and fill, but this was probably a result of inexperience rather than lack of resolve. In setting up the first banking institutions—the exchange firms—government officials relied on their experience, which was mainly with firms that traded commodities (e.g., rice). But these institutions proved to be ill-suited to the country's financing needs and were soon allowed to wither away in favor of the new national banks. The Rice Exchange Regulations of 1876 were an attempt to use past experience with commodities as a basis for regulating money flows, but these too did not work and were amended.

Representatives of the new government made frequent trips to Western Europe in search of useful ideas; the early history of modern Japan is replete with efforts to transplant institutional arrangements found elsewhere. On advice from the French minister of finance, for instance, the government established a central bank in 1882. But rather than use either the leading French or British counterparts as the model, the Japanese decided to use the Bank of Belgium, because it was the most recently established bank and therefore had the most complete set of rules and regulations. The bank's procedures also seemed most appropriate to the Japanese setting. Though the procedures were much amended over the years, they proved to be one of the more successful institutional imports into Japan.

Launching Stock Exchanges

The government bonds given in compensation to the warrior class also played an important role in establishing public securities exchanges. Although initially the bonds were not allowed to be officially traded, many samurai could not live on the income and sold them anyway, often at large discounts, in an informal black market. The government, bowing to the realistic need to provide liquidity for the bonds and mindful of the need to establish a public market for its other financing needs, again turned to Western advisers for help.

9. This is now the Daiichi Kangyo Bank, with its own modern "keiretsu" (interlocked group of enterprises, successor to the zaibutsu).

In 1874, the government commissioned a Frenchman, Gustave Boisonard, to draft a set of proposed regulations for stock exchanges.[10] The draft closely mirrored the rules used by the London Stock Exchange at the time, but financial dealers vociferously criticized it as unworkable in the Japanese setting. Consequently, no group established any stock exchanges. Instead, interested parties circulated their own home-grown proposals, which were viewed as more responsive to local circumstances. Out of this came the Stock Exchange Regulations of 1878 and the founding of the Tokyo Stock Exchange (TSE) and the Osaka Stock Exchange in the same year. The founding of a number of other exchanges soon followed.

At the very outset, trading on the TSE was restricted to several issues of government bonds. A month and a half later, the first stocks were traded—stocks of the exchange itself, followed by stocks of the First National Bank and the Rice Exchange—were traded. Government bonds were traded every day in two sessions, at 10 A.M. and again at 2 P.M., but stocks were traded only twice a month.

Because Japan's public securities exchanges initially were filled with irregularities in trading and the use of information, Hermann Roesler, a German legal adviser to the government, was appointed to devise new rules that would correct the abuses. The reforms, patterned after rules of the Berlin Exchange and tentatively introduced in 1887, were referred to as the "Bourse Regulations." A number of the provisions were unfamiliar to Japan and were seen as punitive by those engaged in public securities trading. In response to the subsequent outcry, the rules were suspended and study groups sent to Europe and the United States to seek further guidance. That effort resulted in the Exchange Law of 1893, which was uniquely Japanese in its provisions and which remained the basic legal regulatory document for the exchanges until 1943.

Spurs to Growth

Necessity, as we know, is the mother of invention. And in Japan, as in the West, progress in financing capacity and inventiveness followed closely on the heels of political and military emergencies. The impetus for Japan's modernization had been the external military threat in the mid-1800s. In 1877, a still-powerful samurai leader attempted to topple the new government, which was then forced to tap the country's fledgling capital markets for large amounts of military

10. T. F. M. Adams and Iwao Hoshii, *A Financial History of the New Japan* (Tokyo: Kodansha International Ltd., 1972), p. 6.

Table 6-1
Ranking by Volume of Transactions on Tokyo Stock Exchange, 1878–1917

	Rank			
	1878–1887	1888–1897	1898–1907	1908–1917
Transaction Type				
Railroads	1	1	1	—
Shipping and shipbuilding	2	3	2	4
Mining	—	2	3	5
Exchanges	3	—	5	1
Sugar refining	—	—	—	3
Banking and insurance	4	5	—	—
Electric power and gas	5	—	—	—
Spinning	—	4	4	2

Source: "50 Years of the Tokyo Stock Exchange," in T. F. M. Adams and Iwo Hoshii, *A Financial History of the New Japan* (Tokyo: Kodansha International Ltd., 1972).

funds to quell the rebellion. In 1894, war broke out between China and Japan over hegemony in Manchuria and Korea (the Sino-Japanese War), and, once again, the capacity of Japan's developing financial markets was stretched by the government's war matériel needs.

Although transaction volume in the early years of the securities exchanges fluctuated widely, the overall activity grew impressively during the late 1800s. National and local government bonds were issued in large quantities; industrial debentures were better received after enforcement provisions of the new Commercial Code (patterned after the German code) were implemented in 1893, thus making the environment somewhat safer for investors. Stock issues also increased substantially.

As in Europe and the United States, the creation of a network of railroads was an essential ingredient of industrial development in Japan.[11] This, in turn, generated a large volume of public bond and stock financing. Not surprisingly, therefore, railroad stocks dominated trading activity in the early decades of the TSE, as shown in Table 6-1.

The Advent of Stockbrokers

Long before the restoration of Emperor Mutsuhito in the mid-1800s, various types of brokers were doing business throughout Japan.

11. See Masaho Noda, *Nihon Shōkenshijō no seiritsushi* (The Historical Development of the Japanese Securities Market) (Tokyo: Seikosha Co., 1980).

Some were engaged in handling fresh produce and acting as middle-men between wholesalers and retailers or between wholesalers and producers. Others were active as money exchangers. In Edo (now Tokyo) and Osaka toward the end of the Tokugawa era, there may have been as many as two thousand money-exchange houses.[12]

A number of these produce brokers and smaller money brokers gravitated toward stocks and bonds as the new financing infrastructure of modern Japan was assembled. In the 1870s, government bonds were traded in a sugar warehouse in Sakai-cho; money exchangers, pawnbrokers, pickle dealers, rice merchants, and second-hand furniture dealers joined in the group trading, which was usually conducted in the evenings, since it was a sideline for most of the participants.[13]

The TSE initially was organized as a private enterprise, and its stockholders expected to receive an annual profit on their invested capital. The stockholders became the official members of the exchange and were distinct from the less favored stockbrokers, who were authorized to trade on the exchange in return for only a small fraction of the commission charged to the investors (the rest went to the stockholders of the exchange). Among the most important TSE stockholders were some of the recently organized national banks and some of the large and well-capitalized foreign exchange houses. Stockbrokers, by contrast, were drawn from the ranks of the smaller money brokers as well as produce and second-hand furniture dealers.

Thus, while the TSE's member-shareholders received large annual returns on their capital (often running to more than 100 percent per year), the stockbrokers operated on the edge of subsistence. With narrow margins and small capital cushions, they were highly vulnerable to violent swings in market prices and volume. Their tenuous position throughout this period may have contributed to their early reputation for sharp—and sometimes shady—practices in securities transactions.[14]

Groups of stockbrokers would create corners in the markets for certain securities in an effort to extract special profits for themselves; others were accused of "crossing" (i.e., matching) buy and sell orders from their own customers without notifying the exchange, thus enabling them to pocket all the commissions on both sides of the transaction. In the stock market boom following the 1894 Sino-Japanese War, some stockbrokers opened branches under various names, and

12. Adams and Hoshii, *A Financial History of the New Japan*, p. 37.
13. Ibid.
14. Ibid., pp. 35, 57, 59.

there were widespread accusations of customer abuse and embezzlement. Turnover in the stockbroker ranks was high, but a few were able to hold on. By 1912, of 107 stockbrokers on the TSE, 12 had survived from their original businesses as money changers, 10 had been rice dealers, and 8 had originally been members of the foreign silver exchange.[15]

Introduction of Securities Underwriting

By 1893, a standard method of stock issue by Japanese private-sector companies had been established. An issue was usually managed by one or two national banks, which would offer the issue for public subscription, with other banks acting as selling agents. For the Kansai Railroad issue in 1893, for instance, the Mitsui and the Daiichi banks handled the issue, but fourteen other banks from around the country accepted applications for subscription.[16]

From 1905 to 1914, the system for public sale of bonds was greatly improved. National banks began either subscribing to whole issues of corporate and government bonds (similar to the practices of J.P. Morgan and other U.S. bankers) or pledging (underwriting) to buy all bonds that remained unsubscribed. Further, a clear distinction arose between "subscription" to an issue (guaranteeing to buy) and "handling" it strictly as a subcontracting selling agent. When government bonds were refunded, the important banks typically would form a single syndicate, with the government as consultant on acceptable procedures and terms. The syndicate approach was subsequently extended to a wide variety of other public and industrial capital raisers, thus further solidifying the dominant role of the big commercial banks (as opposed to the stockbrokers) in the public financing process.

During this period, the Industrial Bank of Japan (IBJ), which the government had created in 1902 as a vehicle for financing the longer-term capital needs of Japanese industry, became an important underwriter of corporate debentures. The IBJ and several other specialized banks were the only institutions authorized to issue long-term debentures and to use the proceeds to lend to private corporations on a long-term basis. Thus, the long-term credit banks accounted for a large proportion of corporate debt securities being publicly issued and were an important conduit for channeling individual and institutional savings into private-sector investment.

Being much weaker than the national and important private

15. Ibid.
16. Ibid., p. 31.

banks, securities brokers were relegated to the role of selling agents in these public financing operations during the early 1900s. In 1910, however, two groups of the largest securities brokers (including present-day Nomura Securities) were invited to participate as syndicate members with banks that were underwriting a refinancing of government bonds. Subsequently, securities dealers began to manage financial debentures issued by the country's special banks (regional banks of agriculture and industry, as well as the Industrial Bank of Japan, Kangyo Bank, Hokkaido Colonial Bank). And in 1911, a syndicate of securities dealers managed, for the first time, the issuance of bonds of the banks of agriculture and industry as original contractors, not just subcontractors.

World War I to the Great Depression

The economic boom in Japan that accompanied World War I and its immediate aftermath was impressive. Japan was selling goods to all the combatants and was able to penetrate markets in Asia, Africa, and Central and South America—regions where European countries had dominated trade. As a consequence of the war, Japan moved into an export-surplus condition and became, for the first time, a creditor nation. The war-years boom also resulted in mergers that marked the emergence of large and increasingly concentrated national banks and industrial companies.

Japan's financial markets also developed. During the immediate postwar years, the volume of both debt and equity public financing accelerated; public stock offerings, for instance, rose from 11 in 1915 to 235 in 1919. Corporations also tapped the public debt-securities market much more heavily; issues of industrial debentures rose 200 percent between 1915 and 1919.[17] Debenture issues by financial organizations, such as the IBJ, also grew, and secondary-market trading on the TSE and elsewhere increased enormously during this period.

Emergence of Leading Securities Firms

As a consequence of the boom, the stockbrokers enjoyed a period of unusual profitability, their yearly incomes rising severalfold. This was due, in part, to the greater volume of market activity and also to their strength vis-à-vis exchange members. Greater strength led to a greater share of the commissions. Moreover, a number of brokers were actively participating in the underwriting of new public offerings. In fact, at the height of this cyclical post–World War I upturn in

17. Ibid., p. 73.

the markets, some forty-three local syndicates of stockbrokers were participating in new stock offerings, either in collaboration or in competition with the national banks.[18]

A new government bond market was developing and some stockbrokers began to specialize in the underwriting of public bonds and corporate debentures. The first of these firms was the Koike Company (reorganized as Koike Bank), the forerunner of the present-day Yamaichi ("first mountain") Securities. The Koike Company had been active in handling bond issues since 1910, when the first stockbrokers' syndicate was formed. Another firm was the Fujimoto Billbroker Bank (now Daiwa—"big harmony"—Securities). In addition, an Osaka spot dealer, Tokushichi Nomura, set up the Osaka Nomura Bank. Its securities department was reorganized as an independent firm, Nomura Securities Co., in December 1925 (see Chapter 11). The bank later became the Daiwa Bank, one of today's biggest Japanese commercial banks.[19]

Imitating the relationship between the then National City Bank of New York and its securities affiliate, the National City Co., associates of IBJ established the Nikko Securities Company in June 1920. Half of the 200,000 shares of the new firm were owned by the Industrial Bank.[20]

The IBJ continued to be an important force in the public markets and a dominant factor in public debt financings; it was itself a principal issuer of financial debt to fund its lending operation. As the scale of bond flotations grew larger, the role of the syndicate formed by the big banks for underwriting the issues became more important. Starting with the ninth bond issue of the South Manchurian Railway Co. (1919), the bank syndicate system replaced the IBJ's role as the sole underwriter and also took over the issues of electric power and chemical companies. All of these issues involved large sums. If foreign bond issues are omitted, the IBJ's share of the flotation of industrial debentures fell from 55 percent in 1919 to 23 percent in 1925.[21] This does not imply that the bank's stature in Japan was diminishing, but rather that the demands of the booming Japanese economy for capital were growing dramatically.

During the early 1920s, "trust companies," Anglo-Saxon institutions unknown in the modern Japanese law, first appeared. Early

18. Ibid., p. 77.
19. Nomura Securities Co., Ltd., *Beyond the Ivied Mountain: The Origin and Growth of a Japanese Securities House, Nomura: 1872–1985* (Tokyo: Nomura Securities Co., Ltd., 1986), p. 35.
20. Adams and Hoshii, *A Financial History of the New Japan*, p. 77.
21. Ibid., p. 85.

trust operations had involved managing collateral, securing corporate debentures, and performing other services on behalf of the issuers of debt securities. But in 1922, a law was passed that codified how trusts should be organized and the scope of their activities.

The Ministry of Finance sought to limit the number of trust companies by setting high minimum-capital requirements. The most important trust institutions were connected with the zaibatsu: Mitsui Trust (founded in 1924), Mutual Trust (later, Yasuda Trust) and Sumitomo Trust (both founded in 1925), and Mitsubishi Trust (founded in 1927). Under the new legislation, these trust companies could manage money and participate in the issuance of new corporate debentures. Some, particularly those connected with the zaibatsu, subsequently gained prominent roles in underwriting new securities offerings of their group-affiliated companies.

Nevertheless, this development should not obscure the general trend toward increasingly large and powerful commercial banks. The wave of bank mergers after World War I had already produced some very large financial institutions.

Meanwhile, the booming stock market had reached its highest level in January 1920, and then the bottom fell out. A frenzy of speculation had resulted in a fundamental overvaluation of securities, creating an opportunity for Japan's moneymen to learn yet another lesson from the West: that speculative bubbles eventually burst. In the ensuing panic, all the country's exchanges were closed down for more than a month and the stock price index fell from its high of 250 in January 1920 to 113 in June of that same year. The stock market crash was the beginning of a long series of crises that included a bank panic in 1922, the Great Kanto Earthquake in 1923 (which destroyed two-thirds of Tokyo and Yokohama and their stock exchanges), a financial panic in 1927, and finally, the global depression of the 1930s. Partial recoveries came and went, but no real upswing ensued. Having experienced the heady prosperity of World War I and its immediate aftermath, Japan found itself locked in the jaws of a chronic depression during the 1920s.

The financial panic of 1927 brought the downfall of many banks and securities companies and caused an even greater degree of concentration in both the banking and the underwriting businesses. Among the thirteen large banks at the time, the "Big Five" (Daiichi, Mitsubishi, Mitsui, Yasuda, and Sumitomo) increased their share of the deposits of the thirteen large banks from almost 60 percent in 1926 to just under 65 percent in 1931.[22] During the same period, their

22. Ibid., p. 87.

percentage of *all* bank deposits rose from over 24 percent to over 38 percent.[23]

With industry so indebted to the big commercial banks, the government felt compelled to provide bailout funds to ailing companies in an effort to avert failures among the important lenders. Nonetheless, a number of banks did fail during the decade, including some prominent names. The failures prompted still further consolidation within the banking sector, and the surviving banks became even more important in the public underwriting arena. In fact, after the financial panic in 1927, only the big banks, the big trust companies, and the biggest securities dealers were left in the underwriting business and in offering securities for public subscription. Among these surviving securities brokers were Koike Bank (as mentioned, the forerunner of Yamaichi Securities), Osaka Nomura Bank, Fujimoto Billbroker Bank (the forerunner of Daiwa Securities), and Nikko Securities.

Stabilization of Securities Prices

In a number of instances in the 1920s, important financial institutions or groups of them, with the support of the Ministry of Finance, attempted to stabilize and prop up prevailing securities prices (a practice still extant in contemporary Japanese securities markets). In the panics of 1920 and 1927, for instance, the Bank of Japan loosened credit to encourage the large banks to extend credit to securities dealers so that they, in turn, could go into the market to purchase securities. In 1930, the IBJ, at the government's behest, extended special credits to TSE members to help support stock prices. A group of thirty-two insurance companies, fearful of having to write down the book values of their large portfolios, also put up a large capital sum for the support of stock prices.

There was a considerable element of speculation in the equity markets during the 1920s. Much of the trading volume was in the form of de facto "futures" transactions, which probably increased the leverage in the stock market and the potential for price fluctuations.[24]

The "Manchurian Incident" to the End of World War II

As was the case in Europe during the 1920s, economic disruption nurtured military ambition. Unemployment and instability in Japan

---

23. Ibid.
24. Kaichi Shimura, *Nihon Shijo Bunseki* (Tokyo: University of Tokyo Press, 1969).

provided the new warlord class with an opportunity to take center stage and to undertake military adventures in mainland Asia.

Japanese banking and industry underwent further transformation during the approximately fifteen years of war fever that gripped Japan, beginning with the 1931 "Manchurian Incident." The incident occurred when elements of the military persuaded the government to attack Chinese positions in Manchuria, signaling the commencement of a buildup in the country's war matériel-related industries, including development of raw material resources and industries in Japan's occupied territories of Korea, Manchuria, and Taiwan.

The cooperation of the private sector, particularly the zaibatsu, old and new, became central to the government's pursuit of its war goals. Aided by formal cartel relationships with their group member firms and permissive government legislation, the zaibatsu evolved into a powerful network of industrial and financial enterprises. Through the government's policy of continuous consolidation and rationalization of different industry sectors during this period, the zaibatsu's share of the total economic activity rose considerably.

The cooperation between the zaibatsu and the government was extensive. The zaibatsu firms provided key executives to serve in various government and quasi-government positions. When the government undertook particular overseas activities, the zaibatsu mobilized to act as implementers, with the government effectively underwriting the risk in the form of tax exemptions, inexpensive credit, special subsidies, guaranteed minimum dividends, and so forth.

Securities Market Activity

The mobilization effort, of course, required a huge amount of financing for key industries. Stock issues grew in importance during this period as many established firms—including zaibatsu—found their internal sources inadequate. Also, a considerable number of newly organized firms were going public to raise equity during the war boom. Publicly issued debentures grew in volume and importance, as firms sought the necessary growth funds. As a result, the private sector's reliance on debt increased markedly, what with the extensive public debt offerings and still-heavy private borrowing.

Government expenditures also rose dramatically during this period, but there was an effort to avoid direct governmental borrowing in the public markets so as not to compete with private fundraisers and thus drive up interest rates. Added to direct government financing was the continuing volume of financial debentures issued by quasi-government agents such as the Bank of Japan, the Yokohama Specie Bank (the forerunner of the Bank of Tokyo), the IBJ, and other special-purpose banks.

Further Consolidation

Although the Ministry of Finance (MOF) induced the big commercial banks to absorb a large amount of the newly issued government bonds and to direct their lending activities in desired directions, the banks benefited from the government's efforts to rationalize the banking industry. The number of banks declined from nearly 700 in 1931, to roughly 400 in 1936, to fewer than 190 in 1941, and ultimately to 72 in 1944.[25] The Financial Enterprises Reorganization Ordinance of 1942 legally sanctioned the MOF to implement its bank merger policy, which previously had to rely on administrative guidance ("gyosei shido") for its teeth.

Japanese thrift institutions and insurance companies also helped fund military expenditures. Japanese savings institutions experienced strong growth during this period, reflecting the inflow of household savings due to both the scarcity of consumer goods and the strong social pressures to save (war bonds were promoted as aggressively in Japan during this period as in the United States and parts of Europe). Thrift institutions increased their purchases of government debt. Japanese insurance companies, which characteristically channeled more of their cash flow to the corporate sector than to government, were also a target of MOF consolidation and rationalization. The total number of life and nonlife insurance companies decreased from sixty-one to twenty-one and from sixty-eight to seventeen, respectively, between 1931 and 1944.[26]

Securities dealers also went through a shakeup. The MOF forced all dealers to become corporations and to increase their capital substantially as a precondition to participation in the issuance market. Consequently, in 1939 there were only eight brokerage firms that qualified as securities underwriters: Yamaichi, Koike, Nikko, Nomura, Fujimoto, Kyodo, Kawashimaya, and Nippon Kangyo.

The Financial Enterprises Reorganization Ordinance of 1942 further affected the securities industry: in September 1943, Yamaichi Securities merged with Koike Securities to form the new Yamaichi Securities; the next month, Kawashimaya Securities absorbed Kawashimaya Company. In December, Nikko Securities absorbed Kyodo Securities, and Fujimoto Securities amalgamated with the Japan Trust

---

25. Goldsmith, *The Financial Development of Japan, 1868–1977*, p. 119.
26. Ibid., p. 121.

Bank to form Daiwa Securities. Then, in March 1944, Nikko Securities merged with Kawashimaya Securities and set up a new Nikko Securities, so that only five underwriters were left: Yamaichi, Nomura, Nikko, Daiwa, and the Nippon Kangyo. Securities dealers who were not members of an exchange were ordered to reduce their numbers by 80 percent. The mold was being prepared for the securities competitor group that would dominate the postwar period.

Government control of the public securities markets culminated in the amalgamation of all the country's exchanges into a single market, the Japan Securities Exchange, in 1944, but the government's intervention in securities price movements on the exchange had started much earlier. During the 1930s, the Japanese government came to view the public securities markets as an important instrument of national policy. At the same time, it viewed any catastrophic price drops as financially and psychologically damaging to its efforts to obtain money to support the war effort. Thus, mirroring both earlier and later periods in Japanese financial history, the government indirectly intervened in the markets at various times to stabilize and support securities prices. In 1937, when securities prices crashed in nervous response to a battle between Japanese and Chinese troops outside Beijing, the government asked the same group of life insurance companies that had purchased equity shares in 1930 to do so again. The government then established the Japan Co-operative Securities Co. and the Wartime Finance Bank in order to stabilize stock prices. To provide them with the necessary liquidity, the government directed the IBJ to buy the securities that the association was already holding. The government again took similar actions, directly or indirectly, in 1940 and 1941. In the last months of the war, when the MOF ordered all the exchanges to suspend business, a government agency (the Wartime Finance Bank) was directed to buy all the securities offered at the last prevailing prices before the closing of the exchanges.

Immediate Post–World War II Period

In the aftermath of Japan's surrender to the Allied forces in May 1945, the victors' initial inclination was to dismantle much of Japan's industrial capacity to prevent any resurgence in external expansionist tendencies. The United States, however, as the leading country in the administration of Japan's postwar affairs, decided to push for reconstruction of Japan so it could become self-sufficient without the potential for making war. The decision was to have a dramatic impact on financial services in Japan.

Table 6-2
Zaibatsu Share of Private-Sector Paid-in Capital, 1945

Zaibatsu	Paid-in Capital	Percentage of National Total
Mitsui	¥3,061	9.4%
Mitsubishi	2,704	8.3
Sumitomo	1,667	5.2
Yasuda	510	1.6

Source: T. F. M. Adams and Iwo Hoshii, *A Financial History of the New Japan* (Tokyo: Kodansha International Ltd., 1972), p. 170.

Japan's industrial base had been heavily damaged by the war. It was estimated that the damage from Allied bombing was five times greater than that caused by the Great Earthquake of 1923; measured in 1935 currency values, the damage came to 34 percent of the national wealth.[27] A surprisingly large part of the productive capacity of certain industries remained intact, but it was, for the most part, obsolete, worn out, and badly in need of repair. By 1945, the real standard of living of the population probably had dropped to about half of what it had been in 1935. The balance sheet for the economy was badly out of kilter. Against physical assets of some ¥189,000 billion, there were claims in the form of stocks and bonds, deposits, war-indemnity claims against the government, and so forth, totaling ¥411,000 billion. That left a shortfall of ¥222,000 billion.[28]

The supreme commander for the Allied powers (SCAP), U.S. General Douglas MacArthur, decided that the Japanese authorities themselves should be responsible for the management and direction of the domestic fiscal, monetary, and credit policies, but that the occupation commander would set a number of broad policies and would approve and review the Japanese authorities' implementation.

One of SCAP's early decisions was to dismantle the prewar zaibatsu. SCAP statistics showed just how important the leading zaibatsu had become by 1945, as measured by shares of paid-in capital within the Japanese private-sector economy (see Table 6-2).

It is interesting to note that the market presence of each zaibatsu varied widely by specific industries. In financial services, the Yasuda group had a 17.2 percent share of assets, the Mitsui group had a 13.9 percent share, Mitsubishi had 12.1 percent, and Sumitomo had 5.4 percent. Overall, the Big Four zaibatsu together controlled 24.5 per-

27. Adams and Hoshii, *A Financial History of the New Japan,* p. 161.
28. Ibid., p. 114.

cent of the paid-in capital of all private-sector firms, 49.7 percent of the capital of finance firms, and 32.4 percent of heavy industry companies.[29]

Not only were the Big Four zaibatsu targeted for such dissolution, but twenty-six others (out of eighty-three holding companies that were initially examined) were also dissolved. SCAP decided to force a sweeping redistribution of stock ownership. The objective was to promote the democratization of share ownership by encouraging small investors (including employees and local residents where the companies were located) to take up the shares that had previously been held by zaibatsu families, their holding companies, and others. It was a slow process, because many individuals lacked the sophistication and the savings to invest in the stocks. Nonetheless, by March 1950, corporate ownership of total domestic equity securities had fallen to 5.6 percent from 24.7 percent in March 1946. Individual ownership increased from 53.1 percent to 69.1 percent over the same period.

The stock ownership positions of the leading financial institutions, however, remained at approximately their pre-occupation levels. This was because, while the final version of the law allowed firms to hold no more than 5 percent of the voting shares of other firms, SCAP failed to apply the same divestment requirements to financial institutions, particularly the zaibatsu banks. This oversight was to have a far-reaching impact on the economic infrastructure of postwar Japan. As we will discuss, the big zaibatsu banks in many respects were able to pick up the dissolved holding companies' leadership roles and orchestrate the reassembling of control positions in their major prewar operating components.

Origins of Article 65

Among other reforms, the occupation forces initiated replacement of the legislation that had governed the securities sector in the prewar period. In 1947, the Japanese Diet passed the Securities and Exchange Law, which included key provisions from the United States' Securities Act of 1933 and the Securities Exchange Act of 1934.[30] Thus, the new Japanese act mirrored concerns paramount in the U.S. market prior to the enactment of the 1933 and 1934 Acts: that the markets

29. Hiromitsu Arisawa, *Shoken Hyakuneshi* (A Hundred Year Securities History) (Tokyo: Japan Economic Journal, 1974), p. 195.
30. See Joseph Auerbach and Samuel L. Hayes, III, *Investment Banking and Diligence: What Price Deregulation?* (Boston: Harvard Business School Press, 1986) for a discussion of the legislative history of the 1933 and 1934 Acts.

were speculative in nature, with financial products being marketed without careful analysis and reporting of value factors, and that outright fraud was not uncommon in the trade.[31]

Included in the Securities Exchange Law is Article 65, Japan's equivalent of the 1933 Glass-Steagall Act:[32]

Article 65. A bank, trust company or such other financial institution as may be designated by a Securities and Exchange Commission Regulation shall not engage in any of the acts enumerated in Paragraph 8 of Article 2, provided that a bank may purchase and sell the securities upon the written order of and solely for the account of clients, and a bank, trust company or such other financial institution as may be designated by a Securities and Exchange Commission Regulation may purchase and sell the securities for its own investment purpose and/or on the basis of trust contracts for its trustors accounts under the provisions of other laws.

The provisions of the foregoing paragraph shall not apply to national bonds, local bonds and corporate debentures with respect to which principal redemption or interest is guaranteed by the government.

Article 2. (paragraph 8) The term "securities business" referred to in the present Law shall mean the business by any person other than banks, trust companies or such other financial institutions as may be designated by a Securities and Exchange Commission Regulation to do one of the following actions:

1. To buy and sell securities,
2. To act as broker, agent or proxy with respect to buying and selling of securities,
3. To act as broker, agent or proxy with respect to the entrustment of transactions on a securities market,
4. To underwrite securities,
5. To sell securities by public offering,
6. To handle the issuance or sale of securities by public offering.

Article 65 prohibited banks from participating in the domestic securities industry (i.e., they were not permitted to sell securities or participate in the underwriting of primary security issues in Japan)

---

31. Ibid., pp. 26–27.
32. Ministry of Finance, Financial Commissioner's Office, pp. 719, 745. English translation of the original law.

and similarly prohibited securities companies from engaging in the domestic banking business (i.e., they were prohibited from taking deposits and extending loans in the Japanese market). Furthermore, banks were prohibited from owning more than 5 percent of any Japanese securities company.

The implementation of Article 65, in effect, not only legitimized the securities companies as the sole executors of securities transactions, but legally barred the banks from competing in the securities underwriting domain. While the banks would continue to find other ways to exercise their influence over the financing activities of Japanese industrial corporations, the act would prove to be a critical ingredient in the future success of the Japanese securities companies.

The new Securities and Exchange Law also called for the re-establishment of the Tokyo, Osaka, and Nagoya stock exchanges on May 16, 1949. During the course of that year, six other exchanges were established in Kyoto, Kobe, Hiroshima, Fukuoka, Niigata, and Sapporo. Unlike the for-profit corporate structure of prewar exchanges, the new stock exchanges were structured as nonprofit membership organizations (as in the United States). Coupled with the various control measures implemented with the Securities and Exchange Law, the re-establishment of the exchanges as nonprofit organizations (with membership confined to licensed securities companies) helped establish the legitimacy of stocks and bonds as investments as opposed to speculative instruments. In addition, the occupation leadership required the establishment of a Securities and Exchange Commission, similar to that already operating in the United States. Although the commission was subsequently abolished following the signing of the peace treaty with the Allies in 1952, the Article 65 "wall" separating commercial from investment banking remained intact. But, as we shall point out later, it did not fulfill all the benefits for which the stockbrokers might have hoped.

In June 1952, with passage of the Long-Term Credit Bank Law, long-term credit institutions such as the IBJ lost their special quasi-government role and, along with the new Long-Term Credit Bank, became ordinary banks authorized to borrow 20–30 times their capital to accommodate corporate borrowers. However, as will be pointed out, this did not quite reduce them to the status of "ordinary" commercial banks in Japan.

The Postwar Recovery Period

Despite the occupation administration's clear-cut intention to dissolve the zaibatsu and thereby enhance competition through decentralization, the breakup of concentration in industrial groups did not succeed. Some scholars of this era suggest that it was because the Allied master plan (embodied in the Antimonopoly Law) ran counter to human nature in Japan. As Adams and Hoshii put it, "The occupation policies embodied in the Antimonopoly Law attempted to make competition the supreme law of an economy for which harmony is the basic value."[33] In fact, the authors point out, concentration had always been the official policy of the Japanese government. That basic philosophy did not change in the aftermath of the Japanese defeat in World War II. Thus, it is not surprising that once the occupation forces had departed and a decent interval of time had elapsed, some of the old industrial groups reconstituted themselves.

The Zaibatsu Banks

The occupation authorities had failed to treat the zaibatsu banks in the same manner as they did the top holding companies during the dissolution process. As a result, each of the "commercial" banks (in the Article 65 sense of the word) was able legally to assume the de facto role of the old holding companies within its business group by acquiring a small percentage (less than 5 percent) of equity in each of the former zaibatsu companies. Other former zaibatsu companies made similar equity purchases, often with funds loaned to them by the group banks. Still other companies, not related to the prewar zaibatsu, modeled their business strategies along the same lines and formed their own bank-centered groups.

This new form of business group was termed "keiretsu" (literally, "business affiliations"). The keiretsu was a much more loosely organized entity than the zaibatsu, with controlling ownership being replaced by cross-ownership of smaller blocks of shares within the group, in addition to cross-directorships and informal business coordination. More important, the central role of the commercial (known in Japan as "city") banks in the postwar economic and financial infrastructure was preserved.

The prevailing postwar method of Japanese corporate funding was termed "overborrowing." Overborrowing is essentially a method by which Japanese companies obtain rolling lines of credit from their commercial banks, not just for relatively short-term working capital requirements but also for longer-term plant and equipment needs. The reliance on commercial bank financing as the principal source of operating and growth funds by Japanese corporations had several important foundations.

First, the bulk of the country's savings then being generated was

33. Adams and Hoshii, *A Financial History of the New Japan*, p. 217.

lodged in savings accounts in the commercial banks. In addition, Japanese city banks traditionally have been much more oriented toward industrial financing rather than consumer credit. It is therefore not surprising that they would go to great lengths to try to preserve this primary line of business with the industrial sector despite their exclusion from the public securities marketplace by Article 65. And, of course, financing could then be controlled within a group and thereby strengthen the ties that bound each keiretsu together. Finally, the Ministry of Finance undoubtedly found it easier to manage, control, and ration the country's scarce credits through a few large commercial banks rather than through a diffuse public securities marketplace.

The government had mandated the IBJ, the Long-Term Credit Bank, and the Nippon Credit Bank to finance the country's postwar reconstruction and industrialization. Through at least the 1960s, these long-term credit institutions provided industries with vital extended-term (five to seven years) financing at the Japanese long-term prime rate. Because of their special status as financers of the industrialization process, the long-term credit banks were given special privileges. Unlike commercial banks, which relied on deposits for funding, long-term banks issued bank debentures with maturities in the three-to-five-year range. Until the 1970s, the long-term banks thus functioned as surrogate capital markets. The government, in effect, had created a tiered banking structure where the commercial banks served the short-to-medium-term funding needs for industrial corporations, while long-term credit banks met long-term requirements. The public securities markets were therefore peripheral to the funding process.

Thus, while Article 65 gave the Japanese securities firms an exclusive franchise on the public securities markets for all but government bonds, the mainstream of industrial financing largely passed them by; they were relegated to a role not totally unlike that in the prewar period—as stockbrokers dealing in equity shares for individual investors and the small but growing institutional investor clientele.

One popular investment vehicle among individual investors was the investment trust, similar to a U.S.-style mutual fund. These trusts had been an important means of raising funds during the interwar period, and, after a slow postwar start, they had grown dramatically. For instance, by 1952 their securities holdings were larger than those of the insurance companies; by the end of 1953, they were larger than the holdings of all other financial institutions combined.[34] Seven secu-

---

34. Ibid., pp. 222–223.

rities firms had the authorization to establish and sell investment trusts: Yamaichi, Nomura, Nikko, and Daiwa (all of which carried over their authorization from before the war) as well as Daisho, Osakaya, and Oi (all of which started their investment trust business after the war). Then, in 1958, seven additional securities firms were authorized to establish and sell the trusts: Tamazuka, Nippon Kangyo, Okasan, Kakumaru, Yamazaki, Eguchi, and Yamakano.

Crisis at Yamaichi

The MOF evidently believed that investment trusts could be an important factor for stabilizing securities prices. But the way securities firms managed the trusts led to financial distress during the 1960s.

In the course of managing these investment "pools," the brokerage firms often borrowed debt securities of the investors and used them as collateral for bank loans to finance stock purchases for their own accounts. In the early 1960s, Yamaichi, in particular, did more trading for its own account than for its customers, relying more on capital gains than on fees for income. The company bought large blocks of shares in smaller growth companies, for many of whom Yamaichi was the original underwriter. In addition, Yamaichi's president had initiated large purchases of vacant land in anticipation of a sharp rise in property values. But a business recession held land prices down and dried up the market for such properties. When the stock market took a nosedive, the firm was unwilling to sell its stocks and recognize the enormous losses. Thus, the firm was stuck with enormous debts and heavy monthly carrying costs.

In 1965, Yamaichi's situation became so desperate that it had to ask its main debtor banks for a moratorium on interest payments. Public disclosure of Yamaichi's situation precipitated panic selling in the equities markets, and the Bank of Japan was forced to extend Yamaichi unlimited credits on an emergency basis. A number of other securities firms also experienced sharp reversals during this period, including Oi Securities, which required a similar extension of emergency government credits. In the case of Yamaichi, the MOF asked the IBJ to enter the picture and formulate a plan of reorganization, and a former senior official of IBJ was subsequently named president of the newly reorganized Yamaichi.[35]

As a result of the crisis surrounding the securities firms, in 1965

---

35. The IBJ has continued over many years to play a special role as link between the ruling government and the financial and business community. It continues to cultivate that special position and is frequently consulted by the government when thorny issues involving the securities markets or banking sector arise.

the MOF pushed through an amendment to the Securities and Exchange Law requiring brokers to go through a more rigorous licensing procedure rather than just registration. The decision to tighten regulations, on top of the operating reverses the securities firms were then experiencing, precipitated still another in a long series of consolidations. In 1960, roughly 600 Japanese securities firms had been registered; by 1965, only 430 remained.[36] In the wake of full implementation of the tightened regulations, the number of securities firms holding licenses dropped to 277 in 1968.[37]

The most demanding aspect of the licensing procedure was the capital requirements. Securities firms had to demonstrate that they had sufficient risk capital before they were allowed to engage in various market-related activities. Four separate licenses could be sought: trading, brokerage, underwriting, and retail selling. The license for acting as lead manager was the most stringent and only the so-called major securities firms ("sogo shoken") were able to qualify; to be only a participant in underwriting syndicates required a much smaller capital base. TSE-member firms had a higher requirement than nonmembers, and those with offices in Tokyo and/or Osaka also had more stringent capital requirements than those in other parts of the country. In addition, the MOF imposed qualitative stipulations that gave it additional leeway in deciding what firms to approve. As a further response to the setbacks experienced by the securities brokers in the 1960s, the MOF also limited the amount of securities the firms could carry in inventory at any one time.

The Period of Internationalization

In 1971, the Law Concerning Foreign Securities Firms was promulgated; for the first time, qualified non-Japanese firms were permitted to apply for branch-office licenses. Merrill Lynch was the first to receive such a license (in 1972), and others followed.

In addition to foreign firms' entry into Japan, the largest Japanese securities firms expanded more aggressively overseas. They established new branch offices in the Middle East, Asia, and Europe. Initially, the bulk of their international business comprised executing orders from foreign investors for the purchase and sale of Japanese securities, but they also experienced increased interest from Japanese investors in foreign securities as a result of the growth of Japan's investment funds.

36. Aron Viner, *Inside Japanese Financial Markets* (Homewood, Ill.: Dow-Jones Irwin, 1987), p. 48.
37. Ibid.

The new-issue markets also internationalized. In 1970, the Asian Development Bank (ADB) succeeded in floating the first yen-denominated bond (so-called samurai bonds) by a non-Japanese issuer. This achievement may have been helped by the fact that the governor of the ADB was a former MOF official and by the fact that Japan was one of the ADB's sponsoring countries. It was not, however, an easy breakthrough. The MOF had to approve an exemption to the normal requirement that the offering be secured by collateral (a cause dear to the commercial banks). In addition, the IBJ had to be placated, since it typically had arranged yen-denominated private placements for such international banks. The MOF approved the collateral requirement exemption by treating the ADB as a supranational organization. The securities companies pacified the IBJ by giving it much of their underwriting fee on the deal.[38] The financing breakthrough, supported by the top leadership of the MOF, was based on the hope of making Tokyo one of the world's major international financial centers.

The International Finance Bureau (IFB) of the MOF, which has been in charge of the balance of payments for Japan, played an important role in this process of internationalization. In the 1970s, Japan experienced current account surpluses in 1970–1972 and again in 1976–1978; deficits occurred in 1973–1975 and again in 1979–1980, coincident with the two massive world oil price increases. In the two surplus periods, the IFB promoted yen bond issues by foreign issuers, but in the 1973–1975 deficit period it discouraged this to stem overall capital outflows.

In the 1976–1978 surplus period, one could observe within the MOF the intraministry contention between the IFB and the Securities Bureau. In 1976, the IFB was promoting bond issues by foreigners to cope with the current account surplus. But the Securities Bureau was arguing for a go-slow approach because of the unstable domestic Japanese-bond markets. The Securities Bureau preferred to require prior approval before securities companies could underwrite issues. Securities firms, in turn, could use the regulatory requirement as an excuse for delay when they wanted to avoid underwriting bond issues in deteriorating market conditions. In the end, however, the top leadership of the MOF sided with the move toward internationalization and took only mildly restrictive measures on international offerings during the 1979–1980 deficit period.

Foreign currency-denominated (i.e., non-yen) bond issues by

---

38. James Horne, *Japan's Financial Markets: Conflict and Consensus in Policymaking* (Winchester, Mass.: Allen & Unwin, 1985), p. 174.

Japanese corporations were permitted beginning in 1974. Corporations started to use non-yen bond issues rather than syndicated loans, indicating their growing sophistication in assembling capital funds.[39]

In this internationalization process, pressure from foreigners helped speed the pace of reforms in Japanese domestic capital markets. When Ito Yokado, a Japanese retail store chain, issued unsecured bonds in New York, Sears, Roebuck argued for a comparable unsecured yen-denominated issue in Japan, saying that the then current system was discriminatory. Not surprisingly, this petition was strongly backed by the Japanese securities firms, which wanted to loosen the grip of the commercial banks' role as agents in secured financings. Opponents of unsecured bond issues were again banks such as the IBJ that acted as trustee and guarantor for secured issues. In a move to achieve an industry consensus on the issue, the MOF asked the IBJ to study the question and come up with a policy recommendation. The IBJ proposed that two Japanese companies and forty non-Japanese companies be permitted to issue unsecured bonds in Japan.[40] Yamaichi's client, Sears, was therefore able to complete an issue in 1979, and Nomura's client, Matsushita Electric, which also had been pushing for permission to do an unsecured issue, also successfully issued, in 1979, the first unsecured Japanese bond since World War II.

There were also important developments in the government-bond markets during this period. Until 1964, the government pursued a balanced-budget policy, as had been strongly urged by the occupation administration after World War II. But the government started issuing long-term bonds to finance projects in the 1960s, and the volume of the bond issues dramatically increased after 1975, in part to stimulate the Japanese economy in the wake of the first oil shock. Because of the much larger volume, the Bank of Japan could not afford to continue its policy of ultimately repurchasing all the bonds from the initial buyer. Beginning in 1975, underwriters were allowed to sell the bonds in the secondary market after their initial required holding period.[41] Thus, liquid bond markets rapidly developed. By 1980, long-term government bonds represented 60 percent of all secondary trading. In 1985, ¥2,404 trillion in bonds was traded, four times the amount traded in 1984 and fifteen times the amount in 1980.

39. Ibid.
40. Ibid., p. 177.
41. By 1981, the initial holding period of government bonds by the banks had been reduced to 100 days.

The Role of the Ministry of Finance

In the history of the building of the modern Japanese state, the MOF has been a principal architect and arbiter of the country's national financing and banking structure. It has shaped fiscal and monetary policy through the Bank of Japan, which, unlike the more independent U.S. Federal Reserve model, is closely allied to the MOF. The MOF not only has supervised the financial institutions that supply credit, but has also actively influenced the financial arrangements of private companies. It collects taxes and customs duties, controls foreign exchange, and has a decisive influence on Japanese investments abroad as well as on foreign investments made in Japan. It has, as we have seen, handled the government's fund raising. By the end of the 1980s, its influence over life in Japan had probably reached its zenith. Many observers believe it has surpassed in influence the Ministry of International Trade and Industry (MITI), the focus of world attention during the 1960s and 1970s. This enhanced visibility may reflect Japan's maturation as an industrial power and its move into the relatively new role of massive capital generator and banker to the rest of the world.

Internal Organization

Internally, the MOF is organized into bureaus, each responsible for a part of the financial sector. Probably the most powerful is the Budget Bureau, which coordinates the government's spending program and with which all parts of the government apparatus must negotiate to obtain funding. Next most powerful is the Tax Bureau, followed by the Banking Bureau, which oversees the activities of the commercial banking sector, the Securities Bureau, which is charged with the oversight of the brokerage industry, and the International Finance Bureau, which handles the country's offshore financing activities.[42] While the nation's financial oversight is concentrated in this government ministry, some of the bureaus have been structured so that they serve as advocates for their particular industry sector, much as the American Bankers Association and the Securities Industry Association operate in the United States. At the same time, the bureaus serve the same regulatory watchdog roles as the U.S. Comptroller of the Currency and the Securities and Exchange Commission.

Decisions in the MOF are reached by consensus, following the

42. Each industry group designates a representative to handle the detailed interactions with the appropriate Ministry bureau. The chairmanship is rotated, for instance, among the four leading city banks and, in the Securities Bureau, among the Big Four brokerage firms.

general custom in Japanese society. Officials are expected to champion the interests of their bureau's constituency in the internal discussions and arguments that precede most important policy decisions.[43] In essence, the process involves a vigorous exchange of views and a "letting off of steam" in the course of assembling the case for each private- and public-sector group whose interests are affected by the proposed move. Like the consensus building that characterizes the Society of Friends in the United States, the process can be long and drawn out, but once a common position has been achieved, all Ministry officials embrace it and do their best to ensure its implementation.

This form of policy resolution is successful, in part, because of Japanese societal mores and, in part, because of the purposefully vague nature of regulatory guidelines. The guidelines are largely unwritten and therefore amenable to evolving interpretation and "administrative guidance." It is probably fortuitous that a gray area exists, because it has provided maneuvering room for both private-sector vendors and regulators to modify rules to keep pace with unfolding developments.

When a private financial intermediary or corporation proposes a financing move in an appropriate section within the MOF, it is not to determine the move's compliance with the letter of the law (usually, the firm has already determined that it does), but rather to determine if the MOF thinks the move is appropriate from the point of view of society.

While the MOF does not have the *statutory* authority to penalize firms for failure to follow guidelines, it has ample means for punishing recalcitrants in the court of public opinion. Many Japanese consider such condemnation and exclusion to be more onerous than monetary or physical penalties.

Overall, the concentration of the decision-making apparatus within one government agency, its consensus-building process for decision making, and the flexibility provided by the underlying regulations appear to have served the country well.

The People Factor

A key to the successful operation of the MOF as Japan's central financial coordinator is the high quality of its personnel. In Japan, government (and MOF in particular) attracts some of the best talent from the country's leading universities. The competitive examination

---

43. Ministry officials are rotated among the different bureaus every two to three years, the move usually taking place in June.

for entry into government service is demanding—only about 3–4 percent of those who take it qualify. Historically, the universities with the highest academic reputations have produced the largest numbers of graduates who qualified under the exam to enter government service, with the University of Tokyo (and its law school in particular) at the top and Kyoto University, second.

Although government pay is low by private-sector standards and working conditions often less favorable, mitigating factors nonetheless impel the best university graduates to enter government service, and to seek out the MOF in particular. Uppermost may be the ethic within Japanese society which puts a high premium on service to the country,[44] an ethic that dates back to the Meiji Restoration, when, we have noted, the samurai class voluntarily gave up its perquisites and some of its status to facilitate the defense of the country against foreign threats. Although Japan is a society of private enterprise, it is private enterprise mobilized for the benefit of the community.[45] Thus, the administrative guidance that the MOF exercises is closely studied and generally followed. The MOF's consequent power to influence matters of national import therefore has a strong appeal to young professionals.

Another motivation for employment is the array of opportunities for the MOF officials.[46] These opportunities include follow-on posts in other government or quasi-government entities, senior jobs in private financial institutions, and the chance to enter politics. It is the convention that once a member of a class of university graduates has reached the level of vice minister in the MOF, all the other members of that class resign (the Japanese say that in resigning, the MOF alumni are "coming down from heaven"). Since that time of retirement is likely to be earlier than normal in private industry (and therefore carries a lower pension prospect for the official), there is a tendency for retirees to take senior positions with other government or quasi-government entities, including the prefecture (regional) banks. Some alumni end up in senior operating or advisory roles at a

---

44. Lodge and Vogel, *Ideology and National Competitiveness*, p. 141.
45. Ezra Vogel refers to "communitarianism" as the central binding idea in Japan.
46. There are two career tracks for officials in the Ministry of Finance. The top track ("carriers") is composed of those few who passed the most rigorous entrance examination. The second track ("noncarriers") includes employees admitted through a less rigorous screen. The carriers are the professionals who help set policy in the bureaus and are rotated from bureau to bureau every two or three years. The noncarrier professionals generally stay with the same bureau for a number of years and are responsible for more of the day-to-day administrative work.

stock exchange or at a commercial bank; still others become senior officials of private-sector companies.

Marriages can also figure prominently in the direction the careers of MOF alumni take. MOF personnel are generally regarded as among the country's most intellectually talented. Because their work has given them a special understanding of the subtleties of the governmental decision-making process and a network of invaluable contacts, they are viewed as ideal spouses for daughters of important families, particularly families without sons able to carry on the political or business positions and traditions of that "house." Because of their long working hours, many young Ministry professionals do not have the time or the opportunity to meet young women, so their supervisors or other senior officials on occasion help arrange suitable marriages. Half-jokingly, some observers have suggested that the personnel department of the MOF maintains two special lists: one contains the names of eligible single men, and the other the names of families looking for a suitable husband for a daughter of the house.

Wealthy businessmen constitute one such group on the second list. There are a number of examples of Ministry personnel who have left government service to take on senior-level responsibilities in a private company of a new spouse's family. Another source of opportunity is with political families. In some parts of Japan, political influence and the local seat in the Japanese Diet are controlled by a prominent family, and the Diet seat typically is occupied by a male member of that family. This is very much in the long-standing tradition of Japanese society, where preservation of the family "House" is an important obligation for each generation. As Vogel points out:

> The head of the household in rural areas was not considered the owner of the property but rather the current custodian or trustee of the House. These rights of use were passed down through the generations from the senior head of the household to one of his sons, usually the first. If the first son were not able, or if the House had no sons, the family would adopt a son. If the House lacked a son and had a suitable daughter, then the daughter's husband would be the heir.[47]

In modern Japan, there is still a strong tradition of marriage alliances that not only meet romantic requirements but also serve the other interests of both families. Thus, if a political family has no son to assume the mantle of political leadership, the family may adopt a young man with good credentials who then marries a daughter of the

47. Lodge and Vogel, *Ideology and National Competitiveness*, p. 146.

family and changes his name to that of the daughter's family. The MOF has maintained strong ties to the long-dominant but weakening Liberal Democratic Party in Japan; thus, the move of a certain number of its young professionals into national politics is not likely to be viewed with disfavor by the Ministry's senior leadership.

Sending Ministry alumni into influential positions in Japanese society has obvious benefits for the individuals involved, but it is also important from the viewpoint of the MOF. With widely dispersed and influential alumni, the Ministry is in an even more advantageous position to promote its long-term policies by obtaining key support during the process of national consensus building.

Societal Political Alliances

Because of the long rule of the Liberal Democratic Party in Japan, decision making in the MOF and other government departments has inevitably involved that party's leadership in mobilizing its influence within the Diet. Not only are the government ministries careful to develop liaisons and relationships with groups of influential legislators to enhance the probability of passage of desired programs, but private-sector interests also cultivate their Diet contacts, not unlike the sophisticated and widespread lobbying activities in Washington. Whereas U.S. special interests have used campaign contributions and the payment of speaker fees to ingratiate themselves to congressmen and senators, until quite recently the Japanese securities industry reputedly encouraged favored politicians to purchase shares of certain companies. The expectation (usually fulfilled) was that the share prices would rise and the politician-investors would realize a profit, which would presumably be utilized for election campaign expenses.

These reputed election stock arrangements were publicly discussed but appeared to be condoned on the presumption that there were no real victims in cases of rising stock prices. Foreign—particularly U.S.—observers expressed surprise at the past public apathy to such alleged insider price rigging but assumed that it was an established convention that they would have to accommodate. But in 1988, an instance of special investor preference erupted in the Japanese news media that suggested there might be more rigorous enforcement of insider trading and prohibitions on political favors in the future. And the hegemony of the Liberal Democratic Party appeared to be threatened.

A relatively new company, Recruit Cosmos, which disseminated information about employment opportunities to college graduates, permitted representatives of dozens of key politicians to purchase shares in the company at bargain prices. Shortly thereafter, an initial public offering of the company's shares produced substantial windfall profits to the politician-investors.

The loud and indignant public outcry gave fresh urgency to the enforcement of a newly promulgated and Ministry-sponsored statute on insider trading. There was a conviction among a number of observers that the country might indeed be moving closer to the ethical standards that had been pioneered in the United States after its own abuses of the 1920s.

Pressures for Financial Reform

Aside from the public outcry over insider trading allegations, the formal and informal aspects of the regulatory structure that have been documented in this chapter were also coming under increasing pressure from market developments, both inside and outside Japan.

As we have seen, the core of the Japanese financial structure involved 1) its segmentation into a series of specialized institutions (e.g., trust banks, long-term credit banks) and 2) the distinction between the commercial banking and the securities businesses, embodied in Article 65 of the Securities Transaction Act. These were the outgrowth of long-standing practice and the directives of the Allied occupation following World War II.

This traditional system worked reasonably well in accommodating the unique economic and community needs of Japan in the postwar recovery period, during which the entire Japanese economy faced chronic fund shortages. Under these circumstances, administrators considered it necessary to assign specific financial institutions (with narrowly defined roles) to direct limited financial resources to targeted growth industries.

Circumstances, however, have been dramatically altered, as discussed elsewhere in this book. The fruits of sustained growth in the Japanese economy and the accumulation of substantial excess financial assets were fundamental. The financial reforms being undertaken in other major financial centers also spurred a rethinking of the domestic Japanese structure. The growth in securitization and the proliferation of alternative financing solutions available to many Japanese capital seekers were at odds with the private sector's traditional reliance on commercial bank credit. Further, the electronic interlinking of markets was broadening the group of financial vendors competing for the available Japanese business.

The Ministry of Finance, therefore, established an initial study group in 1985 to report on changes that might be needed to meet the economy's future financing needs and to maintain the country's competitiveness in the international financial markets.

The findings of that study group—issued in December 1987[48]—dealt principally with the traditional role of specialized financial institutions in Japan. The study noted that this structure's utility was eroding over time and might not be appropriate in the future. It also pointed out that although only the long-term credit banks were able to issue longer-term debentures, the ordinary commercial banks were moving more extensively into longer-term lending, but were barred from creating offsetting liabilities of the same duration. This created a significant interest rate risk for those banks.

The second stage of the investigation focused on the distinction between the country's commercial banking and securities businesses. Recognizing that the historically sharp separation between the two parts of the financing spectrum in both Japan and the United States is an increasing anomaly, the study group suggested that Japan should consider the expeditious elimination of Article 65 and make it possible for financial institutions on either side of the historical wall to engage in financing activities on the other side.[49]

By the end of the 1980s, a consensus was slowly developing within the country's financial sector that some modification of the separation between commercial banking and securities operations was inevitable (even though the securities firms, like their U.S. counterparts, were anxious to delay the day of reckoning as long as possible). But a major unresolved issue was the vehicle by which this should be accomplished. The study group considered—and then dismissed—the possibility of allowing free access to any of the various business sectors through a universal bank framework or a holding company arrangement; this decision was based on the conviction that there would not be adequate protection for depositors and others using the financial markets. Instead, major interest was focused on the establishment of either wholly owned subsidiaries or newly chartered financial institutions by which a parent's operations could effectively be expanded into the desired product and customer areas with greater safety to other parts of the system. While this was still under

48. Study Group on Financial Systems, *Report on the Specialized Financial Institutions System*, submitted to the MOF on December 4, 1987.
49. Second Committee of the Study Group on Financial Systems, *On the New Financial System*, interim report submitted to the MOF on May 16, 1989.

study in mid-1989, there seemed to be a strong likelihood that the MOF would continue to push for an early resolution of differences of opinion so that appropriate reforms could be promptly implemented.

Thus, the market forces that were proving so powerful in shaping the organization and structure of financial markets in New York and London were exercising a similar influence in Tokyo.

CHAPTER 7

THE CONTEMPORARY JAPANESE SECURITIES MARKETPLACE

The financial vendor community in Japan divides into two rough groupings as a consequence of Article 65 (the Japanese counterpart of the Glass-Steagall Act), which the U.S. occupation forces introduced after World War II. On one side of the wall is a group of 13 city banks, 7 trust banks, 3 long-term credit banks, 73 regional banks, and miscellaneous others. While the subgroups historically have played separate roles, in recent years their activities have converged. Today, the subgroups can be thought of as commercial banks in the U.S. sense of the word. On the other side of the Article 65 barrier is a group of some 220 domestic securities firms and a small but growing cluster of foreign securities vendors.

This chapter describes some of the most important activities and competition between the players on both sides of the wall.

The Securities Firms

The competitive structure of the Japanese securities industry has been outwardly stable for a considerable period of time. The Big Four securities firms (Nomura, Daiwa, Nikko, and Yamaichi), which were active participants in the public marketplace even before World War II, are pre-eminent today. Nevertheless, the industry has evolved and consolidated since the war, particularly in response to the speculative excesses of the securities firms in the 1960s, which forced a rescue operation for Yamaichi and a tightening of government regulation of brokerage intermediaries. Today, Japanese securities firms divide into three categories: 1) the Big Four, 2) 21 other large firms directly supervised by the central (Tokyo) office of the Ministry of Finance (MOF), and 3) the large group of small local firms supervised by the branch offices of the MOF.

The Big Four firms dominate the country's public securities business. They account for the bulk of the secondary trading in the stock market, trading in the over-the-counter bond markets and international business. They have extensive domestic branch systems. And

169

the Big Four directly or indirectly control a number of other securities firms.

Among the twenty-one domestic firms directly supervised by the Ministry's Tokyo headquarters, for instance, several are affiliated with the Big Four. These firms are heavily dependent on commission income and play only a small role in the underwriting part of the business (a total of seventy-six firms have underwriting licenses). Their branch-office systems are obviously less extensive than those of the largest securities firms.

The many small securities houses in the third group generally do not have government licenses to underwrite securities. They draw their income almost exclusively from brokerage and secondary-market trading activities. Because many of these small brokerage houses are affiliates of larger securities firms (more than two dozen are believed to be affiliated with Nomura), they are often understood to act for the larger firms to execute orders whose origins the larger firms want to disguise.

Despite the regulatory wall that Article 65 has erected between investment banking and commercial banking, a number of city banks and long-term credit banks have managed to build a significant although indirect position in the securities sector. These commercial banks initially bought equity in a number of securities firms during the 1960s, when many brokerages were in financial distress. In fact, Japanese commercial banks control four of the country's top twenty-two securities firms, as well as a number of smaller brokerage houses, as Table 7-1 demonstrates.

Despite the fact that commercial banks by law are not permitted to own more than 5 percent of any single brokerage firm, they are

Table 7-1
Commercial Bank-Brokerage Connections

Banks	Affiliated Securities Houses
Daiichi Kangyo Bank	Nippon Kangyo-Kakumaru
Sumitomo	Meiko
Fuji	Daito
Mitsubishi	Ryoko
Sanwa	Towa
Takai	Maruman
Taiyo-Kobe	Shinei-Ishino
Daiwa	Cosmo
Industrial Bank of Japan	New Japan, Wako, Okasan
Long-Term Credit Bank	Daiichi

able to control securities firms by distributing controlling equity interest among a variety of collaborating business organizations so as to comply with the letter of the law. In addition, managers and directors of bank securities affiliates are frequently composed of retired or seconded (i.e., temporarily assigned) senior officers of the banks. For example, the presidents of New Japan Securities and Wako Securities, affiliates of the Industrial Bank of Japan (IBJ), are both former IBJ officials. Similarly, all past presidents of Nippon Kangyo Kakumaru Securities, which is affiliated with the Daiichi Kangyo Bank (DKB), are former DKB officers. Although some securities affiliates of Japanese banks are relatively small, the three affiliated firms just mentioned are among the eight largest securities firms in Japan in terms of assets. The net effect of these moves has been to cement the banks' influence within these brokerage firms while at the same time building a base of securities experience that the banks can directly utilize as regulatory barriers further erode.

There is also a group of about forty-five foreign financial intermediaries competing in one or more sectors of the public securities business in Tokyo. Many arrived in the early 1970s, when legislation first opened the door to foreign vendors. As the regulatory environment became more hospitable and the surplus of the Japanese investment capital increased, the numbers and staffing of the offshore vendors grew apace.

The Business Mix

As a group, the Japanese securities firms have enjoyed unprecedented prosperity in recent years. As in both the United States and Europe, the trend of financing activity in Japan has favored the public markets, thus boosting revenues from underwriting and distribution activities. But by far, the greatest boon has been the sharp rise in domestic secondary trading. The combination of increasing share turnover and a persistent fixed-commission structure has produced a rich harvest of commission revenues, growing by almost 400 percent in the period 1983–1987, as shown in Table 7-2.

The greatest part of the revenue growth has accrued to the largest Japanese securities firms, which dominate this market sector. Nomura Securities, the largest brokerage firm, has seen net profits grow from $200 million in 1983 to $1.6 billion in 1987. Such success earned Nomura the distinction of being the most profitable (in absolute terms) Japanese company for 1987 in *any* industry. Profit on invested capital has also produced impressive results. The return on equity for the Japanese securities industry as a whole grew steadily from 11 percent in 1983 to 24 percent in 1987.

Table 7-2
Income Statement for All Japanese Securities Firms
(¥ billions)

	1983	1985	1987
Operating revenues			
Brokerage	¥9,011	¥14,082	¥32,033
Other commissions	3,420	5,416	10,343
Financial income	3,205	4,711	5,625
Trading income	1,657	3,482	4,669
Operating expenses	11,430	16,519	28,172
Corporate overhead	1,818	2,936	2,976
Net income after tax	1,631	3,434	10,136

Source: Japanese Securities Dealers Association.

Brokerage Activities

Japanese securities firms are more heavily dependent on brokerage commissions than are firms in New York or London. Table 7-2 shows that almost 60 percent of composite industry revenues come from secondary-market commissions. Another 10 percent comes from the firms' own principal trading activities in the secondary markets, a smaller proportion than is characteristic of their U.S. counterparts.

As discussed in Chapter 6, Japan has had a long tradition of secondary-market securities trading. At one time, there were as many as 85 separate securities exchanges, in part because of the semi-isolation of many parts of the country. Today there are eight principal exchanges.[1] While both equity and debt securities are publicly traded on exchanges, the greatest activity is in equities, in part because until very recently, little corporate debt was issued in the public market-place; the only large-volume trading in debt securities has been in Japanese government bonds.

The importance of the public secondary markets has grown dramatically in recent years. Trading on the Tokyo Stock Exchange (TSE) has risen impressively;[2] in 1988, all 114 exchange seats were highly coveted. Aside from the considerable prestige that accompanies ownership of a TSE seat, nonmember securities firms had to pay 20 percent of their commissions to the floor member who actually handled

1. The Tokyo Stock Exchange is by far the largest, with 264 billion shares traded in 1987; Osaka is second, with 37 billion shares; and Nagoya is third, with 13 billion shares traded. The others are Kyoto, Hiroshima, Fukuoka, Niigata, and Sapporo.
2. It should be noted, however, that because approximately 70 percent of Japanese equity shares are tied up in illiquid corporate, institutional, and bank holdings, only a fraction of the remaining 30 percent is available for trading. This has led some observers to describe the Tokyo market as relatively "shallow."

Table 7-3
Market Shares of the Big Four, Based on Stock Transaction Volume

	1983	1984	1985	1986	1987	1988
Stock-trading volume on the eight stock exchanges (billions of shares)	123.5	116.2	151.5	225.2	304.6	307.1
Market share (%)						
Nomura	14.8%	14.5%	15.1%	7.7%	18.7%	15.01%
Daiwa	11.4	11.8	10.9	10.7	10.3	9.4
Nikko	10.9	10.4	10.2	10.6	9.7	8.2
Yamaichi	10.6	10.9	10.5	10.3	11.5	9.3

Note: 1988 figures are for TSE only.
Source: Daiwa Securities.

the execution, clearing, settlement, and delivery aspects of their transactions. The largest firms handle the bulk of the trading business, fielding large numbers of trained and highly motivated salespeople to sell securities to both individuals and institutions. (See Table 7-3.)

The rewards to the executing brokerage houses from these trades are particularly lucrative because commission rates have remained relatively fixed, long after they became fully negotiated in New York (1975) and more recently in London (1986). It is true that the stock exchanges (with the approval of the Ministry of Finance) gradually have been lowering the levels of commissions on very large institutional transactions and small retail trades. But a combination of the soaring TSE volume, high stock prices,[3] and the fact that salespeople at the largest Japanese securities firms are paid a fixed salary, has funneled a deluge of commission revenues to the bottom lines of firms' profit-and-loss statements. This situation has provided the largest brokerage firms with an impressive and relatively stable source of profits with which to support new initiatives at home and abroad. In Japan, however, brokers still lack the authorization to undertake bank settlement services. Thus, they cannot directly offer a full range of retail services such as checking accounts, although they

3. While a significant part of the differential in price-earnings multiples may be accounted for by differing accounting rules, the balance has variously been explained away as a function of Japan's excess liquidity and/or the fact that many shares sell more on the basis of their underlying real estate value than on their earnings momentum. With an acre of land in the center of Tokyo selling for approximately $1 billion in late 1988, the theoretical current market value of the 3,300 acres of the Imperial Palace grounds would exceed the market capitalization of the entire New York Stock Exchange by a considerable margin!

do so indirectly through collaborations with local savings and loan associations, much as Merrill Lynch has teamed up with a commercial bank to offer its now-famous cash management account (CMA).

As we have mentioned, Japan's commercial banks entered the securities business through the back door. A number of the securities firms were in financial distress and accepted various forms of bank assistance. Meiko Securities, for example, became affiliated with Sumitomo. Meiko's CEO is one of the directors of Sumitomo, and of its more than 800 employees, 90 are from the bank.

Foreign securities firms with Tokyo offices[4] have worked diligently to capture a share of the lucrative commission business, but with only modest success thus far. During the 12-month period ending September 1987, the total operating profits of all foreign firms as reported to the Ministry of Finance were no more than ¥1,344 million (about $11 million), although these accounting figures are highly arbitrary and therefore suspect. Foreigners have had a number of regulatory and cultural barriers to overcome as, for example, the difficulty in obtaining membership on the TSE. As already mentioned, the fixed number of seats on the exchange are highly coveted by a variety of Japanese nonmember brokers, who, like the foreign firms, have to channel their trading activity through a floor member. After repeated rebuffs, foreign securities firms (including several prominent American firms) finally made a breakthrough in 1986 when the TSE accepted six foreign securities firms as new members: Merrill Lynch, Morgan Stanley, Goldman, Sachs, Vickers da Costa, Jardine Fleming, and S.G. Warburg. This breakthrough was achieved with heavy government-to-government pressure from the United States to Japan, in which the applications of certain Japanese banks and securities firms for appointment as primary dealers in the U.S.-government securities market were said to have hung in the balance. Some observers believe that the Ministry of Finance has used the pressure of the U.S. government as a lever to force reform of the domestic Japanese financial markets.

Subsequently, in March 1988, the TSE announced that it was

4. Tokyo and Osaka are the two major economic and political centers in Japan. While Osaka was the location from which some of the most important financial and industrial firms originally sprung, Tokyo is now the center of future growth. Most of the major business firms have their central offices there, and the most famous universities have relocated there.

Total production of the Tokyo area (TPTA) in fiscal 1985 exceeded the GNPs of Australia, Canada, and Italy. In fiscal 1985, TPTA was ¥55,100 billion, which was equivalent to $229.6 billion using ¥240 to the dollar at the time. If the current exchange rate of ¥130 is used, TPTA equals $423.9 billion and exceeds Italy's GNP of $355.6 billion and Canada's $346 billion and almost reaches the United Kingdom's $459.4 billion.

admitting another sixteen foreign firms.[5] Even so, the penetration of foreign firms into the secondary market for Japanese equities remains nominal. Morgan Stanley, the most active offshore firm in this sector of the market, captured less than 1 percent of the TSE volume in 1987 (compared to 11.5 percent for Yamaichi, for instance, as set forth in Table 7-3).

Legal access to the Japanese market is only one dimension of the challenge to foreign firms. Selling Japanese securities to Japanese investors is another. With the legal barriers down, foreign firms still face the greater hurdles of culture and language. With the exception of Merrill Lynch, no foreign securities firm has developed any significant retail distribution capability in Japan. And that will not be easily remedied, given the skillful retail marketing programs the Japanese securities firms have perfected.

Foreign firms have begun to make modest headway in selling Japanese securities to Japanese institutional investors. These institutional investors manage capital pools worth more than two trillion U.S. dollars and are gradually becoming more active in the management of those funds. In recent years, they have given modest market orders for Japanese equities to foreign firms operating in Tokyo. In some cases, these orders have been in exchange for research generated by the small groups of analysts established by foreign firms to follow Japanese corporate securities. In other instances, the motivation may have been to conceal the portfolio managers' trading intentions from the Japanese securities establishment.

Futures Market

As noted in the previous chapter, there was a thriving de facto futures market in Japanese securities prior to World War II. It is not surprising, therefore, that in the early 1980s when the MOF signaled its willingness to see the futures market reopened, progress was rapid. Japanese government bond futures were introduced on the TSE in October 1985 and, by July 1986, the volume of trading in these bond futures exceeded the volume of the comparable futures being traded on the Chicago Board of Trade.

Futures on the Nikkei Stock Index were introduced on the Osaka Exchange in June 1987 and were followed a little later by options on the Nikkei Stock Index. By 1989, futures based on the TSE Index were being traded on the Tokyo Stock Exchange and, in June 1989, the TSE

5. In May 1988, the TSE admitted six U.S. firms (First Boston, Kidder, Peabody, Prudential-Bache, Shearson Lehman Hutton, Salomon Brothers, and Smith Barney), four British firms (Baring, County NatWest, Kleinwort Benson, and Schroder Securities), and six others.

had introduced interest-rate futures on Euroyen and Eurodollars as well as currency futures on the yen-dollar relationship. It is expected that the Japanese commercial banks will be allowed to participate in the futures market as intermediaries. With their close contacts with institutional investors (including regional banks), they will present formidable competition to the securities firms. Techniques for valuing futures contracts and utilizing them in hedging strategies and the construction of hybrid securities have been well developed by Western investment bankers, particularly those from the United States. Thus, it is not surprising that a Salomon Brothers official in the Tokyo office has the distinction of being the first non-Japanese member of a new committee to oversee the stock futures market in Japan (see Chapter 10).

Japanese Government Bond Underwriting

Although important prefectures such as Tokyo and Osaka have been large public bond issuers, cities and towns have been only modest participants in Japan's pubic securities markets.[6] We have noted in Chapter 6, however, that the Japanese national government has long been an important public debt issuer. It undertook extensive public works projects and incurred large operating-budget deficits in the mid-1970s. The large volumes of public debt issued to finance these outlays were coming to maturity at the end of the 1980s, requiring either refunding or retirement. Some observers believe that the demands of the refunding may have been an important motivation in the Ministry of Finance's moves to liberalize the Tokyo securities markets.

Historically, the Japanese government has required financial institutions to subscribe to new government debt issues at below-market yields set by the Ministry of Finance. Institutions were required to hold that debt for at least one year before reselling it, usually to the Bank of Japan and often at a loss to the selling bank. (Government bonds that originally had been bought by individual investors were often subsequently traded on the over-the-counter market.) Perhaps in part because of this de facto subsidization of the government's borrowing programs, there was no competitive bidding on most government debt. After 1965, a fixed syndicate of Japa-

---

6. Because of strict qualification requirements by the MOF, only twenty-three municipalities qualify to use the public debt markets to raise funds. The rest typically borrow from the regional commercial banks. In fiscal 1987, the total amount of public sector bonds publicly issued was ¥430,476 billion. Municipal bonds publicly issued totaled ¥976 billion. Municipal bonds privately offered totaled ¥1,576 billion. (*Source*: Nomura Securities.)

nese financial intermediaries (initially composed of 90 percent financial institutions and 10 percent securities firms, but now 74 percent financial institutions and 26 percent securities firms, in consultation with the MOF) divided up the bond offerings according to prescribed percentage participations worked out between the two categories.

At the beginning of the 1980s, the government decided to create a more liquid secondary market for its securities. It therefore began moving toward the attachment of market rate coupons on new debt offerings. Further, it authorized commercial banks to begin selling investment units that included government securities to individual investors rather than requiring the banks to hold the securities for their own accounts.

Since 1984, commercial banks in Japan also have been permitted to engage in secondary-market trading of government bonds. Initially, the trading was limited to issues with less than two years to maturity; from 1985 onward, however, the commercial banks' authorization has extended to all maturities. Since 1984, the secondary market in government bonds expanded dramatically from ¥1.4 trillion in 1980 to ¥50 trillion in 1986, and profits from secondary-market trading have been one of the fastest-growing areas for both the commercial banks and the securities firms.[7]

In an era of rising value for Japanese currency, the attractions of risk-free, yen-denominated Japanese government securities have become apparent to many foreign portfolio managers. Heightened foreign interest in the securities produced increased pressures from foreign securities firms in Tokyo for more meaningful participation in the government-bond underwriting process. Questions of reciprocity in other national market centers were also raised. Not surprisingly, Japanese financial institutions have balked at this prospect, arguing that they have earned the right to exclusive access to the bonds because historically they have subsidized issuance of the bonds. They further pointed out that even in the case of fixed-syndicate government bond offerings, negotiations have always been tough, with the government persistently trying to reduce the net cost of the financing.

It has been the government's practice to raise the bulk of its funds in the form of 10-year maturity bonds. In recent years, the government has issued a few experimental 15- and 20-year maturity

7. Only certain benchmark government securities are actually traded on the TSE. The rest of the government debt is still traded in over-the-counter markets. All government bonds are *listed* on the stock exchange, but the big volume is done OTC. Even in the OTC market, over 90 percent of the volume is concentrated in the bellwether 10-year bonds.

issues as well as some short maturities in the 2- to 5-year range. The MOF introduced competitive bidding in the occasional financings and in the open bidding process presented a special opportunity for foreign securities firms. In one surprise result, Salomon Brothers won some 45 percent of the 2-year bonds up for bid in the February 1987 auction (see Chapter 10). Then, in July 1988, Goldman, Sachs won ¥20 billion of a 20-year bond offering. This was as large as the share won by Yamaichi and ranked with or above the major long-term credit, city, and trust banks.[8]

The fixed-syndicate management system was continued for the standard 10-year government bond maturities, until the MOF made a special announcement in September 1988. The government announced that, beginning in April 1989, it would sell 40 percent of each issue of 10-year bonds by soliciting competitive price bids from members of the all-inclusive underwriting syndicate. The remaining 60 percent would be distributed to the syndicate's members under fixed allocations. And, beginning in October 1988, an enhanced share would go to foreign underwriters (increasing to almost 8 percent from the previous 2½ percent). These moves, which had been under protracted discussion with several U.S. government agencies, may well have been given a fresh urgency by the passage of a U.S. trade bill in mid-1988 that required the Federal Reserve to deny primary-dealer status to foreign financial institutions whose home countries denied similar competitive opportunities to U.S. firms.[9]

Corporate Underwriting Activity

The small amount of public corporate-debt issues in Japan until very recently (see Appendix Table C-6) was probably due in large part to the country's past shortage of investment capital and the fact that the private-sector savings were flowing largely into commercial bank savings accounts and therefore were most readily available to corporate users in the form of bank credit. The MOF maintained an artificially low level of interest rates on bank deposits so that bank credit could be allocated at low cost to borrowers approved for priority consideration by the Ministry of International Trade and Industry (MITI) and the MOF. Moreover, until the 1980s, the commercial banks that were the major purchasers of the publicly issued corporates (largely in the electric utility and steel industries) were the self-same commercial banks. Thus, it was undoubtedly easier for the MITI and the MOF to manage the allocation of the historically scarce credit via the banking

---

8. *Nikkei Shimbun,* July 25, 1988.
9. *The Wall Street Journal,* September 7, 1988, p. 3.

system than through the public debt securities market. In more recent years, of course, the country is awash with surplus capital, the government's preoccupation with rationing capital has subsided, and a number of the larger corporations have turned to both the Tokyo public market and the Euromarkets for new capital when needed.

Another cause for heavy private-placement commercial bank financing has been the lenders' insistence on collateral for corporate bonds (administered and monitored by certain commercial banks acting as commissioned banks). As we have mentioned earlier, this practice grew out of a rash of defaults in the 1920s. Only recently has this pattern begun to change. For one thing, the credit ratings of a number of leading Japanese corporations have dramatically improved. The discovery that unsecured financings could be obtained in the Euromarkets and other hard currency markets spurred a reconsideration of the need for secured liens in the home market in Tokyo. For the great majority of Japanese businesses, however, the secured-lien requirement remains.

The inauguration of commercial paper financings in November 1987 also opened up new opportunities. As it had in the United States a decade earlier, the securitization of what had historically been commercial bank credit lines had grown impressively. Though still in its infancy, securitization threatens to erode further the position of the Japanese city and trust banks as principal purveyors of short-term credit.[10] Fortunately for them, the deal struck with the MOF in initiating domestic commercial-paper financings allowed the commercial banks to underwrite and deal in these instruments along with the securities firms, because commercial paper was defined as a promissory note rather than, as in the United States, a security. The securities firms may have acceded to this de facto intrusion onto their turf because they were convinced that the banks would block the introduction of commercial paper without it, which might stall the brokers' campaign to attract corporations away from their substantial dependency on the city banks for short-term credit. Thus far, it appears that Japanese commercial banks have been bidding more aggressively than securities firms for the commercial paper business.[11]

The largest securities firms in Japan dominate the underwriting activity in new debt and equity financings. During the 1980s, for

10. Further, the international move to require higher bank-capital ratios may curtail somewhat the volume of lending by Japanese commercial banks, which have had some of the highest degrees of financial leverage in the world.
11. For instance, the *Nikkei Newsletter on Bond and Money*, April 25, 1988, estimated the banks' share at 65 percent and the securities firms' share at 35 percent. *Nikken-Kogyo*, August 29, 1988, estimated the banks' share at 70 percent and the securities firms' share at 30 percent.

Table 7-4
Underwriting Volumes for Stocks and Bonds by Big Four Japanese
Securities Firms, 1984–1987
(¥ *billions*)

	1984	1985	1986	1987
Nomura	¥1,502	¥2,053	¥1,918	¥2,886
Yamaichi	982	1,240	1,225	1,692
Nikko	921	1,238	1,140	1,673
Daiwa	1,015	1,214	1,184	1,645

Source: Ministry of Finance.

instance, the shares of the Big Four securities firms have been approximately equal in size, with only Nomura having a significantly larger share (see Table 7-4).

In the conventional underwriting process, a committee composed of representatives of securities firms and commercial banks (in consultation with the MOF) decides both the priority of the financing need and the terms of the offering if authorized. The lead managership for the resulting public offerings then rotates among the Big Four.[12]

Although the big securities firms maintain that competition among them is vigorous and that the appearance of a shared monopoly is because of the prerequisites of size, experience, and capital, outside observers remain skeptical about the level of bona fide competition among the leading securities firms in some sectors. The MOF has recently introduced another new financing form dubbed the "proposal method," ostensibly to encourage more competition in the underwriting sector. This form invites potential lead underwriters of a few large companies, such as electric utilities and telephones, to bid on a particular offering, with the most attractive proposal theoretically winning the business on behalf of the lead manager's syndicate. In practice, however, the issuer often undertakes further negotiations with the bidders, and it appears that the rotation among the Big Four continues. Foreign vendors such as Salomon Brothers, Merrill Lynch, Goldman, Sachs, S.G. Warburg, and Kleinwort Benson have been granted minor syndicate positions in this new form of underwriting, which is preferable to being excluded altogether, as typically has been the case with conventional offerings.

In May 1988, the MOF also guided through the Diet another form

12. On yen-denominated debt offerings in Tokyo on behalf of foreign corporate borrowers, the member of the Big Four that serves as lead manager ordinarily accords co-manager status to the other three largest securities firms.

of de facto competitively bid public offering, the shelf registration form, which was introduced in the United States in 1982.[13] Under this innovation (effective October 1, 1988), qualified issuers can preregister securities and hold them ready for an offering on short notice if market conditions become favorable. As part of the use of the shelf registration, securities firms had sought the elimination of the role of the commissioned bank. Such elimination would give securities firms the latitude to manage underwritings with the same freedom and autonomy enjoyed by U.S. underwriters. That appeal failed, however, and the Japanese commercial banks retained their substantive role in public debt underwritings.

Japanese corporations have raised large sums through equity-linked securities offerings. These are obligations with a "sweetener": stock purchase warrants or another provision that allows the offerings to be converted into the stock of the issuer, typically at a small premium over the market price of the stock at the time of issue. The largest proportion of the money recently raised by Japanese corporations through the capital markets has been with this form of instrument. The commissions earned on the equity and equity-linked underwritings have been comparable to levels in the United States and Europe, averaging some 3½ percent on new straight equity offerings and 2½ percent on equity-linked convertibles or bonds-with-warrants financing. Straight debt offerings, by contrast, typically carry a spread of 1.6 percent.

Offshore Corporate Underwriting

Recent years have seen a dramatic increase in the frequency of Japanese corporations turning to the Euromarkets for debt financing, particularly equity-linked securities. Japanese securities houses as well as Japanese commercial banks have become increasingly active in these Euroyen-denominated issues.[14] The policy of MOF has been that such issues could not be sold initially to Japanese investors but, instead, had to be placed with foreign investors (so that this financing would not serve as a dodge around the Japanese domestic-securities market regulations).[15] Recently, the MOF has indicated that it would like to

---

13. Joseph Auerbach and Samuel L. Hayes, III, *Investment Banking and Diligence: What Price Deregulation?* (Boston: Harvard Business School Press, 1986).
14. Some observers believe that the MOF has used the Euromarkets as a safety valve to release some of the pressure from the commercial banks for direct access into the Japanese domestic market, currently barred to them by Article 65.
15. Some foreign securities vendors maintain, however, that the Japanese securities firms manage to find ways to circumvent that restriction and thereby to de facto place these London-issued Euroyen offerings directly with Japanese investors.

see more of the yen-denominated Euroissues migrate back to Tokyo, where initial foreign-investor placement could be dispensed with and where the Japanese vendors could make use of their well-developed infrastructures.[16]

It is, of course, in offshore corporate underwriting where the Japanese commercial banks have sought to make the most explicit inroads into the public securities business. In that overseas arena, Article 65 is much less binding than in Tokyo. Most of the big banks have established subsidiaries in the major offshore markets, particularly in London. To be sure, the commercial banks are still restricted from acting as lead underwriter of Japanese corporate issuers under the MOF's "three bureaus agreement," so named after the Ministry's three bureaus of banking, securities, and international finance (discussed in Chapter 6). But the banks have been permitted to lead manage Euroyen issues on behalf of non-Japanese borrowers, and they have been aggressive in pursuing that business (see Chapter 3, on the contemporary Euromarkets).

Corporate Finance Activities

Historically, corporate finance has not been a strong suit of the Japanese securities firms. In contrast to the United States, where the investment banks forged ahead as the primary financial counselors to U.S. corporations in the post–World War II period, Japanese securities firms were not able to achieve a similar position for themselves.

Indeed, relationship banking is much more complex in Japan than in the United States. The prewar zaibatsu groups reassembled themselves in the post–World War II period despite the efforts of the allied occupation administration to disband them. To be sure, the postwar combinations were substantially looser than the prewar groups, which owed unquestioned allegiance to a holding company and its individual or family chief. But the postwar keiretsu versions of the zaibatsu were nonetheless relatively cohesive and organized around each group's commercial bank. Thus, the influence of that financial institution on the capital-raising activities of the group companies was bound to be strong. We have already chronicled how the postwar industrial groups, led by their commercial banks, bought, on

---

16. See, for instance, Report to the Minister of Finance by the Securities Exchange Council, December 1986, which states that Japanese domestic institutional and cultural constraints, as well as interest-rate differentials, are the reasons for the stagnant domestic corporate-bond issues and the booming Euroissues. The proposed measures to be taken include the "proposal method" of underwriting and more liberalized use of unsecured debt issues.

Table 7-5
*Ranking of Japanese Financial Organizations
by Number of Customer Companies' Shares Owned*

Rank	Financial Organizations	Number of Shares (millions)	Number of Companies
1	Nippon Insurance	10,814	1,064
2	Daiichi Insurance	5,725	655
3	Mitsubishi Trust	5,579	759
4	Industrial Bank of Japan	5,106	606
5	Sumitomo Trust	4,577	815
6	Meiji Life Insurance	4,538	492
7	Nihon Shoken Kessai	4,500	247
8	Sumitomo Life Insurance	4,340	600
9	Daiichi Kangyo Bank	3,798	670
10	Mitsui Trust	3,315	613

Source: Toyo-Keizai, "Kigyo Keiretsu Soran 1989," Triangle Research.

the secondary markets, group company shares that had been initially purchased by individual investors immediately after the war. Much of that stock ownership ultimately became lodged in institutions either connected with or friendly to the keiretsu (see Table 7-5). Ownership realignment further strengthened the community of interest within the group. When a group company needed financing or financial counseling, it would logically turn to the group's own commercial bank and, in the event of a full-blown financial crisis, that main bank would be expected to be the lender of last resort.

In addition to the three groups with the same names as the prewar zaibatsu (Mitsubishi, Mitsui, and Sumitomo), a few other groups are clustered around specific city banks. These include the Fuji Bank group, the Daiichi Bank group, and the Sanwa Bank group. Thus, it is not surprising that the role of the lead commercial bank for Japanese companies assumed a stature in the corporate finance area similar (or perhaps superior) to that enjoyed by investment banks in the United States or merchant banks in the United Kingdom.

Table 7-6 presents a statistical tabulation of the most important corporate-commercial bank relationships in Japan as of 1988. Since in Japan the main bank relationship is key, these rankings are more important than those that chronicle *all* corporate-bank relationships (see Appendix Table C-9), although a comparison of the two lists would not reveal any radical differences in bank rankings. However, when one considers just the corporate clients listed on the first sec-

Table 7-6
Ranking of Japanese Main Banks by Number of Customer Companies, 1988

Rank	Bank	Number of Companies	Share (%)
1	Daiichi Kangyo Bank	7,626	6.9%
2	Mitsubishi	5,839	5.3
3	Sanwa	5,288	4.8
4	Sumitomo	5,000	4.5
5	Fuji	4,970	4.5
6	Tokai	4,038	3.6
7	Mitsui	3,567	3.2
8	Taiyo-Kobe	3,198	2.9
9	Kyowa	2,336	2.1
10	Daiwa	2,100	1.9

Source: Diamond Weekly Magazine, March 5, 1988.

tion of the TSE, a somewhat different ordering emerges. Most significantly, IBJ moves up to share the top spot with DKB, reflecting the fact that IBJ is a wholesale bank in the tradition of a J.P. Morgan & Co. in the United States, with a client list that, while small, is made up of many of the largest and most influential Japanese companies.

Although many observers would consider commercial bank relationships the key ones for Japanese corporations, securities firms also maintain ongoing relationships. Like the commercial bank connections, those relationships are listed in the *Japan Company Handbook*, published quarterly by Toyo Keizai Shinposha.[17] The relationships are typically forged when a firm first goes public. Once having allied with one of the securities houses, it is very unusual for a corporation to switch its public securities business to another brokerage firm. Thus, securities firms aggressively pursue that IPO business. If the company going public is a member of one of the keiretsu, that group's bank would be likely to have a substantial influence over which securities firm would be selected to underwrite the deal. Even if the company was not part of a keiretsu, its lending bank or the trading company ("shogo-shosha") handling the company's raw material supply or product distribution might be a member of such a group and might therefore be in a position to influence the company to select a securities firm allied with that group.

Although the major securities firms are not themselves members of any of the keiretsu, there do appear to be alliances or affiliations between securities firms and commercial banks, as presented in Table 7-7.

17. *Japan Company Handbook* (first section) (Toyo Keizai Shinposha, Autumn 1988).

Table 7-7

Instances in Which Japanese Corporations Have Designated Specific Combinations of Main Banks and Managing Securities Firms

	Security Firm				
Bank	Nomura	Daiwa	Nikko	Yamaichi	Other
Daiichi Kangyo Bank	69	19	38	58	32
Sumitomo	60	74	13	32	3
Fuji	42	19	20	102	16
Mitsubishi	33	14	71	50	11
Sanwa	82	26	13	33	24
Mitsui	84	15	18	19	10
Industrial Bank of Japan	25	12	42	35	14
Long-Term Credit Bank	12	4	5	6	3
Mitsubishi Trust	2	4	10	6	4
Mitsui Trust	9	1	5	8	0
Sumitomo Trust	4	8	9	5	3

Source: Koichi Noda, "Recent Developments and Challenges by the Japanese Banks and Their Strategies for Future Survival," unpublished independent research project, Harvard Business School, May 1988.

While Nomura has a primary relationship with companies utilizing a number of group commercial banks (and a particular relationship with the Daiwa Bank group, which the Nomura family founded), other securities firms appear to share special corporate relationships with only one or two groups. Daiwa Securities, for instance, has very strong relationships with companies that use Sumitomo as their main bank. Nikko Securities has a similar relationship with Mitsubishi and also a fairly strong collaboration with the IBJ (which originally founded that securities firm). Yamaichi Securities has strong links with Fuji, Mitsubishi, and IBJ, which orchestrated its bailout in 1965. These relationships are also strengthened when the same brokerage houses maintain automatic payment settlement for brokerage customers' accounts with the same banks.

Only as corporate issuers have succumbed to securitization and to the tapping of offshore financing sources (direct borrowing accounted for more than half of recent large-company financing),[18] have Japanese securities firms begun the process of building capabilities in corporate finance. These capabilities include the financial engineering skills needed to fashion esoteric securities, the strategic perspective required to help corporations formulate long-term financing planning, and the valuation and financing skills implicit in the expanding area of mergers and acquisitions.

18. The Bank of Japan, *Monthly Research Report*, May 1985.

The leading Japanese securities firms have undertaken major programs of expansion in their corporate finance capabilities, including aggressive recruitment of university graduates for this area of the business. Daiwa Securities, for one, has divided its corporate finance activities into two parts: the "Liability Service Group," which focuses on such activities as raising new capital for corporate issuers, while the "Asset Service Group," focuses on the demand for securities investment generated by cash-rich corporations (referred to as "zaitech" activities).

The big securities firms appear to recognize, however, that corporate finance skills are difficult to build internally without substantial senior talent already on board to train and act as mentors to the younger people. This may account for the decisions several firms have made to acquire an interest in talent-rich Western corporate finance boutiques such as Wasserstein, Perella (see Chapter 11).

The Japanese commercial banks are not, of course, standing by and complacently watching their corporate clients being lured away. They have seen their borrowing costs rise with the liberalization of interest rates, just as competition is lowering lending rates. The banks have consequently taken aggressive action to boost their own capabilities in corporate finance. Mitsubishi Bank, for instance, announced a major corporate reorganization in October 1986. In the course of doing so, it set up a specific securities group as part of a publicly announced effort to build a universal bank in the style of a number of continental European institutions. The securities division was to utilize the resources of both the bank's domestically controlled securities companies as well as its overseas securities subsidiaries. The four divisions within the securities group would deal in issuance of corporate bonds, trading of government bonds, investment in foreign bonds, swaps, and so forth. The staff of 150 would be as large as that of a number of medium-sized Japanese securities houses. Although it was not publicly announced, the bank also set up a strategic team to assist firms in preparing to go public via a listing on the TSE.

In the meantime, facilitation of cross-border M&As is one area where the foreign securities firms in Tokyo have continued to maintain an edge. Japanese corporations and institutions are very sensitive to quality images and by their action have made it clear that they consider the U.S. securities firms to be the premier vendors of this sophisticated acumen. It is understood, for instance, that Nippon Life has been diligent in introducing Shearson Lehman Hutton to Japanese corporations, institutional investors, and securities firms in an effort to drum up business for its 12 percent-owned U.S. investment banking partner. But generating business in the *domestic* Japanese M&A market has proved particularly difficult for the foreign securities firms. To begin with, it is still a relatively small market. In Japan, the general presumption is that a company belongs to its employees at least as much as to its stockholders; therefore, the prospect of a hostile takeover has been considered unlikely.

Most merger activity has been among small to medium-sized businesses, many with owner-managers amenable to cashing out of their shareholding positions. In many such cases, the companies turn to their main bank for advice and facilitation. The informal channels of information about corporate developments often bypass foreign vendors unless they are staffed with knowledgeable Japanese professionals. In addition, the Japanese corporate sector has not, historically, been used to paying substantial fees for these services. Domestic financial institutions traditionally have undertaken the efforts without a fee, relying instead on the revenues of a long-term relationship to reward them for their time and energy. Still another vendor group—the trading companies—have entered the M&A business, drawn in part by the lack of opportunities in their mainstream business.

Financial Performance of Securities Firms

Unlike U.S. investment banks, whose consolidated results have been driven in recent years both by M&A and by trading, Japanese securities firms have negligible M&A-related fees and relatively modest trading revenues (less than 10 percent of total revenues in fiscal 1987, for instance). Their profit streams are therefore regarded by many market observers as more stable and dependable than those of other groups of financial intermediaries, both Japanese and foreign. The firms appear able to sustain a strategic direction in the face of temporarily adverse business conditions. As noted elsewhere in this book, the attractive securities-commission structure plus strong Japanese investor demand for foreign securities have strengthened the hands of the leading Japanese securities firms in their aggressive bidding for increased market share in the very competitive Eurobond and U.S. Treasury markets.

That confidence is reflected in the valuation of the brokerage firms' stocks in the Tokyo marketplace. Recently selling at more than thirty times current earnings, the total market capitalization of Nomura Securities, for instance, is some $60 billion, by itself much more than the market values of all the publicly traded U.S. securities firms combined.[19] While such an observation might appear to be irrelevant

---

19. According to the *Fortune 500* survey of April 1987, among U.S. companies only IBM had a larger capitalization ($68 billion).

to an analysis of competitive factors, it does suggest that if one of the Japanese securities firms wanted to increase its equity capital, a multi-billion-dollar addition could be accomplished with only modest dilution to either ownership interests or earnings.

In fact, a number of the largest Japanese securities firms have been tapping the equity and quasi-equity marketplace in the past several years. Using the TSE as well as the Euromarkets, they have sold some very large (in the range of U.S. $1 billion) convertible bond or bond-with-warrants offerings with interest coupons as low as 3 percent. Because they can put the funds to work at returns of up to 10 percent, and because in Japan there is a tendency to ignore the "cost" of extending to an investor an equity option, the firms' managers calculate that they have earned a net spread on the new funds of up to seven hundred basis points (7 percent).

Capital Position

By international standards at least, the capital positions of the leading Japanese securities firms are already among the strongest in the world. The securities firms' capital bases have grown dramatically in recent years, mostly because of enormous profits and low dividend payouts—thus, most earnings are retained. Daiwa Securities' capital, for example, grew from approximately $650 million in 1980 to $4 billion at the end of 1987, in large part from retained earnings.

These levels of capital are most meaningful when compared to the assets they are supporting and to those of the competing vendors. Appendix Table C-12 shows that as of September 1987 composite assets for all Japanese securities firms were ¥26.8 trillion, compared to equity of ¥4.3 trillion, or 16 percent of assets. For the Big Four securities firms at the same time, composite assets of ¥9 trillion compared to equity of ¥1.9 trillion, or 21 percent of assets. The statistics represent a much more conservative capital structure than that of U.S. securities firms, whose equity usually equals only 6 percent of assets.

The contrast is also notable when Japanese commercial banks are compared to Japanese securities firms. The banks typically earn a fraction of the profits reported by the brokerage firms; from a capital structure point of view, their "book" equity bases are proportionately smaller even than those of some of the U.S. commercial banks. It should be recognized, however, that Japanese banks carry their holdings of Japanese common stocks at original cost, typically incurred many years earlier. Nonetheless, even a liberal adjustment for this undervalued asset category would not bring their capital positions to anything approaching the level of those of the Japanese securities firms.

In sum, the extraordinarily large equity bases of the Japanese securities firms in relation to their balance sheets, the attractive prices at which additional equity shares could be sold, and the size and composition of their profit-and-loss statements provide an impressive source of reserve spending (and staying) power for any domestic or foreign initiative they should choose to pursue.

People

In a country where the human capital input is key to national productivity, the securities sector is no exception. Securities firms have a reputation for delivering a high level of personal service to their client groups while at the same time extracting a particularly heavy commitment from their employees. Even so, productivity has been on the rise in recent years. Total securities industry employment has grown only modestly over the past several years despite sharp increases in its volume of business. The larger firms have set demanding individual performance standards, yet they still compensate their employees on a straight salary basis, rather than the commission basis that characterizes the smaller Japanese firms.

Perhaps because of the nature of the work and the emphasis placed on personal selling, securities firms have recruited new employees from more diverse backgrounds than have the commercial banks (see Appendix Table C-13). Then, too, the status attached to working for a securities firm has historically been lower than that attached to a number of other employer groups. Guided by the counsel of their university (and even elite middle school) administrators, faculty, and alumni groups, young graduates—particularly those from the law and economics faculties of prestigious universities such as the University of Tokyo and Kyoto University—have traditionally expressed greatest interest in the leading government ministries (the Ministry of Finance, the Foreign Ministry, the Ministry of International Trade and Industry). Just below the government in job preference stands the IBJ, because of its perceived leading role in important corporate-financing sectors and its prestigious position as a former quasi-governmental institution. Next come the leading commercial (city) banks (Sumitomo, Fuji, Mitsubishi, DKB, and Sanwa in approximately that order). Securities firms have usually ranked below these, although their extraordinary prosperity has more recently enhanced their attraction to young university graduates. While well-educated job seekers do not relish the prospect of being put into a retail sales slot and having to call on potential investors door-to-door (the traditional career-entry route), they are often quite interested in the entry-level job opportunities that the securities firms offer in research, mergers and acquisitions, and the international arena.

Conclusions

As in New York, the securities brokerage industry in Japan has prospered mightily but is being challenged by at least two groups, one composed of offshore securities competitors and the other composed of nonconventional domestic competitors. Thus far, the foreign firms have made only small inroads into the domestic Japanese marketplace. Their most impressive advances have been in areas where they bring a decided home-market advantage, such as in the sale of U.S. equity securities to Japanese investors or in the delivery of M&A counseling and facilitating services in cross-border transactions.

The minimal progress of foreign firms cannot be explained away strictly as the result of regulatory prohibitions. While obtaining membership on the TSE has been slow in coming for a number of offshore vendors, the domestic financial community has had to solve real membership and office space limitations associated with this. The Japanese government-bond market is in fact opening up, although at a slower pace than some offshore vendors would like. More important barriers have to do with business practices and relationships, which are not likely to be overcome in any quick or dramatic fashion.

The threat from nonconventional *domestic* financial vendors is the more serious threat to the status quo of the securities industry in Japan. This chapter and the previous one have chronicled the historical pattern of bank-corporation financing accommodation in Japan. While the Japanese securities firms have long been adept and successful in selling securities to various kinds of Japanese investors, only recently have they entered seriously into the corporate finance realm that has proved so lucrative to their Western European and U.S. counterparts.

Just as the Glass-Steagall Act created a protective compound within which the fledgling U.S. investment banks could practice and refine their craft, so the imposition of the carbon-copy Article 65 created a similar protected fiefdom for Japanese securities firms with respect to public securities activities. But the similarities are at least equally balanced by the differences. The Japanese commercial banks emerged from the occupation period as the rallying point for a rebirth of the old prewar industrial groups, this time in a looser-organized keiretsu family of companies. With their ability to reassert some of the old discipline of the zaibatsu in this new reincarnation, and buttressed by cross-holdings of equity securities and frequent exchanges of personnel, the post–World War II Japanese commercial banks were in a much more powerful position to influence the national financing scene than their U.S. or European counterparts.

Perhaps as a consequence, the pattern of financing for much of the postwar period showed primary reliance on privately arranged bank credit and a paucity of public debt financings. These patterns now appear to be undergoing important shifts, resulting in new issuer-vendor relationships. Securities firms are working diligently to build the corporate finance side of their businesses, both by internal development and external alliance, such as the investment and joint venture of Nomura Securities with Wasserstein, Perella.

The unfolding competitive environment in Tokyo presents a major challenge for Japan's regulators. By sustaining Article 65 in the years after U.S. occupation forces left, the MOF implicitly signaled that it favored a protected domestic-market environment in which the historically weak group of securities firms could develop and grow vis-à-vis the commercial banks and other financial institutions. That plan, if it was such, succeeded beyond the wildest expectations of most observers. In sheer financial strength, the leading securities firms now rival the commercial banks and almost all other industry groups in Japan.[20]

This has presented a real dilemma for the MOF. Not just the resolution of a turf dispute, the dilemma also has involved the future competitive positions of the trust banks, life insurance companies, and other institutional investors. As for the foreign investment banking and commercial banking entities with offices in Tokyo, these firms have made only very modest inroads into the Japanese domestic marketplace, just as has been the case with foreign vendors in New York trying to crack the domestic U.S. investment banking marketplace.

To be sure, the MOF has used the insistent clamoring of foreign vendors as a lever for effecting regulatory change in the domestic marketplace. But the future requires complex, multidimensional solutions to several complicated questions: how to preserve the viability of a multitude of small, less efficient brokers who depend on fixed brokerage commissions and at the same time rein in the embarrassingly high levels of profits of the giant Japanese securities firms? How to remedy the eroding position of the commercial banks in the Japanese financial equation? How to respond to the demands of the foreign securities firms for greater access to the domestic market, particularly when many of the barriers are not regulatory but cultural and attitudinal and thus slow to change?

---

20. By contrast, the Glass-Steagall Act on which Article 65 was modeled was promulgated for just the opposite purpose: to protect *investors* from the misdeeds of financial intermediaries.

Forward progress is evident, and the reform proposals put forth by the MOF-sponsored special study group are indications of further changes to come. It is an open question as to whether it will be fast enough or extensive enough to maintain Tokyo as *the* Asian center of the emerging global market. Hong Kong, after a long period of decline, appeared to be picking up some business from Tokyo prior to the massacre in Beijing's Tiananmen Square in May 1989. Its laissez-faire market environment, influenced by British administration and the free-wheeling entrepreneurship of the Chinese, were thought to provide the same appealing level playing field and deregulated environment that originally spawned the London Euromarkets. Since the uprising, however, all bets are off. It will take a considerable period of time to discern the long-term financial market repercussions of this troubling turn of events.

CHAPTER 8

FROM EMPIRE TO BIG BANG: THE DOMESTIC U.K. MARKETPLACE

During the hundred years from 1815 to 1915, London enjoyed clear domination of the world's capital-raising markets. This period was the flowering of the British Empire, and the City of London (the counterpart of Wall Street in the United States) was consciously structured to support and nourish the country's worldwide investment and trading activities. Britain's elite "public" schools and major universities were internationally oriented and were, in fact, mandated to train successive generations of young men to go out and administer the affairs of the Empire, upon which, some were fond to assert, "the sun never set."

Britain's world standing waned dramatically after World War I and continued to erode until the late 1970s. For its victories in both world wars, Britain paid an awesome price in dissipation of national wealth and tragic losses within two generations of young men. Equally important, each victory had come at the cost of greatly expanded waves of private and public indebtedness.

The first hard evidence of the decreased role of London as a money and capital center appeared in 1914. At that time, the financial district in the City experienced the closing of its stock exchange and the simultaneous abandonment of the gold standard for international monetary settlements. These two acts raised the stature of the New York market to that of a primary center for international financial arrangements. Although sterling was returned to the gold standard in 1925, the weight of this financial burden was too great, and the linkage again had to be abandoned in 1931.

During the depression of the 1930s and the war years that followed, British investors sustained major losses on pound-denominated international debt securities floated during the 1920s, as well as on equity investments on the European continent and in developing countries. To meet the costs of World War II, the American shares of British investors were sequestered at the beginning of the war for use in meeting the dollar cost commitments of the British government. As part of this program, foreign exchange controls were imposed in 1939, not to be lifted again until 1979. Britain was thus one of the last major countries during the post–World War II period to allow full freedom of international currency convertibility and investment at market exchange rates.

World War II closed the book on Britain's colonial empire. The dislocations resulting from the new reality, coupled with economic policies favoring consumption over domestic investment, led to a decline in the British position in the world economy. Interest rates and inflation were generally higher than in the other major Western economies, and a series of devaluations of the British pound began in 1949, prior to which sterling was at an official parity of $5.60 per pound. This rate was reduced to $2.80 per pound in the 1950s and early sixties and to $2.40 per pound in 1968. When the free floating of international exchange rates began in 1972, the pound fell to below $1.80 during the sterling crisis of 1976 and hit a new low of $1.10 in 1985. Domestic long-term interest rates meanwhile ranged between 13 and 17 percent during the 1974–1981 period. In 1976, the country sought assistance from the International Monetary Fund, including a bridge loan, as part of a program of economic stabilization.

With this sharp rise in domestic interest rates, domestic private-sector borrowers abandoned long-term funding in favor of floating-rate loans from the clearing banks. Foreign issuers, many of whom had had important relationships with the United Kingdom and a long history of borrowing British pounds, were now virtually excluded by the exchange control system set up during World War II, as well as by the Control of Borrowing Order 1958 administered by the Bank of England. Meanwhile, the British government's borrowing needs were ballooning. Britain's horizons had not been so cloudy since the dark days of Dunkirk. Indeed, Prince Philip was quoted as saying that unless something was done to arrest the decline of its economy, Britain would soon find itself in the same boat as the much-lamented third world nations.

The British financial world began to emerge from the darkest of these shadows during the 1970s. First, significant North Sea oil production during a period of rapidly rising energy prices was clearly a factor in re-establishing a better balance of payments for the country. Second, the major merchant and clearing banks in the City had been successful in taking advantage of London's central geographic position to partially reorient their business away from domestic services and toward international operations such as foreign exchange, Eurocurrency lending, and Eurobonds. They were joined by a growing cadre of foreign banks and brokers that established offices in London. Interestingly, a small Eurosterling sector to the Eurobond market, which had been initiated with a single £10-million issue in 1972, was restarted in 1977 with a few issues totaling just over £100 million. The Eurosterling bond market grew gradually in the late 1970s and more vigorously in the 1980s, reaching a volume of £13 billion by 1988 to become a significant source of fixed- and floating-rate sterling finance.

Political Change

The most significant factor in the re-emergence of the British domestic capital market was the 1979 election of a Conservative Party majority headed by Prime Minister Margaret Thatcher to the House of Commons. With a mandate to move away from the socialist policies of the previous thirty years, the new leadership took a number of steps that favored the expansion of British domestic and international financial services. As a follow-up to the election of 1979, exchange controls were eliminated later that same year. Subsequently, specific incentives designed to stimulate domestic investment were introduced, and the country's budget was placed on a more balanced footing. Income taxes, both corporate and personal, were also reduced. As a result of these policies, inflation declined, with interest rates settling in the 9–11 percent area for long-term British gilts. More important, confidence generally returned to the capital markets, although in size the British market has remained modest relative to its American and Japanese counterparts. As we shall see in the following chapter, the British market has been increasingly active as a source of funds for domestic and foreign borrowers during the 1980s.

Regulatory Change

Prior to the enactment of recent legislation, the British regulatory system could be characterized as less formal but slower to change than its American counterpart. Under the U.S. system, fixed stock-brokerage commissions were eliminated in May 1975; this event did not occur in Britain until October 1986. The British financial system also exhibited a multiplicity of different institutional formats including clearing banks, accepting houses, discount houses, stockbrokers, jobbers, and money brokers, all of whose principal functions are described in Chapter 9. The lines of demarcation between these functional units were in some cases established through informal guidelines set by the London Stock Exchange (in England, called simply The Stock Exchange). They were rarely the subject of specific legislation. Instead, the Bank of England, sometimes referred to as The Bank, and The Stock Exchange enforced codes of conduct on their members, who looked to these two organizations for guidance in capital and administrative questions. Thus, there were no British securities laws and no counterparts to U.S. legislation regarding trust indenture, investment advisory, or public utility holding companies.

Entering the 1980s, the British regulatory framework included, in addition to the informal system of guidelines, three specific acts or orders. First, the *Companies Act 1948* contained provisions relating to the contents of prospectuses for the issuance of securities, as well as to such matters as corporate duties of officers and directors. Recognizing the political and economic events of the 1930s, this act was an attempt to legislate protection for investors in a relatively quiet capital market, with strong informal direction from the central bank and The Stock Exchange.

A second act, the *Prevention of Frauds (Investments) Act 1958*, significantly advanced this public policy. It established basic operative provisions for conducting a securities business with respect to both the initial issuance of securities and their subsequent trading markets. The concept of preventing fraud was to an important degree comparable to the two principal U.S. securities laws, the Securities Act of 1933 and the Securities Exchange Act of 1934. In the 1958 British act, the guiding concept was an assurance that securities business was carried on by persons believed to be reliable and that the contents and circulation of documents relating to the offering or trading in securities would be spelled out in adequate detail for the investor.

The third element of regulation was control over access to the British capital market, as administered by the Bank of England under the *Control of Borrowing Order 1958*. Under this order, a new-issue approval arrangement was initiated by the Bank of England for all financings denominated in pounds sterling. In administering this order of priority, The Bank would have regard for the capacity of the market and to the need to maintain orderly arrangements for new issues. Thus, well before the 1980s, the Bank of England was able to direct the timing of new financings in a period when long-term sterling capital was relatively scarce. This role was legislated to avoid a capacity conflict between private or foreign financings and funding requirements of the British government, for which The Bank acted as fiscal agent. Such government credit arrangements represented the bulk of British domestic fund raising during the 1960s and 1970s.

While the Companies Act 1948 and the Prevention of Frauds (Investments) Act 1958 embodied both criminal and civil sanctions, there was still no government watchdog equivalent to the U.S. Securities and Exchange Commission. Together with the Bank of England, The Stock Exchange remained the monitor and overseer of the British domestic securities industry. The Exchange's rules and its authority over its members were expected to guard the public interest.

An issuer seldom attempted a public offering of securities in the London market without concurrently seeking Stock Exchange listing. Indeed, members were prohibited by The Exchange from participating in issuances not made under its rules. The Council of The Stock Exchange was the governing body that fixed the rules to supplement the broad public policy objectives set forth in the acts. The Stock Exchange exercised control over its members, and, as a result, members were free from any direct action by the Department of Trade and Industry.

Interestingly, when the Eurosterling market re-emerged in the late 1970s, The Bank asserted its control over that market as well, confirming that all new Eurosterling borrowings larger than £3 million would be subject to The Bank's timing and consent procedures under the Control of Borrowing Order 1958. A November 1980 notice established that foreign-owned banks could lead manage Eurosterling offerings but only jointly with a British institution, and then only if British banks were accorded equal treatment in the foreign bank's domestic market. These arrangements for timing, consent, and reciprocity have generally been maintained for Eurosterling financings in the 1980s, except that the requirement for a British joint lead manager was dropped in 1987.

Court Action and Change

The impetus for fundamental change at The Stock Exchange was the prosecution by the government of a suit against The Exchange under the Restrictive Trade Practices Order of 1976. The 1976 order was a successor to the 1973 Fair Trading Act, which had been passed by a previous Conservative government with a view to examining existing cartels within the British economy generally and to encouraging competition. The Stock Exchange, finding that it was not exempt from the act, was obliged to register its rules and regulations as well as its dealing code with the Office of Fair Trading, then a part of the Department of Trade and Industry.

Following receipt of this registration and further study, the Office of Fair Trading identified a number of practices it regarded as restrictive. Among them were the practice of enforcing on certain Stock Exchange members a single function (acting either as brokers or jobbers, but not both) and the practice of fixed minimum commissions. When the director of Fair Trading referred these restrictive practices to the Restrictive Practices Court, The Stock Exchange was forced to retain outside legal counsel and to prepare a formal defense. Even at the beginning of this legal action, there were significant doubts within British financial and administrative circles as to whether the Restrictive Practices Court was the ideal forum within which to instigate possible changes at The Exchange. A court victory by one side or the other would presumably result in either dramatic change in practices or no change at all. Many observers therefore recommended a negotiated solution that would also encompass a period of significant reform and modernization at The Stock Exchange. In late 1979, the court documents were served on The Exchange, and opening statements in the case were made before the court in March 1981. Finally in 1983, following a second landslide victory by the Conservative Party in the Parliamentary elections, the new secretary of state for Trade and Industry, Cecil Parkinson, opened direct negotiations with Sir Nicholas Goodison, chairman of the Council of The Stock Exchange, with a view to settling a broad range of controversial matters.

On July 22, 1983, an agreement was announced between the government and The Stock Exchange under which the case before the Restrictive Practices Court would be dropped and The Exchange would agree: 1) to dismantle by December 31, 1986, its rules fixing a minimum commission scale; 2) to establish an independent appeals tribunal that could overrule decisions by the Council; 3) to introduce members from outside The Stock Exchange community to the Council of The Exchange; and 4) to modify rules regarding the membership of the boards of directors of Stock Exchange member firms. Later in 1983, Goodison presented to the firms further proposals to implement these and other major reforms at The Stock Exchange, including the abandonment of the single-function restrictions in firm membership. Subsequently, a date—Monday, October 27, 1986—was chosen for the final implementation of all reforms; the target date became known as "Big Bang." A number of specific results of these Stock Exchange reforms are discussed in Chapter 9.

The Gower Report

At the same time that court action was forcing reform at The Stock Exchange, developments leading to the eventual modification of British securities laws were occurring. While the court action was designed to modify the competitive structure in financial services, modification of the securities laws was intended to make improvements in the old informal style of securities regulation. Although the British financial markets generally encouraged a high standard of ethical behavior, a number of frauds and failures had occurred in the late 1970s and early 1980s. Most notable was the failure of Johnson Matthey Bankers, a well-known London financial group whose banking arm became overextended in real estate loans to Middle East interests that defaulted. Depositors had had no hint of a developing problem despite a supposedly reliable regulatory reporting system. There was a clear need for a change in regulatory procedures. The older practices, sometimes referred to as "the nod and the wink" system, had worked well in a small community of British financiers, but the City roster of firms had grown substantially in the 1980s and also included a large number of non-British firms, some of which were not used to the traditionally informal modes of regulation.

In 1981, Professor L. C. B. Gower, a highly respected academician in the field of securities law, was commissioned by the government to consider the adequacy of the statutory regulation framework. As Gower himself later recalled:

> A couple of years ago, following a series of large scandals in the City . . . the then Secretary of State for Trade commissioned me to carry out an independent review of investor protection with three specific areas of interest. One, to consider the statutory protection now required by both private and business investors in securities and other properties, including unit trusts and open-end investment trusts operating in the U.K. Two, to consider the need for statutory control of dealers in securities, investment consultants and investment managers. And three, to advise on the need for new legislation.[1]

The Gower Report became the underlying basis for a government White Paper in 1985 embodying its proposals and entitled "Financial Services in the United Kingdom: A New Framework for Investor Protection." As the secretary of state for Trade and Industry indicated in his press release of January 29, 1985, "The theme is self-regulation within a statutory framework."

The Financial Services Act 1986

The *Financial Services Act 1986* was introduced to Parliament in December 1985. After an unusually large number of amendments, it became effective by Royal Assent on November 7, 1986. The structure as created was designed not merely to fill a domestic regulatory need but also to ensure comparable world status or even to secure to the

---

1. *Barron's*, March 26, 1984, p. 40.

United Kingdom's financial businesses advantages in relation to competing marketplaces. Analysis of the new structure makes apparent an almost complete departure from traditional practice.

The act bridges the transition from a private system to a governmental regulatory structure but retains in concept the British tradition of self-regulation in the securities industry. At the same time, the public protection deemed essential is accomplished through an oversight system involving layers of review by both those being regulated and those charged with the regulation. The latter function is coupled with governmental rule-making that in principle adopts the idea of the rule book of The Stock Exchange but in practice parallels the rule-making or quasi-legislative functions employed by the Securities and Exchange Commission in the United States. Like the U.S. system, rule-making is not formal legislation, but it achieves a flexible approach to making "laws" that cannot be disregarded easily.

Unlike that of the United States or Japan, the U.K. structure is fundamentally pyramidal; the secretary of state for Trade and Industry (a minister in the cabinet of government) is vested with the full oversight authority and powers of the system. The act states that the secretary will delegate regulatory responsibilities to a second tier, a "designated agency." This agency, which was subsequently named the Securities and Investments Board (SIB), is under the direction of a governing body with a chairman appointed jointly by the secretary of state for Trade and Industry and the governor of the Bank of England. The agency is required to prepare an annual report for the secretary to submit to Parliament.

The SIB has power under the Financial Services Act 1986 to regulate the functioning of a broadly defined financial and investment business in the United Kingdom. It is authorized to establish rules for conducting an investment business and the patterns of required accounting by participants in the financial and investment sectors. The rules in this regard may establish provisions for the holding of a customer's assets, including their location and safety. In general, as in the United States, the agency may intervene directly in financial or investment matters where apparent inaction by one of the self-regulatory organizations is deemed to have jeopardized investor protection.

The rule-making authority of the agency extends specifically to the regulation of the persons who will be permitted to conduct an investment business. Under the act, investment businesses, except for the Bank of England, the insurance market at Lloyds, existing clearing houses, and several recognized investment exchanges, must obtain specific regulatory approval. Authorization is to be granted only to individuals or institutions deemed fit and proper to conduct an investment business.

The Financial Services Act 1986 opened the door to the investment business for not just the regular cast of characters but to members of recognized professional organizations (such as lawyers and accountants) that deal with investment matters, insurance companies, and similar organizations. Individuals or institutions resident in European Economic Community member states and authorized by their own countries to engage in financial activity under standards of investor protection considered equivalent to those of the United Kingdom will also be authorized by the designated agency, in concert with the EEC's 1992 integration goals. Foreign persons or institutions are also eligible to be authorized under the act.

The Financial Services Act 1986 includes criminal sanctions for engaging in the investment business without having obtained authorization, and firms employing unauthorized persons are liable for any losses to investors that might result. In the United States, an appeal from the Securities and Exchange Commission lies with a court of appeals. Similarly, an appeal may be taken in the United Kingdom to a financial services tribunal, created under the act. The tribunal's members, three of whom will sit on any case, are drawn from a panel of persons having the requisite legal background and financial expertise and are appointed by the Lord Chancellor or the secretary of state for Trade and Industry. The tribunal has been given investigatory powers by the act, and its findings are binding on the secretary and the designated agency. Thus, unlike the right of the Securities and Exchange Commission to seek higher judicial review of a court decision it finds unacceptable, the tribunal's decision is final from a regulatory standpoint.

The third tier in the regulatory pyramid is represented by various *Self-Regulatory Organizations* (SROs). The Act provides that organizations created for self-regulatory purposes are responsible for regulating the relationships between their members and their customers. To meet this objective, the SIB may delegate some of its powers and responsibilities to an SRO to establish rules in particular areas of its financial activity, but the SRO remains responsible to the SIB. A significant provision of the act, which may be analogous to U.S. antitrust concepts and Securities and Exchange Commission actions, requires that an SRO's rules do not impede competition unnecessarily or go beyond restrictions needed to protect investors.

Five principal SROs were initially set up to regulate different segments of the United Kingdom's investment business: 1) The Securities Association (TSA) regulates trading in domestic and international securities (including the brokers, dealers, market makers, and large domestic and foreign security houses active on The Stock Exchange in gilts and corporate securities and off The Exchange in Eurosecurities and in dealings with other professionals); 2) the Association of Futures Brokers and Dealers (AFBD) regulates trading in financial futures and commodities; 3) the Financial Intermediaries, Managers, and Brokers Regulatory Association (FIMBRA) regulates smaller securities firms and independent brokers of life insurance and unit trusts; 4) the Investment Management Regulatory Organization (IMRO) oversees investment management firms, including merchant banks and investment trust and unit trust managers; and 5) the Life Assurance and Unit Trust Regulatory Organization (LAUTRO) represents dealers in pooled trusts (including such investments as those sold by insurance companies, unit trusts, and other societies). The operations and powers of the SROs were patterned after those of SIB, including separate industry tribunals.

The next tier of the regulatory structure is constituted by the "recognized investment exchanges." Like the SROs, these exchanges are authorized by and report to the SIB. The former Stock Exchange regulatory group merged with the International Securities Regulatory Organization late in 1986 to form The Securities Association.[2]

The Financial Services Act 1986 assumed that securities firms active in trading would likely become members primarily of one self-regulatory organization and one recognized investment exchange. But the act also recognized that a firm, through diversification of its activities, might well be subject to regulation by more than one SRO or investment exchange. In this event, the act provided that one of the self-regulatory bodies would act as the principal regulator of the member.

The investment exchanges initially chosen included a variety of trading exchanges. Thus, TSA oversees markets for two recognized

---

2. The International Securities Regulatory Organization was formed in 1985 by firms in the international securities community to decide whether there was support for the formation of an international self-regulatory organization. It formed a working party with The Stock Exchange to discuss whether they would jointly create a recognized investment exchange in the fourth tier of regulation for trading international equities. That action led to the question of forming a joint self-regulatory organization in the third tier and, in due course, to an actual merger of the two exchange interests. This merger, according to the organization's leadership, had the approval of the Department of Trade and Industry, the Bank of England, and the Securities and Investment Board. Members of the organization were advised, nevertheless, that each would have to pass the "fit and proper" test to be admitted as a member of the new self-regulatory organization. (*Source:* Letter, dated 15 October 1986, from ISRO [Formation] Ltd. to its members.)

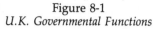
Figure 8-1
U.K. Governmental Functions

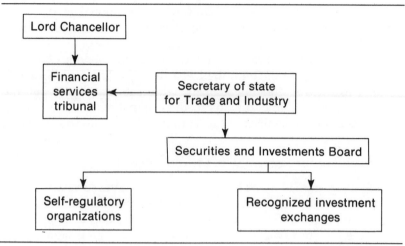

investment exchanges: The International Stock Exchange (formerly The Stock Exchange) and the Association of International Bond Dealers (based in Zurich). The AIBD oversees members often active on three recognized investment exchanges: the London International Financial Futures Exchange; the London Commodity Exchange; and the London Metal Exchange.

Listing of securities on exchanges, as well as trading in the unlisted securities market, is addressed in the fourth regulatory level. The International Stock Exchange continues to determine listing requirements, while issuers of unlisted securities are required by the act to publish a prospectus meeting disclosure requirements established by the secretary of state or the designated agency. The complexities of the regulatory structure of the investment business, even in the initial stages, indicate the likelihood of problems of future identification and exercise of regulatory responsibility in the course of the objective of blending multinational market units into a pragmatic national scheme.

Figure 8-1 illustrates the governmental oversight structure. The key to its function lies in the SIB's right to intervene in the SROs as it deems appropriate. The structure also permits additional organizations to be established and gives the SIB oversight of persons who are *not* members of an organization. The scope of the structure requires a permanent staff of broad financial and market expertise at the SIB.

This aspect parallels a characteristic of the United States' Securities and Exchange Commission since its formation in 1934.

It is worth noting that at the drafting of the original bill there was significant debate as to whether the international securities industry and Eurobond market should be included in the scope of the legislation (Eurobond dealers generally operated outside the previous U.K. domestic oversight). In the end, the Department of Trade and Industry decided to incorporate this segment within its regulatory net and made a number of amendments to the original bill to take into account the unique character of the Euromarkets, as discussed below.

Implementing the Securities and Investments Board (SIB)

In early 1987, the SIB made formal application to the secretary of state for Trade and Industry for appointment as the designated agency under the Financial Securities Act. A rule book and a statement of objectives and procedures were also submitted. The designation of the SIB as the regulatory board under the act was made a few months later.

The SIB's rules have the force of law and set limits on the freedom of SROs in drafting their own rules. In addition to noting disciplinary sanctions and rights of injured persons to sue, the SIB states that it may seek injunctions and other relief on behalf of investors.

The act requires authorization and regulation of all persons conducting an "investment business" in the United Kingdom. The SIB has a much broader universe in types of businesses to be regulated than do any of the individual U.S. regulatory agencies. The SIB's authority covers life insurance sales, stock brokerage and advice, investment advice, and dealing in and managing investments of all types, from unit trusts to complex Euromarket instruments. Various rules have extraterritorial effects; they apply generally, for example, to any firms that seek to procure business from investors in the United Kingdom, or elsewhere, if the firm is operating in the United Kingdom.

The Eurobond market, which had been wholly unregulated prior to Big Bang, is regulated only in principle under the SIB rules. When the rules were being formulated, the Zurich-based Association of International Bond Dealers, which in effect represented dealers in the Eurobond market, jousted with the SIB as to the niche it should occupy in the new structure. The result was an agreement that the association would be deemed "an overseas exchange" under the act. This understanding entailed that the association receive an expression of satisfaction from the SIB stating that the self-engendered trading rules of the association broadly met the investor-protection provisions being installed by the SIB in the United Kingdom. Furthermore, this understanding would not permit individual members of the association to trade Eurobonds in the United Kingdom unless authorized by TSA, which, as an SRO, would oversee the business practices and financial resources of the association's members.

The Eurobond rules apply to authorized U.K. firms doing business with persons oversees. However, an overseas-based firm authorized to do business in the United Kingdom would not be subject to rules on business undertaken overseas. Exceptions are granted when regulatory systems overlap, specific rules remain to be written, Bank of England provisions apply, certain pension schemes are involved, or the Take-Over Code applies. The SIB warns, however, that the "fit and proper" test for authorization to conduct an investment business might still apply even if the conduct rules do not.

In an alteration of past practices, foreign securities firms can gain entry into the U.K. securities business on the same basis as British firms. In any case, authorization must be obtained from the SIB or one of the SROs sanctioned by the SIB.

Specific regulation relates to such areas as the protection of investors (distinguishing between unsophisticated and sophisticated investors); adequate disclosure of fees, commissions, and other such particulars; the policing of potential conflicts of interest; and the potential misuse of insider information. The objective of the regulations was to promote "greater confidence of investors, foreign as well as U.K., greater recognition by foreign regulators," and increased benefits from greater stability and more consistent standards of solvency and behavior.

With publication of the rules, it was possible for the industry to appraise the advantages and to weigh the implications and consequences of compliance with a regulatory structure not heretofore experienced in the United Kingdom. An editorial analysis in the *Financial Times* concluded that "London retains certain freedoms denied in New York and Tokyo in terms of the combination of commercial banking and investment banking. But in most other respects the activities of securities houses in London will be tightly restricted by international standards. So much so that the main risk must be that business will drift away from London to alternative centers where the rules are not so tightly drafted."[3]

The freedoms retained refer, of course, to the Glass-Steagall Act in the United States and the equivalent Article 65 of the Japanese

3. *Financial Times*, July 23, 1987, p. 22.

securities law barring commercial banks from acting as underwriters of securities except in limited areas.[4] While decrying the new regulation, however, the *Financial Times* recognized that the "system will be controlled by practitioners, and the day-to-day operational rules can be changed without the need for new primary legislation." The *Financial Times* further stated that if "a self-regulatory system is operated imaginatively and flexibly it may be possible to retain the more dynamic aspects of the City of London's securities markets."[5]

In addressing the House of Commons on January 29, 1985, regarding the objectives of the proposed Financial Securities Act, the secretary of state for Trade and Industry made it clear that the government was seeking a method to ensure London of international financial industry importance:

> Modern technology and intense international competition are bringing about rapid changes in the financial services industry. . . . The Government's task—in this sector as in others—is to create an environment in which [industry can respond effectively]. This is best done by allowing market forces to operate responsibly but without unnecessary constraints, in a way which promotes efficient and competitive business. A prerequisite for an internationally competitive industry is a clear regulatory framework within which practitioners and customers can deal with confidence. . . . This regulatory framework must be capable . . . of accommodating rather than stifling innovation.[6]

Current Assessment

From the perspective of the late 1980s, we have seen a staged implementation of the new competitive and regulatory environment in

4. Although there has never been a statutory equivalent of the Glass-Steagall Act in the United Kingdom, there has been a pragmatic parallel. Informal guidelines adopted by the Bank of England had the same effect on commercial banks generally until just prior to Big Bang. T. M. Rybeznski, in *The UK Financial System in Transition* states: "While the Bank of England in principle has been willing to see a reasonable degree of concentration among the depository and other similar institutions, until recently it has tended to favor the separation of what in effect was investment banking activity from deposit banking business. The exception was merchant banks, which have managed to combine these two businesses for more than 150 years. . . . This attitude began to change in the mid-1960's, when the Bank of England allowed one clearing bank to acquire one merchant bank."
5. *Financial Times*, July 23, 1987, p. 22.
6. Statement by Norman Tebbit, Official Reports, 6th Series, Parliamentary Debates (Hansard), Commons, vol. 72, 1984–1985, p. 89.

the United Kingdom during the past three years. In October 1986, Big Bang took place with far reaching changes in The Stock Exchange and a reorganization of the gilts market. During 1987, the rules of the SIB were promulgated, and the five principal SROs were authorized. Application deadlines for firms to obtain membership in the SROs were set in February 1988, and applications were processed during the first nine months of that year.

It is still too early to make a complete assessment of the effect of the Financial Services Act 1986 on the British financial scene. No meaningful litigation under the new act has been adjudicated, and the administrative and disciplinary procedures are still being applied only tentatively. Nevertheless, it is clear that the new system is substantially more rigorous than its predecessor and that the original law does not permit the SIB flexibility in administering rules. The legislation is also more exacting in some respects than American securities legislation. Most firms complying with the new framework regard it as both burdensome and costly and hope that, when the regulators have gained more experience, a number of provisions will be relaxed or made more flexible.

Europe in 1992

During 1988, the countries of the European Economic Community made decisions intended to result in a free market in financial services (as well as other products) throughout the twelve nations by December 1992. In the finance area, the new stage of liberalization will include the elimination of all restrictions on the movement of capital, such as exchange controls. It will also permit banks, insurance companies, fund managers, and other financial intermediaries to sell their services in Common Market countries other than their own. Finally, such intermediaries will be able to operate in any Common Market country without local regulation, provided their home-country regulatory regime is considered adequate. (The provision of the Financial Services Act 1986 that allows reciprocal treatment to residents of other EEC countries seems almost prescient.) These changes are generally expected to result in a harmonization of regulatory approach throughout Europe.

CHAPTER 9

THE U.K. MARKETPLACE TODAY

The U.K. domestic securities market has become increasingly important in the 1980s, not only because of the resurgence of Britain in the world economy but because of its interdependence with the growing international securities market. Further, the privatization program initiated by the Thatcher government has pumped new life into the domestic securities market. From 1979 through the spring of 1988, about £18 billion of new securities—primarily equities—were issued in the market. Although slowed by the slump in world markets after the crash in October 1987, the British government has targeted another £5 billion of privatizations each year for the succeeding three years plus the privatization, sometime in the future, of the electricity industry, expected to be worth another £25 billion.

The traditional center of U.K. securities activities has been The Stock Exchange in London, which, following Big Bang in 1986, was renamed the International Stock Exchange. Most domestic U.K. securities, including equities, government debt, corporate bonds, and many foreign securities are listed and traded on The Stock Exchange. An over-the-counter market (including the unlisted securities market, which is comparable to the U.S. OTC market) is becoming an increasingly important factor. In total, over 7,500 securities, representing about 3,000 different entities, are traded in the United Kingdom. At the end of 1988, the total market value of the securities traded on the International Stock Exchange was £1,633 billion, of which £154.9 billion represented debt issued by public sector borrowers and £107.9 billion represented Eurobonds (see Table 9-1). Approximately £408 billion ($715 billion) represented ordinary or preference shares issued by British or Irish companies, ranking the U.K. equity market third behind comparable figures of $3 trillion in Tokyo and $2.5 trillion in New York.

Before the changes in 1986, financial institutions were neatly categorized and differentiated by formal and informal rules. The major players included clearing banks, merchant banks, stockbrokers, and jobbers. Clearing banks, similar to commercial banks in the United States, were primarily engaged in accepting deposits and making loans through their nationwide branch networks. The name

209

Table 9-1
Securities Issues in the United Kingdom, 1979–1988
(£ millions)

	1979	1980	1981	1982	1983	1984	1985	1986	1987	1988
Gross share issues										
Domestic enterprises	£959	£893	£1,876	£1,052	£2,334	£1,597	£4,409	£7,575	£15,661	£5,783
Foreign enterprises	1	62	13	33	116	34	9	78	191	—
Total shares	960	955	1,889	1,085	2,450	1,631	4,418	7,653	15,852	5,783
Gross bond issues										
Public Issues										
Central government	14,115	15,033	12,827	10,576	14,541	14,005	15,192	14,838	14,364	7,491
Local government	638	765	698	876	1,088	775	344	200	69	35
Domestic enterprises	84	87	60	10	1,298	27	64	256	193	401
Foreign enterprises	0	0	189	345	279	638	542	300	0	186
Total public bonds	14,837	15,885	13,774	11,807	17,206	15,445	16,142	15,594	14,626	8,113
Private Placings										
Domestic enterprises	60	195	221	421	495	453	919	1,334	2,075	2,161
Foreign enterprises	0	74	160	219	237	214	110	194	0	0
Total private placings	60	269	381	640	732	667	1,029	1,528	2,075	2,161
Total bonds	14,897	16,154	14,155	12,447	17,938	16,112	17,171	17,122	16,371	10,274
Total financing in domestic market	15,857	17,109	16,044	13,532	20,388	17,743	21,589	24,775	32,223	16,057
Sterling Eurobonds	—	—	—	—	—	5,400	4,700	5,900	10,300	13,100

Source: "Organization for Economic Co-operation and Development."

"clearing bank" derived from the function of transferring and paying drafts and checks drawn on customer accounts. There are several hundred clearing banks in the United Kingdom but the big four are Barclays, National Westminster, Lloyds, and Midland. Although not legally prohibited, securities activities of the clearing banks have historically been restrained by informal understandings and tradition. Nevertheless, beginning in the mid-1970s, the big four clearing banks began to move gradually into the securities business through merchant banking subsidiaries.

Merchant banks concentrated on wholesale financial transactions such as financial advisory services, arranging mergers and acquisitions, and underwriting securities. While there were no official prohibitions against commercial banking activities, the merchant banks tended to forgo straightforward sterling lending and concentrated on export credits, acceptances, leasing, and other specialized forms of financing. The importance and reputation of Hambros, Hill Samuel, Kleinwort Benson, Morgan Grenfell, N.M. Rothschild, J. Henry Schroder Wagg, and S.G. Warburg, all with wealthy and aristocratic leadership, imparted a clubby atmosphere to the industry.

Securities sales and trading, which revolved primarily around The Stock Exchange, were officially the province of jobbers and brokers. Jobbers, which numbered about 500 before Big Bang, were charged with making two-way securities markets, that is, standing ready to buy or sell securities. For every security traded on The Stock Exchange, there were at least two jobbers.[1] The role of the jobber was similar to that of the specialist on the New York Stock Exchange. The largest jobbers included Akroyd & Smithers, Wedd Durlacher, Bisgood Bishop, Wilson & Watford, and Smith Bros.

Jobbers dealt only with brokers, who in turn acted as agents for individual or institutional investor clients for a fixed commission. Of the more than 3,000 brokers before Big Bang,[2] the major firms, who dealt primarily with equities, included de Zoete & Bevan, Strauss Turnbull, Wood Mackenzie, Grievson Grant, Rowe & Pitman, Vickers da Costa, James Capel, Cazanove, Scrimgeour Kemp-Gee, Hoare Govett, L. Messel, Phillips & Drew, and Buckmaster & Moore. In addition, other brokers concentrated on government securities. Jobbers could deal only with brokers who were Exchange members, and brokers agreed to bring all their business to The Exchange and to deal through the jobbers. This arrangement, known as "single capacity,"

---

1. Stuart Valentine, "The U.K. Equity Markets," in Abraham M. George and Ian H. Giddy (eds.), *International Finance Handbook* (New York: John Wiley, 1983), p. 6.3.7.
2. Ibid., p. 6.3.6.

had been a Stock Exchange rule since 1908 and forced firms to choose between making markets and selling securities.

As part of the run-up to Big Bang in October 1986, foreign and domestic institutions were allowed for the first time to acquire interests in member firms of The Stock Exchange. As a result, the British jobbers and stockbrokers, no longer protected by regulation, became acquisition targets. Because this consolidation occurred during a period of buoyant markets and good profitability, high prices were paid for such acquisitions (and for the salaries of the people who worked in them).

The threat of large, well-capitalized foreign entrants, especially American commercial and investment banks, put pressure on the British merchant banks to merge with jobbers and brokers. Although there was a strong cultural fit between members of The Stock Exchange and the British merchant banks, this advantage was offset by the merchant banks' relatively small capital bases. Heavy tax rates and the low profits from the sparse activity in public securities underwriting through the 1970s had contributed to this low level of capitalization.

Nevertheless, most British merchant banks merged with brokers and jobbers to become full-service investment banks. At the same time, the merchant banking subsidiaries of most of the major British clearing banks were making similar moves. For example, Barclays Merchant Bank acquired the broker de Zoete & Bevan and the jobber Wedd Durlacher. Many of the over 500 foreign banks located in London have also become more active in the securities field—either starting up their own merchant banks or buying existing British merchant banks and stockbrokers.

As we shall see, the U.K. securities market presented many business opportunities to merchant and investment bankers, including securities underwriting, U.K. government-securities trading, other securities trading, research, money management, and mergers and acquisitions.

Securities Underwriting

Following the lackluster 1970s, domestic securities underwriting in the United Kingdom increased substantially in volume through the mid-1980s until slowed by the effects of the October 1987 crash. Total share and bond financing raised on behalf of private-sector enterprises grew sixfold, from £3 billion in 1984 to over £18 billion in 1987 before falling back to £8.5 billion in 1988 (see Table 9-1). Unlike in the United States, where equity financings were generally declining during the period, the great majority of those flotations were "shares" (the traditional name for equity in the United Kingdom), with new common-stock issues representing 70–80 percent of total private financing for the years 1984 through 1987. Except for the U.K. government-bond market, fixed-income issues in the domestic market were negligible, a phenomenon attributed by some market observers to traditional requirements of collateral and restrictive covenants, similar to those in Japan, and to aversion by investors to long-term maturities. Further, the expansion of the Eurosterling bond market provided a more suitable alternative to the domestic market for the long-term borrowing needs of British entities. However, despite the resurgence in new equity issues, merchant and investment banks in London could not count on private-sector securities underwriting as a dominant business focus.

The types of securities offered in the United Kingdom are diverse and, in some cases, unique. Further, although many are similar to U.S. instruments, the U.K. varieties are often labeled differently, sometimes leading to confusion and frustration. Therefore, a taxonomy of the large segments of the U.K. private-sector securities market is presented next.

Corporate Equity Underwriting

Equity securities constitute the largest part of the private-sector new issuance market. New shares totaling almost £6 billion were issued in 1988—less than half the amount in 1987 but still larger than 1986 (see Table 9-1). New foreign-share issues, after increasing to £191 million in 1987, fell to almost nothing in 1988.

Corporate equity offerings are usually underwritten by merchant banks. British institutional investors and foreign securities firms frequently participate as members of underwriting syndicates but rarely serve as lead managers. Share flotations may be through an "offer for sale," in which the underwriters each agree to purchase a block and offer them to the public at a higher price (comparable to traditional U.S. underwritings). Less frequently, shares may be privately placed directly with institutions, as in the United States. Most public offerings and private placements are fully underwritten, but a few deals are handled on a "best-efforts" basis—sometimes called "moral underwritings," because of the implicit but not legal obligations undertaken by the lead manager to successfully complete the financing.

"Rights offerings" are the most commonly used method for already listed companies to raise additional equity capital in the U.K. domestic market. Rights are granted to existing shareholders and entitle the holder to buy a certain number of shares at a fixed price within a certain time period. A holder would generally elect to exercise the right to purchase shares if the market price of the shares is greater than the stipulated purchase price on the date the rights expire. Rights issues are popular with U.K. investors and, in effect, give existing shareholders the right of first refusal for new shares (preemptive rights). This protects the existing shareholders' ownership from dilution, provided the shareholders use the rights to purchase new shares. Typically, the purchase price of the new shares is set 15–30 percent below the current market price to ensure their exercise. Shareholders not wishing to exercise their rights may elect to sell their shares on the market. To protect the issuing company against the possibility that the new-share issue will not be fully subscribed, the offering is usually underwritten by a securities firm.

It should be noted, however, that the regulations requiring strict adherence to pre-emptive rights have been relaxed somewhat in recent years. Companies have begun to seek changes in corporate charters requiring rights offerings, commenting that they are more expensive, take longer to execute, and reduce flexibility relative to domestic cash offers and international equity flotations.[3] At the same time, some issuers have been able to bypass rights requirements by issuing convertible securities either domestically or in the Euromarkets.[4] Institutional investors, on the other hand, have banded together on several recent occasions to resist the movement away from rights issues.[5]

Lead-management roles and syndicate memberships are actively sought by merchant and investment banks, as well as by investment funds, for several reasons. One attraction is the presumption of improved chances for future business with the issuer. A second reason is the potential for fees and trading profits. Management fees average only about 1¼ percent for fully underwritten rights offerings and new-share placements, including initial public offerings (IPOs). Although this is relatively low compared to the 4–6 percent range in the United States, the practice of pricing rights offerings at steep discounts to prevailing market prices minimizes the risk that the under-

3. For a theoretical treatment of the arguments for and against rights issues see Richard Brealy and Stewart Myers, *Principles of Corporate Finance* (New York: McGraw-Hill, 1984), pp. 309–317. For a discussion of the practical problems of rights issues see "How Rights Issues Go Wrong," *The Economist*, September 5, 1987, pp. 71–72.
4. For a more detailed discussion and several examples, see "Pre-emption Rights: No Free Lunch," *The Economist*, September 26, 1987, p. 101.
5. "British Firms Offering Shares Overseas Clash with Big Domestic Stockholders," *The Wall Street Journal*, April 17, 1987, p. 20.

writer will be stuck holding unsold securities. Thus, many market observers in the United Kingdom are quick to point out that the fee for rights offerings is "money for old rope." IPOs are conservatively priced, which generally is designed to ensure a moderate price appreciation on the day of the offering, called "impact day"; this is a subtle form of additional compensation for underwriters.

The massive privatization program in the United Kingdom during the 1970s and 1980s provided a rich source of underwriting opportunities. Underwriters for several of these issues made a substantial amount of money as prices soared in the secondary market following impact day. However, the tables were sharply turned in the privatization offering of British Petroleum (BP) shares, which spanned the crash in October 1987. Underwriters, including American and Japanese as well as British firms, incurred gut-wrenching losses, estimated at £1.5 billion, as the price of BP shares plummeted roughly 20 percent below the set offering price. Despite efforts to postpone the issue, thereby letting the underwriters off the hook, the decision was made to go ahead with the deal, perhaps in response to political pressure from Labor MPs. However, the British government did establish a floor price, about 20 percent below the postcrash market quote, at which it was willing to buy back the shares to prevent a collapse in the stock. Despite the losses incurred by the underwriters and the lack of interest among potential investors, the market price of BP ultimately stabilized, and the British government was not called upon to intervene.[6]

Table 9-2 shows the relative standings of various banking intermediaries in shares and rights issues in recent years. In 1988, for instance, Samuel Montagu, the merchant banking subsidiary of Midland Bank, led the list of underwriters, followed by a wide margin, by such firms as Goldman, Sachs, Rothschild, and Schroder Wagg.

Debt Underwriting

With attention focused on the rapidly growing Eurosterling bond market, the British domestic corporate-debt market, like that in Tokyo, is much less active than New York's. The volume of new domestic public issues by British and foreign enterprises averaged only about £600 million per year throughout the mid-1980s, after the opening of the Eurosterling market in 1984. The amount outstanding on

---

6. Craig Forman, "British Petroleum Trading in London Is Subdued as Buy-Back Plan Cuts Fears," *The Wall Street Journal*, November 2, 1987, p. 6.

Table 9-2
Top Underwriters of New Equity Issues—1988
(Volume in £ millions)

Issuing House	Amount Raised	Number of Companies
Samuel Montagu	£2,525	5
Goldman, Sachs	279	1
N.M. Rothschild	279	1
Schroder Wagg	143	5
Lazard Brothers	136	8
S.G. Warburg	111	3
Barclays de Zoete Wedd	60	8
Kleinwort Benson	58	5

Source: Investors Chronicle, January 1989.

The Stock Exchange is quite small, representing less than 1 percent of the total market capitalization for all traded securities. Private placings were slightly more important and growing, averaging about £1 billion per year during the same period.

U.K. corporate bonds are usually registered and may be issued in two forms: as debentures or loan stock. The use of these terms is peculiar to the U.K. market. Debentures, the more common of the two, are secured bonds that rank ahead of all other capital issues in the payment of creditors in the event of liquidation. Thus, use of the term is just the opposite of that in the United States, where debentures are generally unsecured borrowings. Loan stocks, which represent unsecured bonds, rank behind debentures but ahead of equity shares in the order of claims by creditors. Debentures and loan stocks, like shares, are issued through, and usually underwritten by, merchant or investment banks.

Bonds issued in the domestic U.K.-securities markets by non-resident borrowers, known as "bulldog issues," grew in importance following the lifting of exchange controls in 1979. This market peaked in 1984 at £852 million—£638 million in public issues and £214 million in private placements. The public new-issue market then decreased to virtually nothing in 1987 and only £186 million in 1988 (see Table 9-1).

In contrast to the domestic bond market, new issues of Eurosterling bonds grew from about £5 billion in 1984 to £13 billion in 1988. In recent years, both British and foreign issuers have exhibited a preference for Eurosterling over domestic bonds for several reasons. First, they are distributed over a wider investor base. Second, although a substantial proportion of these issues are sold in the United Kingdom, the broader investor base can, at times, produce a lower effective borrowing cost than domestic issues. This might also be due to more aggressive bidding by the broader spectrum of banks competing for Eurobond business. And third, Eurosterling bonds typically avoid the need for collateral or detailed restrictive covenants that are prevalent with domestic issues. While this point might be viewed as an important disadvantage by some investors, the fact that these Eurosterling securities are issued in bearer form attracts investors for whom anonymity is important.[7]

The principal lead managers in the new-issue market for Eurosterling bonds have traditionally been British merchant banks such as Samuel Montagu, Morgan Grenfell, and S.G. Warburg (see Table 9-3). In recent years, however, foreign banks have muscled into the top ranks. Credit Suisse First Boston rose to the number-one spot in the Eurosterling-underwriting league tables in 1987 and 1988 with a 17 and 16 percent market share, respectively. During 1986, it was ranked number four. Salomon took over the fourth-ranked slot in 1987 with an 8 percent market share and the third ranking in 1988, with a 14 percent market share.

The process of securitization that has advanced so dramatically in the United States has been notably slower in the United Kingdom. Asset-backed securities, for example, have gained favor only gradually. Despite the popularity of mortgage-backed securities in the United States, where 30 percent of all outstanding residential mortgages have been repackaged, the idea has been slow to catch on in the United Kingdom. In 1987, three mortgage companies launched six mortgage-backed floating-rate note (FRN) issues worth £700 million, only a tiny portion of the £150 billion total outstanding mortgages in the United Kingdom. The future growth of this market is uncertain. Because of their enormous retail-deposit funding base from extensive branch networks, British building societies (similar to U.S. savings and loan institutions) have not until recently felt the need for securitizing and liquidating assets.[8] At the prompting of British merchant banks and American investment banks, however, receptivity to securitizing assets and liabilities appears to be growing.

Similarly, domestic commercial paper and junk bonds (i.e., high-yield corporate debt) have been slow to catch on in the United Kingdom. Despite the Bank of England's 1986 authorization of sterling-denominated commercial paper and that paper's subsequent rapid

7. See "Recent Developments in the Corporate and Bulldog Sectors of the Sterling Bond Market," *Bank of England Quarterly Bulletin*, February 1988, pp. 62–68.
8. See "Does Britain Need Mortgage-Backed Securities?" *The Economist*, October 10, 1987, p. 77.

Table 9-3
Top Five Lead Managers of Sterling Issues, 1986 and 1987

Rank 1986*	Rank 1987	Bank	1986 Amount (£ millions)	1986 Number of Issues	1986 Share (%)	1987 Amount (£ millions)	1987 Number of Issues	1987 Share (%)
4	1	Credit Suisse First Boston	£1,140	8	11	£2,480	16	17
5	2	S.G. Warburg	964	10	10	2,284	15	16
3	3	Baring Brothers	1,643	9	15	2,053	17	14
—	4	Salomon Brothers	—	—	—	1,209	8	8
2	5	Morgan Grenfell	1,660	14	16	911	10	6

* In 1986, S. Montagu ranked number one, with a 16 percent market share.

Source: Annual Financing Report, *Euromoney*, March 1988.

growth, the total outstanding amount is still only a tiny fraction of sterling acceptances.[9] Further, because of the typical international distribution and placement, this very small market is usually known as the "Eurosterling" commercial-paper market. Junk bonds have not yet gained prominence in the United Kingdom, whereas in the United States they constitute a $180-billion market. To be sure, in the United Kingdom there is no domestic equivalent to the U.S. rating agencies like Standard & Poor's or Moody's, although informal assessments of the investment risks of different bond issues are made. Unlike municipal bonds in the United States, U.K. local government bonds are not given preferential tax treatment and, therefore, tend to yield slightly more than U.K. government gilts of comparable maturity.

U.K. Government Securities Trading

At the end of 1988, approximately 120 gilts issues were outstanding, with a total market value of approximately £140 billion ($250 billion). Of this amount, daily trading volume exceeded £1.5 billion ($2.5 billion). In contrast, at the end of 1988, approximately $100 billion of U.S. government securities were being traded on a typical day. The U.K. government securities have been traditionally classified as short (maturities up to five years), medium (maturities between five and fifteen years), long (maturities over fifteen years), and undated (perpetual). Short and medium gilts each have about 38 percent of the market. Long gilts account for most of the balance.

Gilts are referred to individually by name, coupon, and maturity. Most bonds are labeled either "exchequer" or "treasury" stocks, but a small number, such as the "Gas three percent 1990/95" or the "War Loan 3½ percent (undated)," have names that specify the purpose for which the bonds are issued. Interest on U.K. government bonds, often referred to as a "dividend," typically is paid semiannually net of withholding tax.[10]

Gilts are issued in one of several ways. First, the whole amount of bonds may be issued at a price determined by reference to the prevailing market yields given the coupon set on the bond. Second,

---

9. "Sterling CP: A Healthy Niche Operation," in *Commercial Paper*, a special supplement to the *Financial Times*, February 17, 1988, p. v.
10. Nonresidents, however, may apply to the Bank of England for exemption from withholding tax on a select number of gilts issues. Then, depending on the issue, interest is paid gross, or an amount withheld for taxes can be claimed through tax filings. These different tax features can cause significant yield differences between otherwise comparable gilts issues.

the bonds may be issued on a partly paid basis whereby subscribers are required to immediately pay a fixed portion with additional payments on specified later dates. Third, gilts may be issued on a "tap" basis, in which bonds are sold into the secondary market on a staggered basis over a period of time (perhaps ranging from several weeks to a few months) in response to market demand until the government's financing needs have been met. Finally, in 1987, the British government began experimenting on a limited basis with U.S. government-style bond auctions (as is also occurring in Tokyo).[11]

Although gilts are listed and traded on The Stock Exchange, all of the activity is "upstairs" in the dealing rooms of the banks rather than on the floor of The Exchange. Thus, an over-the-counter market is made among the twenty-four registered gilt dealers, not unlike the market created by primary dealers in U.S. Treasuries. With a highly liquid secondary market, gilts account for over 90 percent of the value of all fixed-income securities trading in the United Kingdom.

Recent developments in the U.K. government-securities trading market also provide an interesting illustration of the simultaneous effects of both deregulation and an influx of international competitors on a major domestic marketplace. Prior to October 1986, virtually all long-term gilts were traded on The Stock Exchange. Markets were made by jobbers quoting bid-and-offered prices to brokers, who collected purchase and sale orders directly from investing institutions and individuals. The two dominant jobbers, Akroyd & Smithers and Wedd Durlacher, shared approximately 80 percent of the market-making activity. Another five firms divided the remainder.

Following the 1983 decision to reregulate the British financial services industry, the Bank of England planned to alter the gilts market to conform to the pattern followed by the larger U.S. government-securities market. The Bank, in its role as fiscal agent for the British government, had a substantial stake in successful implementation of this change and David Walker, a senior executive of The Bank, was given the principal responsibility for the task. It was decided that incumbent as well as new market makers, to be called primary gilts dealers, would be permitted to join the new system and allowed to compete with bids and offers, thus creating an intradealer market to replace the existing Stock Exchange jobber-based market. In the new marketplace, the same firm could perform both the market-making and the sales functions, a role referred to as "dual capacity."

11. See "Britain Discloses Plan for Auctioning Government Bonds," *The Wall Street Journal*, April 14, 1987.

During 1985, the Bank of England interviewed a wide range of potential primary gilts dealers and decided to allow virtually all interested domestic and foreign participants, numbering over thirty, to enter the new market upon application. Although there were no stipulated qualifications, informal discussions with the Bank of England limited the formal applications to those vendors whose participation would be acceptable. A series of regulations was proposed that would require primary dealers to report on a daily, weekly, and monthly basis to the Bank of England regarding their positions, transactions, and operations. In addition, each new participant would be required to conduct operations through a separately capitalized subsidiary (most applicants were part of larger financial entities) with qualified personnel approved by the Bank of England. The "qualified personnel" requirement was significant in that the availability of experienced market makers and back-office staff was limited by the relatively small number of gilts jobbing firms that had operated under the old single-capacity system. The shortage of such personnel gave rise to substantial recruiting efforts and upward pressure on salaries, which were widely reported in the press during 1985 and 1986.

Deregulation and Consolidation

During the period leading up to Big Bang, British jobbing and broking firms were being acquired by larger financial services companies. Wedd Durlacher was acquired by Barclays Bank and Akroyd & Smithers was acquired by S.G. Warburg. In both cases, a substantial premium over book value was paid on acquisition, and various contractual and other methods were employed to retain key trading executives. In addition, various stockbroking firms with substantial gilts-broking business were acquired, including Greenwell by Samuel Montagu (a unit of Midland Bank), Wood Mackenzie by Hill Samuel, Pember & Boyle by Morgan Grenfell, Kitcat & Aitken by Orion Royal Bank, Gilles & Cresswell by Merrill Lynch, Messel & Co. by Shearson Lehman, and Phillips & Drew by Union Bank of Switzerland. Thus, substantial consolidation within the jobbing and broking community took place in 1985 and 1986, almost simultaneously with the selection process for primary dealers in the new gilts market.

In late 1985, the Bank of England announced that a total of thirty-one applications had been approved on a preliminary basis for participation in the new gilts market. This announcement caused concern among both current and prospective participants because of a feared decline in profitability with so many competitors. In the U.S.

Table 9-4
Primary Gilts Dealers Approved by the Bank of England in 1989

Aitken Campbell Gilts
Barclays de Zoete Wedd Gilts (controlled by Barclays Bank)
Baring, Wilson & Watford (controlled by Baring Brothers)
Bankers Trust Gilts
Cater Allen Securities
Chase Manhattan Gilts
Credit Suisse First Boston (Gilts)
Daiwa Europe (Gilts)
Gerrard & National Securities
Goldman, Sachs Government Securities (U.K.)
Greenwell Montagu Gilt-Edged
James Capel Gilts
Kleinwort Benson Gilts
Merrill Lynch Government Securities
J.P. Morgan Sterling Securities
NatWest Gilts
Nomura Gilts
Salomon Brothers U.K.
Shearson Lehman Hutton Gilts
S.G. Warburg, Akroyd, Rowe & Pitman, Mullens (Gilt-Edged)
UBS Phillips & Drew Gilts

---

government-securities market, which was more than ten times as large and more international, there were then only thirty-eight primary dealers. Following The Bank's announcement, four firms—J. Henry Schroder Wagg, Drexel Burnham Lambert, Bank of America, and Union Discount Co.—withdrew their applications. The remaining twenty-seven firms, which began operations in October 1986 as primary dealers, are listed in Table 9-4.

The list in Table 9-4 includes fourteen British-based competitors and thirteen foreign firms, of which ten were American. This list is almost as interesting as a reflection of those that did not apply as well as those that did. Among the major U.S. investment banks, Morgan Stanley alone was absent. None of the major German, Dutch, or Italian banks applied. Swiss Bank Corporation did not join, although its two major competitors established units. Japanese firms, following high-level discussions between the British and Japanese governments regarding reciprocity for financial institutions in each other's markets, were invited to submit applications in the fall of 1987, almost a year after Big Bang.[12]

The 1986 change in the gilts market was the most radical revision

---

12. "Nomura and Daiwa Keep Gilts Powder Dry," *Financial Times*, May 11, 1988, p. 28.

of this marketplace in many decades, so it is perhaps not surprising that there was a great deal of journalistic comment regarding the major houses' motives for participating (or not participating). For non-British firms, it is clear that many regarded the opening as an unusual, and perhaps unique, opportunity to enter a major government-securities market on almost equal terms with local competitors. Many international firms had come to regard a presence in the United Kingdom as a critical building block in a tri-city global strategy with New York and Tokyo. Although the sterling securities market was not as large as its Eurobond counterpart, approximately 12 percent of all gilts were held by non-U.K. investors, which, together with greater international confidence since the 1970s in sterling as a currency, suggested an opportunity for greater internationalization. In addition, several American firms had achieved significant success as trading firms both at home and in the London Euromarkets and saw gilts as a natural expansion of their product line.

For the principal British merchant banks and clearing banks, the opening of The Stock Exchange community to outside ownership was regarded as a major opportunity, and the gilts market, as part of the old Stock Exchange structure, was one of the most important sectors. Three of the four big clearing banks and several of the principal merchant banks entered the field through acquisition of brokerage firms, most of which had some gilts operations.

Hambros, Lazard Brothers, and N.M. Rothschild & Sons did not apply for gilts dealerships. As mentioned earlier, Schroder Wagg indicated an early interest but later withdrew. Most firms that chose not to enter expressed a view that profitability in the field would be depressed, perhaps for years to come, by excessive competition. There is evidence that several British firms that undertook primary dealerships shared these views but felt that this market sector was so central to their long-term strategies that they could not be absent. A number of these firms had substantial existing underwriting and dealing operations in Eurosterling and bulldog bonds and regarded it as unfeasible to continue these activities without a trading desk for gilts, off which these other issues were priced.

In addition to gilts trading and sales, the Bank of England also encouraged the development of interdealer brokers (IDBs), similar to those in the United States, that would arrange transactions between primary gilts dealers on an anonymous basis. Six such firms entered the new submarket, and a screen service was developed to show their bids and offers to which only the primary gilts dealers have access. The IDBs generally charge $\frac{1}{128}$ of 1 percent, or £78 per £1-million transaction. Although they act as principals in shifting positions among primary dealers, they do not make purchases for inventory.[13] Similarly, a handful of money brokers provide services to primary dealers by arranging loans of funds to carry long positions and loans of securities to allow the establishment of short positions. The IDBs and money brokers are often subsidiaries of diversified financial groups but generally have been independent of the major international investment banking groups that own primary gilts dealers.[14]

As many market observers had anticipated, trading conditions in the months following the new market's opening were very competitive and, for most firms, unprofitable on a fully costed basis. Not only did the number of dealers offering trading services increase, but the aggregate capital of the active firms rose from approximately £100 million under the old system to an estimated £700 million under the new regime. Reflecting the increased capital and staff in the new market, the typical dealer margin declined to a differential of ⅛ of 1 percent between bid prices and offer prices. This small amount replaced both the jobber's commission and, for institutional accounts, a broker's commission under the previous system. In these circumstances, it is perhaps not surprising that, amid forecasts of several years of required rationalization, several of the original twenty-seven entrants decided to discontinue operations. Two prominent early departures were those of Lloyds Bank in the summer of 1987 and RBC Gilts in the fall of that same year. Most other firms scaled back their operations in one fashion or another in response to the very competitive market conditions.

Other Securities Trading

Until the 1987 market collapse, secondary-market trading thrived in the United Kingdom, especially as a result of the growing importance of international securities activities in London. In addition to gilts, Eurobonds, domestic equities, and international equities are also traded. Turnover for 1988 on The Stock Exchange was £1.365 billion per day. Turnover for U.K. gilts averaged £2.060 billion per day. In addition to these figures, market sources estimate that roughly three-quarters of the annual $2,200 billion secondary-market turnover of Eurobonds passes through institutions located in the City.[15] (Although it is hard to establish a locus for Eurobond trading, most of the balance is believed to be traded elsewhere in Europe.) Total an-

---

13. "Inter-dealer Brokers: A Mechanism That Will Lubricate Sales," *Financial Times Special Survey: The City Revolution, Part 1,* p. viii.
14. "London Money Brokers: Chasing Fires," *The Economist,* August 8, 1987, p. 71.
15. "Pragmatic Approach to City Rules," *Financial Times Special Survey: The City Revolution, Part 2,* October 27, 1986, p. xxvi.

nual turnover of U.S. Treasury securities traded in London is estimated to exceed $500 billion.[16]

The introduction of new equity-trading arrangements in October 1986, particularly the initiation of The Stock Exchange automated quotation (SEAQ) system, resulted in the movement of the secondary-trading business physically away from The Exchange floor and into dealing rooms, where transactions are made through computer terminals or over the telephone on the basis of information carried on screens.

The International Stock Exchange regulations require member firms to register as market makers in certain securities and it imposes performance requirements accordingly.[17] Equities, for example, are divided into four categories for SEAQ. "Alpha" stocks are the most actively traded U.K. equities, about 150 in number. For these equities, a number of self-appointed market makers maintain continuous, firm two-way prices in a minimum size of 1,000 shares during mandatory SEAQ trading hours. However, with the depressed market conditions prevailing in 1988, market-making and reporting requirements were relaxed.

"Beta" stocks constitute a second rank of some 600 stocks based on volume of trading activity. A small group of registered market makers are charged with offering two-way quotes on SEAQ. Details of trades must be reported to The Exchange and are reported the following day.

"Gamma" stocks are less actively traded than beta stocks. They generally have at least two registered market makers, which are obliged to post only indicative bid-and-ask prices on SEAQ but must quote firm prices on inquiry.

"Delta" stocks, with the smallest trading volume, are the least liquid. The SEAQ screen does not show quotes for delta shares but gives information on registered market makers, which are committed to quote a price on inquiry.

The Exchange has both a listed securities and an unlisted securities market. The securities in the latter group are apt to fall into the gamma and delta categories. There is also an international SEAQ, which quotes prices on selected domestic and foreign-traded securities. Gilts and other fixed-income securities form a separate category, where market makers are required to display mid-prices only on SEAQ.

Transaction costs fell sharply after Big Bang, in part reflecting a

16. "More Products Now Need Round-the-Clock Trading," *Financial Times Special Survey: The City Revolution, Part 2,* October 27, 1986, p. xxvi.
17. This discussion draws on "Change in the Stock Exchange and Regulation of the City," *Bank of England Quarterly Bulletin,* February 1987, pp. 54–65.

reduction in the stamp tax. Also, increased competition from new entrants drove down both commission rates and the spread between the best bid-and-offer price, also called the "market touch." For example, the Bank of England estimated that for an equity transaction in the range of £100,000 to £1 million, commission rates fell from about 0.4 to 0.2 percent.[18]

Trading foreign securities in London has become an important business for merchant and investment banks. Any security listed on a recognized exhange overseas is eligible for trading under the auspices of the International Stock Exchange, whether or not the stock is formally listed in London. Market participants now estimate that more international equity is traded in London than U.K. domestic stock. Perhaps as much as $1 billion of foreign equity from over 600 companies is traded in London daily. In fact, home market governments of several countries, such as France and Germany, are concerned about the migration of share trading of local companies away from their domestic exchanges to London. Such migration means a loss of business in the home market and, potentially, a longer-term diminution in the local market's world standing.

The *Financial Times* surveyed 125 investment managers in October 1986 to rate various firms involved in secondary trading in London.[19] The top three firms in overall equity market making were Rowe & Pitman/Akroyd in first place, Barclays de Zoete Wedd second, and Hoare Govett third.[20] For the special segment of international equities, the top three in descending order were Goldman, Sachs, Rowe & Pitman, and Hoare Govett. The list for market making in gilts was topped by Greenwell Montagu, followed by Phillips & Drew, and then Barclays de Zoete Wedd. On the basis of overall secondary trading for all types of securities, investors rated James Capel first, Phillips & Drew second, and Hoare Govett third.

Research Activities

Traditionally, securities research in the United Kingdom has been the domain of the British brokerage houses. In the 1989 *Institutional Investor (International Edition)* All-British Research Team rankings, James Capel came out on top for the second year in a row, with Barclays de

18. On very large deals, the commission rate might have been as low as 0.125 percent. The market touch for alpha stocks fell from 0.8 percent to 0.6 percent. With the depressed markets and decreased liquidity in 1988, however, spreads and market touch generally increased.
19. "Thirteen Firms Under Scrutiny," *Financial Times Special Survey: The City Revolution, Part 2,* October 27, 1986, p. xxx.
20. Ibid.

Table 9-5
All-British Research Team

Rank		Firm
1988	1989	
1	1	James Capel
3	2	Barclays de Zoete Wedd
3	3	S.G. Warburg Securities
5*	4	UBS Phillips & Drew
2	5	County NatWest Securities
6**	6	Security Pacific Hoare Govett
15	7	Kleinwort Benson Securities
8	8	Kitcat & Aitken
12	9	Goldman, Sachs International
15	10	Morgan Stanley International
9	11	CL-Alexanders Laing & Cruickshank
12	12	Morgan Grenfell Securities
10	13	Smith New Court Securities
7	14	Citicorp Scrimgeour Vickers

* 1988 figures for Phillips & Drew.
** 1988 figures for Hoare Govett.
Source: *Institutional Investor* (*International Edition*), February 1989, p. 56.

Zoete Wedd second and S.G. Warburg third.[21] (See Table 9-5.) Some of the British brokerage houses, including top-ranked James Capel, have forgone market making and positioning securities; instead, they have continued to rely primarily on their research on domestic companies to fuel brokerage commissions.

Now, with the advent of a truly international equities market based in London, things are changing. American and Swiss firms are getting more actively involved in research, although it has proved a time-consuming and difficult task. Some market participants still complain that there is a scarcity of truly international research.[22] For example, there is an ongoing debate about whether researchers should split into teams covering individual markets, as in the United States, France, and Germany or whether each analyst should cover a separate industrial sector such as chemicals or textiles on a global basis. Clearly, international research will be an area of major emphasis in the future for merchant and investment banks in Lon-

21. "The 1989 All-British Research Team," *Institutional Investor* (*International Edition*), February 1989, p. 56.
22. See Martin French, "Room at the Top in Global Equities," *Euromoney*, April 1987, pp. 61–72.

don. However, with commission rates slashed in the wake of Big Bang, the subsidization of research activities may become a controversial issue within many firms. In a survey conducted in October 1986, the *Financial Times* reported that more than 60 percent of the investment managers contacted expected they would have to pay for research in some way in the future.[23]

Money Management

Money management has long been an important activity in the United Kingdom, especially over the past few years with the growth of international institutional funds based in London. It has been estimated that, before the October 1987 crash, $650 billion of assets were managed in London.[24] About $250 billion of this amount was in pension funds.[25] Of the balance, investment trusts accounted for just under $100 billion. Although the absolute amounts under management trail those in the United States, Japan, and Switzerland, London has become the dominant center for the management of international portfolios, with just under 20 percent of the total assets invested in foreign securities.[26]

A wide range of U.K. financial institutions are active in fund management, including insurance companies, pension managers, and merchant banks. Merchant banks with strong commitments to fund management include County Bank, Robert Fleming, Morgan Grenfell, Kleinwort Benson, and, through a 75 percent owned subsidiary, S.G. Warburg.

Annual revenues from management fees, averaging 0.3 percent of assets, total about $2 billion. The revenues from this business represent an attractive sum compared to an estimated combined income of only $800 million for the market makers in British equities. It is not surprising, therefore, that many financial firms have been eager to get into the London fund-management business.

The U.K. market is known for its plethora of unit and investment trusts, which served as models for the development of similar instruments in Japan. Unit and investment trusts are similar to U.S. mutual funds in that a holder owns a portion of a collective portfolio. The trusts typically are established and managed by merchant banks, in-

23. "Fund Managers Take a Wary View," *Financial Times Special Survey: The City Revolution, Part 2*, p. xxx.
24. "Profits with Honour," *The Economist*, August 8, 1987, p. 68.
25. "Pension Funds: Wasting Assets," *The Economist*, October 31, 1987, p. 73.
26. "Costs Under Scrutiny," *Financial Times Special Survey: International Fund Management*, November 19, 1986, p. i.

vestment banks, insurance companies, or independent managers. A unit trust is quite similar to open-end mutual funds, and the share price reflects the net asset value of the underlying securities held in the portfolio. Unit trusts are not listed on The Stock Exchange but can be bought and sold over the counter.

In contrast, an investment trust is a limited company whose shares are quoted and traded on The Stock Exchange. Investment trusts have a fixed capital base and are thus closed-end. They may borrow to leverage their investments to change their risk and return profile. Approximately 500 investment trusts were listed on The Stock Exchange in 1987, with a total market value of £30 billion.

Mergers and Acquisitions

Mergers and acquisitions (M&A) in the United Kingdom traditionally have been gentlemanly affairs generating modest fees for a select group of British merchant banks. Even contested British takeovers were, until recently, orderly affairs. Rules governing the conduct of M&A activities are set by the City Panel on Takeovers, a self-regulatory body closely associated with The Stock Exchange. Economic, competitive, and other aspects of proposed deals are reviewed by the secretary of state for Trade and Industry and the Office of Fair Trading, which may refer deals to the Monopolies and Mergers Commission (MMC). The MMC has the power to stop or dismantle a deal.[27]

As M&A deals in the United Kingdom ballooned in the mid-1980s, however, takeover tactics once considered taboo in London were introduced by some aggressive City merchant bankers. With 1,320 deals in 1986, for instance, the United Kingdom ranked second only to the United States in that year, which had a total of 4,024. Both countries showed a healthy increase over the previous year.[28] Further, 30 percent of the British deals were hostile.[29]

During 1988, the top firm acting as adviser for bids for U.K. and offshore companies was S.G. Warburg, followed by Schroder Wagg and Morgan Grenfell (see Table 9-6). Morgan Grenfell topped the league tables for defense against takeovers, followed by County Nat-

27. See Terry Garrett, "International Mergers and Acquisitions: Mounting a Counter-attack to U.K. Trading Abuses," *Mergers & Acquisitions*, July/August 1987, p. 65.
28. See Steve Coley, Sigurd Reinton, and Jack Welch, "International Mergers and Acquisitions: The High Mortality Rate in Plowing Unfamiliar Turf," *Mergers & Acquisitions*, July/August 1987, p. 58.
29. "The Global Advance of M&A: A Route to Distant Lands," *Mergers & Acquisitions*, July/August 1987, p. 88.

Table 9-6
*Ranking of Advisers for Bids for All U.K. Companies
and British Bids Abroad, 1988*

Rank	Adviser	Total Bid Value (£ millions)	Number of Bids
1	S.G. Warburg	15,446	84
2	Schroder Wagg	14,458	102
3	Morgan Grenfell	12,471	90
4	County NatWest	9,207	78
5	Shearson Lehman	8,668	37
6	Kleinwort Benson	8,117	57
7	Samuel Montagu	7,460	71
8	Lazard Brothers	5,590	56
9	N.M. Rothschild	5,220	62
10	Lazard Frères	5,104	3

Note: Value of some private bids not disclosed by advisers; totals do not include tender offers and buyouts of minority stakes.
Source: Financial Times, January 9, 1989.

Most Active Advisers to the Targets, 1988	
Adviser	Number of Companies
Morgan Grenfell	17
County NatWest	14
Kleinwort Benson	13
N.M. Rothschild	13
S.G. Warburg	13
Hambros Bank	10
Samuel Montagu	10
J. Henry Schroder Wagg	10

Source: Investors Chronicle, January 15, 1989.

West and Kleinwort Benson. However, with the arrival of American firms and their aggressive and sophisticated tactics, British dominance has been challenged on its home turf.

American investment banks, including Morgan Stanley, Goldman, Sachs, Salomon, and Shearson Lehman, have been quick to set up M&A staffs in London to take advantage of the burgeoning international takeover market.

Credit Suisse First Boston, sharing in the M&A strengths of its sister company in New York, has been very active in this area. Goldman, Sachs also became the first American firm to single-handedly advise in a major U.K. deal—the sale of British Caledonia to British Airways. In what may be more of an expression of hope than fact, the British bankers believe the upstart American firms still have to prove themselves to potential British clients. In the words of one S.G. Warburg director, "One swallow doesn't make a summer."[30] But it is evident that the M&A business in the United Kingdom had become much more competitive.

1988 Profit Problems

In the quieter, less buoyant securities markets following the crash of 1987, most equity market makers and gilts dealers experienced severe profitability problems. Those major banking institutions that, through aggressive acquisitions of complementary brokerage companies, had created their own integrated financial houses were, in 1988, faced with fierce competition and considerable losses. These pressures have resulted in some firms embarking on a dramatic slimming-down process in their securities operations.

In July 1988, Citicorp announced the closure of its gilts dealership in London; it has since reduced staff from 1,000 to 400 in its securities area. In August, Citicorp Scrimgeour Vickers and Phillips & Drew, like many others, began narrowing their equity market-making dealing spreads. Significant losses in equities and gilts during 1988 culminated in December, in particular, when Morgan Grenfell announced it was closing both areas simultaneously, resulting in a loss of 450 jobs. Hoare Govett (owned by Security Pacific) and Prudential-Bache also closed their gilts dealerships in December. Chase Manhattan closed its U.K. equities-dealing area at year's end, resulting in the loss of 135 jobs.

Nevertheless, other top market makers such as Barclays de Zoete Wedd, S.G. Warburg, Smith New Court, and Kleinwort Benson have resolved to continue their U.K. securities operations. Many of the integrated financial houses appear to be reverting to more specialist, rather than universal, roles, and the selective emphasis on investment management, banking, and corporate finance activities as a stabilizing influence is apparent. When the situation was eased by stronger equity markets in early 1989, some firms returned to profitability in Stock Exchange operations.

---

30. "A Hot New Export to Europe Takes Hold: The Hostile Takeover," *The Wall Street Journal*, April 21, 1988, p. 1.

Conclusions

The growth of the U.K. securities markets, reflecting the resurgence of the British economy and the increasing internationalization of world capital markets, has provided some attractive opportunities in recent years to a variety of financial services institutions, both domestic and foreign. British merchant and clearing banks, traditionally the main vendors of financial services in the United Kingdom, have been under pressure from the large number of foreign firms—particularly American—that have set up shop in London. By 1989, a general overcrowding had reduced profitability in several key areas, such as gilts trading and equity market making, and resulted in the dramatic closings of certain lines of business by both British and foreign firms.

Each business area has its own set of rules, client relationships, and customs. British firms are likely to continue to dominate those fields dependent on strong domestic relationships, such as U.K. privatizations. (It is difficult to envision for the foreseeable future a situation in which a non-British firm would be chosen to lead manage the U.K. tranche of a government-sponsored privatization.) Aggressive pricing by foreign firms, however, may win more mandates from British corporations, particularly if the demand for British securities increases among Japanese and American investors.

When the impact of the planned EEC market integration in 1992 is added to the already strong international financing movement, the pace of change is bound to further accelerate.

Certain other market areas that have become more like commodity businesses, characterized by high volumes but low profits, will be dominated by low-cost producers, regardless of nationality, as has already happened in the gilts market. A similar development might take place in domestic equity and bond trading. In the past, the Japanese have targeted just such markets in other settings as a means of gaining footholds.

The top British firms, along with the Americans and perhaps a limited number of major continental European institutions, are more likely to seek out high-value-added segments, such as international equity flotations and merger-and-acquisition work. Much to the chagrin of the British, the American firms have already become active in both areas. But it is uncertain whether there will be enough of this more lucrative business to go around. The firms that will remain on top in the London market are likely to be those that retain the flexibility to quickly seize successive new high-value-added segments as they appear.

CHAPTER 10

THE TOKYO CONNECTION: SALOMON BROTHERS' ASIAN STRATEGY

Since its founding in 1910, Salomon Brothers has progressed from an obscure money broker to a world-class securities underwriter and trader. Up through World War II, the firm built on its initial dealing and trading expertise in short-term instruments to become a significant force in a wider array of secondary markets and a more active distributor of new issues. However, it was only with industry changes in the 1960s and 1970s and the timely influx of a new generation of younger managers (William—"Billy"—Salomon and John Gutfreund prominently among them), that the firm ascended to the front ranks of the business. The inflationary pressures of the 1970s, deregulation in the United States, the growth of offshore markets, and "securitization" of formerly illiquid financial assets and liabilities also created openings for the firm.

Before the stock market crash in October 1987, Salomon was one of a handful of leading global investment bankers, with highly visible operations not only in the United States but also in London and Tokyo. Yet by the middle of 1988, the firm was seriously stumbling in important sectors of its business, and the public press was loudly trumpeting the humbling of what had been a seemingly invincible financial giant. A useful way of examining this turn of events is to look at the striking contrast between the parent's performance over time and that of its largely autonomous Tokyo operation. Clearly, Tokyo was now Salomon's "jewel in the crown," and the differences in recent strategies of the two entities are instructive.

A Modest Money Broker Makes Good: 1910–1945

In 1910, at a time when the great European merchant bankers could boast of several centuries of successful operations, and when J.P. Morgan and Jacob Schiff held forth in the United States, the brothers Salomon—Arthur, Herbert, and Percy—set up their firm and capitalized it at a meager $5,000. Later in the year, the founding triumvirate was joined by Morton Hutzler, scion of the Hutzler Department Store family in Philadelphia. The fledgling operation, under the name

233

Discount House of Salomon Brothers and Hutzler, was admitted to membership in the New York Stock Exchange that same year.

Closely patterned after the traditional English discount houses, the startup focused its efforts in the short-term money markets, arranging collateralized loans between commercial banks and Big Board–member firms and making secondary markets in discounted short-term securities, mostly issued by municipalities. With success in these businesses and with the ever increasing depth of the debt markets, the firm subsequently moved from arranging loans for brokers to trading in the short end of the fixed-income sector.

Their competence broadened during and after World War I. In 1915, the firm began trading U.S. Treasuries on the NYSE floor and also engaged in primary underwriting and selling for the first time, though only for foreign governments. In 1917, the firm was designated an authorized Treasury dealer (with the result that by the late 1970s Salomon was the longest-serving dealer in the government market among banks and securities firms). It was already beginning to acquire a reputation as a large block trader of foreign- and domestic-debt securities. In the mid 1920s, it was one of the first brokers to utilize the swapping of old portfolio securities for new ones (a mode of distribution still much used in current markets), in which a dealer buys outstanding securities from an institution to facilitate purchase of a new offering. The firm also dealt in the distribution of foreign bonds in the United States (including such speculative issuers as "Gov't of Argentine Nation," "Republic of Cuba," "Kingdom of Hungary," and "Czecho'Slovakia"). Dealings were undertaken in preferred stock and, in the firm's first move into the long-term end of the markets, municipal bonds. It was also during this period that the firm strengthened its distribution capability by opening regional sales offices in Chicago, Boston, and Cleveland.

Salomon Brothers and Hutzler weathered both the stock market crash of 1929 and the subsequent depression of the 1930s in reasonably good form and continued in most of its business lines. Additional sales offices were opened in San Francisco and Dallas in 1931 and 1932, respectively. Another harbinger of the firm's future development was a $43-million Swift & Co. 3¾ percent first-mortgage issue managed and distributed by Salomon in 1935. The largest single offering since the promulgation of the Securities Act of 1933, the issue was also the first to employ the simplified prospectus form allowed under the Act.

Industry Change Aids Salomon's Rise

Its growth from humble money-broking roots notwithstanding, Salomon entered the post–WWII period as a marginal player in the U.S.

securities markets. The firm's activities remained largely confined to secondary trading and sales, with almost no presence in origination, especially equities, and no position at all in value-added areas of corporate finance as mergers and acquisitions and corporate reorganizations. It is worth noting that Salomon (along with another contemporary distribution leader, the retail-oriented Merrill Lynch) was not even included among the seventeen firms named in the Justice Department's 1947 antitrust suit against the investment banking industry. This omission—and indeed the very filing of the suit—reflected the tight and clubbish configuration of the American securities industry at that time.

The investment banking business had been long dominated by a small group of firms, whose hold was reinforced by the exclusion of commercial banks by the Glass-Steagall Act in 1933. In the wake of Glass-Steagall, the business assumed more clearly the form of an oligopoly that was the province of a handful of private partnerships. Two notable examples were the bluest of the "blue blood" houses, Morgan Stanley (formed by a group of ex–J.P. Morgan partners) and The First Boston Corporation (spun off from the brahmin First National Bank of Boston and the Mellon Securities Corporation). These firms exploited longstanding corporate ties formed before 1933 to preserve paramount positions in the finance-origination business.

Salomon Brothers enjoyed no standing in this group. Along with the myriad retail "wire houses" (the precursors of such firms as Merrill Lynch and Shearson), which had staggered through the depressed 1930s, Salomon was considered beyond the pale. At the time (and indeed through the 1960s), the culture of the firm was "white sock" rather than "white shoe," with employees traveling in from Brooklyn by subway rather than from tonier midtown.

Another key theme of the culture was its trading element. The hustling, "what's-the-spread" flavor did not just reflect the firm's early focus on the secondary-trading part of the business; the milieu also resulted from the absence of other means of obtaining business and revenues. Without the benefits of blue blood or the bonds of old-school ties, the firm depended on what one analyst referred to as "its sixth sense of spread."[1] The trading culture was not genteel, even among its members; at this early point the firm was already known for being fiercely competitive internally.

One enthusiastic exponent of this approach in the postwar era was Gutfreund, a young municipal bond trader who joined the firm in 1953. Gutfreund's background was comfortable and well connected. He grew up in the affluent New York suburb of Scarsdale and

---

1. *Financial Times*, October 13, 1987, p. 21.

attended the good local high school, where he dabbled in thespian and musical pursuits. His father was the prosperous owner of a trucking concern and a wholesale meat business. Gutfreund's father also found time to play an occasional round of golf with Billy Salomon, a member of Salomon's founding family. After graduation from Oberlin College—where he majored in general literature and English—and two years in the Army, the young Gutfreund started in Salomon's statistical department at the invitation of Billy Salomon. Gutfreund soon moved into trading municipals, where he distinguished himself sufficiently to be made a partner at the relatively young age of thirty-four.

Gutfreund was the leading member of a new class of young managers who had joined Salomon in the postwar years. The group had ambitions to elevate Salomon beyond its debt-trading roots to become a force in the underwriting of negotiated debt and equity offerings. Regulatory, market, and macroeconomic developments all helped to make this possible. One business opening for those excluded from negotiated financings was competitive bidding, in which investment banks (singly or in syndicates) bid directly on a lowest-cost basis for debt securities being offered by issuers. The firm would, in turn, reoffer the securities to investors, in Salomon's case to institutions, since it had no retail outlets. The profit for the transaction would be derived from the fee or "gross spread" that was added onto the price paid by investors. The gross spread was composed of: 1) a *management* fee, paid to the managing underwriters for their services in structuring and documenting the deal and in assembling the underwriting syndicate; 2) an *underwriting* fee, paid on a pro-rata basis to all syndicate members for assuming the risk of the underwriting; and 3) a *selling concession* to compensate members of the syndicate for the amounts of the issue they actually sold to customers.

The competitive-bidding business was risky, since the underwriters needed not only to win the bid, but to price it to leave enough money for their fees; this would ensure compensation for the cost of money they were putting at risk. It would hopefully also leave some margin to spare in the event the market moved unfavorably during the time required to offload the securities to investors (usually a period of a few days). Obviously, those firms with the best knowledge of, and contacts with, large investors were able to distribute competitive-bid paper most expeditiously and therefore could be most aggressive on the bid itself. Previous experience in similar situations—such as Treasury security auctions—helped.

Salomon possessed the required resources. Recently, the competitive-bid market had been broadened significantly by regulatory developments. In 1941, the SEC, concerned by the cozy, oligopolistic nature of negotiated underwriting of utilities' debt, had stipulated (under Rule U-50 of the Public Utility Holding Company Act of 1940) that such companies raise their debt capital using competitive-bid financing. In a similar move after 1944, the Interstate Commerce Commission required railroads to employ competitive bidding. Largely at Gutfreund's urging and under his direction, Salomon aggressively entered the competitive-bid side of the underwriting business. The initiative also extended to a broadened presence in competitive bidding for long-term general-obligation municipal bonds (securities that, uniquely, commercial banks were also allowed to continue to underwrite under the Glass-Steagall Act).

Salomon's efforts in these sectors, though risky, quickly began to bear fruit. One factor in its success was a secular change in the markets for investment capital: *institutionalization* of capital. The huge post–World War II growth of financial intermediaries—insurance companies, pension funds (both public and private), and mutual funds—was shifting the locus of the prime source of investment capital, particularly debt capital, away from individual investors and toward large institutions. A number of securities firms focusing on the needs of these investors, especially their information needs, had begun to prosper, including the brash young interloper, Donaldson Lufkin & Jenrette. DLJ had created its own niche by providing institutions for the first time with detailed research reports on the equity securities of publicly traded U.S. companies.

Salomon Brothers and Hutzler focused its research on debt securities. In 1961, it organized its own institutionally targeted bond-market research department, under the stewardship of economist Sidney Homer, who was joined shortly thereafter by a young economist named Henry Kaufman. The department provided large investors with market, interest rate, and economic analysis. Like DLJ in equities, Salomon plowed new ground in debt security analysis, pioneering the new concepts of duration (the weighted-average length of the cash flows from an investment) and convexity (a description of bond-pricing behavior reflecting duration) in an almost academic frame of reference. The theoretical flavor foreshadowed the later days of the quantitatively oriented "rocket scientists," whom Salomon and others recruited from academia in the 1970s and 1980s to synthesize new securities and build the information systems needed to establish liquid markets for trading and arbitrage in a variety of new instruments.

In 1963, Salomon was instrumental in banding together with Blyth, Merrill Lynch, and Lehman Brothers to form the "Fearsome

Foursome" underwriting group. They had broken away from the established bidding groups because their ambitions for advancement within those groups—ambitions they thought were justified by strong performances in the distribution of issues—had been frustrated. Their move was revolutionary because for many years there had existed only two competing syndicates: one led by Morgan Stanley (to which the Fearsome Foursome had belonged and continued to belong for smaller deals); the second led by Halsey, Stuart (itself destined to be later absorbed by the wire house Bache & Co.).

The Fearsome Foursome enjoyed significant success. By 1966, Salomon was the leader in competitive bidding for utility offerings in the public markets. By 1970, its leadership had spread to the entire competitive-bid sector, which Salomon had led for four of the previous five years. Successes on the competitive-bid side and in debt underwriting inspired parallel moves on the equity side. In 1963, the firm entered the equity markets for the first time in a big way with the formation of a commercial bank stock department. Taking the example of the firm's successful entry into debt underwriting, the initial effort was confined to secondary-market making in commercial bank stocks. Salomon gradually built skills in trading so that by the late 1960s, the firm had emerged as one of the leading block positioners and traders in a wide variety of equity securities. Part of this effort involved obtaining membership in regional stock exchanges: in 1965, Salomon became a member firm of the Detroit, Boston, Philadelphia-Washington-Baltimore, and Pacific Coast exchanges. Another initiative, especially to bolster equity credibility with institutions, was the formation of an industry and stock research department in 1969. About that time, a separate corporate finance department had been formed. Previously, such activities had been handled by the statistical research department, where Gutfreund had trained.

As a result of the advances made by Salomon and by Merrill Lynch (the latter was often disparaged by its investment banking competitors as the plebeian "thundering herd" or "we, the people" in view of its retail orientation), these two distribution-oriented firms were gradually accepted into the charmed circle of the "special bracket" of U.S. underwriting firms, which was limited to the top four or five securities firms in the Wall Street hierarchy.

Growing securities businesses can operate only from large bases of capital, and a number of U.S. firms moved to lock in theirs during the late 1960s and early 1970s. Several, including DLJ, Merrill Lynch, Dean Witter, PaineWebber, Bache, Hutton, and Shearson Hayden Stone shocked Wall Street by committing the ultimate apostasy—going public. Salomon, while not joining their ranks, had long been preoccupied with building its capital base. Beginning in 1958, it adopted strict rules on withdrawals by its partners, making them look wealthy on paper but giving them only a modest amount of cash income to live on. Only Goldman, Sachs among the other major partnerships had a similar discipline. The rest of the Street was content, like their British merchant banking cousins, to pay out most earnings to their partners, remaining confident that in relationship investment banking, expertise and long association, rather than capital, were the essential ingredients. This capital-building process was to continue throughout the 1970s.

The Gutfreund Era

In 1978, Gutfreund took over as managing partner of Salomon—succeeding the man who had hired him, Billy Salomon—and accelerated Salomon's diversification into all aspects of the securities business. Despite all its successes, Salomon was still viewed as essentially a bond-trading house. True, the 1970s had seen the beginnings of its international expansion. The firm had opened a regional office in London in 1972 to serve British, continental, and Middle Eastern clients. And in 1973, Salomon started operating in the decade-old Euromarkets for the first time, trading Eurodollar certificates of deposit and Eurodollar bonds in London under the direction of Ed Aronson (who, after leaving the firm at the end of the 1970s, filed a compensation claim against his old firm that became one of the few, uncharacteristic instances of bad publicity for Salomon in the early 1980s). By 1976, it had begun to co-manage and distribute Euro-offerings in a variety of currencies, and in the following year, it established a European syndicate department in London. In 1980, Salomon looked eastward, entering the Tokyo marketplace with a branch that was to grow impressively in size and in perceived presence. The firm's capital then stood at $208.7 million, the largest among the remaining Street partnerships. But Salomon was nonetheless seen as primarily a bond house, respected for its trading prowess but regarded warily for its eccentricity.

In reality, all the ingredients for explosive growth were present, awaiting only an activist hand. The firm's basic competences—trading expertise, institutional-investor ("buy-side") thinking, and distribution capability—were well respected and deeply rooted. Basic macroeconomic factors, notably inflation and the increasing tendency of corporations and governmental units to finance growth with publicly issued debt capital, favored well-capitalized, institutional bond houses like Salomon. Escalating federal deficits in the 1970s and 1980s created growth in the Treasury securities markets and provided another arena for the trader. And the SEC's streamlining of corporate-underwriting procedures (including the introduction of shelf registrations in 1982) likewise shifted the market toward large and quick debt financings, which demanded that underwriters have huge amounts of ready capital and rapid distribution capability for aggressive underwriting commitments.

The practice of securitization, or the creation of tradable securities through the bundling of assets with associated cash flows, also played to Salomon's strengths. In the three years leading up to 1981, Salomon established an overwhelming predominance in the burgeoning mortgage-backed market. This area, headed by Lewis Ranieri, a former mailroom clerk who had joined the firm in 1968, provided well in excess of half the firm's profits during that period. Salomon led the market with most of the important innovations—conventional pass-throughs, GNMAs, and variable pass-throughs—and prospered mightily. Salomon's innovative success was to continue through the 1980s, with the principle of securitization being applied beyond mortgages to automobile-loan receivables, Treasury securities, and computer leases, among other financial assets. These activities benefited from Salomon's highly regarded distribution capabilities, especially on hard-to-place offerings.

Although Salomon continued the aggressive use of its capital during these years to support business expansion, by 1981 Gutfreund had concluded that additional capital beyond its current base of $300 million would be required if the firm was to exploit all the attractive opportunities available. Two feasible means of raising capital were available: a public offering of part or all of the firm's equity or the sale of the whole—or a portion—of the firm to a deep-pocketed outsider. In view of unfavorable equity market conditions, the initial public offering (IPO) option was rejected in favor of a sale of the whole firm for $554 million to Philipp Brothers, a giant (if obscure) commodities trader, broker, and processor with an international orientation, large European operations, and significant South African ownership interests. Philipp dwarfed Salomon in size and was at that juncture riding the cresting wave of historically unprecedented world commodity prices to high profitability. In 1980, the firm had achieved a 45 percent return on its equity.

The timing and handling of the new alliance caused a stir in the public press. Gutfreund negotiated the deal in secret with the acquiescence of the firm's executive committee, which he dominated. Then, the shocked sixty-two general partners were presented with a fait accompli at a hastily called weekend meeting. Billy Salomon, the senior surviving member of the founding family and the man who had recruited, trained, and ultimately tapped Gutfreund as his successor, was informed of the deal only after its consummation. The active partners obtained a premium of more than twice the book value, including a $30-million payment to Gutfreund. Billy received no premium on the ownership stake he had surrendered when he had retired—and was paid the book value of the capital he had in the firm, or roughly $10 million. Gutfreund assumed his new title as co-chairman of the newly merged concern, Phibro-Salomon, holding in addition the office of CEO of Salomon Brothers, which was retained as a separate securities-operating subsidiary.

Gutfreund's ambitions were not long constrained by his subordinate position to David Tendler, the chairman of Philipp Brothers who ruled as sole CEO of Phibro-Salomon. The commodities boom of the 1970s ended virtually as the merger was consummated, and the junior partner—Salomon Brothers—soon displaced its recent acquirer as the principal profit generator of the combination. By August 1984, only three years after the merger, Tendler was unseated in a palace revolution widely thought to have been engineered by Gutfreund; he was blamed for the poor performance of Philipp Brothers and forced out after a plan for Tendler to lead a management buyout of the majority of Philipp's operations proved abortive. Gutfreund became the sole CEO of Phibro-Salomon. The next year, 1985, was Salomon's best ever, with earnings of $557 million.

Overextension and Management Controls

Huge profits and the realization of Gutfreund's expansion goals came only at the cost of a departure from the firm's proven and gradualist trading orientation. On the surface, the firm's performance remained strong. Salomon led the world in underwriting in each of the years 1983–1987, using its finely tuned trading expertise and distribution power to dominate the commodity end of the issuance business (that is, the straight-debt underwritings with very thin margins). However, Salomon's accelerated expansion and diversification efforts created strains. The critical factor was that the trading and distribution culture underlying the firm's success—embodied most of all by "The Room," the football-field–sized trading hall that constituted the firm's nerve center and the site of Gutfreund's principal office—incorporated no managerial control system sufficient to the task of stewarding the firm's expansion in a prudent manner. Indeed, despite a daily net securities position running in excess of $20 billion, the firm was not to adopt a budgeting procedure until March 1987, when it also appointed its first chief financial officer.

The lavish spending plans on people and premises created an overhead level that was especially dangerous in view of Salomon's low-margin business mix and its dependence on favorable markets and trading results. The headlong rush into a variety of businesses, including even sterling mortgage origination in Britain, was a premature extension of the previous pattern of leveraging trading and distribution skills into broadened services and higher value-added expertise. Without internal controls to monitor its pace, Salomon's push into new businesses and high-priced overhead became perilous. The growth in the firm's workforce was dramatic. The head count at Salomon Brothers (not including Philipp Brothers) shot from 2,300 to 6,800 between 1981 and 1987; 40 percent of the increase came in the single year of 1986. In the past, the firm had employed a highly selective recruiting process: it had not done much formal recruiting at colleges and universities, depending instead on referrals and self-directed applicants. Now, the new people did not carry the Salomon culture of gradualism and many lacked basic trading skills. Unconstrained by supervisory control systems, the new hires contributed to a series of disastrous trading losses in 1986 and 1987.

The altered policy on the physical plant seemed even more incongruous. For years, Salomon had existed in cramped offices at 30 Wall Street. Theirs had been a low-margin business—a game where if you watched the dimes and nickels, the dollars would take care of themselves. Then, in 1970, the firm moved to new and larger premises at One New York Plaza. "The Room" was recreated on an even larger scale, complete with a visitors' gallery in the style of the Big Board—a feature put to effective promotional use. By the mid-1980s, however, staff, particularly in the newly expanded areas of investment banking, were once again spilling into the hallways and stairwells.

Clearly, expenditure on expanded accommodations was required to maintain employee effectiveness. What was surprising was the level and the lavishness of the expenditure. Critics questioned whether the firm's leadership had become afflicted by an edifice complex when details of the monumental $1.5-billion Columbus Circle project were made public. It was quickly dubbed "The Shadow" by Jacqueline Onassis and other critics for its projected submersion of vast spreads of Central Park in premature gloom on winter afternoons. Another locus of the spending spree was London. An expensive lease on palatial new headquarters for the London operations, Victoria Plaza, near Buckingham Palace, was signed in November 1985.

Fits of Reorganization and a Tentative Return to Tradition

The most unambiguous evidence of future shock at Salomon was its passage through a period of almost uninterrupted administrative turmoil and personnel turnover. Long before the watershed of the October 1987 market crash, the firm suffered through recurrent reorganizational spasms. Indeed, the years 1984–1988 seemed to have been years of almost continual organizational upset, with an autumnal rhythm gradually emerging centering on October as the preferred month for metamorphosis.

Following Gutfreund's successful coup in August 1984, the autumnal cycle was inaugurated at Philipp Brothers. In October of that year, it was announced that 100 of that subsidiary's 700 U.S. employees would be dismissed by the end of the year.[2] The next reorganization, at Salomon Brothers in January 1985, was presented in an upbeat manner, though its initiatives suggested that communication and coordination were already suffering, with massive growth still in the offing. In that month, the equity sales, trading, and research departments were restructured into two groups to better integrate these functions with investment banking. A new equity group was created encompassing sales, trading, and arbitrage, and a new, equity capital-markets group was established to act as a liaison with investment banking.[3]

October 1985 brought a further, more extensive retrenchment at beleaguered Philipp Brothers. A 600-person reduction in worldwide staffing was announced, with the heaviest layoffs in marketing and distribution.[4] These cutbacks sparked the latest rumors in the following month that Salomon planned to sell Philipp or else go private. Similar rumors had followed the combined firm almost from before the time the ink had dried on the 1981 merger agreement. In January 1983, *Fortune* reported that the 1981 deal might be unwound! In June 1984, *BusinessWeek* enticed Street gossips with claims that a "certain" plan was in motion for the sale of the combined firm's nonenergy commodity–trading businesses to a Tendler-led group for $500 million—the only certain result of which was the swift departure of Tendler and a number of his confederates.[5]

October 1986 brought another management revolution. Prompted seemingly by a gathering sense of reorganizational drift and incipient

2. *The Wall Street Journal*, October 6, 1984, p. 4.
3. *American Banker*, January 7, 1985, p. 55.
4. *New York Times*, October 29, 1985, pp. 33, 45.
5. *BusinessWeek*, June 14, 1984, pp. 114, 118.

insurrection, especially among the firm's investment banking professionals, Gutfreund created a number of new administrative entities
and promoted some key lieutenants. A new nineteen-member board
of directors was created for the principal Salomon Brothers unit, to be
peopled in great part by upcoming stars in hitherto neglected areas
such as corporate finance. The charter of the new board was to assist
the nine-member executive committee in running Salomon Brothers,
especially in determining the firm's future strategic direction. A ten-
member capital-commitments committee was also set up to oversee
the firm's entry into merchant banking. Merchant banking, a term
that originally referred to the trade-oriented financing of British private banks in the eighteenth and nineteenth centuries, in the U.S.
context involved the investment of the firm's capital in transactions as
part of the investment banking service. This participation could take
several forms: short-term (bridge) loans, needed to close a transaction, which would be refinanced later; intermediate loans; purchases
of warrants and options; and direct equity investment. In the early
1980s, a number of Wall Street firms, most notably First Boston and
Merrill Lynch, had become deeply committed to this business, investing both their own capital and money from publicly offered funds
designed for such investment. Even commercial banks of all shapes
and sizes had jumped into the rapidly growing lending avenue.

Though much in vogue, merchant banking, with its long-term
commitments of capital, was a business profoundly different from the
in-and-out type of trading and debt underwriting traditionally practiced by Salomon. Moreover, entry into this sector was deeply opposed by several of the most prominent figures at the firm, including
Wall Street legend Kaufman. Indeed, Kaufman stepped down from
his positions as vice chairman of the parent firm and as member of its
board over the very issue of merchant banking, concluding:

> We cannot escape the fact that we have some financial
> responsibility. We are not just in the business of pushing com-
> panies around. There is the ultimate issue of whether we in the
> financial community should be moving into the area of specu-
> lative capitalism. . . . We are all going to be tainted by this
> entrepreneurial drive. . . .[6]

But the voices of old-guard advocates of restraint were weakened
by a management reshuffle. Three of the firm's brightest stars—
Thomas W. Strauss, the top Treasury trader; Lewis Ranieri, mortgage

6. *New York Times*, November 16, 1986, p. 8.

head; and William J. Voute, head of corporate finance—were made vice chairmen of Salomon Brothers. Strauss was widely hailed as the anointed successor, while Ranieri and Voute were seen as welcome additions to overburdened senior management. Voute in particular seemed game for an aggressive move into new businesses. Speaking of merchant banking, Voute indicated, "It's something we haven't done before, but obviously we're being forced to change; you have to wake up to reality. We're consumed with thinking about it."[7]

Unfortunately, within nine months a different sort of reality became evident. Ranieri left Salomon in the midst of yet another demoralizing reorganization. He was a Horatio Alger-like figure who by that time had become a loose cannon within the firm, exercising vast influence because of the profitability of his operation but accused of being an insurgent factionalist intent on building his own empire. The mortgage innovator's departure also hinted at the extent to which management relationships and communications had become attenuated at the rapidly expanding company. In April 1987, Gutfreund had gone public with some of his worries during an unusual round of analyst presentations and press briefings. While expressing his confidence in Salomon's "strong management relationships" and emphasizing the smooth running of the firm, Gutfreund warned of perils being run by Wall Street firms that were expanding too rapidly, thereby not only losing control over employees and standards, but jeopardizing their very futures in an era of instantaneous commitments of huge amounts of capital.[8] At the time, Gutfreund told a news magazine that "Our problem is symptomatic of Wall Street's problem. The business has grown faster than our ability to manage it."[9] Perhaps more ominously, the same article quoted a former Salomon manager as saying, "The firm has grown so quickly that it's lost any sense of its old culture. They are going to have to spend a fair amount of time putting their arms around all these new people and trying to get them all to work together."[10]

One man not embraced was Ranieri. In July 1987, he was forced out by Gutfreund himself, long seen almost as a surrogate father to the rags-to-riches mortgage pioneer. The broader reorganization brought a sweeping realignment of trading and investment banking activities. Sales and trading of *all* debt—governments, municipals, corporates, mortgage and real estate, and money markets—were consolidated in one new group, while all finance activities—mortgage,

7. Ibid.
8. *American Banker*, April 30, 1987, pp. 3, 11.
9. *BusinessWeek*, April 20, 1987, pp. 72–73.
10. Ibid.

corporates, municipals—were similarly unified. While Gutfreund explained that the restructuring was designed to "eliminate non-economic things, redundancies, and the creation of separate businesses," the specter of factionalism haunted another of his remarks: "We had this huge new business of securitization. When you create one huge new business, securitization, there is a temptation to have it build a separate culture, which we don't want." An executive at a competitor put it more bluntly: "They're showing they will sacrifice 6–9 months' worth of business to get rid of the Ranieri cult."[11]

One question was whether these moves amounted to anything other than the banishment of a charismatic, but troublesome figure who was perhaps threatening to Gutfreund's pre-eminence. In the late summer of 1987, speaking to a group of new hires following Ranieri's sacking, Gutfreund characterized the recent organizational change this way: "It was something like changing from the Sun King to rule by the Office of the Chairman, a Board of Directors, and committees."[12]

But the measures of July 1987 soon proved insufficient. Early retrenchment was required in the wake of the pell-mell expansion of the previous three years. This was the conclusion of a three-month, internally produced strategic study of the firm and its prospects that was launched at the onset of the Ranieri imbroglio and completed in September. The firm had announced a hiring freeze in late August, but in the end, Gutfreund's hand was forced by the threat of a potential hostile bid for his company. The price of Salomon's shares was depressed from previous highs, and the need to keep looking over its shoulder to see who might be sniffing out a bargain was undoubtedly on management's mind. When a large block of stock held by South African interests was put on the block, takeover entrepreneur Ronald Perelman made threatening noises. The end of September brought relief when legendary "value" investor Warren Buffett made a large enough capital investment to allow the hot block of shares to be retired.

The organizational changes of October 1987 were indeed more like the genuine article, occurring at a chaotic juncture externally and sparked by the activities of insurgents and subversives internally. Although announced before the crash—specifically, seven days before Black Monday—the measures came in the midst of a deteriorating market and during a period of poor results for Salomon itself. Inside the firm, a long-brewing battle between the traditionally domi-

11. *The Wall Street Journal*, July 24, 1987, p. 2.
12. *Financial Times*, October 13, 1987, p. 27.

nant sales and trading side and the relative newcomers on the investment banking side was coming to a head. The bankers had long thought that at Salomon they had received little respect and had been starved of the resources commensurate with their proven results and their future potential. This was especially true in light of the large losses reported throughout 1987 in trading, particularly in municipal bonds, and in the British Petroleum underwriting, in which the firm lost over $60 million after taxes (world stock markets crashed three weeks after Salomon and the other underwriters had guaranteed the British Government a fixed price; they, in effect, had pre-bought the deal).

Emotions at the firm were running high when drastic expense cuts of October 12 were announced, just one week before the market crash. The medicine was tough, if tardy, in its dispensing. The most important measures included a 12 percent reduction in the head count to save $150 million, with postcut levels to be maintained through 1988; total abandonment of the municipal, commercial-paper, and short-term bank liability markets; a scuttling of the plan to move to "The Shadow"; and a $60–$70 million write-off to net worth to provide for expenses associated with the retrenchment. Additionally, Bruce Carp was appointed as hatchet man, with responsibility only to Gutfreund. A member of the Salomon Brothers board, Carp was charged with pursuing additional draconian economies over the intermediate term.

The brunt of the October 1987 cuts fell on the London office, where the departure from Salomon's traditional developmental patterns was the most striking. The office head count had surged from 200 to 650 in the three years prior to November 1985, when the Victoria Plaza lease was signed. It appeared that the new facilities might themselves soon be inadequate, as staff expanded another 40 percent in 1986 in the heady pre-Big Bang City atmosphere. By October 1987, the London employee total was 1,000. In its business mix there, Salomon had followed no consistently logical plan other than espousing the then-fashionable nostrum of the necessity of "across the board/ around the globe" competence and scope in the emerging global market of the 1980s. Caught up in the hoopla of Big Bang, the firm entered a broad variety of markets, from gilts to sterling commercial paper to Eurocommercial paper. Salomon even opened a mortgage origination subsidiary, The Mortgage Corporation (TMC), to generate the raw material for sterling mortgage-backed securities. Building societies, the British equivalents of American thrifts and the primary lenders to the housing market, were prohibited by law from selling mortgages off their books. Lacking this source, Salomon executives believed a captive originator was necessary. In its first substantial foray into the retail side of financial services, Salomon aggressively promoted TMC's services, including extensive mailings and even television commercials to promote mortgages-by-mail. True, the subsidiary's solicitation efforts were limited to the mail-order medium, with slim staffing and minimal "bricks-and-mortar" facilities. The link with Salomon itself was downplayed, and the staff employed were exclusively British. Nevertheless, the entry of Salomon into a retail business in a market of questionable size, which could easily be monopolized by local players with only a minor change in the regulations, must have struck some observers as perverse.

By contrast, the decision to exit overnight both the entire municipal finance sector (clients who called about deals already in process were peremptorily told to look elsewhere) and the short-term money market business dumbfounded the investment community. Salomon had held what was generally conceded to be the number-one position in municipal finance and was a strong competitor in the short-term instruments area as well. Despite management's contention that these were marginal businesses likely to be overwhelmed by the entry of commercial banks into the securities area, other securities firms had made good profits servicing these sectors and were additionally convinced that there were synergies with other parts of the securities business that mandated at least a modest presence in those market sectors.

Gutfreund's public image was also undergoing a change. Historically, Salomon executives had maintained a reserved public profile and relatively modest personal lifestyles. Gutfreund had assumed such a posture until the 1980s, when he and his second wife became more active in society and adopted a much more prominent public role. His new manner had both its favorable and unfavorable aspects. Increasingly, Gutfreund was willing to provide leadership and support for arts and charitable organizations. At the same time, the publicity that his wife attracted was often at odds with the sober image of a Salomon managing partner.

The deep cuts of October 1987 left the formerly confident leaders of Salomon chastened. In a long, somewhat introspective profile in the Sunday *New York Times Magazine* on January 10, 1988, Gutfreund explained what he thought had been the problem administratively:

> At the end of 1986, the numbers of people we had doing things did not make sense. Only when I really examined these things did I realize how far off track we were. I came to my

senses cumulatively. . . . Central control was lacking. The business [had] gotten beyond my simple abilities. . . .[13]

Gutfreund also saw reasons for the difficulties in the strategic direction the firm had pursued in the preceding few years:

> The world has changed in some fundamental ways, and most of us were not on top of it. . . . We won't be so arrogant as to think we can become a factor in [all significant] indigenous markets. We had been seduced into thinking we could. . . . We'll operate in businesses that are cost effective. Is being No. 1 in all of the markets something that we can or want to do now? We will always want to be, but we have to consider what would be more profitable. I can see us coming back to the top in profits, but we won't be No. 1 in all of the markets. . . .[14]

President Strauss expressed similar sentiments in announcing the cutbacks to the London staff:

> In a global environment—to think that everyone can do everything . . . we know we can't. . . . This would have happened even in a bull market. This is not a sudden realization that we have a problem. We have grown very quickly over the past seven years, and the time has come for a strategic reassessment. If we made a mistake, it was that we should have acted sooner.[15]

But it was Henry Kaufman who drew the most sobering lesson from the experience. After having resigned in December 1987 from all his posts at Salomon, the man the press liked to dub "Dr. Doom" phrased the message in characteristically stark words:

> It is always oh so pleasant to expand. It expresses virility, drive, the profit motive. But it is so difficult to consolidate, to reassess where you want to be. True, you do have to take advantage of some of the fluff that comes along, the new businesses where there are substantial profits. But you cannot veer from your main course.[16]

---

13. James Sterngold, "Too Far Too Fast," *New York Times Magazine*, January 10, 1988, p. 22.
14. Ibid., pp. 18, 22, 27, 59.
15. *Financial Times*, October 13, 1987, p. 1.
16. Sterngold, "Too Far Too Fast," p. 59.

From the statements of those remaining at the firm, it was un-
clear whether these lessons had truly been taken to heart. In announcing the October 1987 cuts, Gutfreund had emphasized that
there existed "a clear management consensus concerning our tactical
priorities and the proper future deployment of our assets," centering
on "the historic basis of the firm's strength." He then went on to
outline a new focus on "advisory, high-margin corporate finance
businesses, including merchant banking." In the January 1988 *New
York Times Magazine* article, he emphasized the importance of strengthening ties with corporate clients: "One of the things we're going to
look at very hard is to reaffirm relationship banking."[17]

The editors of the "Lex" column of the *Financial Times* perhaps
put it best in their analysis of the October 1987 reorganization:

> A year and a half ago Salomon was the most powerful
> house on Wall Street, and London bankers watched in awe
> as it quadrupled the size of its London operations. Given the
> size of its capital base and the well-publicized creativity of its
> staff, it seemed only a matter of time before the firm conquered
> the London markets. However, yesterday's humiliating an-
> nouncement of major cutbacks at Salomon only served to
> underline the speed with which even the biggest players in the
> global financial markets can come unstuck. . . . It is now pul-
> ling out of such basic businesses as commercial paper and
> municipal bonds, which will only serve to reinforce European
> prejudices that Wall Street firms are fair-weather friends. . . .[18]

Salomon in Tokyo

In contrast with the problems besetting Salomon in New York and
London, the firm's Tokyo operation was considered a bright jewel.
Whereas Salomon's London operation suffered from a departure
from the firm's gradualist and trading-centered strategy, the Tokyo
operation benefited from the reaffirmation of Salomon's traditional
approach. At the beginning of the 1980s, Salomon found itself with
neither a presence in the pecking order of Japanese domestic underwriting nor relationships with Japanese corporate or governmental
issuers. Consequently, the firm decided to enter through distribution
rather than origination, at least initially. The firm adopted a strategy
of first gaining experience in secondary-debt trading as a direct *principal*, not just agency, participant. After mastering the secondary-

17. Ibid., p. 27.
18. *Financial Times*, October 13, 1987, p. 26.

market trading dynamics of that most basic of financial markets in any advanced economy—the securities of the central government— Salomon built up its distribution contacts and capability by moving into government securities underwriting. The current stage of the strategy is the development of similar competences and capacities on the equity security side, with the ultimate intention of selectively leveraging the combination of these market activities into the higher-margin corporate finance businesses, such as mergers and acquisitions.

In Tokyo, Salomon was definitely a latecomer, but it had made the most of its situation since arriving in 1980. Although the firm could claim to have sold American bonds as early as 1910 to Japanese insurance companies anxious to diversify their investments away from the earthquake-prone Japanese mainland,[19] Salomon had, like many of its peers, selected Hong Kong as the initial locus of its Asian business efforts. The Hong Kong office was opened in 1976 as the focal point for a jumble of theretofore uncoordinated activities in the region, a nucleus that became the parent firm's unit for the area, Salomon Brothers Asia.

Conventional wisdom held that Hong Kong, with its British financial, legal, and regulatory practices, would turn out to be the pivotal Asian outpost of an emerging global capital market, eclipsing admittedly powerful Tokyo because of Japan's rigid centralized control over that country's financial markets and the clannish practices of the Japanese business and financial sectors. Hong Kong was already an offshore banking center of some magnitude and the only place where large non-Japanese Asian companies could raise funds locally. As such, Hong Kong had become the base from which most European and American securities firms and banks attempted to exploit non-Japanese domestic financial markets and serve Asian clients, including Japanese companies seeking to raise offshore funds.

However, doubts about Hong Kong's continued viability as an unfettered financial environment after its reversion to mainland China's control in 1997 and Japan's own growing awareness of the attractive potential for centering Asian financial activity in Tokyo caused a shift in vendors' thinking. Initially, Salomon was able to obtain Japanese Ministry of Finance approval to open only a "representative office," not the full-branch capability already enjoyed by some of Salomon's competitors.

The other firms had gotten to Japan earlier than Salomon, even though they, too, had been betting on Hong Kong as the Asian out-

19. *Tokyo Business Today*, November 1987, p. 46.

post of the financial world of the future. Numerous British and continental firms had long maintained operations in Asia, and many had well-established representative offices in Japan. Merrill Lynch, the dean of American brokers in Japan, had established its initial presence in Japan more than three decades previously, principally as brokers to American military personnel. Smith Barney had had an active liaison office since the 1960s, when Yankee bonds (bonds for Japanese companies sold in New York) became fashionable for a time among Japanese utilities. Other prestigious firms, such as Goldman, Sachs, First Boston, and Morgan Stanley, had opened representative offices in the 1970s. Salomon did beat a few of its peers to a Tokyo presence, including Shearson Lehman, which finally set up shop in the mid-1980s.

In 1982, Salomon received Ministry of Finance approval to upgrade its Tokyo office to branch status, and it relocated its Asian operations to Japan. The concentration of resources in Japan happily coincided with a series of favorable economic and regulatory developments in Japan on which Salomon capitalized in a manner similar to its earlier days in New York. Most obvious was the impressive economic performance of Japan during the 1980s, which for the first time freed up excess cash for potential investment abroad.

This improvement rested in great measure on a series of favorable contextual factors. Indeed, in the 1980s, a variety of forces lined up very favorably for Japan. The decade was marked by low and steadily falling commodity prices; during the 1970s, high raw-materials prices had brought repeated current-account deficits for resource-poor Japan. On the output side, Japan was favored through much of the decade by an overvalued dollar, facilitating exports to America. Perhaps most important was the willingness of the United States to provide both incremental world demand by its tolerance of large budget deficits and additional world trading liquidity via trade deficits, all within the context of an international trading order that was liberal by historic standards. With Western Europe in recession after forty years of debilitating interventionism and the United States indulging in a complacent orgy of consumption, foreign markets were ripe for the plucking.

These factors produced huge capital surpluses that, because of favorable regulatory developments, could now be invested, at least partially, abroad. Prior to 1980, capital exports from Japan were virtually impossible, because of the exercise of strict official oversight of foreign exchange transactions. In 1980, the capital controls were lifted; by 1986, liberalization had produced annual investment outflows of $130 billion. At the same time, the new openness encouraged foreign investment in Japan, which by 1986 had reached $30 billion.[20]

The most important exporters of investment cash were the various Japanese financial intermediaries. Because of the high propensity of the Japanese for savings, insurance coverage, and retirement plans, these institutions controlled huge cash flows, which to this point had been required for domestic investment. The most important single intermediary group was the life insurance industry. Over the years 1980–1987, life insurers first were granted the right to invest abroad and then had the allowable portion of assets investable abroad increase from 5 percent to 25 percent. To their chagrin following the collapse of the dollar after 1985, much of the exported funds were invested in U.S. Treasury securities. Such investment had been made more attractive by another regulatory change, this time by American authorities. In August 1984, the Treasury, faced with the need to attract truly heroic amounts of money into the U.S. Treasury market to finance current government deficits and anxious about potential crowding out and interest rate impacts on domestic U.S. capital seekers, eliminated the 30 percent withholding tax on foreign holdings of. U.S. Treasury securities (and also *reintroduced* bearer-form securities targeted especially at foreign buyers, who would be attracted by their tax evasion potential!).

The Japanese capital exports, though not as large as those of Great Britain at her imperial height, nevertheless represented important business opportunities for American investment banks. The sale of large blocks of Treasury securities was one such immediate opportunity; another was arranging investment in American real estate. Although it developed much more slowly, there was also growth in the investment of Japanese funds in foreign equities. Moreover, the more receptive climate that had attracted greatly expanded levels of foreign investment in Japan had been accompanied by a more open attitude toward the operations of foreign securities firms in Japan. A number of Western firms, including Salomon, were eager to exploit that opening.

The Wisdom of Salomon:
Gradual Domestication, Not Expatriate Agency

The Salomon-Tokyo strategy did not hinge on the exploitation of opportunities arising from external flows. Rather, the Salomon orientation was toward the development of a free-standing subsidiary that

---

20. *The Economist*, May 14, 1988, p. 86.

operated essentially as a *domestic* firm in domestic markets, while benefiting where applicable from the New York link. Instead of functioning largely as an *agent* for *"gaijyn"* (i.e., foreign) transactions in Japan and for Japanese investment overseas, Salomon-Tokyo would compete as a *principal* player from the start and would build domesticization gradually. First would come the development of secondary-market institutional investor activity in banks, followed by the buildup of securities-distribution capability and expansion into equities, and capped by the establishment of a corporate underwriting and finance franchise. The first phase of this business strategy was the buildup of expertise in the relatively unfettered area of Japanese government-bond trading. Just as the short-term markets of New York had been free of the cultural constraints of the "white shoe" pedigree, the Japanese government-bond markets were seen as markets where pure trading expertise could earn profits and, more importantly, a high profile. Once a profile was established through *trading,* Salomon could justifiably make an effective case for a bigger piece of the actual government-bond primary *underwriting* business.

A key step was to hire prominent local talent. In this respect, the entrepreneurial leader of Salomon's effort in Japan in the early 1980s, Eugene Dattel, exhibited considerable foresight. With a cosmopolitan background of his own—equity trading in the United States, bond trading in London, and stewardship of the Hong Kong office's development—Dattel understood the need to obtain the best Japanese talent if top positions in markets were to be obtained. Upon arriving in Tokyo in 1980, Dattel hired away Shigeru Myojin, a bond trader at Yamaichi, one of the Big Four Japanese securities houses. Myojin, nicknamed "Sugar," became the chief of yen-bond trading for Salomon Brothers Asia and a director of the subsidiary. Another important recruit was Toshihide Sakamoto, like Myojin a long-time veteran of Yamaichi. Sakamoto was ultimately hired to be head of Tokyo equities following a 10-month period of agonizing over his departure from the firm that had been his employer for seventeen years. Sakamoto finally decided to make the move—highly risky in Japan even in the relatively opportunistic securities industry—after seeing that Salomon had demonstrated the necessary commitment to (and staying power in) the Tokyo markets.[21]

This talent, augmented by the addition of several other traders from Yamaichi, Daiwa, Wako, and other securities firms, equipped Salomon to launch the first phase of its Tokyo strategy. This phase centered on providing liquidity for customers in the cash government-

---

21. *Institutional Investor,* May 1987, p. 302.

bond markets and in the government-bond futures markets. By 1986, Salomon was clearly the leading foreign house in yen bond trading and ranked among the top three (Japanese firms included) in yen-bond futures trading.[22] The firm's success and sizable presence prompted Salomon to establish a separate offshore yen bond book (that is, house trading account) run from Tokyo. In February 1987, Salomon moved into even tougher company when it directly challenged the Big Four Japanese brokers in a government two-year-note auction. In an unprecedented coup for a foreign firm, Salomon won over 40 percent of the issue, two and a half times as much as that obtained by Nomura, the largest domestic bidder.

Unfortunately for Salomon, pure pricing prowess was not sufficient to establish the firm as a kingpin in the more lucrative long-term government-bond market. Unlike the short-term government markets, which were organized along the lines of the U.S. Treasury's auction system, the Japanese long-term government-bond underwriting system was essentially closed. Not only was the list of specific firm participants in the government's bond syndicate fixed, so were their percentage shares in each underwriting. The percentages, infrequently changed, reflected past performance in large measure. Nevertheless, the Salomon strategy of pursuing a high profile in government-bond trading apparently convinced the Ministry of Finance to reward it with the largest syndicate share accorded any foreign firm. In May 1987, new percentages were assigned as part of a broader increase in the amount of each issue—from 1.19 percent to 5.72 percent—to be assigned to foreign firms. In the reshuffle, Salomon obtained 1 percent of the aggregate 5.72 percent, with six other major foreign firms included in the syndicate (First Boston, Goldman, Sachs, Jardine Fleming, Merrill Lynch, Morgan Stanley, and S.G. Warburg) each receiving only 0.5 percent.

Still another breakthrough occurred in August 1988 when, partially in response to the threat of U.S. congressional trade sanctions, the Ministry of Finance announced a further liberalization in its government-bond issuances procedures. Beginning in 1989, a part of the bellwether 10-year maturity issues would also be let out to competitive bid, and the composition of the fixed underwriting syndicate to distribute the balance of the offerings would be altered to increase foreign security vendors' share to 8 percent from 5.72 percent.

As Salomon achieved pre-eminence among foreign firms in government-bond and note underwriting and in yen bond futures, the firm also began to build a presence in Japanese equity securities mar-

22. *Euromoney*, March 1987, p. 146.

kets. Its entry, tardy compared to that of several of its foreign competitors such as Merrill Lynch and Morgan Stanley, was apparently insufficiently developed to merit Salomon's assignment of one of the half-dozen Tokyo Stock Exchange (TSE) memberships awarded in December 1985 to Merrill, Morgan, Goldman, and three British firms. Salomon thus continued to suffer from the significant disadvantages of exclusion from the TSE floor, having to execute its trading transactions through member firms (with attendant commission and market impact costs) and missing much of the floor intelligence crucial to the open outcry system employed by the TSE for the most active stocks.

The failure to gain a seat sparked a major effort to build a presence in the Japanese equity markets designed to be of such a magnitude as to make a lengthy delay of membership politically impossible for the Japanese. The heart of the effort centered, as it had earlier in New York, on the secondary markets. It was two-pronged: a beefed-up presence in Japanese equity trading and a greatly expanded effort in Japanese-based equity research. Resources were made available for Sakamoto to increase his equity-trading staff through additional recruiting of veteran Japanese nationals.

In research, the firm had a daunting problem in view of the vast resources dedicated by the Big Four and other indigenous firms to investment analysis. The Big Four generally maintained broad coverage not only through conventional economics, debt, and equity research departments, but also through separate research institutes. Owned and funded by their respective associated firms, these groups enjoyed significant autonomy and were considered a fairly objective contact point for companies potentially interested in securities services. Because the institutes also performed both pro bono and contract work for central and local government entities, they served as useful intermediaries for their parent securities firms wishing to call matters to the attention of public officialdom. Finally, the think tanks performed unique analyses of many issues relevant to the securities business: economic trend analysis, both domestic and international; futurist scenario exercises and projections; demographic studies; political analyses; and more theoretical work in fixed and debt markets and instruments.

Despite such formidable Japanese forces, Salomon nonetheless moved to allocate greater resources to its Japanese research effort. Prior to the first quarter of 1986, Salomon maintained no equity or fixed-income analysts in Japan. Some of the firm's American and European research product had been distributed among Japanese institutional investors, but not on a significant scale. By March 1987, the firm had organized a Japanese Equity Group in Tokyo, staffed by eight equity analysts. The new employees, along with the addition of three fixed-income analysts, marked the end of what the firm called the first phase of its equity buildup in Tokyo.[23] The next phase was designed to expand the number to twenty. Robert Salomon, Jr., co-director of the stock research department, characterized the overall effort thusly:

> At the beginning of 1986 we began a serious push into the secondary market in Japanese equities. We began in Europe, which is the most internationally oriented of the capital markets. Now we're building up that capacity in the U.S. and Japan. [We plan to] use the secondary market among Japanese institutions to build a presence in Japanese stocks.[24]

The most recent element in Salomon's secondary-equity effort—the Osaka futures market—played even more directly off the firm's traditional expertise in trading. The Osaka Futures Exchange, the first and only equity futures market in Japan, was opened in June 1987, with trading in the "Stock Futures 50" contract. In September, Salomon successfully closed its first contract on that exchange. By the end of the year, the firm was engaging in highly profitable arbitrage between the Osaka "50" contract and the underlying cash market in the basket of TSE-listed stocks composing the "50."

This activity, along with Salomon's sizable commitment to the Tokyo equities market in the form of its new Equity Group and its beefed-up trading effort, may have prompted Salomon's inclusion among the foreign institutions selected to participate in the privatization of Nippon Telephone and Telegraph (NTT). In November 1987, the Japanese government sold the first tranche (in a planned series of phased offerings) of its 100 percent holding in the national long-distance communications monopoly. Although the seven foreign firms admitted to the underwriting syndicate were allocated in aggregate only 4½ percent of the offering, their participation was highly significant since, despite what appeared to be stratospheric pricing, the issue was vastly oversubscribed. Interestingly, it easily could have been sold exclusively by the Big Four securities firms without any help from other Japanese securities firms, much less foreign vendors.

While Salomon's inclusion in the NTT underwriting syndicate was a feather in its cap, its admission to TSE membership a month later, in December 1987, indicated that Salomon's commitment to

---

23. *Japanese Economic Journal,* April 18, 1987, p. 14.
24. Ibid.

Tokyo had finally won the confidence of the Japanese Ministry of Finance. Salomon's exclusion from the ranks of the newly admitted in December 1985 had been a humiliation in the firm's eyes. Injured pride might well have explained in part the broad and intensive publicity campaign Salomon orchestrated during its two years in purgatory. The photogenic Deryck Maughan, who replaced Dattel as Salomon's Tokyo head in August 1986, graced the pages of Japanese, American, and European business and financial publications on a seemingly uninterrupted basis. The most senior Salomon executives, including President Strauss, were flown in for elbow-rubbing encounters with the highest-level regulators and politicians. Maximum publicity was extracted from anything, reflecting the traditional publicity consciousness of the firm, as typified by "The Room" and its ingenious use as a promotional tool.

The promotional gloss notwithstanding, Salomon's commitment to the Tokyo marketplace had been steadfast, as the firm attempted to establish its Tokyo operation as a free-standing entity. The basis of the commitment in Salomon's eyes was that the Asian marketplace is, in itself, an opportunity worthy of pursuit, regardless of the speed or extent of global financial integration. Maughan characterized the Pacific Rim market as a viable stand-alone proposition:

> We believe the Asian markets are legitimate business opportunities in themselves. I think that's what is a little different with Salomon Brothers. Many other foreign firms are here to market their own foreign products—here's an American stock, here's a European bond. But we are making a serious attempt to approach the national capital markets of Japan.[25]

Evidence of this long-term perspective was seen in a number of actions. The clearest indication was the announcement of a tenfold increase in Salomon-Tokyo's capital in January 1987. The subsidiary's capitalization was increased from roughly $35 million to $350 million, in yet another carefully scripted public relations flourish designed to impress Japanese regulators, investors, and issuers. The increase not only pushed Salomon past all its foreign competitors in one sweep (Merrill Lynch had been by far the best-capitalized at approximately $100 million), but it also prompted speculation (or wishful thinking) that the Big Four securities firms in Japan might become the Big Five, since the capital infusion (temporarily) put Salomon's Tokyo operation on the same plane as Yamaichi, the smallest of the Big Four, with capital of about $500 million. With credit lines from Japanese commer-

25. *Euromoney*, March 1987, p. 145.

cial banks, Salomon's capital base could potentially support large securities-inventory positions that would hopefully permit Salomon's traders to exploit their skills in debt, equity, and derivative products trading more aggressively than their foreign firm counterparts. By year-end 1987, Maughan was able to proclaim publicly that Salomon-Tokyo was now self-financing, with future expansion expected to be funded by retained earnings and no foreseeable need for additional capital infusions from its U.S. parent.[26]

The achievement of financial self-sufficiency reflected in part the significant profits being generated by Salomon on its Tokyo activities. Despite its comparatively late arrival to Japan and particularly to the TSE, Salomon was almost certainly the most profitable foreign securities firm in Japan in 1986 and 1987. Figures are difficult to establish because few firms break out the performance of their Japanese units and maintain that accurate revenue and profit assignments are often impossible to make. In December 1987, the *Nikkei Kinyu Shimbun* published estimates of foreign firm profitability garnered from data released by the Ministry of Finance. For what those estimates are worth, in the financial years ending September 30 in 1986 and in 1987, Salomon-Tokyo was thought to have earned ¥1.69 billion (U.S. $12 million) and ¥2.26 billion (U.S. $16 million), respectively. The next two runners-up among foreign securities vendors were not even within shouting distance. In those same years, Merrill Lynch reportedly made ¥492 million (U.S. $3.5 million) and ¥317 million (U.S. $2.3 million), respectively, while Morgan Stanley came in at ¥404 million (U.S. $2.9 million) and ¥428 million (U.S. $3 million).[27]

Organizationally as well as financially, Salomon-Tokyo had been given an independent existence. Part of the independence came from its broad-ranging responsibility for the parent firm's Asian, not just Japanese, operations. It has already been noted that with the upgrading of the Tokyo office from representative to branch status in 1982, Asian operations were moved there as part of the firmwide policy of concentrating resources in multiservice central offices. Thereafter, Salomon's operations in the sixteen Asian countries in which the firm does business were covered from Tokyo. The Hong Kong office, formerly the management seat of Salomon in Asia, was closed, with only one other Asian office—in Australia—maintained because of time zone differences. Asianwide competence was given a symbolic boost and a deeper managerial dimension in 1987 with the establishment of a separate insider board of directors for the Tokyo subsidiary (at the

26. Ibid.
27. *Nikkei Kinyu Shimbun*, December 8, 1987, p. 1.

same time, a board was also created for the London-based subsidiary overseeing European operations).

More subtle support of Salomon-Tokyo's independence was noted in its human resource policy and its attitude toward responsibility and advancement. In its early stages, the Tokyo operation focused on recruiting proven professionals for key positions from established Japanese firms. The policy was effective because of the firm's success in luring top performers from big Japanese brokers such as Yamaichi, Wako, and Daiwa, and the subsequent performance of the new hires in key positions. Following the initial period of building critical mass, however, the firm shifted its focus in 1984 to entry-level recruiting among newly graduated Japanese nationals. By the 1986–1987 academic year, annual inquiries from graduating seniors had reached 3,000, with 800 interviews being conducted. During that year, Salomon hired twelve graduates, including seven from prestigious Tokyo University.[28]

The influx of new employees has been part of a dramatic buildup of staff that was not interrupted by the parent's retrenchment in other areas. When the Tokyo representative office opened in 1980, Salomon's staff in Japan totaled nine (including Dattel and Myojin). By 1985, the number had grown to 35, and by year-end 1987 to 200. Salomon-Tokyo was thus exempted from the round of cutbacks recommended in the parent's 1987 strategic review.[29]

Interestingly, Salomon was not the largest employer among the foreign firms operating in Japan. That title went to Morgan Stanley, which had 430 people working in Tokyo just before the October 1987 crash and 500 by mid-1988. Despite the significant retail business it conducted at its three branches in Tokyo, Osaka, and Nagoya, Merrill Lynch employed only 400 at the end of 1987. First Boston, with 185 people, was another foreign firm with a sizable contingent at the time of the 1987 crash.[30]

Personnel policies on responsibility and advancement reinforced the independence of Salomon-Tokyo at the same time key elements of the parent's culture were being introduced. As in New York, management emphasized the delegation of responsibility in a competitive, if supportive, atmosphere. Among the early experienced hires, "Sugar" Myojin proclaimed that "here everybody has the authority to do whatever he has to do; we delegate authority."[31] Maughan identified the same attitude among the new university-graduate

28. *Euromoney*, March 1987, p. 145.
29. *Tokyo Business Today*, November 1987, p. 46.
30. Ibid., p. 47.
31. Ibid., p. 146.

hires, who were sent to New York for the standard six-month training program also given new American professionals: "Half the people I hire don't ask about money. They say, 'whatever is appropriate.' They want to work for a company like this because we give responsibility early. They get jobs they would not get for 15 years in a traditional Japanese securities company."[32]

A troublesome issue for any company operating in a foreign country is both the mix of locals and expatriates and the role of locals in senior management. Because of its policy of recruiting senior professionals from Japanese firms, Salomon-Tokyo had by the end of 1987 attained a relatively advanced level of integration at all levels, which contributed further to the subsidiary's independence. At that time, 85 percent of the Tokyo office employees were Japanese. Japanese nationals held a number of the most senior positions: sales manager, head bond trader, equities chief, and head of operations. Richard Grand-Jean, the head of the unit's capital markets group and a ten-year veteran of Salomon in Asia, concluded in early 1987 that "in the future, the management of this office will be Japanese."[33]

Existing and Potential Problems

The success of Salomon in establishing itself as a profitable foreign securities firm in the Japanese markets notwithstanding, significant continuing obstacles remain to achieving the firm's longer-term objectives. Cultural and regulatory barriers may inhibit the firm's further integration into, and ultimate leadership in, the Japanese domestic markets, now overwhelmingly dominated by the large domestic securities firms. In addition, the competences and commitment of other foreign firms, particularly Morgan Stanley, Goldman, and Merrill, are another challenge to Salomon in its aim to be a pre-eminent "gaijyn" participant.

Cultural barriers are the most intimidating because they could be tenacious enough to block the establishment of a broader Salomon Japanese franchise. In the New York market, old-school ties gradually yielded in the face of incontrovertible evidence of Salomon's competence and concurrent reinforcing deregulation and economic change. In Japan, traditional skepticism of foreigners is only one of many barriers to entry. The interorganizational links binding the key large industrial groupings in Japan—successors to the pre–World War II "zaibatsu"—include cross-shareholdings, common directors, and other ties. The tenor of these corporate interrelationships in Japan

32. *Euromoney*, March 1987, p. 146.
33. Ibid.

meant that there has been comparatively little available business in the highest-margin areas, such as mergers and acquisitions. The financial needs of even the largest corporations have historically been served by the commercial banks associated with those corporations. Indeed, the post–World War II industrial groupings have generally been considered to be *led* by the commercial banks linked with them. As a result, the corporate debt-issuing markets in Japan have been exceptionally thin compared to those in the United States or Britain.

Nor will Salomon's foreign competitors be sitting still while it attempts to consolidate its Tokyo position. With $100 million in capital, 400 people, and an honored name among the Japanese, Merrill Lynch is one key rival. Morgan Stanley, with $35 million and 430 people, is busily selling its famed expertise in the high-margin advisory work, as is blue chip Goldman, Sachs. And First Boston, with $15 million in capital and roughly 200 people, is touting its future Euromarket prowess in the wake of its merger with Credit Suisse First Boston (see Chapter 12). These rivalries were further heightened recently by bad blood over attempts by the foreign firms—but resisted by Salomon— to orchestrate a coordinated push with the Ministry of Finance for regulatory reform. A number of the other foreign firms, for instance, had unsuccessfully approached Salomon to join a campaign to get the Ministry of Finance to adopt an auction system for its long-term bond offerings. Instead of spending management time and political and social capital there, Salomon went ahead to become the most active trader of governments so as to secure by performance a larger role in the fixed-syndicate system, to the disadvantage of the other foreign firms.[34]

Another potential difficulty is the firm's relatively late arrival in Japan. In a country where time is most often considered the true barometer of commitment and legitimacy, Salomon has suffered. The Salomon-Tokyo's capital-markets group chief, Grand-Jean, expressed reservations about the impact of the firm's short tenure in an otherwise confident assessment of its prospects:

> Certainly we were here in force for this tidal wave of capital export that has occurred here only in the last couple of years. But were we late? I suppose you could say we wish we had been here in the 1970s and developed the relationships with Japanese companies that some of our competitors have. Had we done that, we might have been better able to exploit the interest of certain Japanese investors in making direct investments in real estate in America. Certainly there probably

34. *BusinessWeek*, September 7, 1987, p. 90.

were more opportunities we missed by not being here early. But, taken as a whole, being here the last four years has been highly significant to the firm's overall business and to its international business. And because a lot of what has happened to Tokyo has come suddenly, our lack of history here does not seem as damaging in certain ways as it might have been.[35]

But perhaps the most critical variable will be the future willingness of Japanese regulatory authorities to sustain the momentum of financial deregulation in Japan. This concern has two dimensions: the deregulation of Japan's financial markets *domestically* and the liberalization of foreign participation in those deregulated domestic arenas. The 1980s have seen some strides toward both the opening of Japan's financial markets and their modernization, the most notable being the admission of foreign firms to the TSE. But the Japanese have not taken these moves with either the doctrinal commitment or the pragmatic enthusiasm of similar initiatives implemented during the same period in New York and London. This perception was shared by a number of other foreign vendors operating in Tokyo. They are now hedging their bets: Morgan Stanley had recently reopened an office in Hong Kong and was now doing a considerable volume of business with the non-Japanese sectors of the Asian market. Salomon Brothers moved shortly after to reopen its own Hong Kong operation, with a special emphasis on trading in various Asian securities. Other foreign vendors that had not, like Morgan Stanley and Salomon Brothers, earlier shut down their entire operations, are now beefing up their Hong Kong offices, although the longer-term consequences for Hong Kong of the Tiananmen Square massacre in Beijing are still to be determined. Salomon executives like Maughan argue for change, using polite tones in the Japanese way:

> Clearly it is in Japan's interest to maintain its presence in capital markets overseas. The question is how much it would lose by opening up at home. In my view, very little. Foreign companies are generally only scratching the surface. Japan should be an advocate of open markets, not a defender of closed ones.[36]

And in the way of financiers in all three cities of the world's financial triumvirate at the end of the 1980s, those same executives, in this case Grand-Jean, speak in the language of globalized optimism:

35. *Euromoney*, March 1987, p. 46.
36. *Tokyo Business Today*, November 1987, p. 48.

If financial services are an important key to the Japanese future, as we think they are, then you have to ask yourself if the Japanese really will be satisfied, given the importance of their capital base, their economy, their position in the world, to have Tokyo be a capital market any less than fully equal with New York and London.[37]

Conclusions

Anyone who seriously studies the financial services sector in relatively deregulated markets will appreciate just how fragile the equilibrium of firms can be. The major asset of the business is not the capital that a particular vendor can mobilize, even though the absence of sufficient capital can be a substantial restraint and a factor in the maintenance of market position. The essential ingredient is people. People take the elevators to go home each night and you hope they will choose to return the next morning. Managing a group of entrepreneurial professionals (some could be labeled "prima donnas") is difficult. Too much organizational control can stifle the creative drive that has allowed firms like Salomon to grow so impressively over a relatively short period of time.

Perhaps it has been Salomon's preoccupation with its capital that has been, in the end, its biggest stumbling block. Its initial decision to go public by merging with Philipp Brothers may well have been, as it stated, to ensure adequate capital for future growth. However, that decision set the firm on the path of a stereotypical publicly owned U.S. company, with the attendant preoccupations with quarterly earnings and potential threats to management control. Salomon's logical decision to allow its major overseas operating units a great deal of autonomy came to haunt them in the case of London, where the markets have been at least temporarily shrinking. On the other hand, in the still-booming Tokyo market, the autonomy and the focus on cracking the domestic Japanese marketplace are serving the parent firm quite well.

Managing the downside of any market cycle is clearly the more challenging part of the top executives' assignment in these kinds of financial services firms. If you can find a way to juggle the need for a relatively flat and decentralized organizational structure to encourage individual initiative and the countervailing need for controls, which can identify potential problems early on, then the required capital is likely to take care of itself. Over long periods of history, capital has followed the path of talented people who can use it productively.

37. *Euromoney*, March 1987, p. 148.

CHAPTER 11

NOMURA SECURITIES COMES TO WALL STREET

By the end of the 1980s, Nomura Securities Co., Ltd. had assumed the proportions of an international phenomenon. It was recognized as the leading securities firm in Japan and an entrant into the London Euromarkets that had just grabbed away the number-one underwriting position from long-established Credit Suisse First Boston. Its far-flung financial services operations reached into Australia, Switzerland, Singapore, and Bahrain. And a principal focus was on its rapidly growing subsidiary in New York. Nomura's worldwide profits in 1987, at $2 billion, topped those of any other Japanese company in any industry and were some five times that of Merrill Lynch, its closest U.S. counterpart and rival.

Despite evidence of success, Nomura was still struggling to transform itself from a domestic Japanese stockbroker, with only secondary links to the Japanese corporate community, into a full-service investment bank in the tradition of comparable U.S. firms. Progress was slow, and Nomura was being hounded by new potential competitors. Both Japanese commercial banks and foreign securities firms were clamoring for regulatory approval to expand their involvement in the Tokyo home securities market and the Ministry of Finance was circulating a plan for deregulation that would do just that.

Nowhere were the early signs of Nomura's transformation more evident than in New York. The subsidiary had grown rapidly by leveraging off Nomura's traditional strengths as broker and trader, funneling the gusher of cash from Japan into U.S. and other foreign securities. Forward progress on the corporate finance front had been disappointing, however, and the firm had recently taken the extraordinary step of spending $100 million to buy a minority position in a newly formed U.S. mergers-and-acquisitions boutique, Wasserstein, Perella.

Early History

There is no denying that Nomura has come a long way from its humble beginnings. The firm's early history is primarily the story of

Tokushichi Nomura.[1] Born in 1878, he was the adopted first son of a modestly successful money changer in Osaka, then the major center of domestic commerce and finance in Japan. Since there was not a single currency in the country, money changers played a key role in all commercial activities. Nevertheless, they were considered to be the lowest-ranked and socially least respectable class in Japan.

In 1904, the young Nomura joined the family firm, which had turned its attention toward stock trading. (With the appearance of a national currency after the Meiji Restoration in 1868, most of the large money changers had gone into national banking, while the smaller firms gravitated toward the stock exchanges.) Although the stock market was on the periphery of the financial system, Japan's success in the 1904 war against Russia in Manchuria acted as a powerful stimulus to the market, and the Nomura firm profited and grew along with it.

Securities underwriting, which guaranteed to the issuer that an entire offering would be successfully sold, dated only from the 1890s in Japan and had been the exclusive domain of the national banks. Beginning in 1910, the securities firms had sought to act as primary underwriters of major Japanese government-bond and corporate equity issuers; however, they could obtain only positions subordinate to the large banks. By World War I, Nomura's business had broadened to include some underwriting, trading, and sales of fixed-income as well as equity securities, but it remained primarily a retail-oriented stockbroker. Tokushichi Nomura was not averse to taking big risks. He timed the market correctly in 1917 and recorded the largest trading gains in the history of the firm. Despite a string of successes, he was painfully conscious of the superior status accorded the national banks in Japan's financial system and envied the close relationships between securities firms and commercial banks in other countries. As a result, the Osaka Nomura Bank was founded in 1918 not only to edge into the commercial banking sphere but also to handle the underwriting and sales of government bonds and corporate debentures—areas dominated by the national banks.[2]

The move toward bonds was fortuitously timed. In the early 1920s, the Japanese government responded to a slump in the equity market by attempting to revitalize the dormant government-bond market. Like other banks controlled by securities firms, the Osaka

1. The material in this section has been drawn largely from *Beyond the Ivied Mountain: The Origin and Growth of a Japanese Securities House, Nomura: 1872–1985* (Tokyo: Nomura Securities Co., Ltd., 1986).
2. It was later renamed the Daiwa Bank (no relation to the present-day Daiwa Securities Company).

Nomura Bank reaped the benefits of this expanding market. The bond business was on a roll, and by 1922 it had become evident that a separate organization would be needed to service it. The result was The Nomura Securities Co., Ltd., headquartered in Osaka, in December 1925.

The new firm was originally chartered primarily to underwrite and distribute government bonds, corporate bonds, and stocks and to trade already issued public and corporate bonds, but it soon encompassed all securities activities. Nomura, along with the Osaka Nomura Bank and several other family-controlled enterprises, was part of a nascent zaibatsu controlled by Nomura Company, a holding company, established in 1922.

The next twenty years were extremely difficult for Japan's securities industry. The Great Kanto earthquake in 1923 devastated Tokyo. There were massive financial panics in Japan in 1927 and again in 1929. Many securities firms folded and, prodded by the Ministry of Finance, the securities industry began a dramatic process of consolidation that lasted through the end of World War II. During this period, Nomura continued to grow, establishing eight domestic branch offices by the late 1920s. In March 1927, Nomura also opened a New York representative office to act primarily as an agent for the sales and related clearing functions of dollar-denominated Japanese government bonds. But the U.S. depression seriously eroded the demand for foreign currency bonds, and the New York office was closed in December 1936.

The early 1930s were years of political uncertainty in Asia, and Japan prepared for military conflict, which erupted in full-scale war in 1937. Like other parts of the private sector, securities firms and national banks were mobilized by the government in support of the war effort. The Ministry of Finance instituted regulatory changes in 1938 that forced further consolidation in the securities industry; by the end of the decade, only eight firms qualified as securities underwriters. Although not the largest, Nomura was a powerful and respected member of the group. While this development enabled Nomura and other members of the securities oligarchy to expand their role in the business of underwriting and distributing government bonds, the market remained dominated by the big national banks. The government had come to rely more and more heavily on the zaibatsu and their affiliated banks. These major national banks, along with the Industrial Bank of Japan, occupied pre-eminent positions as capital market vendors, counselors, and strategists for the Japanese corporate establishment.

The climate was nonetheless favorable for stock brokering. With increasing government control of the bond market and the rise in inflation resulting from the wartime economy, investors turned their attention to stocks, and Nomura profitably stepped up its activities in secondary-market stock trading.

A major new business with far-reaching implications was created in 1941 when the Ministry of Finance authorized the establishment of equity investment trusts, patterned after those in Britain and similar to present-day U.S. mutual funds, as a means of bolstering prices (and civilian morale) on the stock market and thus assisting the war effort. Nomura successfully offered the first Japanese investment trust and took the unusual step of guaranteeing that investors would suffer only a limited capital loss if the securities in the trust declined in value. Other securities firms were quick to follow.

The year 1945 was devastating for both Japan and Nomura. During the final months of the war, Nomura lost over half of its fourteen domestic branch offices as a result of Allied bombing, including the new head office that had been moved from Osaka to Tokyo during the war. Almost half the staff had taken temporary leave to join the armed forces, and many never returned. The Nomura zaibatsu's investments in the fallen Japanese colony of Manchuria were lost, and many critical documents were destroyed in fires from the bombings. The measurable losses incurred by Nomura totalled ¥25 million—more than twice its total capital.

As part of the reforms instituted by the occupation forces after the war, the Nomura zaibatsu and holding company were dissolved, separating Nomura from its banking affiliate. Several of the group's senior officers and directors were forced to resign. Nomura, like some other securities firms, avoided having to change its name by procrastinating on the implementation of this Allied order, thus preserving the valuable retail customer franchise associated with it.

Then, in 1948, the Allied occupation instituted a number of financial reforms, including Article 65, the Japanese equivalent of the U.S. Glass-Steagall Act. The separation of investment from commercial banking gave the surviving securities firms—including what came to be known as the Big Four (Yamaichi, Nomura, Nikko, and Daiwa) the exclusive privilege of underwriting new issues of corporate bonds and equity. After decades of playing second fiddle to the national banks, the privilege was perceived to be a rich prize indeed. And while a number of the occupation administration's reforms were dropped or substantially modified following the signing of the peace treaty in 1952, the separating of public securities business from commercial banking business was retained by the Ministry of Finance, perhaps in recognition of the historically weak position of Japanese securities firms vis-à-vis the commercial banks and the ministry's desire to achieve a better future balance between the two groups of financial intermediaries.

The period of the occupation and its reforms resulted in a shift in share ownership. As the zaibatsu were dismembered, their share holdings were more broadly distributed. This development played to the strength of retail brokers. Nomura responded to the revitalization of the retail market by re-establishing and expanding its branch network across the country. "Investment consultant centers" were opened throughout Japan in department stores and other locations, and the firm's capital base was also increased. With these moves, Nomura firmly established itself as a major postwar retail force among Japan's securities firms.

Spurred initially by the economic boom associated with the Korean War, the 1950s and early 1960s were generally years of prosperity and growth for Japan. At the same time, the accompanying boom in its securities markets accelerated activity among individual shareholders. Nomura, through its promotion of investment trusts, assorted savings schemes, and investment seminars, was in the vanguard of the movement. Equity investment trusts had been reintroduced in 1951 and were heavily marketed by the major firms to individual investors. Nomura had soon established a network of 620 agencies, called "service stations," across Japan to accept applications for investment trust and bond subscriptions from individual savers. An important factor in Nomura's success with investment trusts was its development of various savings plans. One such scheme, the "Million Ryo Savings Chest" plan, was launched in 1953.[3] Small cash boxes were lent to individuals who used them like piggy banks. The catch was that Nomura retained the key and employed a staff of 150 women as collectors. In exchange for a full box, the customer received an investment trust certificate. Over a million chests were distributed through the plan, which continued until 1962.

Nomura also increased retail securities sales through investment seminars, investor clubs, and publications. In the mid-1950s, Nomura adopted a policy of identifying and recommending growth stocks. Remarkably accurate predictions, considered by some critics to be a result of price manipulation, further enhanced the firm's image among investors and kept the stream of money coming in.

With business brisk at home, Nomura began looking beyond its borders for new opportunity. Restrictions on the sale of Japanese

---

3. The ryo was an ancient Japanese unit of currency. The expression "I'd like to have a million ryo" was commonly used to indicate an ambition to be wealthy.

equities to foreign investors were loosened in 1951 and sales to non-residents became increasingly important. In March 1953, Nomura became the first Japanese securities firm to open a branch in New York after the war. In 1959, the Japanese government issued its first foreign currency-denominated bonds in twenty-eight years, and Nomura participated in the underwriting syndicate with several major U.S. securities firms, lead managed by First Boston. About that time, Nomura also began to send some personnel to be trained by Merrill Lynch in the United States.

The interest shown by foreigners in Japanese securities enabled Sony Corporation to issue the first Japanese-American depository receipts (ADRs) in the United States in 1961.[4] Nomura co-managed the deal along with the American firm of Smith Barney & Co. and, over the next few years, was involved in several other ADRs for Japanese companies. At the same time, Nomura helped underwrite Japanese corporate bonds in New York. A 1962 convertible issue for Mitsubishi Heavy Industries, for instance, was co-managed by Nomura, with First Boston running the books.

Back in the home market in Tokyo, however, corporate fund raising was sparse in the public markets. The corporate community remained closely wedded to their main commercial banks, relying on them for financing and advice on matters of corporate finance. It is no wonder that Japanese securities firms viewed with envy the more favorable corporate relations enjoyed by their U.S. counterparts.

Other regulatory changes did have an important positive influence on Nomura's growth. Government- and corporate-bond trading on the Tokyo and Osaka exchanges was officially restarted in April 1956. In 1961, corporate-bond syndication procedures were revised. Previously, the Big Four securities firms each underwrote 20 percent of every issue. Now the lead manager's share was increased to 23 percent, and the other three firms were allotted 19 percent. Nomura, as a frequent lead manager, benefited substantially from this change. "Second sections"[5] were added to the Tokyo, Osaka, and Nagoya stock exchanges in 1961, making it easier for medium-sized companies to be publicly traded. This move also served to expand the base of business for firms like Nomura.

Nomura's strong financial position served it well through the major recession and depressed markets of 1965. In contrast, several of

---

4. ADRs were certificates, denominated in dollars, that represented a specific number of shares of a non–U.S. company denominated in a foreign currency and listed on a foreign stock exchange. The shares underlying the ADRs, while not actually traded, were held in trust.
5. Roughly equivalent to the NASDAQ over-the-counter market in the United States.

Nomura's competitors, including the largest—Yamaichi Securities—had to be rescued with government-secured loans. As a result, Nomura emerged for the first time as the undisputed leading securities firm in Japan.

The disasters of the war had left Japan's economy starved for capital. While the Ministry of Finance was pleased to open the door to capital that wanted in, it closed the door to capital outflows during the decades of economic recovery. The early 1970s saw the beginning of two-way capital flows into and out of Japan. In 1970, the Ministry of Finance authorized, for the first time, the purchase of foreign securities by Japanese investment trusts. A few years later, restrictions were lifted on the purchase of foreign securities by individual Japanese investors, and foreign securities were approved for listing on the Tokyo Stock Exchange (TSE). Foreign investment trusts also started to be actively sold in Japan. Nomura profited from the Japanese appetite for foreign securities and, in 1973, established Fund America of Japan, Inc., an investment trust jointly managed with Merrill Lynch.

The 1970s were a boom time in the issuance of Japanese government bonds, particularly after the government undertook extensive infrastructure development as an antidote to the shock of the massive oil-price increases in 1974 and 1979. New issues, along with reduced restrictions on sales of secondary-market government bonds by financial institutions, turned up the heat on trading volume. With their tradition in trading, securities firms made the most of this opportunity, although Japanese commercial banks were far larger holders of government bonds in their own portfolios. Nomura scored impressive successes, partly through its door-to-door efforts that employed 2,500 women to sell the securities the way Avon sells beauty products to U.S. housewives.

Bond trading was also facilitated by official recognition of "gensaki" transactions, the Japanese equivalent of U.S. Treasury securities-repurchase agreements ("Repos"). In this type of arrangement, bonds were sold with an agreement to repurchase them at a fixed future date, perhaps in one day or one week, at a price slightly higher than the original sale. Nomura and the other securities firms, seeking an inexpensive and convenient way of funding their bond-trading positions, played a significant role in such transactions. However, government bonds continued to be underwritten by a fixed syndicate dominated by the commercial banks, and so the securities firms' (and Nomura's) share of that underwriting volume remained comparatively small.

At the same time, some Japanese corporations (like their counterparts in Europe and the United States) were becoming less reliant on bank loans as both their external financing needs diminished and their access to lower-cost public bonds increased. In particular, the Eurobond markets provided attractively priced financing opportunities. Nomura, with the other big securities firms, had become active as underwriters in the London market and therefore benefited substantially from this trend.

Nomura was instrumental in the development of the samurai bond market, the name given to yen-denominated bonds issued publicly in the domestic Japanese market by foreign borrowers, such as other governments, supranational organizations, and a limited number of well-known foreign corporations. The first samurai bond deal was led by Nomura in 1970, and the firm quickly seized a large share of this market.

In the samurai market, the securities firms claimed a modest but satisfying tactical victory over the Japanese commercial banks by breaking some of the banks' control over the underwriting syndication process. Previously, an issuer's main Japanese commercial bank would typically be appointed "commissioned bank," to represent the interests of the bondholders and to be responsible for safekeeping the collateral (since most such bonds were secured by real assets). The commissioned banks were therefore often influential in decisions regarding the underwriters' final allotments of bonds to different members of the distribution syndicate, thus giving them a hand in the critical role of running the books for the syndicate. The new arrangements negotiated by Nomura for samurai bond issues clarified the responsibilities of the underwriters and limited the ability of the commissioned bank to interfere in the syndication process, thereby strengthening the hand of lead managers such as Nomura. Nonetheless, the commissioned banks continued to be influential as syndicators for other forms of domestic corporate debt financing.

Other important changes served to strengthen the position of the securities firms relative to the commercial banks. By the mid-1970s, unsecured corporate bonds had gained some acceptance. Without the need to keep track of collateral, the role of the banks acting as commissioned agents in bond underwriting was further diminished. At the same time, small and medium-sized financial institutions and individuals (both prime sales targets for the securities firms) increased their absorption of new government- and corporate-bond issues, relative to purchases made by the big commercial banks for their own portfolios.

Nomura, with its vast retail sales network, benefited from the growing pool of individual investors in Japan, many of whom had a special interest in bonds. Meanwhile, institutional investors were becoming a growing factor in the equity markets. In 1949, individual investors owned 70 percent of the listed shares in Japan. This figure fell to 32 percent by 1972 and decreased even further to about 25 percent by the mid-1980s, forcing Nomura to pay increasing attention to equity sales to institutions and companies in addition to its historical commitment to individual investors.

Thus, by the end of the 1970s, Nomura was already the undisputed leader among the Big Four Japanese securities firms as well as a major player, with the commercial banks, in the domestic financial markets. However, its strength was still primarily in selling stocks and bonds to Japanese investors. Ahead lay struggles to improve the balance of its service mix, particularly to increase its corporate finance capabilities, and to position itself as a leader in the increasingly global financial marketplace.

Nomura Today

Nomura came into the limelight as a truly international firm in the 1980s. Historically, its overseas network in the 1950s and early 1960s consisted primarily of branch and representative offices that were merely extensions of Tokyo. With the increasing internationalization of capital flows, Nomura decided to expand its foreign subsidiaries and give them greater autonomy in local decision making. Reorganizations took place in New York (1969), London and Amsterdam (1972), Frankfurt (1973), and Paris (1979). New representative offices were opened in Bahrain and Sidney (1980), and a number of joint ventures were established in Southeast Asia, Australia, and the Middle East.

In 1981, Nomura Securities International, the official name of the U.S. operation, became a member of the New York Stock Exchange, the first Japanese securities firm to be admitted. At the same time, Nomura International (Hong Kong) Limited was formed. Securities operations were established in Canada following that country's regulatory reform (dubbed "Little Bang") in 1987. New representative offices were also established in Beijing, Brussels, Lugano, Kuala Lumpur, and other locations.

Through its extensive domestic-branch network and overseas operations located in twenty countries, Nomura was active in securities underwriting, sales, trading, brokerage, and research in most major markets around the world. Further, it was actively trying to enhance its corporate finance activities by building a merger-and-acquisitions advisory business. In 1988, roughly 20 percent of total revenues came from international operations, most from either international securities sales in London and Hong Kong or Eurobond underwriting commissions. But highlighting its global ambitions, Nomura's president, Yoshihisa Tabuchi, one of the youngest chief executives in Japanese financial circles and who was featured on *Time* magazine's cover in August 1988, declared his intention of increasing the figure to 50 percent.[6]

Perhaps its most impressive international presence was in the London Euromarkets. Nomura International Limited, having grown from a small branch office first established in London in 1964, was chartered in 1981 to act as the center of the firm's European operations. With the growth in Japanese issuers in the Eurobond market, as well as its placing power for leanly priced Eurodollar bonds among Japanese investors, Nomura steadily climbed in the underwriting league tables. As a result of Big Bang, Nomura became a member of the International Stock Exchange (earlier the London Stock Exchange) and was granted a commercial bank charter. In 1987, Nomura supplanted Credit Suisse First Boston as the top-ranked Eurobond underwriter.

By the late 1980s, Nomura was the largest and most profitable securities firm in the world. Revenues (see Table 11-1) in 1987 totaled ¥1,073 billion ($8.5 billion), and net income was ¥268 billion ($2.1 billion). Shareholders' equity (see Table 11-2) exceeded ¥1,100 billion (almost $9 billion), dwarfing by comparison the major investment banks and securities firms from other countries. But, as competing global investment banks were quick to point out, size was not everything. Nomura's international successes, especially in the Eurobond market, were built primarily on its strong domestic franchise with Japanese investors. Critics pointed out that the firm still lacked entrée into top-ranked multinational corporate board rooms,[7] and, even among Japanese corporate issuers, Nomura and the other large Japanese securities firms were still struggling to dislodge the commercial banks from their long-standing roles as primary corporate financial counselors, especially in the area of mergers and acquisitions.

Securities sales continued to dominate the firm's activities. Commission income from securities brokerage, primarily in Japan, traditionally accounted for just over half of Nomura's total revenues. Although there were over 200 securities firms in Japan, the Big Four dominated trading at the TSE: directly, they handled more than half

6. "Yen Power," cover story, *Time*, August 8, 1988, pp. 42ff; see also, "Nomura: Biggest and Most Profitable," *Euromoney Special Supplement*, September 1987, p. 70; and Peter Hall, "Yoshihisa Tabuchi," *Financial World*, December 1986, p. 22.
7. David Fairlamb, "Nomura Securities' Global Ambitions," *Dun's Business Month*, November 1986, p. 44.

Table 11-1
Nomura Securities Co., Ltd. Consolidated Income Statements, 1982–1988
(¥ million except per share figures)

	1982	1984	1986	1987	1988	1988*
Revenue						
Commissions	¥97,950	¥212,480	¥503,651	¥583,253	¥459,031	$3,763
Underwriting and distribution	51,620	55,141	106,476	176,452	184,872	1,515
Net gain on trading	44,839	58,664	138,365	128,998	135,000	1,107
Interest and dividends	69,752	107,071	191,046	176,494	173,128	1,419
Other	4,058	3,599	2,026	7,810	7,764	63
	268,219	436,955	941,561	1,073,007	959,795	7,867
Expenses						
Compensation and benefits	68,327	89,109	115,480	137,055	144,419	1,184
Commissions and floor brokerage	7,938	11,558	20,124	24,205	19,215	158
Communications	8,428	11,000	13,773	16,436	19,025	156
Interest	35,479	60,873	127,649	98,412	85,485	701
Rental and maintenance	17,298	21,775	26,745	30,364	34,504	283
Advertising and publicity	6,315	6,791	7,496	10,902	9,878	81
Taxes other than income taxes	11,541	18,005	39,466	75,284	67,158	550
Other operating expenses	35,363	53,667	95,122	96,822	109,446	897
	188,689	272,778	445,855	489,480	489,130	4,009
Income before taxes	79,530	164,177	495,709	583,527	470,665	3,858
Income taxes	37,914	91,106	274,853	315,437	256,528	2,103
Net income	41,616	73,071	220,856	268,090	214,137	1,755
Net income per 1,000 share	24.8	40.6	121.6	145.9	112.0	918.23
Dividends per 1,000 share	6.5	6.9	10	12.6	13.1	107.64

* Equivalent U.S. dollars (millions); calculated at 122 yen per U.S. dollar.

Table 11-2

Nomura Securities Co., Ltd. Consolidated Balance Sheets, 1985–1988

(¥ million)

	1985	1986	1987	1988	1988*
Assets					
Cash and deposits	¥641,551	¥702,673	¥969,420	¥1,150,156	$9,428
Loans receivable from customers	347,583	689,787	905,786	976,084	8,001
Other loans and receivables	212,802	217,068	393,601	372,682	3,055
Trading securities:					
Stocks	34,142	13,161	35,340		
Government bonds	413,163	638,565	420,109	1,416,226**	11,608**
Corporate bonds	149,748	145,703	83,420		
Other	153,214	171,908	241,093		
Investment securities	77,131	167,511	208,246		
Other assets	148,492	180,113	228,655	291,443	2,389
	2,177,826	2,926,489	3,485,670	4,206,591	34,480
Liabilities and equity					
Bank and other loans	603,641	551,698	662,365	759,785	6,227,746
Bonds and notes	78,338	123,117	123,478	256,440	2,101,967
Time deposits	313,482	481,704	516,694	620,958	5,089,820
Payables to customers and others	391,764	629,825	792,518	961,494	7,881,098
Accrued liabilities	153,879	304,718	281,180	296,601	2,431,156
Shareholders' equity	636,722	835,427	1,109,435	1,311,313	10,748,467
	2,177,826	2,926,489	3,485,670	4,206,591	34,480,254

* Equivalent U.S. dollars (millions); calculated at 122 yen per U.S. dollar.
** Disaggregation not available.

of the daily volume; indirectly, including the trading of their affiliates, they controlled approximately 70 percent. Of this amount, Nomura and its affiliates accounted for about 30 percent.[8] However, with the growth of smaller Japanese firms and the appearance of foreign brokers, the proportion of trading handled directly by the Big Four declined in the 1980s. Nomura's trading strength in brokerage was a result not only of its extensive retail-distribution network but also its control of a substantial number of investment trusts and investment funds. The firm's almost five-million customer accounts, most of whom purchased at least some investment trusts, were serviced by an army of sales people, including door-to-door saleswomen, operating out of over 100 locations in Japan. Of the total of over ¥42 trillion ($300 billion) of outstanding investment trusts in Japan, Nomura's sales accounted for about one-quarter. In addition, assets totaling ¥14 trillion ($100 billion) were managed by its subsidiary, Nomura Investment Management Co., Ltd.

The Nomura culture demanded hard work, dedication, and relentless selling. Young sales people were exhorted to follow in the tradition of President Tabuchi, who apocryphally had made at least 100 calls a day and wore out a pair of shoes a week during his years as a broker.[9] But some market participants accused the Japanese brokers of abusing the trust of small investors through churning—the execution of unnecessary trades in a client's account to generate excessive commissions. The practice appeared to be more widespread in Japan than in the United States and largely ignored by the authorities.

Securities trading in which Nomura took a principal position represented about one-eighth of total revenues. In the important secondary market for Japanese government bonds, Nomura's share usually represented twice the volume of any other firm.[10] In equities, Nomura was just as dominant; in fact, its competitors complained Nomura could move the markets by rumor.[11]

Although fixed-commission rates were reduced in Japan for large trades following London's Big Bang, there was continuing pressure for further liberalization. Institutional investors, who accounted for roughly three-quarters of the total Japanese market volume, were particularly vocal. However, it appeared that the TSE, backed by the government, was committed to maintaining fixed-commission rates for the present, ostensibly to keep order in the markets, but practi-

8. Brian Robbins, "Tokyo Market Dominated by Rumour and Nomura," *Euromoney Special Supplement*, September 1987, p. 46.
9. Fairlamb, "Nomura Securities' Global Ambitions," p. 44.
10. "Nomura: Biggest and Most Profitable," p. 70.
11. Robbins, "Tokyo Market Dominated by Rumour and Nomura," p. 46.

cally to protect the revenue streams of the politically powerful smaller Japanese brokerage houses with higher cost structures. Fixed rates also had the effect of preserving the lucrative revenue streams of the leading brokerage firms. Nevertheless, the Ministry of Finance had indicated its intention to periodically review commission rates with the aim of maintaining Tokyo's relative competitiveness with other major markets around the globe.

Nomura also had a sizable underwriting business, both domestically and in the Eurobond market, which in 1988 accounted for about 15 percent of revenues. In addition to its top ranking in Eurobonds, it led the league tables for both domestic Japanese equity share and bond issues.

Nomura's revenues from merger-and-acquisition-related business were, however, still nominal in relation to its overall operations, reflecting a number of factors. Historically, Japanese corporations had not paid for counseling services, extended in large part free of charge by their main banks, which counted on the revenue from the total relationship to compensate for an array of counseling and other unbilled services. Thus, it was difficult for the Japanese securities firms, striving for access to Japanese corporate board rooms, to charge fees in addition to gross spreads earned on public financing. Then, too, the volume of mergers and acquisitions in Japan was much smaller than in either the United States or Europe and tended to involve small to medium-sized companies with strong ties to their main bank, which usually had a recently organized staff of M&A specialists.

The most important potential source of M&A fees was from cross-border activities, typically involving a Japanese purchaser and a foreign (often American) seller. In these instances, Japanese corporate executives would turn to U.S. investment banks or British or continental merchant banks with an internationally recognized expertise and franchise in the field. Only in recent years had Nomura focused its attention on penetrating the M&A market, and it recognized that a key to achieving that objective domestically was to demonstrate its full-service investment banking capabilities offshore with a variety of foreign corporate clients. This was one reason for the special focus on its New York-based operation, which provided the opening to the huge potential of the U.S. marketplace for financial products and services.

Nomura (U.S.)

Nomura's postwar American operations, dating back to 1953, were involved originally in facilitating the import of capital to Japan through the sales of Japanese securities to foreign investors. However, because most of these sales went through London or Hong Kong, one senior manager at Nomura (U.S.) labeled the early New York operations as merely a "tourist bureau." It was not until the mid-1980s that the American subsidiary was positioned to play a substantial role in Nomura's global aspirations.

The Federal Reserve's designation of both Nomura and Daiwa Securities as primary dealers in 1986 was an important breakthrough and marked the first major business expansion of the Japanese securities firms in the United States. Nomura's New York operations grew rapidly from under 200 employees in 1986 to a peak of over 600 in late 1987. (By early 1988, total employment at Nomura [U.S.] had fallen to about 550 through attrition and layoffs, a level it maintained through 1989.)

An important goal for Nomura—and for the dozen or so other Japanese securities firms with New York operations, including the other Big Four—was to Americanize operations by hiring U.S. professionals. The Japanese term for this, "dochaku-ka," is roughly translated as "becoming deeply rooted" or "homesteading." At Nomura (U.S.), only about 12 percent of the staff in 1988 represented Japanese, who were on loan from the Tokyo office, and the percentage had fallen from over 20 percent just a few years before. Daiwa had achieved a similar ratio, although Nikko, Yamaichi, and some smaller firms had a comparatively larger percentage of Japanese in New York. One senior executive at Nomura (U.S.) stated his belief that only after his firm had become a truly American securities firm, with a substantial business in U.S. securities with U.S. issuers and investors, would the parent Nomura be able to achieve its goal of becoming a globally pre-eminent investment bank.

Despite Nomura's success in Japan and in the Euromarkets, New York was still considered the weak link in its global network. Masaaki Kurokawa, until mid-1989, the head of Nomura (U.S.), was aiming to increase the contribution to Nomura's profits from New York, estimated at only about 2 percent of Nomura's 1987 worldwide total.[12] To do this, he noted, "We aim to be a solid member of the Wall Street Clan!"[13] Until recently, the U.S. operation had relied primarily on the strength of its U.S. government-bond sales to Japanese investors. However, former Nomura (U.S.) chairman Yoshio Terasawa, noting

---

12. Michael R. Sesit, "Kurokawa Looks to Expand the Territory," *The Wall Street Journal*, October 5, 1987, p. 28.
13. "Yen Power: Nomura Flexes Its Global Financial Muscle," *Time*, August 8, 1988, p. 46.

that the firm did not want to get stuck as a niche player, once commented, "We don't want to be a Japanese restaurant in New York serving only sushi and sukiyaki."[14]

Throughout the mid-1980s and up until the crash of October 1987, equity sales and trading grew in importance for the New York firm. By the late 1980s, Nomura (U.S.) derived about 50 percent of its revenues from the sales and trading of fixed-income securities, 40 percent from the sales and trading of equity securities, and 10 percent from investment banking. Although officials at Nomura (U.S.) stated that all three areas were equally targeted for expansion, Nomura appeared especially sensitive to the underweighting of investment banking revenues. The following sections discuss the various operations of Nomura (U.S.) in more detail.

Treasury Securities

Sales and trading of U.S. Treasuries, especially with Japanese investors, was the most important targeted growth area for Nomura (U.S.) beginning in the mid-1980s. Following the repeal of U.S. withholding taxes in 1984 and Nomura's success in selling Treasury issues into Japan, the firm made a major commitment to this market that culminated in primary-dealer status in 1986. Starting with only a handful of sales people, a U.S. government-securities dealing operation was built that, by the late 1980s, comprised about a dozen traders and over twenty salespeople. The head of this group, Robin Koskinen, and the majority of his staff were Americans. Sales and trading of U.S. government bonds contributed three-quarters of the revenues from fixed-income sales and trading, or about 35 percent of the U.S. operation's total revenues.

The Big Four Japanese firms accounted for roughly 20 percent of $100 billion per day long-term U.S. government-bond secondary-market turnover.[15] Although not public information, Nomura's market share was believed to be well above the ¾ percent minimum share required by the Federal Reserve for primary dealership. Observers estimated that Nomura ranked fifteenth out of the forty primary dealers in terms of transaction volume. Further, Nomura (U.S.) reportedly won as much as 10 percent of some auctions of new U.S. government bonds.[16]

At first, most of this business was in selling 10- and 30-year

14. *The Wall Street Journal*, April 1, 1987, p. 1.
15. "Japan on Wall Street," *BusinessWeek*, September 7, 1987, p. 82.
16. Bernard Wysocki, Jr., "Big Dealer: Tough Japanese Firm Grows in Importance in Securities Markets," *The Wall Street Journal*, April 1, 1987, p. 1.

Treasury bonds to Japanese institutions. However, with Japanese participation crucial at U.S. Treasury auctions, U.S. institutions began to contact Nomura to get the Japanese investor's perspective on the Treasury market before making their own moves. As a consequence, by the late 1980s, one source estimated that as much as 75 percent of the Big Four's government-bond transactions in New York were with major U.S. investors compared to less than one-third barely two years before.[17] With Nomura and Daiwa Securities battling neck and neck in this market, it was not clear who would be the winner. Some observers believed that, despite Nomura's tremendous capital backing and investor franchise in Tokyo, their network of institutional investors in the United States lagged behind that of Daiwa.[18]

To avoid problems with profit allocation, Nomura maintained separate dealing books in New York, Tokyo, and London. Unlike some other global investment banks, particularly some of the American firms, there was no single integrated book (or portfolio of outstanding securities positions) encompassing the profits and losses on Treasuries trading worldwide on a twenty-four-hour basis. Instead, each Nomura location passed its book to the next location with strict instructions for defensive trading. For example, when New York closed, Tokyo watched over the American firms' positions, mindful of the New York desk's established loss limits for various positions, but used only the Tokyo book for its own market-making activities. The Tokyo book was so large that several traders from the home office were stationed in New York just to trade Tokyo's positions during the American work day.

One important ingredient in Nomura's success with U.S. government bonds may have been the high quality of its professional staff, including some well-known experts from the Street and government. For example, Nomura (U.S.) was able to recruit John J. Niehenke, the former deputy assistant secretary of the Treasury who handled U.S. Treasury auctions, for Nomura's sales force. However, the other Japanese firms in the U.S. had also attracted top names. Scott E. Pardee, a vice chairman at Yamaichi, was formerly with the New York Federal Reserve Bank. Nikko vice chairman Stephen H. Axilrod had been the Fed's staff director under Paul Volker. And Mary R. Clarkin, Nikko's new bond-sales manager, was formerly the New York Fed's chief domestic-securities trader. Nomura was quick to add that it did not

17. "Japan on Wall Street," p. 84.
18. "Nomura's Three Major Japanese Rivals," *The Wall Street Journal*, April 1, 1987, p. 24.

buy the talent; on the contrary, many of its stars were hired at lower guaranteed salaries but higher potential earnings from bonuses and commissions than they were making at their former employers.

Nomura (U.S.) also believed it had a unique compensation system for securities firms that encouraged the cooperation of bond traders and sales people. Traders were paid a salary plus bonus, determined by departmentwide profits. The wrinkle was, however, that the traders took home only two-thirds of their bonus—the rest was paid over to the sales staff. The sales staff were paid on straight commission, but one-third of this was withheld and given to the traders. It was hoped that the mix would enhance the chances of success of future marketing efforts for product-line extensions, such as T-bills and derivative products (including bond futures and options), targeted at U.S. institutional investors as well as central banks in Central and South America.

Other Fixed-Income Securities

In addition to U.S. government securities, Nomura (U.S.) was actively involved in the sales and trading of a wide range of other fixed-income securities, contributing another 15 percent of its total revenues. A dozen professionals, only one of whom was Japanese, traded U.S. and Canadian corporate bonds, Eurodollar bonds, mortgage-backed securities, Japanese government bonds, and Euroyen bonds. The same sales staff that handled U.S. Treasuries also sold these other fixed-income products, and most of their business was with U.S. institutions.

Nomura's U.S. corporate bond-trading business, a relatively small operation that had been developed only recently, began to be profitable by the late 1980s. A big push was underway into mortgage-backed sales and trading, because Nomura had fallen behind Daiwa as the first Japanese securities firm to venture into this area. Also, Nomura (U.S.) was considering expanding its coverage to include municipal bonds and medium-term notes. To handle the growth in fixed-income securities business, Nomura (U.S.) planned to double its current sales and trading staff over the next few years.

Equity Securities Sales and Trading

Equity sales, including selling Japanese stocks to U.S. investors and American stocks to both Japanese and U.S. investors, was an increasingly important growth area for Nomura (U.S.)—at least until the October 1987 market crash. A strong point for Nomura (U.S.) had always been selling Japanese stocks to U.S. investors, contributing about 30 percent of the New York operation's total revenues. Nomura (U.S.) estimated that it controlled about half of all Japanese equities sold by the Big Four in the United States. However, these flows were still low compared to London, where there were more internationally oriented portfolios. In the United States, Nomura contacted about 90 institutions per day, while the London office had over 300 on its call list. Eventually, as U.S. portfolio managers become more international, this business was expected to grow, but it did not appear to be a near-term major objective of the firm.

In contrast, the sales of U.S. equities, not only to Japan but also to U.S. institutions, represented only 10 percent of total revenues but was considered a potential hot new growth area. In total, the Big Four Japanese securities houses accounted for an estimated 5–10 percent of all trading on the NYSE. Nomura estimated that its share was normally ½–1 percent, about the same as the American firm Merrill Lynch had on the TSE. On certain days, Nomura (U.S.)'s share was considerably larger because of its involvement in "macho trading" of million-share blocks to execute dividend capture strategies for some of its Japanese customers.[19]

Nomura (U.S.) believed it controlled 20–25 percent of the Japanese capital flowing into U.S. equities, with the other major Japanese securities firms and some American investment banks with strong Tokyo operations handling the rest.

The equity sales staff increased from just over ten in 1986 to over 50 by 1989; most of the growth reflected the emphasis on U.S. equities. In New York, about ten Americans handled sales of U.S. equities to U.S. institutions. Nine Japanese sold U.S. equities to Japan. Another group of nine professionals was involved in selling Japanese securities to U.S. investors.

All position trading was done through the dozen or so traders located in New York, the majority of whom were Americans. Nomura (U.S.), having first obtained a seat on the Boston Stock Exchange in 1970, gained a coveted seat on the New York Stock Exchange in 1981 as already mentioned. By the late 1980s, Nomura (U.S.) had expanded its exchange memberships to include the American and Pacific Stock Exchanges, the two major futures markets in Chicago, and the New York Futures Exchange.

The real emphasis for the future, the New York office believed,

---

19. For a time, Japanese institutions, particularly insurance companies, were keen to receive the high current income from dividends. Therefore, they bought high-yielding U.S. stocks on the dividend date of record, with firm agreements to resell them immediately when the stock went ex-dividend.

would be in selling U.S. equities to U.S. institutional investors. Yoshitaka Yamashita, executive vice president in charge of equities at the U.S. operation, hoped "to capture 5 to 6 percent of the U.S. institutional equity business by 1990, up from a minor share today."[20] Nomura, he believed, was in an excellent position to capitalize on the large volume of the flow of two-way deals between the United States and Japan. American investors would be interested in dealing with Nomura (U.S.) primarily to learn the appetite in Japan for U.S. equities. Also, with its trans-Pacific connections, Nomura was often able to arrange large block trades (that is, large institutional-investor transactions, usually in excess of 10,000 shares) between U.S. and Japanese institutions.

Another potential advantage for Nomura (U.S.) in dealing with American investors was its international equity research, a part of Nomura Research Institute, formed in 1965 as a think tank along the lines of the Stanford Research Institute. Five Japanese analysts followed about 120 blue-chip U.S. firms in several industries and prepared reports for Japanese investors in a format familiar and comfortable to them. Another eight analysts, all American, reported on selected U.S. firms and supported the equity sales effort to U.S. institutions. They were selective in their industry coverage, following companies in industries where Japan had a particular strength, such as the automotive, banking, electronics, and telecommunications fields.

Expanding this business was not going to be an easy task, however. First, Nomura was in tough competition with the other Japanese firms, especially Daiwa. Further, the Japanese selling effort in the United States had to overcome the unfavorable reputation that lingered from the early days. In the past, U.S. institutional clients were often left cold by Nomura's "hucksterism." One U.S. fund manager commented, "Nomura's research is workmanlike, but its salesmen are incompetent. I keep telling them they can't talk to us as though we were a retail customer in Yokohama. We're not interested in the stock of the week."[21] This statement echoed the often heard criticism that foreign securities firms in the United States, including the Japanese, were, in some cases, burdened with second-rate talent that had not been able to make the grade at premier American firms.

20. "Foreign Firms Are Eager to Capture Bigger Chunk of U.S. Equity Market," *The Wall Street Journal*, February 16, 1988, p. 51.
21. Lee Smith, "Japan's Brokerage Giant Goes International," *Fortune*, March 19, 1984, p. 70.

Underwriting

Despite its remarkable success in the Euromarkets, Nomura had been able to make only limited headway in investment banking activities in the United States. Nomura's New York investment banking staff currently numbered about fifty professionals, roughly a threefold increase from the 1984 levels. About eighteen corporate finance specialists, of which four were Japanese, called on U.S. corporations and public sector enterprises in search of business. Another six, five of whom were Japanese, worked with the U.S. subsidiaries of Japanese firms. In addition, the investment banking group included syndication, mergers-and-acquisitions, new products, and swaps professionals. Corporate finance professionals covered the top 200 U.S. companies. With a planned doubling of its corporate finance staff over the next few years, Nomura (U.S.) hoped to be able eventually to call on the entire *Fortune* 500.

Nomura, however, had barely made a dent in the domestic U.S. underwriting-league tables. It was a co-manager for five bond issues in 1987, down from 12 in 1986 (Table 11-3). Although most of the issues it co-managed in the early and mid-1980s were for Japanese firms or their U.S. subsidiaries, by the late 1980s Nomura (U.S.) had managed to get involved in deals for several major borrowers such as General Electric and the Federal Home Loan Mortgage Corporation as well as several U.S. utility firms. Unlike in the Euromarket, U.S. investment banks did not feel the need to invite Nomura (U.S.) into domestic offerings as co-managers. Rather, Nomura usually was only a syndicate member, albeit as a "major-bracket" participant, a real step up from the past. What Nomura brought to these deals was Japanese distribution: normally, half its syndicate allocation was sold in Japan.

The fact that Nomura had captured only one lead management— that for General Electric Credit Corporation (GECC) in the fall of 1986—was a sore point with top management in Tokyo. And other participants alleged unusually aggressive price undercutting in the deal with GECC. Hitoshi Imuta, head of investment banking at Nomura (U.S.), admitted, "There were about ten basis points between our bid and the next one. It took us a month to sell, and half of it went to Japan. We took a loss on it."[22] In addition to the problem of establishing relationships with U.S. borrowers, Nomura also had to overcome a perception by many market participants that it lacked creativity and

22. "Investments Flood into US Markets," *Euromoney Special Supplement*, September 1987, p. 38.

Table 11-3

Co-management by Nomura (U.S.) on Bond Issues in the U.S., 1981–1987

1987 (five deals)
Export Import Bank of Japan
Pacific Gas and Electric
Associates of North America
Connecticut Light & Power
Narragansett Electric

1986 (twelve deals)
Federal Home Loan Mortgage Corporation (five deals)
General Electric Company (three deals)
General Electric Credit Corporation (lead manager)
Southern California Gas
California Power & Light
Southern California Edison

1985 (two deals)
Japan Development Bank
Federal National Mortgage Corporation

1984 (two deals)
Japan Development Bank (two deals)

1983 (no deals)

1982 (two deals)
Sony Corporation
Honda Motor Company

1981 (three deals)
Sumitomo Metal Industries Ltd.
Ito-Yakado
Hitachi

innovativeness. "Their product scope is limited. They're pretty provincial . . ." quipped another competitor.[23]

Still, Nomura had the advantage of being able to place what many considered to be very leanly priced securities with its relatively unsophisticated and cash-heavy retail customers in Japan. As one U.S. investment banker complained, "Nomura was the single largest institution with the dumbest customers. And they're using their customers to subsidize their entry into international corporate finance."[24] But Nomura was not the only firm to be criticized in this respect. Daiwa, in its first U.S. domestic-bond underwriting for Rockwell, faced basically the same circumstances.[25]

23. *"Mighty Nomura Tries to Muscle in on Wall Street," BusinessWeek,* December 16, 1985, p. 76.
24. Ibid., p. 77.
25. "Investments Flood into US Markets," p. 38.

Nomura's performance in equity underwriting was even less spectacular. The co-management with Goldman, Sachs of a 1986 initial public offering (IPO) for EXAR, the California subsidiary of a Japanese firm, was its first success. In 1987, it was co-manager, with L.F. Rothschild Unterberg Towbin, of a small $3.8-million IPO for Plant Genetics, a U.S. firm.

The strategy for the corporate finance group was to try to leverage off Nomura's impressive Eurobond and samurai-bond underwriting successes to establish relations with U.S. companies and win domestic underwriting mandates. Another technique used in relationship building was to get American firms to list their stock in Tokyo. By the end of 1987, Nomura had sponsored thirty-six of the eighty-eight listed American companies. Still, it was not clear how long—if ever—it would take before Nomura's New York operation regularly got the nod from U.S. corporations to lead manage domestic issues. Within Nomura, the possibility of acquiring a well-established U.S. firm with strong origination business had been mentioned, and there had been rumors in the past of preliminary talks between Nomura and both E.F. Hutton and Kidder, Peabody, prior to their acquisitions by Shearson Lehman and General Electric, respectively.

Real Estate

As a small nation with a dense population, Japan commands some of the highest real estate prices on earth. In view of its stratospheric property prices, it is little wonder that cash-rich Japanese investors were drawn to the U.S. real estate market. Properties in New York, San Francisco, and Los Angeles—whose prices made even free-spending Americans blanch—were inviting to Tokyo's investors. The growing strength of the yen made them even more appealing.

Real estate became a growing business area within Nomura's investment banking operations. In 1987, for instance, it handled Japanese purchases of U.S. real estate of about $10 billion. As Japanese money increasingly poured in, such famous landmarks as the Tiffany building in Manhattan were bought. Nomura (U.S.) entered the leveraged leasing and real estate business in the United States in 1986 by entering into a co-operative agreement with Babcock and Brown, a U.S.-based leveraged leasing specialist. Then in 1986, it acquired a 50 percent stake in Eastdil, the premier real-estate finance firm of the 1970s, for $50 million. In this venture, Nomura brought to the table a strong capital base in addition to contacts with Japanese investors, while Eastdil had the ability to design imaginative financing techniques. If the partnership remained amiable, observers suspected that Eastdil could leap once again into the forefront of real estate finance along-side the American investment banks.

Mergers and Acquisitions

The mergers-and-acquisitions team, which at Nomura was referred to as the corporate strategy and services group, was a small part of the investment banking group. Three professionals—two Japanese and one American—worked closely with the corporate finance officers calling on Japanese corporations in Tokyo and at the offices of their U.S. subsidiaries. Nomura had not been involved in any American-style hostile takeovers, preferring to work with Japanese companies who, particularly with the strong yen, were casting their nets for friendly acquisitions, licensing arrangements, and joint ventures in the United States.

Japanese financial institutions, including Nomura, were latecom-ers to the M&A field for several reasons. Merger-and-acquisition ac-tivity in Japan, as already mentioned, was much smaller than in the United States and represented a radically different service mix.[26] His-torically, counsel and assistance in this area had typically been pro-vided free by the commercial banks, the traditional financial advisers to Japanese companies. Hostile takeovers just were not done. In the international arena, Japanese companies traditionally preferred to build up overseas operations from scratch rather than buy existing operations in order to avoid buying troubled, overpriced companies. With the accumulation of experience in operating in foreign environ-ments, this reticence to acquire had only recently begun to change, thereby offering potential opportunities to the Japanese securities firms.

Although a couple of Japanese commercial banks, Sanwa Bank and Long-Term Credit Bank, had taken an early lead in assisting Japanese companies investing in U.S. firms, the securities houses, including Nomura, were determined to leap to the forefront. In 1988, Nikko Securities purchased a minority interest in Blackstone Group (a Lehman Brothers spinoff), and Yamaichi Securities purchased a simi-lar interest in Lodestone Group, the new boutique started by a former senior merger-and-acquisition banker from Merrill Lynch.

In August 1988, Nomura also announced the purchase for $100 million of a 20 percent equity interest in a new start-up mergers-and-acquisition boutique, Wasserstein, Perella. Bruce Wasserstein and

26. "Mergers and Acquisitions in Key National Markets," *Mergers & Acquisitions*, July/August 1987, p. 58.

Joseph Perella were both Harvard Business School graduates who, as co-heads, had catapulted First Boston into a leading role in the lucrative and rapidly growing mergers and corporate-restructurings area. Disgruntled in part by First Boston's tolerance for large losses in the trading area and convinced that the appropriate strategy for a firm of First Boston's profile was to fortify a specialized niche position in the global M&A area (see Chapter 12), they resigned from the firm in December 1987 and within a few weeks hung out their "Wasserstein, Perella" shingle (soon jocularly referred to in the industry as "Wasserella"), with the intent of implementing their M&A boutique strategic concept.

Because both men had high public profiles and personal followings that were unusual even by Wall Street standards, they were able to get off to a running start by signing up some impressive companies for monthly retainers in exchange for M&A and strategy counseling. Within a few months, they closed their first billion-dollar leveraged buyout. But because their initial equity was small, they were limited in their ability to exploit the corporate-restructuring investment opportunities that were coming their way. They talked with a number of potential outside capital sources and, not surprisingly, their quest took them to Tokyo. They quickly learned that it had been a mistake to have printed their Japanese-language calling cards identifying themselves as "securities brokers." It was made clear to them that in Japan stockbrokers were historically identified with shady business practices. They made out much better with new cards explicitly associating themselves with M&A activity, which was then attracting a great deal of favorable interest in the Japanese financial and business community.

Their ultimate deal with Nomura, which placed a total value of some $500 million on "Wasserella" after only a few months in business, caused a sensation in international investment banking. There was active speculation as to just how the two parties intended to collaborate to realize benefits from the hookup, which included jointly owned subsidiaries in Tokyo and London to service the M&A potential in those regions. From Wasserstein and Perella's viewpoint, the benefits were obvious: an enormous infusion of capital, a spectacular "market" valuation for the firm, and a partner with very deep pockets and the muscle to open doors in the Far East and elsewhere.

From Nomura's perspective, immediate payoffs would likely come from shared U.S. and foreign M&A deals and the opportunity for both the parent and the Nomura (U.S.) organizations to edge into the potentially lucrative merchant banking business as co-venturers with Wasserstein, Perella. There were, however, a number of unanswered questions. First, it was not clear how the two groups would cooperate on a day-to-day basis. For example, which organization would act as the primary adviser in a deal involving a Japanese purchaser of an American corporation, the Tokyo joint venture or Wasserstein, Perella in New York? The decision would undoubtedly have an important impact on the allocation of the fees from the deal. Such ambiguities could lead to potential conflicts between the parties, which can sow the seeds for later difficulties as happened with First Boston and Credit Suisse First Boston (see Chapter 12). Over the longer term, the question still remained how Nomura would build a world-class in-house corporate finance capability. Was there the possibility, through its collaboration and exchange of personnel with the small but highly skilled boutique, to graft onto its own organization the corporate finance skills and culture that would eventually fill the gap in its service portfolio? This goal would require a relatively long and harmonious relationship. Or was Nomura trying to get the best "bang for the buck" in the near term, using the luster from the Wasserstein, Perella name to quickly win over new clients?

The Talent Challenge

More than almost any industry, the securities business runs on human energy and talent. Because its products are intangible, the output of a securities firm's human resources is paramount. It is in this area that Nomura and other Japanese firms face their greatest challenge. For all their success in product development, management, manufacturing, and foreign trade, Japan's corporations have not been notably effective in reproducing clones of themselves on foreign soil. As management consultant and observer Kenichi Ohmae has noted, the failure of Japan's subsidiaries to fully empower their native talent—always reserving key decision-making authority for native Japanese—constitutes a major roadblock to successful internationalization.[27] Nowhere, perhaps, is this challenge greater than in the international securities industry.

The cultures of Wall Street and Japan's securities firms could not be more different. Wall Street is practically a caricature of American frontier values, strangely transported through time and space to the canyons of Manhattan. Its youthful gunslinger traders and investment bankers brashly confront each other across the deal table, confident of success and rewards that push the limits of common sense.

27. Kenichi Ohmae, *Beyond National Borders: Reflections on Japan and the World* (Homewood, Ill.: Dow Jones Irwin, 1987).

Talent is for hire. Personal allegiance is to one's craft, not to a firm. This ambience is a far cry from the culture of Japan's security industry, which, like that nation's corporate mentality in general, honors the virtues of teamwork, subordination of individual agendas to those of the group, a get-rich-slowly attitude, and the "good soldier."

With so much of Nomura's future strategy in the United States dependent on the quality of its professional staff, the firm took measures to strengthen its human resources management. Stan Lomax, an American, was hired early in 1986 from a competing U.S. investment bank to establish a human resources department. According to Lomax, Nomura gave him relative freedom to establish policies that were appropriate in New York but at odds with those in Tokyo.

Salary, bonus, and commission arrangements that were competitive in New York contrasted sharply with lower pay, primarily in the form of salaries, for Japanese professionals both in Tokyo and on temporary assignment in New York. It was difficult to get a handle on these differences, however, since the Japanese in New York were paid housing allowances and other perks for living abroad. Nomura, along with the other Japanese securities firms, rationalized these differences by emphasizing the employment guarantees implicit for Japanese professionals. In fact, the layoffs at Nomura (U.S.) early in 1988 affected only Americans. (When Nikko Securities and Sumitomo Bank made earlier similar decisions to lay off Americans in New York, fired employees filed a class-action suit against them, charging discrimination.) But the pay differentials did not go unnoticed. Several of Nomura's key Japanese professionals in New York, who were suspected of resenting the higher earnings of their American counterparts, defected to American competitors, where they were offered top jobs with the Tokyo offices of Drexel Burnham, Morgan Stanley, and Merrill Lynch. Over time, Nomura believed that salaries for the Japanese would rise. In fact, Tabuchi, the president of the parent Nomura in Tokyo, publicly admitted that he expected some employees to earn more than he did—quite a radical concession for a Japanese firm that historically based pay on seniority.

At the same time, many American employees of the Japanese securities firms complained of limited autonomy and excessive direction from Tokyo. Nomura's New York subsidiary was hurt by the resignation of thirty-four American traders, analysts, and salespeople in 1986 and 1987 over disputes involving pay and differing U.S. and Japanese management styles.[28]

Perhaps the greatest personnel problem facing Nomura and all

28. "It Won't Stop With the Shearson Deal," *BusinessWeek*, April 6, 1987, p. 36.

Japanese securities firms in the United States was the nationality and tenure of senior management. No American headed up the U.S. operations of Japanese securities firm. There was also the problem of lack of continuity of senior management from Japan. Japanese management in most Japanese firms usually came from Tokyo or other overseas posts on assignments of three–six years. Nomura's normal overseas posting for a Japanese executive was at the short end of that range—about three years.[29] When Terasawa, the former head of the New York operation, was replaced in late 1986, there was some hope within the firm that he would be succeeded by an American. But, for reasons that were not made clear, he was not. As one ex-employee of a Japanese securities house commented, "Even if you get on marvelously with the present regime, you just don't know who's coming through the door the next time."[30]

Conclusions

Nomura's role as a truly global investment bank has depended not only on its successes in Tokyo but also its activities in London and New York. Despite all the activity, the only solid success in the domestic U.S. market has been the U.S. Treasury–bond sales operation, a commodity-like business primed by Nomura's strong franchise with Japanese investors. With a large volume of home market demand for bonds, Nomura (U.S.) has been able to gain credibility and develop business with American institutions in this area.

However, the firm continues to struggle in its attempt to build on this success and move into more value-added product segments, such as sales and trading of corporate bonds and equities. The key to developing these areas is the recruiting and retention of skilled professionals, particularly Americans. Nomura has made an effort to differentiate its personnel practices in America from those in Japan. However, without an American at the helm, it seems likely that a number of talented individuals will shy away from a firm that could be viewed as heavily directed by Tokyo.

There are even more serious problems facing Nomura in its efforts to build corporate finance relationships with American firms to handle securities issuance and merger-and-acquisition advice. Corporate treasurers and CEOs maintain loyalty not only to individual investment bankers, because of talent and personal chemistry, but also to the issuing house themselves, because of a variety of capabilities

---

29. "Nomura May Shift Top U.S. Officers," *New York Times*, November 13, 1986, p. 3.
30. "Investments Flood into US Markets," p. 39.

and past services. Even if it were able to hire the right people, Nomura's entrée into corporate treasury staffs and board rooms in the United States is likely to be slow and difficult. It is doubtful that this type of business can be built from scratch over a reasonable period of time. An alternative strategy, purchasing or forming a joint venture with an American firm with strong corporate-finance capabilities, would be worthwhile only if the two cultures were able to mesh and the skilled professionals do not leave. Nomura's purchase of Eastdil, the American real-estate finance specialist, and the joint venture with Wasserstein, Perella in M&A, are interesting experiments to see if such relationships can work.

No one doubts Nomura's long-term commitment to becoming a globally pre-eminent player or to boosting its position in New York. Like the other Japanese securities houses, Nomura is willing to stick it out over the long haul and, in its methodical manner, take its lumps along the way. As President Tabuchi has said, "We are like a marathon runner trying to get into the lead."[31] It appears likely to be a long race.

---

31. Fairlamb, "Nomura Securities' Global Ambitions," p. 44.

CHAPTER 12

CS FIRST BOSTON

By an agreement signed in October 1988, and publicly announced as completed on December 23, 1988, a new global securities-firm holding company, CS First Boston, was created by the dramatic merger of First Boston, one of the top New York investment banks, and London-based Credit Suisse First Boston (CSFB), a premier underwriter in the Euromarkets. Although CSFB's roots date back before World War II, its formation was a result of a joint venture in 1978 between Credit Suisse, the oldest and third-largest of the three dominant universal banks in Switzerland, and First Boston. Credit Suisse had held a majority interest in this joint venture and had indirectly controlled a sizable interest in First Boston through the equal cross-shareholdings between CSFB and First Boston.

CSFB had long played a leadership role in the origination, underwriting, sales, and trading of Eurobonds and, in the mid-1980s, had also become active in international equities and cross-border M&A activities—areas that First Boston was also pursuing. The venture was highly successful: record profits followed year after year for much of the 1980s as CSFB dominated the Eurobond market, until Nomura Securities grabbed the top spot in 1987. Further, CSFB's sales and trading operations were highly rated by competitors. The surprising success of this rather unusual partnership was attributed to a number of factors, including the unique and clearly defined role for CSFB in the international securities markets. Unlike most of its competitors, CSFB did not have a domestic market on which to build. Yet both First Boston and Credit Suisse, with strong positions in their home markets, recognized the need to work with one another and CSFB to exploit their relative strengths and overcome their individual weaknesses. In addition, the success of CSFB was a testimony to three key leaders in the firm—Michael von Clemm, John M. Hennessy, and Hans-Joerg Rudloff—who, by contributing unique skills and vision at critical points in the organization's history, propelled CSFB forward.

However, as the barriers separating world markets fell, conflict between First Boston and CSFB was inevitable. The quarrels frequently resulted in highly publicized departures of senior staff. After several years of negotiations, in 1988 the two firms decided to merge and create a single bottom line, thereby resolving the territorial and compensation disputes that were absorbing an increasing amount of valuable management time. Nevertheless, the announcement of the deal in which a Swiss bank would indirectly control a major U.S. investment bank jolted the international financial community.

The global operations of the new CS First Boston would be conducted by three geographically focused subsidiaries: First Boston in North and South America; CSFB in Europe, the Middle East, and Africa; and First Boston Pacific in Japan, Hong Kong, Australia, and other parts of the Pacific Basin. Through this network, CS First Boston would provide a full line of investment banking services to securities issuers and investors in every corner of the world. The structure mirrored the judgment of CSFB's management in London that it was impossible for a group of professionals sitting in one capital market, such as New York, London, or Tokyo, to make sound and timely judgments about foreign markets. In fact, it was the London operation that had first appreciated the growing significance of the international markets and the need for a well-coordinated strategy. The importance of the London operation to the future of the newly formed structure was clearly highlighted when its top executive, Jack Hennessy, was chosen to head this privately owned CS First Boston.

Early History of CSFB

The origins of CSFB date back to the international operations of White Weld & Co. Ltd., an old and respected New York investment bank with a solid corporate finance tradition.[1] A London office was established in 1934 to trade and sell securities in Europe. In the late 1950s, White Weld AG was set up in Switzerland to handle private-investor client business and to participate in the growing dollar-denominated foreign bond market. Shortly thereafter, White Weld AG was sold to Credit Suisse to avoid potential regulatory problems in both the United States and in Switzerland. White Weld, having developed a close relationship with Credit Suisse, was given the option of ultimately repurchasing the subsidiary.

Following the opening of the Eurobond market in 1963, White Weld's London operation became heavily involved in Eurobond underwriting and trading. Its rankings in the underwriting league tables steadily improved from eighth in the early days of that nascent

---

1. Parts of this section have been drawn from Padraic Fallon, "The CSFB Interview," *Euromoney*, March 1984, p. 50.

market to second in 1972. Its performance reflected, to a degree, the firm's close relationship with Credit Suisse. Although certain regulations in Switzerland effectively blocked the direct participation of Swiss banks in the early years of the Eurobond business in London, Swiss institutions were important links in the distribution and sales of these international securities. It was estimated that, in certain years, Swiss banks alone accounted for the placement of 50–80 percent of Eurobond issues (see Chapter 2).

Credit Suisse, the oldest of the major Swiss banks, was founded in 1856 as a domestic initiative to counter the strong foreign financial interests then controlling Switzerland's economic development. The immediate catalyst was the pressing need for capital to finance the growing Swiss national railroad, a pattern similar to the key role played by railroad financings in the development of the U.S. securities markets in the 1800s and, later, the Japanese markets. Initially, a portion of Credit Suisse was owned by a German bank that was later acquired by Deutsche Bank. Although Credit Suisse's current ownership was predominantly Swiss, some observers believed that a special relationship continued to exist between Deutsche Bank and Credit Suisse up until the mid-1980s.

Over time, Credit Suisse, which originally focused on promoting new business ventures, diversified to become a true universal bank, with activities spanning a broad service range, including commercial lending, deposit taking, securities underwriting, trading and sales, and investment management. Credit Suisse, like the other two big Swiss banks—Union Bank of Switzerland and Swiss Bank Corporation was known for the sizable amount of individual investment funds it controlled on behalf of both Swiss citizens and foreigners seeking anonymity. Its ability to place new Eurobonds with these investors earned the bank an important role in the growing international securities market. To be sure, some critics accused the major Swiss banks of "stuffing" the accounts by purchasing bonds at a discount in the primary market and then selling them into these investment funds at par, thus securing potentially sizable profits for themselves.

As a traditional and conservatively managed institution and one of only seven AAA-rated banks in the world, Credit Suisse's consistent profitability enabled it to accumulate substantial capital and undisclosed reserves with which to buttress its influence in the financial arena. Its embroilment in the "Chiasso affair," perhaps Switzerland's biggest banking scandal, provided a rare opportunity for a public glimpse at the enormous size of its hidden reserves. The incident came to light in 1977 with the disclosure of extensive losses at the

Chiasso branch of Credit Suisse, located on the Swiss-Italian border, that arose from unauthorized lending activities and resulted in a top management shake-up. Although the losses totalled almost Sfr 1 billion, Credit Suisse emerged from the fray untattered. It was able to cover the entire amount with a charge to its substantial hidden reserves rather than decreasing current earnings or the equity capital carried on its balance sheet.

Changes in regulations enabled White Weld in 1969 to buy back from Credit Suisse its former Swiss operation, which had, in the interim, been renamed Clariden Finanz AG. As part of the deal, Credit Suisse took a small interest in White Weld Trust, a Swiss holding company set up in Zug to control White Weld's European activities. A few years later, in 1974, Credit Suisse increased its share of White Weld Trust to a majority stake, and, in turn, White Weld Trust took a minority ownership position in White Weld & Co. Ltd. in New York. A group of managing directors was also allowed to purchase a limited number of voting shares. To reflect the participation of the Swiss bank, the name of the holding company was changed to Société Financière du Crédit Suisse et de White Weld (CSWW). As a result, a powerful joint venture, based in London, was formed between a major Swiss bank and a well-regarded U.S. investment bank.

After weathering the contraction in the Eurobond market in 1973 and 1974, the joint venture CSWW was able to profit from the expansion of new-issue volume throughout most of the remainder of the decade. The firm was especially active in floating-rate notes (FRNs), a type of security in which the amount of the periodic coupon (interest rate) payments was based on the level of a floating benchmark rate such as LIBOR (the London interbank offered rate). Although CSWW did not invent FRNs, its championing of the instruments led to their explosive growth in the mid-1970s.[2] CSWW was especially successful in developing the market for bank FRNs and, in 1977, created floating-rate certificates of deposit.[3] Partially due to its success in the FRN sector, CSWW held on to third place in the Eurobond league tables for the combined years 1976 through 1978 against stiff competition, trailing only two of the leading German universal banks,

2. The first FRN, for the Italian state-owned enterprise ENEL in 1970, was lead managed by Bankers Trust and S.G. Warburg. White Weld, Credit Suisse, and Banca Commericale Italiana were co-managers.
3. For a detailed history of the development of the market for floating-rate securities, see Georges Ugeux, *Floating-Rate Notes* (London: Euromoney, 1985). For a discussion of the role of CSWW and Michael von Clemm in the development of this market see Charles Grant, "Michael von Clemm: The End of a Legend," *Euromoney*, March 1986, pp. 18–23.

Deutsche Bank and Westdeutsche Landesbank Girozentrale, which, like the Swiss banks, had formidable placing power by virtue of their large number of bank-controlled investment funds.

The Alliance with First Boston

The working relationship among White Weld & Co. Ltd., Credit Suisse, and CSWW was shattered in April 1978 with the sudden announcement that White Weld was being purchased by Merrill Lynch. Merrill Lynch, which had only three years before reorganized and consolidated its international investment banking operations in London, was more interested in White Weld's U.S. operations than its Euromarket joint venture.[4] This suited Credit Suisse and CSWW fine: neither was interested in a joint venture with a lumbering giant like Merrill Lynch. After much negotiating—and, some say, subtle threats by CSWW to use its share holding in White Weld to delay the sale—Credit Suisse was allowed to repurchase the minority share of CSWW that Merrill would acquire through White Weld, thus giving Credit Suisse about 90 percent ownership of CSWW.

The deal left CSWW with $32 million in cash (the proceeds from the sale of its shares in White Weld to Merrill Lynch) but without an American connection. Although several other initiatives were considered, it was concluded that CSWW's first need was to re-establish a major American presence.[5] This was considered crucial because of the important two-way business traffic that brought U.S. issuers to the Eurobond market in London and foreign issuers to the Yankee bond market (that is, the U.S. market for overseas issuers) in New York. If CSWW was to get a meaningful piece of that business, it would need a credible U.S. outlet. Building an operation in the United States from scratch was ruled out as likely to absorb too much management time; the only unsettled question was with which well-established U.S. investment banking firm to build a new relationship.

John Craven, head of CSWW's London operation, favored a deal with a relatively small firm. In particular, he was keen on Dillon, Read, a prestigious and "white shoe" firm that was in a period of relative decline on Wall Street (it had recently been demoted from the "special bracket" to the "major bracket" in the U.S. underwriting hierarchy). However, von Clemm, then CSWW's vice chairman, pre-

4. "The Credit Suisse White Weld Deal: How Gut and Craven Got What They Wanted," *Euromoney*, July 1978, pp. 101–104.
5. Parts of this discussion of the CSWW alliance with First Boston are drawn from Padraic Fallon, "Dissecting the Credit Suisse First Boston Alliance," *Euromoney*, March 1979, pp. 75–85.

ferred one of the special bracket firms that enjoyed pre-eminent status in U.S. investment banking.[6] Wanting to do as big a deal as possible, von Clemm urged Credit Suisse's Rainer Gut, who had taken over the top position at the parent Swiss bank in the wake of the Chiasso scandal, to "write the biggest hydrogen bomb deal in our power."[7]

Morgan Stanley, with an extremely strong client list, had already firmly established itself in London and had been prominent in the Eurobond league tables in the late 1960s and the 1970s (see Chapter 2). Thus, there would likely be little enthusiasm at Morgan Stanley for a joint venture with a Swiss bank in the Euromarkets. Salomon Brothers, which had built a strong international presence through its trading prowess (see Chapter 10) and was interested in a deal with the Swiss bank, was not seriously considered by Credit Suisse; apparently, there was not the right culture fit between the two. Preliminary talks with Goldman, Sachs, an ascending firm with strengths in relationship investment banking and domestic U.S. equities, did not result in the right personal chemistry with the CSWW leadership either.[8] Thus, with Merrill Lynch also out of the running, the logical choice appeared to be First Boston.

First Boston, a product of the 1933 Glass-Steagall Act, was formed in 1934 as the first publicly owned securities firm in the United States.[9] It grew out of the securities affiliate of The First National Bank of Boston, along with some key corporate finance experts, from the old-line investment banking firm of Harris, Forbes. In 1946, Mellon Securities Corporation also merged into First Boston, further expanding both the client base and the capital resources. Building on already established relationships that had carried over from before Glass-Steagall, First Boston quickly became a major underwriter for a diverse group of companies, including blue-chip manufacturing firms such as Alcoa, Gulf Oil, and Koppers (all former Mellon family start-ups), major financial institutions, and utilities. In the postwar 1950s and early 1960s, First Boston was also active in bringing foreign issuers to the Yankee bond market in New York. In 1959, for instance, the company reintroduced the credit of Japan to the U.S. capital markets by managing two offerings of Japanese government bonds—the first such Japanese issues since 1930. Despite this foreign activity,

6. The five special-bracket firms at that time were Merrill Lynch, Salomon, Goldman, Sachs, Morgan Stanley, and First Boston.
7. Quoted in Fallon, "Dissecting the Credit Suisse First Boston Alliance," p. 75.
8. Ibid., p. 80.
9. No other major U.S. securities firm would go public until 1970, over four decades later, when Donaldson Lufkin & Jenrette (DLJ) did so. Interestingly, the DLJ issue was managed by First Boston.

First Boston was probably the most domestically focused of the major U.S. investment banks. Although a London office had been established in the 1960s, it was not until the early 1970s that First Boston Europe began to build, on a limited basis, an international presence.

As one of the original four special-bracket underwriters (along with Morgan Stanley, Dillon, Read, and Kuhn Loeb) following the Second World War, First Boston had a list of traditional clients for whom it did securities origination and merger-and-acquisition advisory work, which could only have impressed von Clemm and Credit Suisse. However, as the discussions went forward, First Boston was still recovering from internal and market-related problems that had arisen in the mid-1970s. Net earnings had fallen from $18 million in 1976 to an anemic $3 million in 1977, with scant improvement expected for 1978. Further, First Boston's international operations, with the possible exception of its role as an arranger for syndicated loans, had been lackluster. To give the firm real clout in Europe and to improve its standing in the Eurobond league tables, Jack Hennessy, then president of First Boston International and head of investment banking at First Boston, was rumored to have been looking for a European universal-bank partner. The possibility of a deal with giant Credit Suisse and its London subsidiary seemed a fortuitous opportunity.

Craven, however, opposed an alliance with First Boston. He believed that, because of excessive overhead, the New York firm's profitability was too low. Further, he believed First Boston, unlike a firm such as Dillon, Read, was too big for CSWW to control effectively, a concern that at least some of the other members of CSWW's management apparently also harbored. However, Credit Suisse's Gut, a former investment banker with experience at Lazard Frères in New York, made the final decision that an alliance with First Boston was the best available alternative. First Boston, seeing an opportunity to dramatically expand its international presence, agreed wholeheartedly. In July 1978, an agreement was reached in which First Boston purchased from Credit Suisse 40 percent of CSWW, leaving the Swiss bank with just over a majority interest in the joint venture. CSWW, in turn, purchased a 40 percent shareholding in First Boston, creating an offsetting cross-shareholding arrangement between First Boston and CSWW. Thus, Credit Suisse indirectly controlled 40 percent of First Boston through its majority interest in CSFB. Shortly thereafter, the name of the joint venture was changed to Credit Suisse First Boston (CSFB). Frustrated by the turn of events, Craven resigned a few months after the deal and was succeeded as chief executive officer by von Clemm.

Von Clemm quickly established himself as one of the dominant figures at CSFB and became its most public persona. Over the years, the tall and imposing American had enjoyed a varied career. Holding a degree in anthropology from Harvard and a doctorate from Oxford, he had subsequently lived with the Wachagga tribe in Tanzania for just over a year.[10] After a stint as a reporter with the *Boston Globe*, he joined Citibank in 1963, where, while working in its London operation, he pioneered the Eurodollar certificate of deposit. In 1968, von Clemm left Citibank to lecture at the Harvard Business School and to do some part-time consulting work for the London joint venture. Stanislas Yussukovich, chief executive of White Weld & Co. Ltd., hired von Clemm away from Harvard in 1972, shortly before the formal establishment of the Credit Suisse White Weld (CSWW) joint venture in 1974.

At CSWW and later at CSFB, von Clemm was given the chance to further exercise his creativity. He personally pushed for the development of the bank floating-rate note (FRN) market, successfully arguing that FRNs—with coupons of ¼ percent over LIBOR—were an attractive and relatively stable funding alternative to LIBOR-based deposits. Von Clemm became known as a skillful deal maker, spending much of his time traveling widely in the course of visiting the firm's long list of current and prospective clients. A forceful and unique person, von Clemm frequently entertained friends and business associates at La Gavroche, a three-star Michelin-rated French restaurant in London in which he had a financial stake.

CSFB's Successful Marketing of the "Bought Deal"

Following the consummation of Credit Suisse's alliance with First Boston, CSFB piled up successive record profits throughout the early and mid-1980s as it reinforced its leadership in the London-based Euromarkets. The initial impetus for its success, according to von Clemm, was CSFB's perfection of and aggressive marketing of the "bought deal." In a bought deal, a variation of the "fixed-price" or "firm-bid" issues that had previously surfaced in the Eurobond market, one investment bank (or a small group of banks) agreed to buy immediately an entire issue from a borrower at a fixed price and coupon. By contrast, traditionally underwritten deals took much longer to execute: after a financing mandate had been awarded, a large underwriting and selling syndicate had to be formed that would then market the bonds for several weeks before establishing the final

---

10. This discussion of Michael von Clemm's history is drawn from Grant, "Michael von Clemm," pp. 18–23.

price and consummating the sales. Not only was this syndication process more cumbersome and more expensive, it sometimes caused the issuer to miss an important window of opportunity in the market, given the speed with which economic conditions shifted.

CSFB's success with executing the bought deal was largely the work of Hans-Joerg Rudloff, hired from Kidder, Peabody's Geneva office by von Clemm in 1980. Compact, slightly balding, and full of energy, the German-born Rudloff was brought up in Switzerland and, in addition to German, English, and French, was fluent in Schweizerdeutsch, the special German dialect spoken in parts of Switzerland, including the important banking circles in Zurich. He started his career as a trainee at Credit Suisse, then joined Kidder, Peabody. After a year in Kidder's New York office, he returned to Switzerland and worked his way up to the position of manager of the U.S. firm's Geneva office. At Kidder, Rudloff developed an exceptional sense for the public debt markets and began experimenting with the prepriced deal, the predecessor of the bought deal.

One early CSFB bought deal was done in April 1980 with GMAC. From London, von Clemm telephoned Thomas Patton, GMAC's executive vice president, and offered to buy $100 million of five-year bonds with an annual interest payment of 13⅛ percent, which at the time was a very attractive rate. The catch was that GMAC would have to decide quickly, because CSFB was concerned that market conditions could deteriorate. Patton accepted the offer within a half hour. The GMAC deal was quickly followed by others like it. With increased market volatility, many borrowers responded enthusiastically to the ability to launch a bond issue quickly when a financing window temporarily opened, and the bought deal soon became a regular feature of the Eurobond market.

Of course, the commitment to buy an entire issue exposed the bank to substantial risk should the market turn downward before the bonds could be sold. In June 1980, for example, CSFB was caught holding a huge chunk of bonds from a bought deal for European Investment Bank; interest rates soared, and the price of the bonds fell from par, or 100, to below 93 in only ten days.[11] About the same time, CSFB incurred a similar loss on $150 million it bought from the Export Development Corporation. But CSFB had earned the reputation for boldness and the willingness to commit its capital on short notice. One CSFB executive commented, "We take big risks here. We don't

---

11. David Shirreff, "The Warrior Style of CSFB's Rudloff," *Euromoney*, December 1981, p. 31.

have to wait for someone to wake up in New York to say if they can buy an issue."[12]

Despite these occasional losses, von Clemm and Rudloff were convinced that the advantage of having total control over an issue outweighed the inherent risk of capital exposure. Lead managers of traditionally syndicated deals often suspected that some syndicate members who were included at the borrower's request but who lacked any real placing power were quick to offload their commitments in the "gray market."[13] This put downward pressure on new-issue prices and often necessitated costly price-stabilization maneuvers and caused embarrassment for the lead managers at their miscalculations. With a bought deal, the situation was different. As one CSFB executive put it, "We weren't prepared to go out and discuss with the issuer which banks should be included in the management group. We eliminated the whole syndicate discussion which normally takes place with the borrower."[14] The bought deal permitted CSFB to eliminate its exposure to losses from uncontrolled selling by syndicate members. Although awed by CSFB's capacity for quick and aggressive commitments to borrowers, many banks were nonetheless irritated by being eliminated from such comfortable and lucrative syndicate positions.

Internal Dissension at CSFB

Despite its business successes, CSFB had a long history of internal friction and staff dissension that frequently found their way into the press. After the alliance with First Boston in the summer of 1978, there was scarcely time for a honeymoon before Craven, head of the London operation, resigned. Over the succeeding years, internal bickering and power plays led to a steady stream of high-level resignations.

A central figure in many of the internal spats was Rudloff. After his arrival at CSFB and the subsequent successes with the bought deal and new-issue business, friction developed between the market-oriented Rudloff and some of the firm's relationship-oriented corporate finance professionals. With von Clemm increasingly on the road seeking new business, Rudloff's market expertise was required to execute the transactions. As Rudloff explained, "The theory changed

---

12. Jack Hennessy, quoted by Fallon in "The CSFB Interview," p. 59.
13. The gray market is an unofficial secondary market for bonds that have not yet been officially issued.
14. Quoted in Nigel Adams, "Behind the Bravado of the Bought Deal," *Euromoney*, August 1980, p. 15.

from getting a mandate through your personal relationships, the services you offered the client. You now had to get a mandate at a price, which someone else had been fixing. That was a totally new experience for the old type of banker. And that doesn't go without any change in mentality. It does create frictions. Some people adopt it very easily. Some don't."[15]

Unhappiness with the new style of business and personal conflicts with Rudloff were suspected to have caused well-publicized mass defections of key people in 1981 and 1984. Nevertheless, Rudloff's keen sense of the market was an important ingredient in CSFB's success. Over the years, he held numerous titles, most revolving around new-issue business and syndication. In 1986, Rudloff was named deputy chairman of CSFB. By 1987, he and Gut at Credit Suisse were the only two officers to sit on all three key boards: First Boston, CSFB, and Credit Suisse. After the merger in 1988, Rudloff was given command of the CSFB part of the combined operation.

Part of the internal dissension may have resulted from a lack of consistent top management direction. CSFB was considered by some to be a loose collection of stars, with management tasks taking a back seat while the firm's leadership was out on the road soliciting new deals. Von Clemm, long recognized as primarily a deal maker, gave up the title of chief executive at the end of 1981 when Hans-Ulrich Doerig, a senior official at Credit Suisse, was brought in temporarily as the top administrator. (Von Clemm served thereafter as chairman, with the job of helping to bring in new business, until he left the firm in 1986 to join Merrill Lynch.)

It wasn't until Jack Hennessy, by then vice chairman of First Boston, took over in 1982 that CSFB had a strong, respected, and capable chief executive. Before joining First Boston, Hennessy, a graduate of Harvard College and MIT's Sloan School of Management, was assistant secretary for international affairs at the U.S. Treasury during the turbulent period of the Nixon administration when the United States closed the window on the sale of gold at a pegged price. A staunch Republican and consummate politician, Hennessey was later a finalist in the Reagan administration's search for a new head of the World Bank in 1986. Although a senior executive at First Boston, his progress to the top spot of the New York firm was apparently blocked, and so he elected to take the offer of president and chief executive officer at CSFB. His delicate balancing of the powerful egos within CSFB, including those of von Clemm and Rudloff, contributed substantially to the firm's success.

15. Quoted in Fallon, "The CSFB Interview," p. 56.

CSFB's Continued Success throughout the Mid-1980s

One of Hennessy's first tasks was to review CSFB's overall strategy and to make some tough decisions about its operating structure. Within CSFB, there were eight different legal entities, each carefully guarding its independence and product turf. Several unprofitable businesses were shut down, including a commodity-trading operation and a French bank. Getting everyone to pull together was no easy task. For example, it was not until 1984 that Hennessy was able to convince the Eurobond-dealing operation to change its name from White Weld Securities (a holdover from the CSWW days) to CSFB Securities.

Hennessy eventually defined three strategic business areas that mirrored the firm's primary sources of revenue: 1) investment banking, which encompassed securities underwriting and distribution, as well as international M&A activities; 2) securities sales, trading, and research; and 3) investment management. In addition, CSFB was entitled to its 40 percent share of First Boston's annual net profit. Although CSFB's revenues and net profit in turbulent 1987 declined 7 percent and 19 percent, respectively, the downturn fortunately came on the heels of a string of seven straight years of record revenues and profits.[16]

CSFB's success throughout the mid- and late 1980s was due to its clearly defined mission, its international franchise, and the synergies it generated working through its parents in different parts of the world. From its very beginning, CSFB was designed as a truly international investment bank. Although committed to the development of a global capital market, the firm believed it could not ignore the subtle differences arising from the diverse nationalities of the various players. As von Clemm once commented, "You cannot be influential in the different capital markets if you're trying to do it from one location."[17] He believed that many of his competitors, especially the American investment banks, considered their international operations less important in their overall strategy. Overseas offices of those firms, he thought, were often revolving doors through which professional staff cycled periodically on their route to the top at the home office.[18]

---

16. CSFB's financial statements were reported in Swiss francs. Since most of its revenue is denominated in dollars, a large part of the decline in 1987 operating results was probably due to the appreciation of the Swiss franc against the dollar.
17. Quoted in Fallon, "The CSFB Interview," p. 52.
18. Ibid.

Investment Banking

CSFB's strategy was to build a broad geographical network, in cooperation with Credit Suisse and First Boston, so that it would be able to respond to the often unpredictable public financing and M&A activities of companies and governments of various countries and to the constantly evolving currency preferences of issuers and investors. CSFB tried to avoid relying on a single currency or on issuers from any single country. Table 12-1 shows the broad geographic and currency mix of Eurobond, foreign bond, and international equities that were lead managed by either Credit Suisse or CSFB during 1987. Only 36 percent of the turnover was denominated in U.S. dollars and only 38 percent in Swiss francs. Similarly, issuers from continental Europe represented only 33 percent. Roughly equal percentages for issuers from Japan, America, the United Kingdom, and Australia/New Zealand further demonstrated CSFB's broad client base.

That CSFB would eventually fall from the number-one slot in league-table rankings and market share was anticipated by everyone, especially CSFB. In 1984, Rudloff had predicted, "The more people who get into the market, the more people who participate, the more sophisticated it will get. So our market share is going to go down."[19] At the same time, von Clemm had added, "Our objective is very specifically that we want to be, every year, one of the top. We know we can't be number one every year. . . . But every year we want to be one of the top three firms: year after year."[20] In 1987, CSFB lost its top slot to Nomura.

Merger-and-acquisition activities, which became increasingly important in the mid-1980s, were conducted by a special, separate joint venture between First Boston and CSFB consisting of some two hundred professionals, most of whom made up First Boston's domestic U.S. M&A group. Only about twenty-five of these professionals were based in London. One of the major strengths of this special joint venture was its ability to draw on both First Boston's and CSFB's international experience to identify acquisition and divestiture targets in a broad range of countries. The group was particularly successful in representing European buyers in U.S. acquisition programs and U.S. companies divesting parts of European operations.

The team advised in sixty-five international transactions valued at $23 billion during 1987, 36 percent higher than in 1986. *Euromoney* ranked the group as number one for worldwide mergers and acquisitions in 1986 (see Table 12-2), although the largest part of the total

19. Ibid., p. 64.
20. Ibid.

Table 12-1

CSFB/Credit Suisse New Issues: Geographic and Currency Balance, 1987 (U.S. $ millions)

Currency	Domicile of Issuer							
	Japan	United States	Continental Europe	United Kingdom	Canada	Australia/ New Zealand	Other	Total
Yen	—	—	—	—	—	—	—	—
U.S.$	—	2,036	1,992	376	150	675	150	5,378
DM	—	56	110	83	110	83	—	442
SFR	2,132	293	2,219	163	267	131	434	5,640
STG	—	—	—	1,608	—	877	—	2,486
Other	—	53	624	49	37	331	—	1,093
Equity	—	386	445	12	92	337	62	1,334
Total	2,132	2,824	5,390	2,291	656	2,434	646	16,373

Note: Includes all Eurobond, foreign bond, and international equity issues lead managed (booked) during 1987.
Source: CSFB 1987 Annual Report.

Table 12-2
Financial Advisers for Worldwide Mergers and Acquisitions in 1986

Rank	Company	Number of Deals	Value of Deals (U.S.$ billion)
1	CSFB/First Boston	203	$59.5
2	Morgan Stanley	129	50.3
3	Drexel Burnham Lambert	187	43.0
4	The Lazard Houses*	137	40.7
5	Salomon Brothers	131	33.5

* Combined activities of the three affiliated Lazard operations in London, New York, and Paris.
Source: Euromoney, February 1987, p. 132.

originated in New York. The fees from these activities were split between First Boston and CSFB in a subjective manner based on relative effort. However, because the venture drew heavily on First Boston's strengths, First Boston undoubtedly got most of the income.[21]

CSFB's broad investment banking customer base was a reflection not only of its own marketing skills but also of the cooperation between CSFB and its two parents. First Boston brought to the partnership an impressive list of U.S. clients, which helped feed CSFB's Eurosecurities underwriting and syndicated loan-arranging businesses. CSFB, in fact, rode the crest of the wave of U.S. borrowers in the Eurobond market during the mid-1980s (see Chapter 3). Further, First Boston's domestic expertise in equity underwriting, trading, sales, and research, as well as its mergers-and-acquisitions work, complemented CSFB's international thrust in these areas.

In return, CSFB helped First Boston build relationships with foreign firms that wanted to access the New York securities markets or that were looking for American acquisitions, thereby helping to propel the New York firm to the top in several important league tables. Further, Credit Suisse's effective control position shielded First Boston from the possibility of a hostile takeover attempt, such as the one that bedeviled Salomon Brothers in 1987 (see Chapter 10).

On the other side of the partnership, Credit Suisse's Sfr 6.4 billion of disclosed capital ($4.5 billion) and Sfr 104 billion of total assets ($72 billion), in addition to the large hidden reserves and investment funds not carried on the balance sheet, offered enormous resources

21. "Trying to Patch Up a Family Quarrel in Banking," BusinessWeek, February 2, 1987, p. 66.

that, at critical times, aided CSFB in managing its aggressive under-writing positions as well as its work in arranging syndicated loans and bridge financing. Credit Suisse, as investment adviser to a substantial number of privately controlled investment funds (known as "fiduciary accounts" in Switzerland), was at times a major investor-customer for CSFB's Eurobond underwriting business. The Swiss bank also provided a powerful base for the direct retail distribution of Eurosecurities through some two hundred branches and subsidiaries in Switzerland as well as its nearly seventy offices abroad.

Credit Suisse, which ranked second in the league tables for Swiss-franc bond issues, benefited from the wider issuer contact base through its CSFB and First Boston connections. Also, by delegating most international investment banking to CSFB and First Boston, Credit Suisse effectively separated the two unique and differentiated cultures of traditional commercial banking and investment banking while enjoying the advantages of both.

Trading and Sales

Together with Credit Suisse and First Boston, CSFB traded and sold a full range of domestic and Eurosecurities denominated in U.S. dollars, pounds sterling, Japanese yen, Australian dollars, Swiss francs, Deutsche marks, Dutch guilders, and ECUs. Further, the group made markets in foreign exchange and precious metals options. Turnover reached over U.S. $3 billion per day in a worldwide organization that operated on a twenty-four-hour basis.

Eurobond secondary-market trading was officially the function of the London-based Credit Suisse First Boston Securities, a separate subsidiary of CSFB. This distinction, dating back from the White Weld days, was maintained to foster accountability for trading operations as a separate profit center. Throughout the mid-1980s, CSFB's trading operation had made a special commitment to expand the depth of its coverage of nondollar Eurobonds, especially in the Euro-sterling, Euroyen, and ECU markets.

Domestic securities trading and sales for various countries, including government bonds and equities, were primarily parceled out to branches and subsidiaries in the home markets. In many locations, professionals from the three firms sat side by side in dealing rooms, providing a degree of cooperation that was often masked by formal reporting boundaries. In the United Kingdom, CSFB (Gilts) was established as a primary government-bond dealer following Big Bang. The U.S. domestic market was under the umbrella of First Boston, while the Swiss-franc domestic market was the province of Credit

Suisse. In Frankfurt, the German subsidiary traded a full range of domestic and EuroDeutsche mark securities. In 1987, an important new trading and sales market was tapped in Amsterdam by Credit Suisse First Boston Nederland N.V., where 40 percent of all continental European pension funds were managed.

The Japanese market was handled by First Boston (Asia) Limited in Tokyo, which was awarded a seat on the Tokyo Stock Exchange early in 1988. Similarly, First Boston had offices in Sydney and Melbourne, Australia. Sales and trading in other Asian markets were carried out by various offices of CSFB: Credit Suisse First Boston (Asia), headquartered in Singapore, and Credit Suisse First Boston (Hong Kong), formed in 1987. The Singapore operation began trading as one of the first three registered dealers in the Singapore government-bond market in 1987.

The CSFB sales team, supporting both the primary and the secondary trading operations, was drawn from fifteen countries and spoke over twenty-four languages. Although the sales force covered a wide range of products, specialist sales teams were established in certain areas, such as sterling financial instruments (Eurosterling bonds, CDs, and FRNs, as well as gilts). In addition to its own sales force, CSFB relied heavily on First Boston's international network, especially in Europe, Japan, and Australia, to move international equities.

The sales force, as well as the trading operations, was backed by the extensive research operations at First Boston. First Boston had made an effort to further strengthen its equity research to service the increasingly global demand for international equity and equity-linked securities. In addition, CSFB had its own research effort, which primarily covered Eurobonds and the U.K. domestic market.

Investment Management

CSFB's investment management operation provided a relatively small but steady source of revenues for CSFB and was handled globally by four different subsidiaries. Clariden Bank, a fully licensed Swiss bank with offices in Geneva and Zurich and representatives located in other offices around the world, advised private clients. During 1987, J.M. Blewer, Inc., a New York-based, SEC-registered investment management firm, was acquired to work with Clariden Bank to expand private-client business in the United States.

CSFB Investment Management Limited (CSFBIM), established in London in 1982, specialized in the management of international fixed-income funds worldwide for clients that included central banks, commercial banks, government agencies, supranational organizations, multinational corporations, and insurance companies. CSFBIM also acted as adviser to the four Credit Suisse money market funds, reportedly the largest in Europe, denominated in U.S. dollars, Deutsche marks, sterling, and Japanese yen. The U.S. dollar fund was the only European money-market fund given the "AAAm" rating by S&P. In addition, Credit Suisse appointed CSFBIM adviser to several bond funds denominated in U.S. dollars, Deutsche marks, ECUs, and Dutch guilders.

Credit Suisse First Boston Asset Management Limited, CSFBIM's sister company, was registered as an investment adviser with the SEC in the United States and worked with U.S. resident investment institutions. The group concentrated on fixed-income management for pension funds of U.S. multinational corporations and public sector institutions.

Developing Frictions among the Venture Partners

Despite the general pattern of cooperation and the resulting synergies, the relationships between CSFB and its partners, particularly First Boston, were far from smooth. Instead, numerous territorial disputes seemed to increase in frequency and intensity over the years. When the joint venture was formed in 1978, separate operational spheres were carved out: CSFB devoted itself to the Euromarkets, Credit Suisse focused on Switzerland, and First Boston got most of the rest of the world.[22] As the once separated U.S., European, and Japanese capital markets became more integrated, overlap was inevitable. The three firms—First Boston, CSFB, and Credit Suisse—were required to coordinate their activities more closely, leading to predictable confrontations. CSFB and First Boston often looked on one another as competitors rather than as partners. For example, after making a pitch for a domestic debt issue to a Houston oil company treasurer in the early 1980s, a First Boston team was astonished to see a representative of CSFB waiting in the reception area to try to sell the same client an alternative Eurobond deal.

First Boston's leadership in M&A had often been challenged by CSFB. For example, when a CSFB director brought to First Boston the proposed U.S. $631-million acquisition of Squibb Corporation's Charles of the Ritz Group by the much smaller Paris-based Yves Saint Laurent, Joseph Perella, then an executive vice president who co-

22. Ibid., p. 66.

headed the mergers-and-acquisitions group at First Boston, regarded the idea as "ridiculous, like a minnow swallowing a whale."[23] After a heated debate, CSFB finally persuaded First Boston to pursue the possibility of a merger. The deal was ultimately consummated and brought in over $10 million in merger advisory fees; the takeover itself was financed by a loan syndicate that included Credit Suisse and a series of debt and equity securities issues arranged by CSFB, thus generating still further fees to the group.

There were also problems in the international equities area. In late 1985, a First Boston equity-sales professional confronted Rudloff and said he was not about to share a piece of First Boston's equity business with CSFB. "We're like wolves," explained the man from First Boston in a later press interview. "We think territory."[24] Rudloff favored a cooperative worldwide assault—with an important role for CSFB—on the new market in globally syndicated new-stock issues. A compromise was eventually worked out, but not before the meeting ended in a heated shouting match.

By the end of 1986, both CSFB and First Boston recognized that better coordination of their investment banking activities would be necessary to compete globally against full-service investment banks like Salomon Brothers, Goldman, Sachs, Nomura Securities, and Deutsche Bank. A focused and coordinated plan was needed to attack the growing businesses of international mergers and acquisitions as well as international equity sales. "An approach that focuses on a single market just doesn't work anymore," said Hennessy.[25]

As a step in that direction, Rudloff was put in charge of international stock and bond underwriting at the three firms in late 1986, and a global profit-and-loss statement was generated. First Boston managing director David Batten was sent to CSFB to improve relations between the two firms. Further, two special but separate joint ventures—one for international mergers and acquisitions and the other for Euroequities sales and research—were established. Each venture became a profit center with specific rules for dividing income between First Boston and CSFB. Nevertheless, fee allocation remained a highly contentious issue between the groups.

The division of fixed-income capital raising, sales, and trading responsibilities along product and geographical lines required delicate informal cooperation and coordination. For example, ten CSFB

23. Matthew Winkler, "First Boston Venture with Swiss Thrives," *The Wall Street Journal*, April 29, 1987, p. 26.
24. Ibid.
25. "Trying to Patch Up a Family Quarrel in Banking," p. 66.

professionals in New York sold Euromarket products to U.S. issuers, while a much larger First Boston staff pitched domestic deals to the same clients. (One of the CSFB professionals in New York described this situation as "creative tension.")

Yen-denominated bond-trading operations were another example where cooperation was essential. Euroyen securities trading was officially the province of CSFB in London; however, the trading of Japanese government bonds was handled by First Boston in Tokyo. In fact, Tokyo was the geographic arena where some of the most serious conflicts arose. With all the pretenders to pre-eminence in global investment banking realizing that a sizable presence in the fast-growing Japanese markets was a necessity, there was a rush among foreign institutions to set up shop and/or rapidly expand operations there (see Chapter 7). Although First Boston had the largest presence in Tokyo of the First Boston/CSFB/Credit Suisse group, including a seat on the Tokyo Stock Exchange, both CSFB and Credit Suisse also had operations there. It appeared that none of the three partners wanted to be wholly dependent on the other two for their access to this large and important financial center.

Reorganization as a Remedy

Like many Wall Street firms, First Boston was battered in 1986 and 1987 by adverse market conditions. During 1986, the firm lost more than $100 million in its mortgage-backed securities business, one of the firm's fastest-growing operations, when interest rates swung sharply.[26] Not quite a year later, First Boston lost another $100 million in its trading of options on Treasury bonds. Shortly thereafter, in October 1987, stock markets around the world crashed, resulting not only in portfolio losses from long positions but also reduced revenues from sales and trading.

In late 1987, the departure from First Boston of several key merger-and-acquisition professionals, including former department co-heads Bruce Wasserstein and Joseph Perella, to set up their own boutique firm left unanswered questions about which part of the joint venture would assume the mergers-and-acquisitions leadership role. Moreover, the new firm established by the departed First Boston partners set out in a direction which promised to put it into direct competition with CSFB and its two owners. Wasserstein, Perella, colloquially referred to as "Wasserella" even by some of its own staff,

---

26. Steve Schwartz and Matthew Winkler, "Loss of Control: First Boston's Slide into Swiss Hands Is Laid to Poor Management," *The Wall Street Journal*, October 14, 1988, p. 1.

announced its intention of becoming a global player in implementing mergers and acquisitions, a niche in which the troika of CSFB, First Boston, and Credit Suisse had held a leading position. Soon thereafter, Nomura Securities announced that it had purchased a 20 percent interest in Wasserstein, Perella for an eye-popping $100 million and that the two new confederates would establish a joint venture in London specifically to pursue cross-border M&A business, with a special emphasis on European clients (see Chapter 11). "Wasserella" was also raising a large pool of risk capital to permit it to engineer leveraged buyouts in situations where merchant banking capabilities were required.

With increasing friction among the partners, mounting losses, and the defection of key players at First Boston, the three related firms began in early 1988 to seriously reconsider their long-standing operating relationship. As one insider put it: "We made an assessment we'd better change our structure. We didn't feel we had to do something because we were hurt or dying or desperate. We thought anything we were going to do would be done out of offensive, not defensive reasons."[27]

The upshot was a decision in late 1988 to merge First Boston and CSFB into the new holding company CS First Boston. First Boston "went private" in the process and reaffirmed through the new ownership structure the community of interests among the organizations, under the watchful eye of Credit Suisse's near-controlling equity interest. CS First Boston was given the exclusive, worldwide responsibility for capital markets underwriting, sales and trading, and merger-and-acquisition activities, including merchant banking, except that Credit Suisse retained the sole right to handle Swiss franc–denominated capital markets activities as well as merger-and-acquisition transactions where both parties were Swiss. Hennessy, the head of CSFB, was chosen to run the new organization.

In the arrangement, Credit Suisse purchased approximately 44 percent of CS First Boston (a level acceptable to U.S. regulators), with an option of increasing its share to 51 percent if and when U.S. regulations were changed. CSFB and First Boston management owned approximately 25 percent of the new entity. The remaining 31 percent was bought by Suliman S. Olayan, a temporary investor, who provided financing for the balance of the transaction until permanent investors were found.

CS First Boston's global operations were conducted through three wholly owned but independent subsidiaries. First Boston Cor-

27. Ibid.

poration, headed by former First Boston head of sales and trading William E. Mayer, retained the rights to North and South America. CSFB, under the leadership of Rudloff, was given Europe, the Middle East, and Africa. Finally, a new entity, First Boston Pacific, was created to cover the immense Pacific Basin. A chief executive was not immediately named for this group, pending the search for permanent equity investors. "We are looking for financial partners in the Far East and perhaps for some distribution," commented Mayer shortly after the merger, although he stressed that the 31 percent stake owned by Olayan was not going to be sold to an "operating partner" and would likely be split from four to seven ways.[28]

The new structure of regional geographic responsibility was obviously an attempt to maintain a high degree of responsiveness to local markets. In Hennessy's words, "You have the people who were the closest to the market of execution . . . have authority to commit capital, to make offers, to buy issues, to distribute issues, to do whatever was necessary in order to be successful in that market." The structure was also designed to resolve the increasingly difficult problems with coordination and cooperation between First Boston and CSFB, problems that their managements attributed to the reporting of separate bottom lines to two different groups of stockholders.

CS First Boston: Looking to the Future

Even with its new structure and enthusiastic top management, CS First Boston's future is far from assured. On the bright side, the turmoil in the world capital markets seems to have subsided at least temporarily. First Boston, although not always number one, certainly excels in U.S. capital-markets transactions. Further, the disruptions in the Eurobond markets that began in the spring and summer of 1987 might actually have helped CSFB's Eurobond new-issues underwriting business. As institutional investors abandoned the Eurobond market to traditional retail investors, it grew smaller, less liquid, and less competitive.[29] With so many banks—particularly American—pulling out of competitive bidding on new Eurobond issues, there was less of a tendency for the remaining players to bid cut-priced deals to increase market share. For CSFB and the other strong firms that have remained committed to the market, this turn of events could eventually translate into more profitability on a per-deal basis

---

28. Quoted in Erik Ipsen, "Mastering the New CS First Boston Empire," *Institutional Investor* (International Edition), January 1989, p. 49.
29. "The Markets Discover Eurobondage," *The Economist*, November 7, 1987, pp. 83–84.

although, because of less volume, lower total profits. It is also possible that these persistent firms could increase market share as borrowers turn increasingly to the leading firms with good records in tough markets. In fact, by mid-1988, CSFB had, at least temporarily, regained its lead in the Eurobond league tables, followed closely by Nomura.

With the crash of the world equity markets in October 1987, the market for international equities went into a period of hibernation. This was a particularly cruel blow to First Boston and CSFB, because, in the view of many market participants, they had built equity teams that were the best in the business.[30] In line with its strategy of geographically diversifying its client base in the Eurobond market, First Boston and CSFB had been awarded international equity-financing mandates from a wider range of client nationalities than any other firm, including issuers from the United States, Austria, the United Kingdom, Italy, Canada, the Netherlands, Switzerland, Spain, Finland, and Australia.

Few observers doubted that international mergers and acquisitions would continue to grow and play an increasingly important role in the combined operations of First Boston and CSFB. The consolidation is expected to eliminate the antagonism between the two. And with an estimated 80 percent or more of all international merger and acquisitions having one component in the United States,[31] First Boston's continued strength in the market is essential. However, with an increasing number of buyers from Japan, the new firm has to figure out how to build a solid presence in Japan, similar to that in the other two major market centers. Other vendors are well ahead of CS First Boston in Tokyo, and with tie-ups like Nomura–Wasserstein, Perella already in place, there is obviously cause for concern.

Despite substantial losses during 1987 in its various trading operations—a fate shared with most other market players—CS First Boston is likely to continue its predecessors' leadership in global securities sales and trading. Its strategy of geographical concentration gives it a competitive advantage in searching out new pockets of investor demand. However, the geographic and product boundary lines drawn among the three operating groups might continue to constrain operations. Rationalization, as part of the merger, will be necessary to better coordinate the sales and trading of Eurobonds and

30. Rosamond Jones, "CSFB Awaits Upturn," *Markets '88*, a special supplement to *Euromoney*, March 1988, p. 31.
31. Kevin Muerhring, "Gearing Up for Global M&A," *Institutional Investor* (International Edition), April 1986, pp. 99–101.

domestic government bonds denominated in the same currency, such as Euroyen and Japanese government bonds. Further, although it was originally believed that international equities could be distributed through the same network as Eurobonds, most market participants eventually conceded that that is not always possible. CSFB needs to incorporate more closely the strengths of First Boston's international equity-distribution network into its own operations in order for the new firm to remain at the top when and if the market for new international equities reawakens.

One of their continuing weaknesses is dealing with the Japanese. CSFB is not a player in the Euroyen new-issue market, despite its rapid growth in the mid-1980s. Further, although Credit Suisse controls a healthy chunk of Japanese new issues in the Swiss-franc foreign-bond market, CSFB is not involved in Japanese issues in other currencies. In fairness, however, it has to be noted that this highly competitive and low-margin business is dominated by the Japanese securities firms and banks. Nevertheless, this void must eventually be addressed if CS First Boston is to reach its full potential. And this need will put an even higher premium on effective cooperation between the newly formed First Boston Pacific and the other two operating companies.

CHAPTER 13

VENDOR STRATEGIES FOR THE FUTURE

In previous chapters, we have examined the operations of investment banks in several key countries and market settings. One of our overarching conclusions has been that those firms that have survived and thrived over time have been ones that were able to adapt readily to changing conditions both in their home markets and in the broader international environment. In this chapter, we bring together several dimensions of our investigation to draw some generalizations and conclusions about investment banking firms in different competitive settings and to examine alternative firm strategies and their possibilities.

In reviewing the influence of competitive settings, we have utilized a framework somewhat similar to one Michael Porter developed to examine the comparative advantages specific industries enjoy from one country setting to another.[1] We have therefore divided our review into several parts: 1) "factor" conditions which distinguish the resources of one host country from another; 2) the organizational structure of the firms competing within a particular country's investment banking sector; 3) the nature of the rivalry between firms in a country's securities and investment banking marketplace; 4) the domestic demand conditions of the market, including the degree of sophistication and the demands imposed by both capital users and investors; 5) the extent to which supporting industries reinforce and/ or influence the direction of the country's investment banking business; and 6) the role of government as it influences the evolution of the country's investment banking environment.

Specific Country Factors

Each of the three countries featured in this study has, at one time or another, enjoyed pre-eminence as an industrial power and subsequently become a generator of substantial surplus investment funds. Britain held that position for much of the nineteenth and early twentieth centuries and was supplanted by the United States in the post–

---

1. Michael E. Porter, *The Competitive Advantages of Nations* (New York: Free Press, 1989).

World War I period. At the beginning of the 1980s, Japan's industrial momentum began to generate substantial capital surpluses, which are expected to persist through the end of the century.

Each country's currency has also enjoyed a special status. Britain's pound was the international reserve currency until World War II, when it was replaced by the U.S. dollar. The Japanese government has thus far been reluctant to allow a similar fate for the yen, but it seems inevitable that it will move in that direction in the future.

Each of the three countries also has an ample supply of professional financial talent trained in the business traditions of that country, practiced in its contemporary financial-services activity and seemingly capable of adapting to a variety of changing market conditions.

Other countries that also have possessed significant industrial bases and savings surpluses from time to time include France, Germany, and Holland, but their financial resources have never been as large as those of our three countries. Switzerland deserves special mention as a smaller country with a highly developed banking industry based on the entrepôt function of receiving savings from foreign investors (mostly because of the country's banking laws, which until very recently have allowed anonymity) and investing such funds abroad with non-Swiss counterparts. However, as other markets have grown with the trend toward globalization, the relative position of Switzerland has declined somewhat.

Organizational Structure of Firms

Management styles within securities firms in Tokyo, New York, and London present remarkable contrasts. In the United States, as Eccles and Crane have described, the organizations tend to be decentralized, relatively loose, and compartmentalized, with ad hoc task-directed teams calling on the assistance of specialized departments only as required.[2] American personal motivation is heavily oriented toward the furthering of individual financial and performance goals, with small groups (or, in some cases, solo performers) building visible stature in a particular market or product specialty. Thus, the firms tend to be collections of entrepreneurial individuals. In addition to overall profits, the major unifying elements within decentralized firms are the allocation of capital, which is typically closely controlled at the top, and senior management's ability to redeploy staff to take advantage of emerging opportunities in a constantly shifting market environment.

2. Robert G. Eccles and Dwight B. Crane, *Doing Deals* (Boston: Harvard Business School Press, 1988).

Japanese brokerage firms, in contrast, tend to be quite central-ized. Employees, as is generally true in Japanese industry, have a highly developed sense of personal identification with their firm and its overall objectives. Teamwork is emphasized, and communication and collaboration between units are highly developed. Compensation patterns also downplay individual financial rewards.

In Britain, merchant banking firms tend to be individualistic and loosely organized, not unlike their American equivalents. Their tradi-tional perspective is even more global than that of their U.S. counterparts, given Britain's long history of active international trade and finance.

From our examination of the structure and the culture of invest-ment banking firms in the three countries, it appears that both loose and more structured organizations can succeed in the domestic and international investment banking arenas, depending on the traditions and expectations of the employees. However, while a firm's organiza-tional structure may not be indicative of success per se, it may exert an important influence in determining the types of products and services with which individual firms are likely to have the greatest success. The Japanese are excellent merchandisers of securities to a mass market, while the Americans are particularly adept in devis-ing new products, innovative financings, and successful acquisition strategies.

Firm size and governance structure can also be an important determining factor. In our view, investment banking operations that function as departments or subsidiaries of larger, diversified financial services organizations—such as universal banks—tend to be less in-novative than stand-alone firms. Stand-alone firms are more flexible because of their independence, and they are not hampered by the potential clashes between disparate cultures of the parent and the subsidiary. In that connection, it is all the more remarkable that a joint venture of the proportions of Credit Suisse First Boston not only survived but positively *thrived* for a number of years. But it is equally noteworthy that no successful copy of the CSFB model has since surfaced. In such co-ventures, neither prospective partner is likely to be enthusiastic about giving up power, influence, or name position in the operations of the offspring. It is apparent that each partner often would prefer to be the sole owner of something smaller rather than a partner in something larger and potentially more powerful.

Interfirm Rivalry

We believe that a helpful predictor of success in international invest-ment banking is the degree of interfirm rivalry among strong competitors in the home market. In reviewing not only the domestic investment banking markets in our three countries but also research and interviews we conducted in Belgium, Canada, France, Germany, Italy, Spain, and Switzerland, we found that countries characterized by a high degree of interfirm rivalry, particularly in the area of new-product development, tended to produce more successful competitors in the international arena. In certain continental European countries where financing cartels operated or where a handful of government-owned banks divided the domestic marketplace, competition was reduced, as has been the case in France, Spain, and Italy. Until the late 1980s, Switzerland also had a structure of fixed commissions and syndicates, which tended to retard innovation and competition within that domestic market environment.

In Japan, the Ministry of Finance in many respects fostered strong competition among the major securities firms (including the Big Four). Competition there was heavily sales-oriented, with stock brokerage as the central product together with mutual fund sales to a domestic investor-client base. While the Japanese commercial banks traditionally had a hammerlock on the primary relationships with Japanese corporations, the spread of securitization in Japan and the increasing opportunities for offshore financings have fostered a spirited competition between the commercial banks and the securities firms for corporate finance-related services, increasing the overall level of service in the process.

In the United States, a strong rivalry among traditional and other vendors of corporate financial services went on for more than two decades. The result was a high level of developed skill by investment banks in a number of areas, including secondary-market trading and M&A-related services and products. These products proved remarkably exportable and, together with the interest rate and currency-swapped products that American firms also had developed, the U.S. investment banks enjoyed a strong advantage in the worldwide market of the late 1980s.

Domestic Demand Conditions

In examining the competitive strengths with which various national firms approached the global market, we found the product-demand conditions faced at home can be a significant determinant of strength and comparative advantage. The United States unquestionably has the largest, most sophisticated, and most demanding set of constituencies. As discussed in Chapters 4 and 5, the U.S. corporate community has grown increasingly sophisticated and savvy about the public financial markets. U.S. corporate financial executives in the 1980s, with the spread of takeovers and restructurings, have become much more knowledgeable and results-oriented in using investment banking services. They have continuously accelerated their product and service demands on the investment banking community. The growing cadre of U.S. institutional investors has also escalated its service and product expectations from the investment banking community while at the same time squeezing down the scale of fees they are willing to pay.

Investment banks have responded to these demands with massive investments of people and capital. In the process, they have developed formidable capabilities in such areas as M&A, restructurings, new flotations involving innovative securities, swaps, and bond trading, which also propelled them to develop sophisticated balance sheet management techniques. It is not surprising that U.S. firms have enjoyed great success in the international arena during the 1980s. Their newly honed skills were well suited to a decade of increasing international acquisitions and volatile interest rates.

In Japan, the situation evolved somewhat differently, both in timing and complexion. Corporations and institutional investors escalated their expectations later than had been the case in the United States, and they had a different vendor focus. Because Japanese securities firms were shut out of corporate finance by commercial banks, they concentrated instead on the brokerage side. In recent years, securities firms have aimed at getting a foot in the door with corporations. At the same time, their commercial banking rivals have been looking hungrily at the public securities marketplace, from which they have been officially barred by Article 65. A similar situation obtains in the Japanese institutional-investing services area, where the securities firms have a formal regulatory mandate but where the commercial banks also have aspirations. Financial services vendors on both sides of the Article 65 wall have worked assiduously to increase their competitive capabilities in the domestic Japanese market. In the process, they also have developed skills that afford them competitive muscle in important offshore securities markets.

The demand conditions in Britain, though different from those prevailing in the United States and Japan, have also honed the skills of that country's investment banking competitors. In Britain, as in America, institutional investors (particularly pension funds) have come to account for the lion's share of the brokerage business. In addition, Britain has maintained its long-standing international perspective. As the premier center of international finance for a century and as the base for the modern Euromarket, London has nurtured the international equities business, even during the difficult years of the 1970s. With the abolition of U.K. exchange controls in 1979 and the movement toward a more international stock exchange at the time of Big Bang, London has developed a strong position in the market for international equity-investment services.

In parallel fashion, the British merchant banks, in physical proximity to the Euromarkets, capitalized on a strong knowledge base and trading ability in international debt securities in the Eurobond market. The effective closure of the New York market to foreign lenders in the decade 1963–1973, following the imposition of the interest equalization tax, only increased their advantage. Thus, despite relatively meager domestic demand from the corporate sector during part of the period under review, London developed as a vigorous marketplace for international equity and debt underwriting and trading. Encouragement by the British government and facilitating leadership from the Bank of England were essential in this process. As a result, the British economy benefited from a position in banking, brokerage, and insurance representing a net balance-of-payments advantage of approximately $10 billion per annum by the mid-1980s.

Supporting Industries

Investment bankers and other deal makers often make the headlines, particularly in America. A few have reached the status of superstars in the business community. But behind the news clips and the mega deals is an army of accountants, lawyers, filing clerks, stock custodians, specialized printers, and record-keeping and computer experts without which there would be no story and no deal. The infrastructure of supporting industries does not appear overnight but grows only over time. In fact, the development of a cost effective infrastructure can be a limiting factor in the expansion of financial services as a whole. Nowhere has this been made more clear than during Wall Street's frenetic 1960s. Stock trading was so fast and furious that the back offices of leading securities firms were literally buried in paperwork. The NYSE, in desperation, closed each Wednesday in an effort to unclog the logjam of record-keeping, broken trades, and handling of certificates. When supporting services are highly developed and well managed, however, they enhance competitive advantage.

The modern accounting profession, a key supporting industry, traces its origins to the flourishing British Empire, when Scottish accountants kept track of the widespread investments and commerce between Britain and its colonies. That competence was imported into the United States, originally by British investors, and took root as a domestic hybrid in the wake of the reform legislation of the 1930s, which called for a more accurate, timely, and detailed accounting of corporate affairs for investors. In the half-century since then, the Big Eight (at last count, six) accounting firms, which sprang from that mandate, have set up offices all over the world, and the accounting standards that originally had been an Anglo-American phenomenon are rapidly becoming the global standard. Thus, the New York and London financial markets have reaped benefits from the accounting industry's service to the investment banking business. The Japanese are now moving to adopt a congruent approach to financial reporting.

Of course, no country comes close to the United States in numbers or the activity of its lawyers. The completeness and sophistication of documentation in the U.S. financial-services area are positive benefits. In addition, a high level of statutory protection for investors (admired by many other countries) is promoted by a cadre of lawyers especially trained in that watchdog role. Nonetheless, there are many who view the large and high-priced population of lawyers in the United States and the national predisposition to litigation as impediments to the efficient production of goods and services.

It is worth noting that the growth of computer technology, particularly the personal computers so widely used in investment banking, has spread to the major countries under study but not uniformly so. It is undoubtedly true that a greater proportion of young entrants to investment banking in the United States and the United Kingdom have computer training, compared to those in Japan. In addition, the use of such technology in the internal management of the securities firms appears more advanced in the two English-speaking countries. In 1987, Coopers & Lybrand surveyed senior executives in investment banking, commercial banking, and brokerage firms in the three centers. Among the questions asked was, "Does your organization currently use electronic technology for calculating and monitoring risk capital on a global, firmwide consolidated basis?" The responses to the question were positive from 46 percent of the U.S. respondents, 40 percent of the U.K. respondents, but only 29 percent of the Japanese respondents.[3] However, no one seriously doubts that the Japanese will catch up.

Government as a Force

We have discussed at length the degree to which domestic markets in all three countries have been shaped by government action. It is, however, worth noting that government attitudes toward the desirability of creating international financing centers in the three capitals

---

3. Coopers & Lybrand, *Opportunity and Risk in the 24-hour Global Marketplace*, Executive Summary, October 1987, p. 11.

do differ. The British authorities have been especially proactive in supporting London as a global financial center, whereas both the U.S. and Japanese authorities have been more ambivalent about undertaking the required modifications in regulatory policies. In some cases, American authorities have been constrained by existing legislation, which limits the degree of feasible accommodation. The Japanese reluctance to deregulate in some areas appears to be a special concern over the possible loss of government management control over the domestic financial marketplace.

Competitive Strategies

As we have indicated, the competitive positions of individual firms as well as national groups of firms are heavily influenced by "where they're coming from"; thus, we emphasize financial market history, firm history, national culture, and government regulatory policies. The direction and the magnitude of capital flows, currency movements, relative inflation rates, and the economies of various countries also play important roles in determining the opportunities open to individual investment banking firms. Within these parameters, investment banking firms nonetheless exercise considerable latitude in how they mobilize and deploy people, capital, and financial products.

The Organization and Development of People

Market observers generally agree that people are an investment bank's most important resource. The individuals recruited and developed by the industry have a high level of personal competence, an aggressive, results-oriented, deal-doing philosophy, and well-developed communications skills with both clients and colleagues. Such professionals express a clear preference for decentralized operations with a maximum amount of autonomy at the business-unit level. In traditional investment banks, such autonomy generally is accomplished by individuals working in small teams covering specialized fields such as municipal bonds, commercial paper, or corporate bond underwriting. Often, the heads of the individual business units are shareholders or partners in the investment bank, know one another well, and have worked with the top managers of the firm, perhaps in different business units, for many years.

Commercial banks with investment banking units, in contrast, often have difficulty in effectively managing the people in these units. In most such organizations, the managers of the investment banking divisions do not have a significant ownership interest in the bank, and senior bank executives have little experience in managing investment banking operations and are understandably preoccupied with the main-line bank-lending strategy. Thus, top commercial banking executives often find it difficult to effectively monitor and assist their investment banking units in developing their quite different product and relationship activities. It was this lack of adequate supervision by National Westminster Bank of its merchant banking subsidiary, County NatWest, which led to the July 1989 censure and resignation of its chairman and three senior bankers following the Blue Arrow financing scandal in the United Kingdom.

Even more important, the culture of commercial banking has not mixed well with the culture of investment banking subsidiaries. The heritage of conservatism, bureaucracy, and wait-your-turn attitude of commercial banking contrasts sharply with the risk-taking, star-oriented ambience of the investment bank. One can well imagine the unrest of commercial bank officers when they learn of the high salaries and bonuses earned by their colleagues on the other side of the wall. BMWs nestled among the Oldsmobiles in the bank's parking lot is a visual image of the problem that commercial banks have in managing their investment banking subsidiaries.

A number of interviewees remarked that the investment banking business is sufficiently taxing by itself without the added problems of the organizational complexities that often occur with a commercial banking parent. Nevertheless, a number of the European universal banks have a long tradition of working in both the securities markets and the commercial banking markets and seem to have dealt successfully with this management challenge. The Japanese commercial banks and long-term credit institutions also appear to us to be making progress in bridging the differences between investment and commercial banking, assisted by their highly developed communications and consensus-building skills. However, they have not yet fully reconciled their predisposition toward centralized control with the need for decentralized responsibility to encourage the maximum level of individual initiative at the level of the single business unit.

Continued recruitment and training of the highest-quality individuals who will provide the future competence, enterprise, and communications skills necessary to achieve success are obviously an important long-term goal for investment bankers everywhere. The U.S. investment banks have been singularly successful in growing professionals from raw university or business school recruits, as have the Japanese. The British clearing banks and the U.S. commercial banks, on the other hand, have often recruited a high proportion of their investment banking staffs from other securities firms.

With the importance of individual initiative and the strength brought to investment banking by the long-term relationships among individuals within a firm, it is not surprising that acquisitions of operating investment banking units have not always been successful in achieving substantial and lasting gains in market share and profitability. A critical issue faced by both investment and commercial banks in seeking by acquisition to achieve footholds in the investment banking industries of other countries is whether the target firm would benefit or suffer from integration within the larger, acquiring enterprise.

Employment of Capital

In comparison to most manufacturing enterprises, capital is a much more complex equation in investment banking. Equity (or subordinated debt) capital serves a multiplicity of functions within an investment bank. In a business where earnings fluctuate sharply from year to year, capital can be a reserve against lean years. Capital also serves as a cushion against underwriting or securities trading-position risks. Adequate capital is a prerequisite for new businesses, particularly in recent years as many firms have entered merchant banking, and needed to commit their own funds in acquisition-related deals. Capital is also required by regulatory authorities, including stock exchanges and self-regulatory organizations within the country jurisdictions in which the firm operates. Capital reallocations are a means by which management redeploys resources from less productive to more productive businesses. Growth in a firm's capital per-ownership-share is viewed as a staff incentive at many investment banks with employee ownership plans. In firms where share-incentive plans are not available, cash bonuses and elaborate profit-sharing plans often take their place.

In addition to the allocation of capital, management must confront the question of how much total capital will be required to run the business. Capital committed to investment banking activities has grown dramatically in recent years. A number of firms have borrowed in both public and private markets; others have sought additional equity capital by selling shares to the general public or undertaking private placements with large and presumably friendly investors. The different approaches raise the issue of the type of capital most desirable within an investment banking context. In this connection, it is worth noting that there are significant qualitative differences between management-provided capital and public shareholders' capital. The former may be uncertain in its tenure but sophisticated in its assessment of how the business is being managed. The latter is more or less permanently locked in but oftentimes naive and prone to overreaction in its response to period results of the firm's operations. There also may be significant differences between "patient" capital injected by long-term holders and "immediate results-oriented" capital injected in expectation of rapid returns.

In looking at the list of the most important international investment banking enterprises, one is struck by the difference in capital strategies of the firms, where the capital form ranges from the public share ownership of the universal banks, to the family ownership of smaller niche players, to the high proportion of management ownership in a number of other investment banks. Clearly, success in the field is related to the raising and employment of capital, but there are a variety of possible successful capital deployment solutions. While different formulas for capital raising and allocation have been successful, it is worth noting that the character of a firm's capital is often closely related to its long-term business strategy.

Although many of our interviewees felt that financial capital was an important resource for an investment banking organization, virtually all agreed that human capital was even more important. It was often pointed out that new firms with high-caliber executives, such as Wasserstein, Perella and the Blackstone Group, generally have little difficulty obtaining sufficient capital for their operations. In sum, in this business capital tends to seek out capable people.

Repositioning Products and Firm Strategy

In addition to the organization and development of people and the employment of capital, investment bank senior management has a certain amount of control over product positioning and firm strategy for expansion or contraction of business units. We qualify the degree of discretion that management can exercise because, in most instances, regulatory and cultural barriers to a transformation are formidable. In addition, each vendor usually has an incumbent book of business and is loathe to abandon current clients and successful products in favor of an untried and risky alternative. Nevertheless, firms are able to undertake incremental repositionings to shift the emphasis among current lines of business or to enter adjacent business areas. The rewards of repositioning, if successful, can be significant, and clearly the success of Drexel Burnham in developing the U.S. market for junk bonds is indicative of just such a successful repositioning. It is also an indication of the difficulties of repositioning a product line. Other major U.S. investment banks initially had great difficulty in duplicating Drexel's junk bond efforts when those products really began to flourish in the early 1980s.

The Strategy-Formulation Process

Historically, investment banks have given relatively low priority to strategic planning. Their strategy flowed from their style and geographic or market specialization. Business was opportunistic. Partners could be gotten together on short notice to discuss a new type of operation, which often sprang from efforts to solve a current problem for an existing client. In some cases, a new business direction resulted from simply fulfilling a client need in a product or service area adjacent to existing lines and then attracting other clients to use it. Occasionally, junior people at the firm would originate a new financing idea or product and convince the firm to give it a try; if the idea or product was successful, it would be added to the firm's existing product line. Larger, universal banking entities had a more established tradition of planning and strategy formulation, especially with respect to geographic expansion, but had less interest in the smaller entrepreneurial areas of investment banking and securities transactions.

Beginning in the late 1960s and early 1970s, attitudes within the American investment banking community toward planning and strategy began to change in response to the growth of the industry. Management noted that larger amounts of capital were necessary for expansion and that expansion produced larger organizations increasingly segmented and separated by both geography and proliferating lines of business. Annual planning meetings utilizing proposed position papers became more common at firms like Morgan Stanley and Goldman, Sachs as a means of setting firm strategy and direction and of keeping the executives current as to developments and opportunities in areas of the business with which they were not directly associated.

Expansion also brought with it the need to allocate capital among competing areas of the business, and consensus building among partners was necessary for this process to occur. Generally, a consensus was reached only on the broad outlines of a revised strategy, and implementation of specific decisions was left to the senior management of the particular areas. Often, such changes required recruitment of outside personnel or transfers of existing staff from one area to another; implementation of such changes inevitably required time and negotiation. Assembling new teams of individuals required significant team balance and harmonious working arrangements. The implementers were then typically called upon for a postaudit of the new initiative at a subsequent planning meeting.

Some of the more significant strategic moves in investment banking in recent years have already been mentioned in this book. They include:

- Drexel Burnham's development of a specialization in placing, trading, and later originating junk bond issues in the United States in the late 1970s.
- Morgan Guaranty's early 1980s entry into the Eurobond market using corporate relationships and swap- and option-based products.
- S.G. Warburg's penetration of the Eurobond field beginning in the mid-1960s, ahead of more established British merchant banking competitors.
- White Weld's initiative to establish with Credit Suisse in the early 1970s a jointly owned international investment banking firm (later Credit Suisse First Boston) to combine the Eurobond origination and placing strengths of the two parents.
- Nomura's concerted move into the U.S. securities marketplace in the 1980s.

Other initiatives failed, in some cases because of faulty research and estimates or a late entry. Indeed, timing is viewed by most investment bankers as critical to the success of new-product strategies. Being first and pre-empting a commanding position in junk bonds were key to Drexel's success, while in other already expanding service areas, a major presence was sufficient to be successful. An example of the latter would be the M&A activities of U.S. investment banks. They have been so profitable and have required so many different investment banking advisers to represent an array of targets, acquirers, and major shareholders that there was room for a whole group of significant vendors.

In other instances of product launch, firms have had difficulty obtaining the right mix of individual talent to compete effectively. Sometimes product specialists recruited from outside have had difficulty obtaining the cooperation necessary to create a successful operating unit, or they have had difficulties with subordinates. Obviously, in these instances, the sponsoring firm must decide whether an effective cure would involve minor repairs to the organizational structure or full-blown surgery. In other instances, key individuals or teams of people became dissatisfied with the culture in which they were working and left the firm, in some cases jumping to a competing entity. Sometimes personnel problems have been exacerbated by distant locations and cultural differences.

In certain cases, successful new-product areas have been copied so effectively that they have evolved into commodity-type businesses with many participants, reduced commissions, and sharply declining profitability. Commercial paper in the United States is one such example.

Future Strategic Options

For all the fits and starts in past strategic planning and positioning, there are only a few broad viable strategic options for international investment banks in the future. In terms of customers, markets, and products,[4] these options separate essentially into the universal bank with an investment banking component, the global investment bank, and the global niche player.

Universal Banks

Deutsche Bank reputedly first coined the term "universal bank" to describe its competitive advantage in covering all major customers in major product and geographic markets around the world. Universal banks are typically domiciled in countries in continental Europe and the United Kingdom, which have no effective regulatory barriers to such comprehensive coverage. They are characterized by very large capital bases and usually have special distribution advantages (e.g., in West Germany, the universal banks have significant stakes in most of the institutional investors; in Switzerland, the Big Three universal banks have impressive placing power within the accounts they manage for individuals). In the management of client relationships, the universal banks enjoy certain advantages. First, a number of investment banking transactions originate from lending situations in which the universal banks play a dominant role. They have become increasingly aware of such opportunities and are now tying much of their lending to opportunities to earn future fee-based business in investment banking transactions with the same borrowers. In addition, in high-volume, commodity-type investment banking businesses such as government bond trading and swaps, the giant banks are able to obtain some economies of scale, and the lower funding costs they possess in comparison with investment banks can be used to advantage. Finally, the idea of full-service commercial and investment banking entities appears to appeal to certain clients.

As has been mentioned earlier, the problems large banks have in

---

4. See, for instance, Ingo Walter, "Competitive Performance and Strategic Positioning in International Financial Services," unpublished manuscript presented at the International University of Tokyo, September 1986.

managing investment banking entities are significant in the recruitment of personnel, the establishment of the necessary lines of communication, and the management of capital to contain losses and enhance returns. A further disadvantage relates to response time. It may take universal banks longer to respond to a shift in the environment than their investment banking competitors. The necessarily more substantial bureaucracies with which they control their lending and other credit services can prove stifling to many investment banking executives.

Consequently, most universal banks that operate investment banking units segregate them from their commercial banking activities and separate them physically by distance in an effort to preserve the required entrepreneurial atmosphere. This was the pattern Credit Suisse followed with CSFB. Deutsche Bank, UBS, and others have also headquartered their investment banking units in London rather than in their home market complex.

Global Investment Banks

Global investment banks are securities firms that offer a comprehensive array of services associated with the public securities markets, on the model of Salomon Brothers, CSFB, and Nomura Securities. The line of demarcation between them and the commercial banking side of financial services is often fuzzy and varies from setting to setting, depending on regulatory constraints and local tradition.

While not of the size of universal banks, global investment banks nonetheless are substantial organizations, given their decision to field a wide variety of products and services in multiple geographic markets around the world. They draw strength and benefit from a system of interconnecting lines of business that provide not only economies of scale but also vital market intelligence. Typically organized with a horizontal and decentralized reporting structure, they go to great lengths to preserve both the entrepreneurial environment and the quick response time that have been the hallmarks of the successful investment/merchant bank.

At the same time, comprehensive coverage entails a mammoth job of coordination and control. The organizational structure most conducive to individual initiative is also the most vulnerable to negligence or abuse. Single or small groups of employees can plunge a firm into difficulties; such activity is difficult to police as the range of product markets participated in and the geographic distances between units become greater. Moreover, the costs of maintaining this global network are prodigious. The breakeven points for the firms keep rising, and a relatively modest downturn—or even a plateauing in activity—can mean a sharp fall in operating results because of the semifixed nature of many of the costs.

Global-Niche Investment Banks

The global-niche investment bank specializes in some segment of the international investment banking market. Typically, it has a comparative advantage over other competitors, often because of a specialized knowledge base relating to a service or product, but occasionally because of a unique access to a customer or client group (after the integration of the European Economic Community in 1992, it is possible that that self-contained market might offer such an opportunity for European investment banks vis-à-vis securities firm vendors from other parts of the world).

The niche player is by definition narrowly focused and therefore more vulnerable to a change in market conditions than a more diversified full-service firm. While the fees in the niche business are likely to be lucrative, they are also likely to be under continuing pressure, as other vendors perceive the profit opportunity and push to get a piece of the business. In the absence of insuperable barriers to entry, erosion in the level of fees can be expected as more vendors enter the market. Niche players have to innovate constantly, looking for the cutting edge of the technology to maintain their positions with their clients and their fees.

Wasserstein, Perella is an example of such a firm. CSFB, too, was originally established as a niche player to exploit the Euromarkets on behalf of its parents. Lazard Frères is still another international investment banking niche player focusing on M&A and corporate-financing facilitation.

Implementing a Strategy

Our studies have also explored how financial services vendors go about positioning themselves in one of the three basic competitor slots. At the most fundamental level, the choice is "make" or "buy." U.S. investment banks and the U.K. merchant banks mostly have grown their own through internal training and development, although there is considerably more senior-personnel switching and talent raiding between competing investment banking firms than there was two decades ago.

Some firms have attempted to move quickly into a new market sector by buying experts or teams of specialists with an established record in the desired area. This is what Salomon did when it came to Tokyo in the early 1980s and what Nomura has been doing to obtain greater penetration of the New York markets.

Other vendors have made the leap by buying whole firms. Nomura and Daiwa both bought primary government-bond dealers in New York as the most effective way to get a foothold in the important U.S. government-bond business. In anticipation of 1986's Big Bang in London, a number of British merchant banks and offshore investment banks bought both jobbers and brokers in order to strategically position themselves in the U.K. domestic markets. An important uncertainty in a purchase of this type is knowing what you will end up owning. As discussed earlier, in any service business where the major "assets" take the elevators to go home each night, you hope they will return the next day. And given what we have already described as the importance of the operating environment within which these highly entrepreneurial individuals work, the task of holding onto the human assets over time is a challenging one.

Still others have tried joint ventures. As we pointed out earlier, this was how a number of banks originally entered the Euromarkets in the late 1960s and early 1970s. Virtually all of these alliances have been replaced, usually by one party buying out the other(s). The joint venture was also the form employed in the First Boston-Credit Suisse alliance that created CSFB in the late 1970s. In fact, that formal joint venture was actually the outer wrapping for several specific product-area joint venture collaborations between CSFB and one or the other of the parents, including M&A facilitation and money management. And, as has been noted, that particular joint venture sustained itself longer than any other in the international investment banking arena.

The extensive research on the dynamics of joint ventures suggests these required ingredients for sustaining a joint effort among two or more partners: a relatively specific and limited business mandate and a stable operating environment within which to carry it out. What ultimately forced a change of organization in the CSFB joint venture (and contributed to the demise of the earlier Euromarket consortia) was that CSFB outgrew its original mandate; with rapidly changing conditions in the international marketplace, the owners found themselves bumping heads with a progeny that was itself growing toward global status.

Because joint ventures are most likely to bear fruit when they are targeted at a specific niche in the market, it would be difficult to envision how such collaborations could be used to create a global investment bank, given the overlaps of markets and the potential conflicts of interest that beset CSFB as time passed on.

It is a little difficult to slot precisely the Nomura-Wasserstein, Perella alliance. While there are two specific joint ventures that came out of the arrangement (M&A boutiques in both Tokyo and London), there is also Nomura's 20 percent equity investment in Wasserstein, Perella. Given the announced global-niche aspirations of Wasserstein, Perella and the undoubted global investment-banking strategic positioning of Nomura, the arrangement could turn out to be of only transitional value for both parties. Sorting out the specific mandates that the joint ventures will pursue and how the spoils will be divided will be a challenging task for the parents.

Implications

Although the markets have become increasingly integrated from the viewpoints of both the capital user and the investors, considerable segmentation and nationalism remain within the investment banking community. Even in the Euromarkets, there is still considerable evidence of intervention by national governments and their central banks, often with the effect of protecting or promoting their national vendors. And the major national markets in New York and Tokyo provide further evidence of the barriers to offshore vendor entry.

Thus, when we are talking about a strategy for investment banking vendors, it is more illuminating to talk about an *international* strategy rather than a *global* strategy. Vendors must fight one battle at a time to gain access to the different markets; each market presents its own barriers to entry. The vaunted financial muscle of the universal bank is of only limited significance. Experience has shown the need to maintain a separate and independent entity for the investment banking unit; as a practical matter, it has been mainly the assurance of the parent's deep pockets for capital and the potential for a distribution bailout in difficult financings that has given the investment banking units of large universal banks any kind of edge at all.

When all is said and done, the basic choices appear to boil down to either the comprehensive worldwide coverage of the global investment banking unit or the niche strategy, in which only a piece of this broad market pie is bitten off. In assessing the merits of each option, two countervailing trends have to be taken into account:

- As high-margin products and services mature, they tend to attract increased competition and suffer shrinkage in those margins. Economies of scale may, in some cases, be a remedy for the profit erosion; and the value of size may imply a concentration of the business among large organizations with the broader distribution and bigger capital bases that characterize the global investment banks and the investment banking units of universal banks.

- As the corporate-user and the institutional-investor constituencies have adopted an increasingly sophisticated approach to the markets, their natural predisposition is to want to unbundle services and look for multiple vendors with special pockets of expertise, rather than rely on a single investment bank to take care of all their needs. Thus, it could be expected that specialized (i.e., niche) vendors would keep picking off pieces of high-margin business from the clients of global investment banks.

In field interviews, the majority of the investment bankers we talked to said they intended to position themselves as global investment bankers rather than as niche players. Yet we also observed that the investment banks are, as a group, quintessentially entrepreneurial and very much profit-oriented (some of the U.S. securities firms are, sadly, distracted by "quarterly earnings-per-share" fixations). When investment banks suffer setbacks, they naturally reassess their situations and usually take remedial actions to preserve both their profitability and their capital, even at the possible expense of long-term market positioning. Salomon Brothers reacted this way to the downturn in the Euromarkets and to the setbacks they experienced in the United States. That firm was willing to abandon its leading roles in municipal bonds and in the marketing and trading of short-term money market instruments to trim overhead and protect capital.

By contrast, the Japanese securities firms, while not hurting for overall profitability by anyone's standards, nonetheless have tended to view the market dislocations of the late 1980s as an opportunity to build a larger market-share position at the very time that some international investment banks were defensively circling their wagons. It is not clear whether a Salomon Brothers could re-enter any of the abandoned markets once better times have returned. It is not clear, either, whether maintaining a token presence in these sectors is any better a means of keeping your nose under the tent. But it is also possible that some of the investment banks—particularly some of the U.S. firms—might be satisfied to remain in a niche position indefinitely. The lure of merchant banking, with its lucrative fees and extraordinary capital gains potential, is very strong. In that event, we could expect vendors from other countries, particularly the Japanese, to pick up the slack in the abandoned areas and come to occupy a leading position in still another important global industry.

CHAPTER 14

GLOBAL BANKING AND ITS IMPLICATIONS FOR GOVERNMENT POLICY

This book is about investment banking and its evolution in the public market settings in London, New York, and Tokyo. We have noted that developments and advances in these markets have, in many instances, been tied to extraordinary political events, such as wars, and to major economic developments.

The twentieth century, an epoch of two world wars and subsequent growing global economic interdependency, has witnessed giant strides in the developments of public securities markets and the vendor firms that compete in them. Moreover, the establishment of the first bona fide supranational market (the Euromarket) in the early 1960s was possible not just because of U.S. balance-of-payments deficits, but also because of other propitious circumstances. Its time had come. That entrepôt marketplace has played an important role in encouraging deregulation and internationalization of the world's other financial markets in the years since then.

There has been much debate in the business literature over the prospects for the development of integrated global markets in a variety of manufactured goods and services. We would postulate that, from the point of view of many of the world's more substantial capital users and investors, a global market in financial products has already arrived. Even medium-sized companies in a number of industrialized countries are now able to routinely tap into the international supermarket of capital in search of the cheapest and most appropriate financing arrangements.

Technology has hastened the globalizing process. Computers and state-of-the-art telecommunications have vastly increased the quantity and sped the flow of information. Investment and merchant bankers have long served as vendors of information, going back to the days when Rothschild used a string of semaphore stations to transmit critical intelligence from one city to another, and when other bankers used carrier pigeons for the same purpose. Today's technological breakthroughs in information exchange have enabled individuals and organizations to comparison shop in different geographic markets in a manner unimaginable only a generation ago. And, as we have noted, swaps between currencies and offering terms have been an impressive facilitator in the process of quickly arbitraging many of the differences in market settings around the world. In a very real sense, the efficiency of information exchange has created a giant global electronic grid tying markets ever more tightly together. It is true that some important barriers and pockets of inefficiency remain, but capital is fungible and relatively easily shifted from one part of the globe to another. U.S. government securities are already traded uniformly all over the world twenty-four hours a day, and other parts of the market for capital are likely to approach such commodity status in the not-too-distant future.

Differentiation among Investment Banks

By contrast, the investment banks operating in the increasingly integrated markets are showing themselves to be much slower to merge into a homogenous group of global competitors. The patterns of evolution exhibited by subgroups of these firms have been different and more complex. Investment banks and securities vendors of various stripes and nationalities are not at all uniform in their organizational structures, their internal resources, or their offerings of products and services. Our research suggests that national and regional differences are very much influenced by the investment banks' origins, early history, and the status accorded them in their home market environments.

Securities firms in the United States have evolved in a fashion markedly different from that in Japan or Great Britain. U.S. investment banks, by virtue of their long-time pre-eminence as financial counselors to U.S. companies, have developed highly sophisticated skills in the areas of corporate finance and institutional trading. Japanese securities firms, by contrast, historically have occupied only a secondary role vis-à-vis the corporate community in Japan and have therefore developed their most impressive credentials in merchandising securities to individual investor-savers.

Footprints of each country's investment banking competitor group are obviously shaped by their regulatory environments and prevailing business customs. Those countries where vigorous interfirm competition has been encouraged tend to foster not only more cost-efficient and innovative domestic solutions for capital savers and users, but also to produce effective competitors in the offshore markets. This has almost certainly been the case with both the United States and Japan. By contrast, some European countries have a few large universal banks that dominate both the commercial and the investment banking sides of their home markets. They often have produced neither vigorous domestic competition nor a group of lean and hungry investment banking competitors in the international arena.

An environment that fosters vigorous home-market competition does not necessarily provide a fertile field for foreign vendors. In a number of countries, foreign vendors confront barriers that effectively exclude them from significant penetration. While some of the impediments are formal government-initiated curbs, others are more subtle and relate to deeply ingrained cultural and business practices.

The Role of Government

As we have seen throughout this volume, the interplay between government action and securities markets is a constant reminder that politics and finance are inextricably intertwined. The relationship manifests itself in various ways.

Most governments since the eighteenth century have treated *access to deficit financing* as a strategic resource. Thus, politicians in both developed and less developed countries have sought to maintain an ability to mobilize funds far beyond the immediate powers of taxation of their citizenry. As we said in the Introduction, William Pitt recognized the availability of finance in London as a great advantage to Britain and its ally Austria in the wars against France in the 1790s. Similarly, the ability of the U.S. government in the 1980s to finance the twin deficits in its balance of payments and budget was a significant boost in achieving other economic objectives of the Reagan administration.

Governments and investment bankers have learned to love each other, but it is, at times, a rocky romance. While modest amounts of deficit financing have been welcomed by bankers, excessive amounts have created tensions. In addition, the differences in style (with the bankers often reflecting entrepreneurial and private values, while the bureaucrats profess public interests) have created distrust and ambivalence, especially when right-left ideological extremes are involved. Nevertheless, the basic relationship has been symbiotic and necessary for both sides.

As a chaperon of the banker-government relationship, a central bank or finance ministry, knowledgeable in market practice and acting as fiscal agent for the government in the sale of its debt, often has been interposed between the two parties. And that banker-government dialogue often has been cast in the form of debates about the method of sale (for instance, whether to use auctions, prevalent in the United States, or fixed domestic syndicates, prevalent in Japan and Canada). Governments have often sought to avoid dependence on even their own securities dealers by the use of alternative channels of distribution. Selling savings bonds to individuals through commercial banks or, in the case of a number of European governments, the flotation of bond issues in other marketplaces through foreign investment banks are examples. Occasionally, other sources have included the International Monetary Fund, as in the case of Britain in 1976. Political circumstances have, of course, always influenced the abilities of governments to mobilize finance, and wartime patriotism has been a major ingredient.

Another facet of the dialogue between a government and its domestic investment bankers has been the debate about the amount and the type of finance to be employed and the impact of various financing levels on interest-rate policy and inflation in the country. Occasionally, when the domestic market has become saturated with government issues, domestic bankers have even encouraged governments to seek funding abroad. Many of the landmark international bond underwritings of the nineteenth and twentieth centuries have occurred in this context, including the $500-million issue in the United States by the British and French governments at the start of World War I.

With the birth of the Euromarkets in the early 1960s, a new avenue of financing appeared. This source was originally regarded by a number of governments as a possible threat to their efforts to mobilize funds in their home markets. Naturally, citizens investing funds in the Euromarkets and outside their own borders represented a leakage of savings from the domestic financing pool. This could be particularly troublesome if financings denominated in the home country currency could be readily floated in the Euromarkets. Some governments moved vigorously to control such home currency financings; others (especially the United States) adopted a hands-off policy that ultimately allowed the nascent market to grow and mature. In the deregulated era of the 1980s, governments have become more accustomed to (that is not to say better at) dealing with the problems of international financial flows, and they have, in most cases, readily accepted the Euromarkets as an alternative avenue for fund raising.

Another facet of the relationship between government and the financial markets has been *the attitude of government officials toward foreign government borrowing in their markets.* As mentioned earlier, in the eighteenth and nineteenth centuries, Britain often welcomed financings by other countries in the London market. Such operations provided an avenue for profitable investment of the surplus savings generated by the industrial revolution, and they could also be used to enhance Britain's trade and colonial relationships elsewhere in the world. This general attitude and the consequent heavy volume of foreign government financing created an enduring tradition of international underwriting in the City of London, which assisted in the City's late-twentieth-century resurgence, this time as the home of the supranational Euromarkets.

With the closing of the British and Continental markets at the onset of World War I, the U.S. investment banking community welcomed the opportunity to undertake financings in the New York market for other countries, particularly Britain and France, with the active support of the U.S. State Department. This trend continued until the Great Depression but opened up once again following World War II.

During the 1960s, President Kennedy effectively closed the U.S. market to foreign financing as part of the remedy for improving the country's balance of payments. As an unintended consequence, his actions resulted in the buildup of an alternative Eurobond market outside the direct control of any formal regulatory authority. As this market was increasingly tapped by savers and governments, the free movement of capital became a much more accepted reality than it had been in the highly compartmentalized world markets of the 1940s and 1950s. The accompanying deregulation of some of the most important national markets in the 1970s and 1980s and the intellectual support for free movement of capital appear to have been further buttressed by the agreement of the European Economic Community to unify its markets (including the one for capital) by December 1992. Although these developments do reflect a free-market view of economics, they are also indicative of the difficulty of enforcing rigid capital controls in a world of modern communications technology and funds transfer.

Another level of the relationship between government and the investment banks has been *government acting as a sponsor for its home country investment banking industry.* With the growth in investment banks' international operations in recent years, the relevant competitive arenas have been extended abroad, and there have been corresponding efforts of foreign vendors to make inroads into others' home markets. Thus, the governments of most of the leading industrialized countries have become involved in refereeing competitive struggles between foreign and domestic firms. Naturally, the governments often have been enlisted to aid their domestic investment banking industries. A host of arguments for government aid have been brought to bear by the firms concerned. Some firms, in seeking to hold onto home market turf, have argued that monetary and credit policies may be more difficult to manage if too many nondomestic firms are allowed to gain standing. In other instances, firms have lobbied their governments to intervene on their behalf to obtain reciprocity for their operations in other countries. The forms of argument in these cases have ranged from special pleading involving particular firm or market situations to broader representations that 1) a strong international investment-banking industry can be a major national asset and foreign currency earner, and 2) a strong international investment banking industry can be an effective interlocuter with foreign sources of funds in placing, trading, and explaining the debt of the government and its agencies.

The range of government responses to such requests for aid have been varied and have reflected their own special preoccupations. As noted earlier, the United States exerted pressure on Japan for concessions to U.S. securities firms as the price for acceptance of Japanese securities firms and banks as primary U.S. government-bond dealers. In France, during the late 1970s and early 1980s, it was clear that the Ministry of Finance, in orchestrating borrowings for French agencies in foreign capital markets, wanted to include French banks in prominent positions in the managing syndicates for such financings, even in instances where the issues were led and placed almost entirely by currency specialist firms from other countries.

As our chapters on the United Kingdom have shown, national objectives have sometimes included the enhancement of a major financial center (London); in other instances, however, where there were no such ambitions, governments concentrated on obtaining reciprocal privileges for their investment banks in foreign centers. In these matters, a host of regulatory concepts such as "most-favored nation" treatment, "national" treatment, or purely "reciprocal" relationships have been used to justify governments' approaches to such issues. And as already mentioned, a multilateral approach to these areas currently is being attempted in connection with the efforts by the European Economic Community to create a free and competitive market in financial services within the community after 1992.

Government action also touches securities markets deeply in the area of *regulation of market practices*. This activity in the major countries often has a range of different objectives, including the following:

1. controlling fraud;
2. providing a level playing field for different categories of investors through such methods as enforced disclosure; and
3. shaping the securities and banking industries through laws,

such as the Glass-Steagall Act in the United States and Article 65 in Japan, that have controlled access to the securities business.

The regulatory approaches of governments in these areas arise fundamentally from cultural attitudes regarding the correct and proper way of channeling savings and investment. As our examinations of the three most important financial-market centers indicate, the consequences of such cultural bias yield different results. In the United States, for instance, one has to factor in the unique populist sentiment that has colored this country's approach to regulation over an extended period of its history. Immigrants to the United States were often political or social refugees from countries with heavily centralized authority; thus, they had a natural antipathy to large government and business institutions. In the United States, when corporations and banks grew to a size where they developed countrywide operations, the political response was to pass antitrust legislation as well as restraining state banking laws. But regulatory authority was also compartmentalized within the different sectors of the financial services field, with the result that the government as watchdog was often curbed in its growth and potential power. This historical political phenomenon has resulted in a hodgepodge of state and federal regulations as well as the presence of more than 12,000 separate U.S. commercial banks, compared to a handful of much larger financial institutions in most other developed countries.

In Japan, by contrast, a firm government hand via the monolithic Ministry of Finance has been accepted, from the beginning of the Meiji Restoration, as necessary for the effective direction of saving and investment. The consensus produced a concentrated financial-services industry that was formally split into banking and securities sectors only following legislation (Article 65) instigated by the postwar occupation forces.

A further significant difference between the regulatory frameworks in the individual countries is the degree to which there is reliance on formal and informal regulation. Within the United Kingdom, the organizational structure was relatively informal until 1986, when the Financial Services Act more formally codified it. Nevertheless, by choosing to regulate principally through the medium of five self-regulatory organizations, the British government has attempted to avoid some of the more rigid aspects of the more formalized U.S. securities laws. It may have observed that both legislatures and regulatory bodies tend to guard their awarded prerogatives jealously, and laws, once in place, inevitably become difficult to modify or replace. It is just this situation that has, in our view, created difficulties for the American financial system in adapting to major changes in the world system of securities distribution and banking during the past two decades. While the United States has led in the deregulation of financial services, there nonetheless have been serious difficulties in making regulatory modifications that involved statutory alterations. This sometime legislative gridlock may be a vexing millstone for the United States in the future if, as a consequence of inattention to certain needed reforms, we see international financing activity bypass New York even more than is now the case.

It does seem inevitable that the increasing economic interdependencies among countries means that national idiosyncrasies will have to subside in importance to accommodate the increasing ease with which both capital suppliers and capital users flit from geographic market to geographic market in search of the best available deal. And the prospect of an integrated EEC in 1992 may provide an early test of that notion. Annoying intercountry barriers will not be tolerated easily, and market participants will either find ways to circumvent them or else bypass the offending countries altogether. That often gets the attention of the political leadership. For politicians and government bureaucrats, the only thing more distasteful than having their powers curtailed is to have their functions become irrelevant.

Despite the efforts of both the United States and Japan to open up their financial markets as a means of enhancing their national prestige and as a source of economic momentum and employment (witness what the Euromarkets have done for London), neither has been able to move with sufficient dispatch to clear away the regulatory and cultural barriers to create a market environment comparable to that of the City of London.

New York will continue as an important national financial center because it is the gateway to one of the world's biggest and richest consumer marketplaces and an attractive locus of direct investments. Still, it is unlikely to supplant London in the role as entrepôt for cross-border financing activity. This will particularly be the case if, as expected, London grows in importance as the EEC financial center in a post–1992 world of lowered barriers to the movement of both capital and vendors from country to country within Europe. Regulatory constraints and the realities of business practice are likely to continue to make for slow going for foreign investment banking and other non-conventional vendors in the United States, even with the Glass-Steagall barrier effectively removed.

By the same token, Tokyo, for all its enormous annual surpluses of exportable capital and cadre of aggressive banking and securities firms, also has had real difficulty in establishing itself as a bona fide international-financing center. To be sure, the Ministry of Finance is in the process of implementing a broad reform and deregulation of its financial services sector (including the effective removal of the "teeth" of Article 65). It is also dismantling a number of restrictions that have been identified by foreign vendors as barriers to doing business. But these same vendors also allege that Japanese business practices and cultural idiosyncrasies are major hurdles to doing business in Tokyo.

In fact, after shutting down or sharply curtailing their Hong Kong offices and moving lock, stock, and barrel to Tokyo in the early 1980s, several international securities firms rethought that decision and reactivated their Hong Kong operations. Their reasoning was that it is going to continue to be difficult and expensive to penetrate the Tokyo market, particularly with the presence of such powerful home-based competitors as Nomura, Daiwa, and the Industrial Bank of Japan. While they believed they would always need to have a powerful presence in Tokyo because of the importance of that national market, some felt they could do potentially more of the available non-Japanese Asian (particularly Chinese) business from another location with a more sympathetic regulatory environment (similar to that of London) and a level playing field free of the shadow of giant indigenous financial institutions. If the Chinese government plays its cards carefully to ensure a friendly operating environment in Hong Kong after the colony reverts to mainland rule in 1997, Hong Kong could be a significant Asian entrepôt center for global finance. The bloody massacre of May 1989 in Beijing's Tiananmen Square has suspended all bets on these prospects, however. But if not Hong Kong, then another center—such as Singapore—might rise.

In sum, while the process of international rationalization of country market regulations and practices is proving to be an arduous process, it is making some forward movement. But one should not look for a complete melding of the various national environments anytime soon. Powerful forces remain, both within governments and in the domestic private sectors of the financial markets, that will continue to resist such a coalescence. Instead of homogenization of the various markets, it is more likely that we will see a harmonization of the national market links. Overriding national concerns and preoccupations will probably continue to sustain discrete geographic and currency market segments for some time.

How the internationalization of investment banking and the growing linkage of financial markets will affect the fates of nations, corporations, and the man on the street is, at this point, a matter of speculation. Theory tells us that where markets are free and open, efficiency prevails. The borrowers and investors from around the world who meet in the Eurobond market would certainly confirm that notion. And the drive to pull down barriers to trade and competition in the financial centers we have just studied suggests that, with a number of reservations, the free-market societies see global integration as a good thing and in their long-term interests.

One wonders how the Soviet bloc countries, which have historically opted out of the circle of free-market finance, will manage to capitalize their own national developments. With the West and the Pacific Rim piling up capital at a fearsome pace and the Eastern bloc woefully short of financial resources, it would seem logical for them to want to join the circle. And, in fact, they are now sending some strong signals of just such an interest. Whatever the economic merits of such a change, the prospects for international peace and harmony would undoubtedly be enhanced, because, as the saying goes, "Borders that commerce cannot cross, armies will."

But these are subjects for another book.

APPENDIX A

EUROMARKET STATISTICS

Table A-1

All Eurobond Issues—Rank and Market Share of Principal Lead Managers, 1980–1988

Rank	1980		1981		1982		1983		1984	
	Lead Manager	Market Share (%)	Lead Manager	Market Share (%)	Lead Manager	Market Share (%)	Lead Manager	Market Share (%)	Lead Manager	Market Share (%)
1	Deutsche	13.6%	CSFB	13.6%	Deutsche	15.3%	CSFB	21.6%	CSFB	16.6%
2	CSFB	7.4	Morgan Stanley	7.4	CSFB	12.1	Deutsche	16.2	Morgan Guar	7.7
3	Morgan Stanley	6.3	SG Warburg	6.3	Morgan Stanley	9.8	SG Warburg	4.5	Deutsche	7.4
4	SG Warburg	6.2	Deutsche	6.2	Salomon	4.6	Morgan Stanley	3.7	Morgan Stanley	6.5
5	Goldman, Sachs	5.0	Salomon	5.0	SG Warburg	3.3	Dresdner	3.3	Salomon	6.0
6	Banque Paribas	3.8	Merrill Lynch	3.8	Union B Switz	3.0	Morgan Guar	3.0	Merrill Lynch	5.4
7	Salomon	3.4	Cred Comm Fr	3.4	Swiss B Corp	2.9	Merrill Lynch	2.8	Nomura	3.3
8	Soc Generale	3.2	Nomura	3.2	Soc Generale	2.8	B Nat Paris	2.8	Goldman, Sachs	3.1
9	Orion Royal	2.7	Morgan Guar	2.7	Morgan Guar	2.8	Nomura	2.3	SG Warburg	2.4
10	B Nat Paris	2.7	Hambros	2.7	B Nat Paris	2.3	Goldman, Sachs	2.2	Dresdner	2.2
11	Dresdner	2.6	Goldman, Sachs	2.6	Merrill Lynch	2.2	Commerzbank	2.2	B Nat Paris	2.2
12	Daiwa	2.5	Union B Switz	2.5	Goldman, Sachs	2.2	Orion Royal	1.9	Banque Paribas	1.9
13	West LB	2.3	Soc Generale	2.3	Nomura	2.0	Swiss B Corp	1.7	Daiwa	1.8
14	Citicorp	2.2	Yamaichi	2.2	Ams Rotterdam	1.9	Cred Lyonnais	1.7	Soc Generale	1.6
15	Hambros	2.1	Swiss B Corp	2.1	Commerzbank	1.8	Salomon	1.7	Shearson	1.6
16	Commerzbank	2.1	Wood Gundy	2.1	BankAmerica	1.6	West LB	1.6	Swiss B Corp	1.6
17	Union B Switz	2.0	Daiwa	2.0	Dresdner	1.5	Ams Rotterdam	1.5	Orion Royal	1.5
18	Yamaichi	1.9	Orion Royal	1.9	Daiwa	1.5	Cred Comm Fr	1.4	Commerzbank	1.4
19	Swiss B Corp	1.7	West LB	1.7	Cred Comm Fr	1.5	Soc Generale	1.3	Nikko	1.4
20	Cred Lyonnais	1.6	Dillon, Read	1.6	Banque Paribas	1.4	Wood Gundy	1.2	Barclays	1.2
	Others	24.7	Others	24.6	Others	23.5	Others	21.4	Others	23.2

	1985		1986		1987		1988	
Rank	Lead Manager	Market Share (%)	Lead Manager	Market Share (%)	Lead Manager	Market Share (%)	Lead Manager	Market Share (%)
1	CSFB	14.3	CSFB	11.4	Nomura	13.0	Nomura	9.9
2	Merrill Lynch	6.0	Nomura	8.0	CSFB	7.0	CSFB	7.8
3	Morgan Guar	5.9	Deutsche	6.6	Deutsche	6.0	Deutsche	6.7
4	Salomon	5.8	Morgan Guar	5.4	Nikko	5.7	Daiwa	5.3
5	Deutsche	5.7	Daiwa	4.9	Yamaichi	5.2	Yamaichi	4.3
6	Morgan Stanley	5.0	Morgan Stanley	4.9	Daiwa	5.1	Nikko	4.0
7	Goldman, Sachs	4.1	Salomon	4.3	Morgan Stanley	3.6	Banque Paribas	3.4
8	Nomura	3.8	Banque Paribas	4.0	Morgan Guar	3.4	Merrill Lynch	3.4
9	Union B Switz	2.8	Merrill Lynch	3.2	Salomon	3.1	JP Morgan	3.3
10	Banque Paribas	2.5	Nikko	2.9	Banque Paribas	3.0	Indus B Japan	3.2
11	Orion Royal	2.2	Union B Switz	2.7	Indus B Japan	3.0	Union B Switz	3.1
12	Daiwa	2.2	Yamaichi	2.4	SG Warburg	2.9	Bankers Trust	2.9
13	SG Warburg	2.2	Shearson	2.3	Union B Switz	2.3	Salomon	2.8
14	Swiss B Corp	1.9	Goldman, Sachs	2.0	Commerzbank	1.8	Swiss B Corp	2.4
15	Shearson	1.9	Soc Generale	1.7	Dresdner	1.7	SG Warburg	2.3
16	Bankers Trust	1.8	Indus B Japan	1.6	Swiss B Corp	1.7	Goldman, Sachs	2.2
17	Commerzbank	1.8	Swiss B Corp	1.6	Goldman, Sachs	1.5	Dresdner	2.1
18	County Bank	1.7	SG Warburg	1.5	Baring Bros	1.4	Morgan Stanley	2.0
19	Lloyds	1.7	Commerzbank	1.5	Long-Term Credit	1.2	Commerzbank	1.9
20	Yamaichi	1.7	B Nat Paris	1.4	Merrill Lynch	1.2	Hambros	1.5
	Others	25.0	Others	25.7	Others	26.2	Others	25.5

Sources: Securities Data Company database; *Investment Dealers' Digest* database.

Table A-2

Eurobond Issues by Currency of Denomination, Percentage of Total, 1980–1988

Currency	1980	1981	1982	1983	1984	1985	1986	1987	1988
U.S. dollar	69.1%	82.0%	82.2%	74.9%	78.1%	70.4%	63.0%	42.2%	40.8%
Japanese yen	1.1	1.4	0.9	0.6	1.4	5.3	10.3	16.0	9.4
British pound	3.8	2.0	1.7	4.4	5.4	4.7	5.9	10.3	13.1
Deutsche mark	17.9	4.8	9.4	11.9	7.5	7.3	8.2	9.8	12.4
Australian dollar	0.3	0.0	0.0	0.5	0.4	2.3	1.7	6.3	4.6
European currency unit	0.0	0.7	1.6	3.8	3.5	5.0	3.7	5.3	6.5
Canadian dollar	1.4	2.7	2.6	2.5	2.5	2.1	2.9	4.2	7.3
Dutch guilder	1.9	1.7	1.2	1.3	0.8	0.5	1.3	1.3	2.1
New Zealand dollar	0.0	0.0	0.0	0.0	0.1	0.8	0.2	1.1	0.4
French franc	3.6	2.1	0.0	0.0	0.0	0.8	1.9	1.0	1.4
Danish krone	0.0	0.0	0.0	0.0	0.0	0.3	0.6	1.0	0.5
Austrian schilling	0.0	0.0	0.0	0.0	0.0	0.0	0.1	0.6	0.3
Italian lira	0.0	0.0	0.0	0.0	0.0	0.2	0.2	0.5	0.8
Kuwaiti dinar	0.1	0.5	0.3	0.0	0.0	0.0	0.0	0.3	0.0
Finnish markka	0.0	0.0	0.0	0.0	0.0	0.0	0.0	0.1	0.0
European unit of accounts	0.4	0.4	0.0	0.0	0.0	0.0	0.0	0.0	0.0
Hong Kong dollar	0.0	0.0	0.0	0.0	0.1	0.2	0.0	0.0	0.0
Luxembourg franc	0.0	0.0	0.0	0.0	0.0	0.0	0.0	0.0	0.0
Norwegian krone	0.3	0.2	0.1	0.1	0.2	0.1	0.0	0.0	0.0
South African rand	0.0	0.0	0.0	0.0	0.0	0.0	0.0	0.0	0.4
Special drawing rights	0.1	1.5	0.0	0.0	0.0	0.0	0.0	0.0	0.0
Singapore dollar	0.0	0.0	0.0	0.0	0.0	0.0	0.0	0.0	0.0
Total U.S.-dollar equivalent (millions)	$18,716	$25,511	$48,079	$47,251	$79,355	$134,468	$183,079	$141,665	$180,398

Note: This table and those that follow include all Eurobond issues and exclude any "foreign" issues. Eurobond issues are usually defined as broadly offered financings underwritten by vendors in a number of countries. Foreign issues refer to financings of foreign obligors that are generally offered in a single national market by vendors domiciled in that country. Swiss franc issues by foreign borrowers, for example, are required to be offered in Switzerland and are not clasified as Eurobonds.

Sources: Securities Data Company database; Investment Dealers' Digest database.

Table A-3
Eurobond Issues by Country of Borrower, Percentage of Total, 1980–1988

Country of Borrower	1980	1981	1982	1983	1984	1985	1986	1987	1988
Japan	7.2%	9.3%	4.4%	9.8%	12.8%	10.6%	12.8%	25.8%	20.1%
Great Britain	7.6	4.9	2.3	3.6	5.6	11.5	10.6	7.5	12.9
United States	19.8	22.7	27.5	13.3	26.7	27.2	20.6	12.7	9.8
Supranational institutions	14.3	9.4	9.6	17.0	7.8	7.4	6.0	8.8	7.9
France	7.8	7.1	13.4	12.7	8.6	8.1	7.2	5.0	6.7
Canada	8.5	19.8	4.3	8.1	5.7	5.4	7.4	3.8	5.5
West Germany	0.0	0.2	3.0	5.2	2.2	2.4	6.1	5.6	5.4
Australia	1.5	1.8	2.5	2.5	2.0	2.8	3.7	4.1	4.6
Sweden	7.4	4.2	2.9	6.8	5.1	3.3	2.6	2.9	4.1
Italy	5.2	3.4	1.5	1.5	3.9	3.5	2.2	4.6	3.7
Austria	2.4	1.8	2.0	1.8	2.1	1.5	1.5	2.7	3.3
Norway	2.3	0.6	0.7	1.0	1.2	1.7	2.9	2.2	2.5
Netherlands	3.1	1.2	1.6	2.0	1.2	1.0	1.4	1.5	2.4
Finland	0.7	0.8	0.8	0.7	1.3	1.0	1.6	1.7	2.1
Denmark	1.6	0.6	1.6	2.7	4.6	2.0	4.9	2.4	1.5
Belgium	1.1	0.7	0.2	1.7	2.0	1.4	1.9	2.2	1.2
New Zealand	0.6	1.2	1.8	0.2	0.6	0.9	1.8	1.0	0.9
Switzerland	1.3	0.0	1.6	1.6	0.8	0.5	1.4	0.7	0.5
Spain	0.8	0.6	0.5	1.8	1.4	0.9	0.8	0.1	0.4
Ireland	0.4	1.5	1.2	1.4	1.0	1.0	1.0	0.5	0.1
Mexico	1.6	5.7	2.7	0.0	0.0	0.0	0.0	0.0	0.0
Others	4.8	2.5	3.9	4.6	0.4	5.9	1.6	4.2	4.4
Total U.S.-dollar equivalent (millions)	$18,716	$25,511	$48,079	$47,251	$79,355	$134,468	$183,079	$141,665	$172,832

Sources: Securities Data Company database; *Investment Dealers' Digest* database.

Table A-4
U.S.-Dollar Eurobond Issues—Rank and Market Share of Principal Lead Managers, 1980–1988

Rank	1980 Lead Manager	Market Share (%)	1981 Lead Manager	Market Share (%)	1982 Lead Manager	Market Share (%)	1983 Lead Manager	Market Share (%)	1984 Lead Manager	Market Share (%)
1	CSFB	13.8%	CSFB	16.3%	CSFB	14.8%	CSFB	28.8%	CSFB	20.9%
2	Morgan Stanley	8.3	Morgan Stanley	8.5	Deutsche	13.6	Deutsche	13.8	Morgan Guar	9.6
3	SG Warburg	7.8	SG Warburg	6.8	Morgan Stanley	11.7	Morgan Stanley	4.7	Morgan Stanley	7.8
4	Goldman, Sachs	6.5	Salomon	6.1	Salomon	5.6	Morgan Guar	3.9	Salomon	7.6
5	Salomon	5.4	Deutsche	5.3	Union B Switz	3.3	Merrill Lynch	3.6	Merrill Lynch	6.5
6	Banque Paribas	5.3	Merrill Lynch	4.6	Morgan Guar	3.3	Goldman, Sachs	3.0	Deutsche	4.5
7	Soc Generale	3.8	Cred Comm Fr	3.8	Swiss B Corp	3.2	B Nat Paris	2.8	Goldman, Sachs	4.0
8	Orion Royal	3.5	Morgan Guar	3.3	SG Warburg	2.9	Nomura	2.7	Nomura	3.4
9	Citicorp	3.1	Goldman, Sachs	3.2	Goldman, Sachs	2.7	SG Warburg	2.4	B Nat Paris	2.5
10	Daiwa	2.8	Nomura	3.1	B Nat Paris	2.6	Salomon	2.1	Banque Paribas	2.1
11	B Nat Paris	2.3	Union B Switz	3.1	Soc Generale	2.2	Dresdner	2.0	Shearson	2.0
12	Union B Switz	2.3	Hambros	2.8	Merrill Lynch	2.2	Swiss B Corp	2.0	Soc Generale	1.6
13	Swiss B Corp	2.1	Yamaichi	2.7	Nomura	2.1	Cred Lyonnais	1.8	Nikko	1.6
14	Cred Lyonnais	1.8	Swiss B Corp	2.6	BankAmerica	1.9	Cred Comm Fr	1.6	Daiwa	1.5
15	Yamaichi	1.7	Wood Gundy	1.9	Ams Rotterdam	1.7	BankAmerica	1.5	Yamaichi	1.5
	Others	29.5	Others	25.9	Others	26.2	Others	23.3	Others	22.9

	1985		1986		1987		1988	
Rank	Lead Manager	Market Share (%)	Lead Manager	Market Share (%)	Lead Manager	Market Share (%)	Lead Manager	Market Share (%)
1	CSFB	18.3	CSFB	15.9	Nomura	15.6	Nomura	18.9
2	Merrill Lynch	8.1	Morgan Stanley	7.2	CSFB	9.9	CSFB	10.4
3	Salomon	7.8	Morgan Guar	7.2	Nikko	9.5	Daiwa	9.6
4	Morgan Guar	6.7	Nomura	6.0	Yamaichi	8.9	Yamaichi	8.7
5	Morgan Stanley	6.2	Salomon	5.8	Daiwa	6.9	Nikko	7.7
6	Goldman, Sachs	5.5	Merrill Lynch	4.9	Morgan Stanley	6.6	Merrill Lynch	5.7
7	Union B Switz	3.6	Daiwa	4.6	Salomon	4.1	Goldman, Sachs	4.1
8	Deutsche	3.2	Deutsche	3.7	Morgan Guar	3.1	Indus B Japan	3.5
9	Nomura	2.6	Banque Paribas	3.5	Union B Switz	2.9	JP Morgan	3.4
10	Shearson	2.6	Shearson	3.5	Goldman, Sachs	2.7	Bankers Trust	3.1
11	Lloyds	2.3	Union B Switz	3.3	Banque Paribas	2.6	Banque Paribas	2.9
12	County Bank	2.3	Nikko	3.2	Merrill Lynch	2.1	Morgan Stanley	2.7
13	Swiss B Corp	2.1	Goldman, Sachs	2.6	Deutsche	2.1	Swiss Bank	1.9
14	Bankers Trust	1.9	Yamaichi	2.3	Indus B Japan	1.8	Deutsche	1.7
15	BankAmerica	1.8	Bankers Trust	2.0	Bankers Trust	1.5	Long-Term Cred	1.6
	Others	25.0	Others	24.3	Others	19.7	Others	14.1

Sources: Securities Data Company database; *Investment Dealers' Digest* database.

Table A-5
Deutsche Mark Eurobond Issues—Rank and Market Share of Principal Lead Managers, 1980–1988

	1980		1981		1982		1983		1984	
Rank	Lead Manager	Market Share (%)	Lead Manager	Market Share (%)	Lead Manager	Market Share (%)	Lead Manager	Market Share (%)	Lead Manager	Market Share (%)
1	Deutsche	63.0%	Deutsche	36.6%	Deutsche	43.9%	Deutsche	49.0%	Deutsche	49.9%
2	Dresdner	12.7	West LB	30.7	Dresdner	16.4	Dresdner	14.6	Dresdner	18.4
3	West LB	10.3	Commerzbank	16.2	Commerzbank	15.1	Commerzbank	11.8	Commerzbank	13.3
4	Commerzbank	9.2	Dresdner	12.8	West LB	12.8	West LB	11.5	West LB	8.3
5	BHF-Bank	4.2	BHF-Bank	2.1	BHF-Bank	6.2	BHF-Bank	6.7	BHF-Bank	5.6
6	DG Bank	0.6	Bayer Vereins	1.4	DG Bank	2.9	Bayer Vereins	3.8	Bayer Vereins	2.7
7	—		—		Bayer Vereins	2.7	DG Bank	2.1	DG Bank	1.8
8	—		—		—		Bayer Landes	0.5	—	
9	—		—		—		—		—	
10	—		—		—		—		—	
Others	Others	0.0	Others	0.0	Others	0.0	Others	0.0	Others	0.0

	1985		1986		1987		1988	
Rank	Lead Manager	Market Share (%)	Lead Manager	Market Share (%)	Lead Manager	Market Share (%)	Lead Manager	Market Share (%)
1	Deutsche	45.7	Deutsche	46.9	Deutsche	44.2	Deutsche	33.5
2	Commerzbank	20.1	West LB	12.2	Commerzbank	15.0	Dresdner	15.1
3	Dresdner	12.4	Commerzbank	12.1	Dresdner	12.6	Commerzbank	13.5
4	CSFB	6.4	CSFB	8.1	West LB	6.0	West LB	7.3
5	West LB	5.0	Dresdner	7.4	Morgan Guar	4.4	Trinkhaus	4.0
6	BHF-Bank	4.4	BHF-Bank	3.2	Trinkhaus	3.7	Bayer Vereins	3.3
7	Morgan Guar	2.6	DG Bank	2.7	CSFB	3.2	Deutsche Genos	3.3
8	DG Bank	2.3	Morgan Guar	1.8	Bayer Vereins	2.6	Berliner Handels	3.0
9	Industrikred	0.6	Trinkhaus	1.4	Morgan Stanley	2.3	Morgan Stanley	2.8
10	Bayer Vereins	0.5	Union B Switz	1.0	Swiss Bank	1.4	CSFB	2.4
Others	0.0	Others	3.2	Others	4.6	Others	11.8

Sources: Securities Data Company database; *Investment Dealers' Digest* database.

Table A-6
Japanese Yen Eurobond Issues—Rank and Market Share of Principal Lead Managers, 1980–1988

Rank	1980 Lead Manager	Market Share (%)	1981 Lead Manager	Market Share (%)	1982 Lead Manager	Market Share (%)	1983 Lead Manager	Market Share (%)	1984 Lead Manager	Market Share (%)
1	Yamaichi	29.3%	Daiwa	55.6%	Daiwa	57.1%	Nomura	50.3%	Nomura	47.4%
2	Daiwa	26.5	Nomura	44.4	Nomura	28.1	Yamaichi	28.4	Daiwa	37.5
3	Nomura	25.6	—	—	Nikko	14.8	Daiwa	21.3	Nikko	7.9
4	Nikko	18.6	—	—	—	—	—	—	CSFB	7.2
5	—	—	—	—	—	—	—	—	—	—
6	—	—	—	—	—	—	—	—	—	—
7	—	—	—	—	—	—	—	—	—	—
8	—	—	—	—	—	—	—	—	—	—
9	—	—	—	—	—	—	—	—	—	—
10	—	—	—	—	—	—	—	—	—	—
	Others	0.0	Others	0.0	Others	0.0	Others	0.0	Others	0.0

Rank	1985 Lead Manager	Market Share (%)	1986 Lead Manager	Market Share (%)	1987 Lead Manager	Market Share (%)	1988 Lead Manager	Market Share (%)
1	Nomura	36.6	Nomura	42.5	Nomura	38.9	Nomura	21.0
2	Daiwa	23.2	Daiwa	19.6	Daiwa	11.8	Daiwa	15.9
3	Nikko	14.6	Nikko	8.6	Indus B Japan	10.8	Indus B Japan	15.5
4	Yamaichi	9.8	Yamaichi	8.4	Nikko	10.0	Yamaichi	8.6
5	Indus B Japan	3.8	Indus B Japan	4.2	Yamaichi	7.8	Nikko	8.0
6	Long-Term Cred	2.6	Bank of Tokyo	2.8	Long-Term Cred	5.3	Long-Term Cred	6.8
7	Morgan Stanley	2.5	Mitsubishi	1.9	Bank of Tokyo	3.1	Bankers Trust	6.1
8	CSFB	2.0	Long-Term Cred	1.2	Mitsubishi	1.9	Nippon Credit	2.9
9	Bank of Tokyo	2.0	Tokao	1.2	Union B Switz	1.7	Sanwa	1.6
10	Banque Paribas	1.2	Sumitomo	.2	Nippon Credit	1.1	Mitsui	1.5
	Others	1.7	Others	8.4	Others	7.6	Others	12.1

Sources: Securities Data Company database; *Investment Dealers' Digest* database.

Table A-7
British Pound Eurobond Issues—Rank and Market Share of Principal Lead Managers, 1980–1988

Rank	1980 Lead Manager	Market Share (%)	1981 Lead Manager	Market Share (%)	1982 Lead Manager	Market Share (%)	1983 Lead Manager	Market Share (%)	1984 Lead Manager	Market Share (%)
1	SG Warburg	18.9%	SG Warburg	37.3%	SG Warburg	47.2%	SG Warburg	58.0%	SG Warburg	30.5%
2	CSFB	16.1	Kleinwort	19.2	Baring Bros	16.0	Hambros	19.1	Morgan Gren	10.5
3	Morgan Gren	14.0	CSFB	11.1	Kleinwort	10.5	Baring Bros	11.0	Baring Bros	9.9
4	Lloyds	12.7	Schroder	10.7	Hambros	6.7	Hill Samuel	4.4	County Bank	8.3
5	Hill Samuel	8.0	County Bank	8.5	Swiss B Corp	6.7	Lloyds	3.8	Hambros	7.8
6	Merrill Lynch	7.1	Hambros	5.2	Morgan Guar	6.5	Morgan Guar	2.2	Lloyds	6.2
7	Salomon	5.3	Baring Bros	4.4	Hill Samuel	6.4	County Bank	1.5	S Montagu	5.4
8	Kleinwort	5.2	Morgan Gren	3.6	—	—	—	—	Schroder	3.9
9	PaineWebber	5.1	—	—	—	—	—	—	Swiss B Corp	3.4
10	Hambros	5.0	—	—	—	—	—	—	Manuf Hanover	3.0
	Others	2.6	Others	0.0	Others	0.0	Others	0.0	Others	11.1

Rank	1985 Lead Manager	Market Share (%)	1986 Lead Manager	Market Share (%)	1987 Lead Manager	Market Share (%)	1988 Lead Manager	Market Share (%)
1	SG Warburg	28.2	S Montagu	16.1	CSFB	17.1	CSFB	16.2
2	Morgan Gren	10.0	Morgan Gren	15.6	SG Warburg	16.1	SG Warburg	15.4
3	Hambros	8.4	Baring Bros	15.4	Baring Bros	14.0	Salomon	14.8
4	S Montagu	8.3	CSFB	10.7	Salomon	8.3	Baring Bros	9.6
5	Schroder	7.7	SG Warburg	9.6	Morgan Gren	6.5	Kleinwort	8.1
6	Morgan Guar	6.9	Morgan Guar	6.0	Kleinwort	6.0	Union B Switz	7.6
7	CSFB	6.7	Salomon	4.8	Barclays	4.1	JP Morgan	5.5
8	Baring Bros	6.5	Kleinwort	4.5	Swiss Bank	3.9	Hambros	4.4
9	Citicorp	4.0	Hambros	3.4	County NatWest	3.9	Barclays	3.4
10	County Bank	2.8	Schroder Wagg	3.3	Schroder Wagg	3.7	Merrill Lynch	3.3
	Others	10.5	Others	10.6	Others	16.4	Others	11.7

Sources: Securities Data Company database; Investment Dealers' Digest database.

Table A-8
European Currency Unit Eurobond Issues—Rank and Market Share of Principal Lead Managers, 1980–1988

Rank	1980 Lead Manager	1980 Market Share (%)	1981 Lead Manager	1981 Market Share (%)	1982 Lead Manager	1982 Market Share (%)	1983 Lead Manager	1983 Market Share (%)	1984 Lead Manager	1984 Market Share (%)
1	—		Kredietbank	57.9%	Kredietbank	32.6%	Soc Gen Banq	21.5%	Kredietbank	22.4%
2	—		B Nat Paris	24.9	Soc Generale	17.8	Kredietbank	19.6	Soc Generale	10.5
3	—		Cred Lyonnais	17.2	Cred Lyonnais	12.7	B Nat Paris	15.7	B Nat Paris	7.6
4	—		—		Cred Comm Fr	12.2	Soc Generale	11.7	Cred Lyonnais	6.8
5	—		—		B Nat Paris	8.9	Cred Lyonnais	9.8	Cred Comm Fr	6.7
6	—		—		B Indosuez	6.2	B Brux Lamb	6.8	Banque Paribas	6.5
7	—		—		Banque Paribas	5.9	Banque Paribas	5.7	B Indosuez	5.5
8	—		—		SG Warburg	3.7	Algemene	3.3	Swiss B Corp	4.9
9	—		—		—		SG Warburg	3.0	B Brux Lamb	4.6
10	—		—		—		B Indosuez	1.6	Deutsche	4.1
Others	Others	0.0	Others	0.0	Others	0.0	Others	1.3	Others	20.4

Rank	1985 Lead Manager	1985 Market Share (%)	1986 Lead Manager	1986 Market Share (%)	1987 Lead Manager	1987 Market Share (%)	1988 Lead Manager	1988 Market Share (%)
1	Banque Paribas	18.1	Banque Paribas	37.0	Banque Paribas	25.2	Banque Paribas	18.5
2	B Nat Paris	9.1	B Nat Paris	11.0	Morgan Guar	8.5	Deutsche	13.7
3	CSFB	8.7	Soc Generale	5.3	Cred Lyonnais	6.1	Swiss Bank	9.5
4	Cred Lyonnais	6.1	Kredietbank	4.9	Daiwa	5.4	CSFB	7.9
5	Morgan Guar	5.8	Morgan Guar	4.4	Morgan Stanley	5.2	Bankers Trust	7.8
6	B Brux Lamb	4.7	Cred Lyonnais	4.2	Bank of Tokyo	4.4	Union B Switz	6.6
7	Cred Comm Fr	4.1	IB San Paolo	3.5	Salomon	4.3	Cred Comm Fr	5.3
8	Kredietbank	3.7	Salomon	2.9	Soc Generale	4.1	Morgan Stanley	4.6
9	Bankers Trust	3.6	Can Imperial	2.8	Cred Comm Fr	4.0	Cred Lyonnais	4.0
10	Soc Generale	3.3	BankAmerica	2.6	Yamaichi	3.8	Soc Generale	3.4
Others	Others	32.8	Others	21.3	Others	28.9	Others	18.7

Note: First ECU financings took place in 1981.
Sources: Securities Data Company database; *Investment Dealers' Digest* database.

Table A-9

Canadian Dollar Eurobond Issues—Rank and Market Share of Principal Lead Managers, 1980–1988

Rank	1980 Lead Manager	Market Share (%)	1981 Lead Manager	Market Share (%)	1982 Lead Manager	Market Share (%)	1983 Lead Manager	Market Share (%)	1984 Lead Manager	Market Share (%)
1	Morgan Stanley	39.5%	Soc Generale	31.5%	Soc Generale	27.9%	Wood Gundy	28.4%	Wood Gundy	28.4%
2	Hambros	38.4	Wood Gundy	22.0	Merrill Lynch	15.9	Orion Royal	18.6	Morgan Stanley	11.0
3	Wood Gundy	15.6	Morgan Stanley	14.5	Union B Switz	11.5	Soc Generale	13.8	Swiss B Corp	10.6
4	Kuwait Inv	6.5	Orion Royal	13.0	Orion Royal	9.2	Swiss B Corp	8.6	Merrill Lynch	9.6
5	—		Hambros	9.3	Wood Gundy	8.8	Morgan Stanley	6.2	Orion Royal	8.4
6	—		Cont Illinois	6.0	Morgan Stanley	6.0	Merrill Lynch	5.5	Soc Generale	8.1
7	—		B Nat Paris	2.5	Kredietbank	4.8	Salomon	5.5	Salomon	4.9
8	—		B Int Luxem	1.2	Swiss B Corp	4.1	Cred Comm Fr	4.5	Can Imperial	4.3
9	—		—		Hambros	3.3	B Nat Paris	4.2	Indus B Japan	3.3
10	—		—		Soc Generale	3.0	Kidder, Peabody	2.5	Morgan Guar	2.9
Others		0.0	Others	0.0	Others	5.5	Others	1.3	Others	8.5

Rank	1985 Lead Manager	Market Share (%)	1986 Lead Manager	Market Share (%)	1987 Lead Manager	Market Share (%)	1988 Lead Manager	Market Share (%)
1	Orion Royal	22.7	Wood Gundy	18.1	Wood Gundy	16.0	Union B Switz	13.2
2	Wood Gundy	15.2	Union B Switz	16.6	Union B Switz	11.9	JP Morgan	11.4
3	Soc Generale	8.3	Orion Royal	12.9	Morgan Guar	8.5	Banque Paribas	10.3
4	Merrill Lynch	7.7	McLeod	7.4	McLeod	5.5	Wood Gundy	8.0
5	Union B Switz	7.6	Can Imperial	5.9	Orion Royal	5.2	Deutsche	6.6
6	Yamaichi	7.0	Goldman, Sachs	4.5	Goldman, Sachs	5.2	McLeod Young Weir	5.9
7	Bank of Tokyo	5.5	Swiss B Corp	4.1	Deutsche	4.9	Merrill Lynch	5.3
8	Can Imperial	5.4	Morgan Guar	3.8	Soc Generale	4.9	Bankers Trust	4.9
9	Salomon	5.0	Soc Generale	3.3	Banque Paribas	3.9	Soc Generale	4.2
10	Swiss B Corp	4.4	Daiwa	2.8	Merrill Lynch	3.5	Goldman, Sachs	4.0
Others		11.2	Others	20.6	Others	30.5	Others	26.2

Sources: Securities Data Company database; Investment Dealers' Digest database.

Table A-10

Australian Dollar Eurobond Issues—Rank and Market Share of Principal Lead Managers, 1980–1988

Rank	1980 Lead Manager	1980 Market Share (%)	1981 Lead Manager	1981 Market Share (%)	1982 Lead Manager	1982 Market Share (%)	1983 Lead Manager	1983 Market Share (%)	1984 Lead Manager	1984 Market Share (%)
1	Hambros	71.5%	—	—	—	—	Orion Royal	76.9%	Orion Royal	35.6%
2	Morgan Guar	28.5	—	—	—	—	Nikko	12.4	Morgan Stanley	22.1
3	—	—	—	—	—	—	Hambros	10.7	CSFB	11.7
4	—	—	—	—	—	—	—	—	Citicorp	9.4
5	—	—	—	—	—	—	—	—	SG Warburg	8.0
6	—	—	—	—	—	—	—	—	Hambros	7.0
7	—	—	—	—	—	—	—	—	S Montagu	6.2
8	—	—	—	—	—	—	—	—	—	—
9	—	—	—	—	—	—	—	—	—	—
10	—	—	—	—	—	—	—	—	—	—
Others		0.0		0.0		0.0		0.0		0.0

Rank	1985 Lead Manager	1985 Market Share (%)	1986 Lead Manager	1986 Market Share (%)	1987 Lead Manager	1987 Market Share (%)	1988 Lead Manager	1988 Market Share (%)
1	Orion Royal	33.0	Orion Royal	21.7	Hambros	9.9	Hambros	12.6
2	Bankers Trust	13.1	Morgan Stanley	10.4	Deutsche	9.8	Deutsche	8.4
3	Hambros	6.2	Salomon	9.5	CSFB	8.7	CSFB	6.3
4	Banque Paribas	4.9	Can Imperial	7.2	Orion Royal	5.8	Aust NZ Bank	5.2
5	Morgan Stanley	4.9	Deutsche	6.5	SG Warburg	5.6	Westpak Bank	5.0
6	Swiss B Corp	4.9	Hambros	5.7	Swiss B Corp	5.0	Nomura	4.3
7	Morgan Guar	3.6	Morgan Guar	4.4	County NatWest	3.6	Salomon	4.1
8	Deutsche	2.8	Bankers Trust	4.3	Banque Paribas	3.6	West LB	3.8
9	Schroder	2.5	BankAmerica	4.1	Indus B Japan	3.6	Indus B Japan	3.1
10	Merrill Lynch	2.5	Ams Rotterdam	3.1	Commerzbank	3.4	Wood Gundy	3.0
Others		21.6		23.1		41.0		44.2

Sources: Securities Data Company database; *Investment Dealers' Digest* database.

Table A-11

French Franc Eurobond Issues—Rank and Market Share of Principal Lead Managers, 1980–1988

Rank	1980 Lead Manager	Market Share (%)	1981 Lead Manager	Market Share (%)	1982 Lead Manager	Market Share (%)	1983 Lead Manager	Market Share (%)	1984 Lead Manager	Market Share (%)
1	Cred Comm Fr	32.4%	Banque Paribas	25.6%	—	—	—	—	—	—
2	Soc Generale	20.4	B Indosuez	23.0	—	—	—	—	—	—
3	B Nat Paris	19.1	Soc Generale	19.0	—	—	—	—	—	—
4	Banque Paribas	10.8	Cred Comm Fr	17.0	—	—	—	—	—	—
5	BUE	10.2	BUE	15.3	—	—	—	—	—	—
6	Cred Lyonnais	3.9	—	—	—	—	—	—	—	—
7	Caisse Agricole	3.2	—	—	—	—	—	—	—	—
8	—	—	—	—	—	—	—	—	—	—
Others		0.0	Others	0.0	—	—	—	—	—	—

Rank	1985 Lead Manager	Market Share (%)	1986 Lead Manager	Market Share (%)	1987 Lead Manager	Market Share (%)	1988 Lead Manager	Market Share (%)
1	Cred Comm Fr	28.0	Cred Comm Fr	41.1	Cred Comm Fr	48.1	Cred Comm Fr	39.0
2	B Nat Paris	24.4	B Nat Paris	18.1	B Nat Paris	17.6	Cred Lyonnais	19.1
3	Soc Generale	23.8	Soc Generale	15.8	B Indosuez	9.9	Soc Generale	13.1
4	Cred Lyonnais	10.8	Banque Paribas	11.5	Soc Generale	9.8	B Nat Paris	10.5
5	Lazard	4.9	Cred Lyonnais	7.6	Lazard	8.9	Banque Paribas	9.5
6	Banque Paribas	4.9	Lazard	3.0	Banque Paribas	5.6	Caisse Agricole	8.8
7	B Indosuez	3.2	B Indosuez	2.1	—	—	—	—
8	—	—	Caisse Agricole	0.8	—	—	—	—
Others		0.0	Others	0.0	Others	0.0	Others	0.0

Note: During the first three years of Mitterrand administration (1982–1984), no French franc-denominated Eurobonds were authorized.
Sources: Securities Data Company database; *Investment Dealers' Digest* database.

Table A-12

Dutch Guilder Eurobond Issues—Rank and Market Share of Principal Lead Managers, 1980–1988

Rank	1980 Lead Manager	Market Share (%)	1981 Lead Manager	Market Share (%)	1982 Lead Manager	Market Share (%)	1983 Lead Manager	Market Share (%)	1984 Lead Manager	Market Share (%)
1	Algemene	25.5%	Algemene	68.0%	Algemene	41.7%	Algemene	52.1%	Ams Rotterdam	49.1%
2	Bank Mees	24.0	Ams Rotterdam	12.2	Ams Rotterdam	39.7	Ams Rotterdam	30.6	Algemene	22.8
3	Ams Rotterdam	19.3	Bank Mees	6.0	Bank Mees	9.4	Rabobank	5.3	Bank Mees	11.4
4	Ned Midden	8.2	Pierson	5.4	Ned Midden	6.1	Ned Midden	5.3	Rabobank	7.6
5	Rabobank	8.2	Rabobank	4.5	van Lanschot	3.1	Bank Mees	4.0	Ned Midden	5.5
6	Pierson	6.6	Ned Cred	3.9	—	—	Pierson	2.7	Pierson	3.6
7	van Lanschot	5.4	—	—	—	—	—	—	—	—
8	Ned Cred	2.8	—	—	—	—	—	—	—	—
	Others	0.0	Others	0.0	Others	0.0	Others	0.0	Others	0.0

Rank	1985 Lead Manager	Market Share (%)	1986 Lead Manager	Market Share (%)	1987 Lead Manager	Market Share (%)	1988 Lead Manager	Market Share (%)
1	Algemene	36.3	Ams Rotterdam	47.9	Algemene	45.7	Ams Rotterdam	32.9
2	Ams Rotterdam	32.2	Algemene	46.8	Ams Rotterdam	42.0	Algemene	28.0
3	Ned Midden	12.5	van Haften	2.4	Swiss B Corp	5.4	CSFB	14.1
4	Pierson	7.4	Rabobank	1.5	Pierson	4.1	Bank Mees	6.8
5	Rabobank	5.0	Bank Mees	1.4	CSFB	2.8	Ned Midden	6.4
6	Bank Mees	4.4	—	—	—	—	Swiss Bank	4.8
7	van Lanschot	2.2	—	—	—	—	Cred Lyonnais	4.3
8	—	—	—	—	—	—	Rabobank	2.7
	Others	0.0	Others	0.0	Others	0.0	Others	0.0

Sources: Securities Data Company database; *Investment Dealers' Digest* database.

Table A-13

U.S. Dollar Fixed-Rate Issues—Rank and Market Share of Principal Lead Managers, 1980–1988

Rank	1980 Lead Manager	Market Share (%)	1981 Lead Manager	Market Share (%)	1982 Lead Manager	Market Share (%)	1983 Lead Manager	Market Share (%)	1984 Lead Manager	Market Share (%)
1	CSFB	16.4%	CSFB	17.5%	Deutsche	19.3%	Deutsche	23.4%	CSFB	15.6%
2	Morgan Stanley	14.3	Morgan Stanley	12.5	CSFB	15.3	CSFB	14.9	Morgan Stanley	13.1
3	Goldman, Sachs	10.6	Salomon	9.6	Morgan Stanley	13.2	Morgan Stanley	7.0	Salomon	12.6
4	SG Warburg	9.7	Deutsche	8.4	Salomon	7.8	Morgan Guar	5.8	Deutsche	8.8
5	Banque Paribas	8.4	SG Warburg	6.0	Union B Switz	5.0	SG Warburg	4.9	Goldman, Sachs	6.6
6	Salomon	7.7	Union B Switz	5.2	Morgan Guar	3.9	Goldman, Sachs	4.9	Morgan Guar	6.6
7	Orion Royal	3.4	Morgan Guar	5.1	Goldman, Sachs	3.8	Salomon	4.2	Merrill Lynch	3.6
8	Union B Switz	2.8	Goldman, Sachs	5.0	SG Warburg	3.0	Merrill Lynch	2.7	Banque Paribas	3.4
9	Wood Gundy	2.4	Hambros	4.5	Merrill Lynch	2.9	Swiss B Corp	2.5	Shearson Lehman	2.9
10	Swiss B Corp	2.2	Cred Comm Fr	4.3	Swiss B Corp	2.7	B Nat Paris	2.3	Nomura	2.4
	Others	22.1	Others	21.9	Others	23.1	Others	27.4	Others	24.4

Rank	1985 Lead Manager	Market Share (%)	1986 Lead Manager	Market Share (%)	1987 Lead Manager	Market Share (%)	1988 Lead Manager	Market Share (%)
1	CSFB	11.0	CSFB	9.5	CSFB	16.9	CSFB	16.1
2	Morgan Stanley	10.5	Morgan Stanley	9.4	Morgan Stanley	8.3	Merrill Lynch	8.8
3	Salomon	10.4	Deutsche	6.3	Nomura	8.1	Nomura	8.6
4	Goldman, Sachs	8.0	Morgan Guar	6.0	Morgan Guar	7.1	JP Morgan	6.7
5	Union B Switz	7.5	Nomura	5.9	Goldman, Sachs	7.1	Indus B Japan	6.1
6	Deutsche	7.4	Salomon	5.3	Union B Switz	5.5	Goldman, Sachs	6.0
7	Morgan Guar	4.9	Union B Switz	5.1	Deutsche	5.1	Bankers Trust	5.7
8	Merrill Lynch	4.9	Merrill Lynch	4.8	Salomon	4.4	Banque Paribas	4.3
9	Swiss B Corp	3.9	Daiwa	4.0	Banque Paribas	3.9	Morgan Stanley	3.8
10	Nomura	2.9	Long-Term Cred	3.5	Indus B Japan	3.2	Daiwa	3.6
	Others	28.6	Others	40.2	Others	30.4	Others	30.3

Sources: Securities Data Company database; Investment Dealers' Digest database.

Table A-14

U.S. Dollar Floating-Rate Issues—Rank and Market Share of Principal Lead Managers, 1980–1988

Rank	1980 Lead Manager	Market Share (%)	1981 Lead Manager	Market Share (%)	1982 Lead Manager	Market Share (%)	1983 Lead Manager	Market Share (%)	1984 Lead Manager	Market Share (%)
1	Citicorp	10.2%	CSFB	16.8%	CSFB	15.5%	CSFB	51.8%	CSFB	23.5%
2	Soc Generale	10.2	SG Warburg	9.6	Morgan Stanley	9.1	Merrill Lynch	5.8	Morgan Guar	14.5
3	CSFB	8.5	Merrill Lynch	7.5	B Nat Paris	6.9	B Nat Paris	4.4	Merrill Lynch	10.5
4	B Nat Paris	7.6	Swiss B Corp	5.8	Swiss B Corp	4.5	Cred Comm Fr	4.2	B Nat Paris	5.0
5	SG Warburg	7.1	B Nat Paris	4.9	Soc Generale	4.3	Cred Lyonnais	4.0	Salomon	4.3
6	Daiwa	6.4	Manuf Hanover	4.4	BankAmerica	4.2	Deutsche	3.6	Morgan Stanley	4.3
7	Barclays	5.1	S Montagu	3.8	Banque Paribas	4.0	Nomura	2.5	Barclays	3.3
8	Salomon	3.8	Cred Comm Fr	3.8	S Montagu	3.7	Morgan Stanley	2.4	BankAmerica	3.1
9	S Montagu	3.8	Nomura	3.8	Manuf Hanover	3.7	Morgan Guar	2.2	Soc Generale	2.8
10	Orion Royal	3.2	Morgan Stanley	3.5	Nomura	3.6	BankAmerica	1.8	Goldman, Sachs	2.2
	Others	34.1	Others	36.1	Others	40.5	Others	17.3	Others	26.5

Rank	1985 Lead Manager	Market Share (%)	1986 Lead Manager	Market Share (%)	1987 Lead Manager	Market Share (%)	1988 Lead Manager	Market Share (%)
1	CSFB	25.4	CSFB	27.6	Salomon	11.3	CSFB	20.0
2	Merrill Lynch	11.8	Morgan Guar	11.8	Nikko	11.2	Merrill Lynch	12.4
3	Morgan Guar	9.0	Salomon	7.8	Banque Paribas	8.8	Goldman, Sachs	11.7
4	Salomon	6.5	Merrill Lynch	7.1	Yamaichi	8.7	Banque Paribas	8.4
5	Lloyds	4.6	Shearson	5.0	Bankers Trust	8.6	Chase	8.3
6	County Bank	4.1	Banque Paribas	4.9	Daiwa	5.6	Swiss B Corp	6.7
7	BankAmerica	3.7	Morgan Stanley	4.8	Merrill Lynch	5.4	Morgan Stanley	4.2
8	Goldman, Sachs	3.1	Soc Generale	3.4	Indus B Japan	4.6	Sanwa	3.8
9	Morgan Stanley	3.0	Chase	3.3	Shearson	4.2	Shearson	3.3
10	Shearson	3.0	Goldman, Sachs	2.3	Sanwa	3.9	Daiwa	3.0
	Others	25.8	Others	21.0	Others	27.7	Others	18.2

Sources: Securities Data Company database; Investment Dealers' Digest database.

Table A-15

U.S. Dollar Equity Convertible and Warrant Issues—Rank and Market Share of Principal Lead Managers, 1980–1988

Rank	1980 Lead Manager	Market Share (%)	1981 Lead Manager	Market Share (%)	1982 Lead Manager	Market Share (%)	1983 Lead Manager	Market Share (%)	1984 Lead Manager	Market Share (%)
1	CSFB	15.3%	Yamaichi	24.0%	Daiwa	21.6%	Dresdner	14.5%	CSFB	33.0%
2	Yamaichi	11.2	Nikko	17.3	Nomura	17.3	CSFB	11.3	Nomura	17.6
3	Nomura	6.8	Nomura	16.8	Deutsche	17.3	Nikko	9.8	Nikko	13.9
4	Swiss B Corp	6.6	Daiwa	14.2	Morgan Stanley	6.9	Daiwa	8.4	Daiwa	10.2
5	Smith Barney	6.0	CSFB	7.5	Nikko	5.2	Nomura	8.1	Yamaichi	9.3
6	Kidder, Peabody	4.9	Salomon	4.1	Yamaichi	5.1	Deutsche	8.1	Dresdner	4.6
7	PaineWebber	4.9	Merrill Lynch	3.4	Banque Paribas	4.4	Ams Rotterdam	4.6	Swiss B Corp	2.6
8	Goldman, Sachs	4.4	SG Warburg	2.1	Salomon	4.1	Swiss B Corp	4.1	Morgan Gren	1.8
9	Orion Royal	4.4	Goldman, Sachs	2.1	Hambros	3.3	Morgan Stanley	3.5	Union B Switz	1.6
10	Nikko	4.1	Banque Paribas	1.6	CSFB	2.8	Pru-Bache	3.5	Nippon Sec	1.4
	Others	31.4	Others	6.9	Others	12.0	Others	24.1	Others	4.0

Rank	1985 Lead Manager	Market Share (%)	1986 Lead Manager	Market Share (%)	1987 Lead Manager	Market Share (%)	1988 Lead Manager	Market Share (%)
1	Nomura	14.6	Nomura	17.1	Nomura	25.0	Nomura	35.0
2	Daiwa	13.3	Daiwa	14.0	Nikko	15.9	Yamaichi	19.7
3	CSFB	11.3	Nikko	12.5	Yamaichi	15.5	Daiwa	19.2
4	Nikko	10.4	CSFB	11.9	Daiwa	11.7	Nikko	16.8
5	Yamichi	7.8	Yamaichi	9.8	Morgan Stanley	6.8	New JP (Europe)	1.8
6	Goldman, Sachs	7.7	Morgan Stanley	4.7	CSFB	6.1	CSFB	1.3
7	SG Warburg	7.4	Union B Switz	3.4	Salomon	2.2	Morgan Stanley	1.1
8	Swiss B Corp	7.1	Banque Paribas	3.0	Union B Switz	1.6	Mitsui-Fin	0.7
9	Union B Switz	3.1	Salomon	2.8	Mitsubishi	1.0	Nippon Sec	0.7
10	Kleinwort	2.5	Dresdner	2.5	Sanwa	1.0	SG Warburg	0.7
	Others	14.8	Others	18.7	Others	13.1	Others	3.0

Sources: Securities Data Company database; Investment Dealers' Digest database.

Table A-16

All Eurobond Issues—Rank and Market Share by Country of Lead Manager, 1980–1988

Rank	1980 Country	Market Share (%)	1981 Country	Market Share (%)	1982 Country	Market Share (%)	1983 Country	Market Share (%)	1984 Country	Market Share (%)
1	United States	24.8%	United States	27.7%	United States	30.1%	West Germany	25.1%	United States	36.1%
2	West Germany	18.6	Switzerland	18.5	West Germany	20.9	Switzerland	24.4	Switzerland	18.8
3	United Kingdom	14.7	United Kingdom	13.6	Switzerland	18.2	United States	19.2	West Germany	12.5
4	Switzerland	13.5	Japan	10.3	France	9.3	United Kingdom	8.7	United Kingdom	9.6
5	France	12.8	France	9.7	United Kingdom	7.7	France	8.4	Japan	8.9
6	Japan	6.0	West Germany	9.6	Japan	5.6	Japan	5.6	France	7.5
7	Canada	3.8	Canada	4.0	Canada	2.8	Canada	3.1	Canada	2.5
8	Netherlands	2.7	Netherlands	2.3	Netherlands	2.7	Netherlands	2.6	Netherlands	1.4
9	Kuwait	1.3	Belgium	1.6	Belgium	0.8	Belgium	1.8	Belgium	1.4
10	Norway	0.5	Kuwait	0.7	Norway	0.4	Sweden	0.3	Norway	0.3
	Others	1.3	Others	2.0	Others	1.5	Others	0.8	Others	1.0

Rank	1985 Country	Market Share (%)	1986 Country	Market Share (%)	1987 Country	Market Share (%)	1988 Country	Market Share (%)
1	United States	34.8	United States	27.7	Japan	38.8	Japan	32.2
2	Switzerland	19.0	Japan	24.3	United States	17.2	United States	18.6
3	Japan	12.4	Switzerland	15.7	West Germany	11.6	West Germany	14.6
4	United Kingdom	10.6	West Germany	11.0	Switzerland	11.0	Switzerland	13.3
5	West Germany	9.7	France	8.7	United Kingdom	9.6	United Kingdom	8.0
6	France	8.0	United Kingdom	7.1	France	5.6	France	6.5
7	Canada	3.0	Canada	2.6	Canada	1.9	Netherlands	2.1
8	Netherlands	0.9	Netherlands	1.6	Netherlands	1.3	Canada	1.8
9	Belgium	0.6	Sweden	0.5	Denmark	0.7	Italy	0.7
10	Sweden	0.2	Denmark	0.4	Australia	0.5	Australia	0.5
	Others	0.8	Others	0.9	Others	1.8	Others	1.7

Sources: Securities Data Company database; *Investment Dealers' Digest* database.

APPENDIX B

U.S. SECURITIES INDUSTRY STATISTICS

Table B-1
Consolidated Revenue for NYSE Firms, 1975–1988
(Percentage by Category)

	1975	1976	1977	1978	1979	1980	1981	1982	1983	1984	1985	1986	1987	1988*
Securities commissions	50%	46%	42%	43%	35%	35%	27%	26%	28%	23%	21%	21%	25%	18%
Trading and investments	15	20	19	17	24	23	24	28	26	26	28	27	20	25
Interest on debit balances	8	8	11	13	15	13	15	9	7	9	7	6	7	6
Underwriting	13	12	11	8	7	8	8	10	12	9	11	12	10	10
Mutual fund sales	1	1	1	1	1	1	1	1	3	2	5	6	4	3
Commodity revenues	3	3	4	4	4	4	3	3	3	2	2	2	2	3
Other income, securities related	8	8	10	11	11	12	16	19	17	23	21	22	26	30
Other income, securities un-related	2	2	2	3	3	4	6	4	4	6	5	4	6	5
Total	100	100	100	100	100	100	100	100	100	100	100	100	100	100

* January–September.
Sources: NYSE Fact Book, various years.

Table B-2
Market Standings of Fifteen Current Volume Leaders
Negotiated Corporate Debt Offerings, 1982–1988
Full Credit to Lead Manager
($ millions)

	1982			1983[c]			1984[b]			1985			1986			1987			1988		
	Rank	Volume	No. of Issues	Rank	Volume	No. of Issues	Rank	Volume	No. of Issues	Rank	Volume	No. of Issues	Rank	Volume	No. of Issues	Rank	Volume	No. of Issues	Rank	Volume	No. of Issues
Goldman, Sachs	4	$5,252	54	4	$5,418	53	5	$4,939	53	3	$11,194	92	6	$22,200	180	5	$23,332	230	1	$32,330	345
Merrill Lynch[d]	3	5,510	61	5	5,134	52	4	7,028	65	5	9,936	104	5	23,391	190	4	24,183	209	2	31,685	327
Salomon Brothers	1	8,442	91	1	10,479	92	1	21,058	158	1	25,207	224	1	42,418	356	1	36,713	281	3	31,133	279
First Boston	5	4,264	39	2	6,602	54	3	8,595	102	2	18,609	233	2	40,045	366	2	32,141	205	4	27,565	277
Morgan Stanley	2	6,002	54	7	2,741	25	6	3,172	30	6	6,469	57	4	23,408	188	3	24,474	243	5	21,094	211
Shearson Lehman Hutton[a]	—	—	—	—	—	—	—	—	—	7	5,642	102	7	11,639	196	7	15,003	189	6	19,300	257
Drexel Burnham Lambert	7	1,827	35	3	5,522	70	2	10,299	83	4	9,974	126	3	24,004	176	6	16,788	153	7	18,738	215
Bear, Stearns	18	—	—	13	508	9	11	977	9	13	782	20	9	3,202	54	9	4,608	57	8	8,915	118
Prudential-Bache	—	—	—	—	—	—	9	1,644	23	12	870	17	12	1,946	46	10	3,631	64	9	7,555	166
Kidder, Peabody	12	680	10	10	1,070	13	10	1,265	17	8	2,302	48	8	7,234	128	8	7,494	101	10	6,021	106
Smith Barney[e]	11	748	21	12	517	17	14	525	20	11	910	12	11	2,055	29	11	3,460	32	11	3,845	51
Citicorp	—	—	—	—	—	—	—	—	—	—	—	—	—	—	—	13	2,530	44	12	3,449	70
PaineWebber	—	—	—	—	—	—	12	914	10	9	1,780	33	10	3,172	68	—	—	—	13	3,323	57
Chemical Bank	—	—	—	—	—	—	—	—	—	—	—	—	—	—	—	—	—	—	14	2,129	10
Donaldson Lufkin & Jenrette	—	—	—	—	—	—	—	—	—	—	—	—	—	—	—	—	—	—	15	2,068	51

Table B-2
(Continued)

Historical Rankings of Predecessors and Other Firms

1982	1983	1984	1985	1986	1987
6 Lehman Brothers Kuhn Loeb	6 Lehman Brothers	7 Lehman Brothers/ Shearson Lehman	10 Dillon, Read	13 Dillon, Read	12 Dillon, Read
8. Blyth Eastman Paine Webber	8 Blyth Eastman	8 Lehman Brothers	14 Dean Witter Reynolds	14 E.F. Hutton	14 L.F. Rothschild
9 Dillon, Read	9 A.G. Becker Paribas	13 Dean Witter Reynolds	15 E.F. Hutton	15 Dean Witter Reynolds	15 E.F. Hutton
10 Dean Witter Reynolds	11 Shearson/Amex and Affiliates	15 Edward D. Jones			
11 Smith Barney Harris Upham	14 E.F. Hutton				
13 Shearson/American Express	15 Dillon, Read				
14 E.F. Hutton					
15 Warburg Paribas Becker A.G. Becker					

a. Reported under title *Shearson Lehman Brothers* in 1985, 1986, and 1987.

b. *Lehman Brothers* (*Shearson Lehman*) #7 and *Lehman Brothers* #8 had between them total volume of $5.327 and number of issues of 62.

c. *Lehman Brothers* had volume of $3.511 and number of issues of 29. *Shearson/Amex and Affiliates* had volume of $760 and number of issues of 7.

d. Reported under title *Merrill Lynch White Weld* in 1982.

e. Reported under title *Merrill Lynch Harris Upham* in 1982.

Sources: *Institutional Investor,* various issues; IDD Information Services, Inc.

Table B-3
Market Standings of Fifteen Current Volume Leaders
High-Yield Corporate Debt Offerings, 1982–1988
Full Credit to Lead Manager
($ millions)

	1982					1983					1984					1985				
	Rank	Volume	% of Total	No. of Issues	% of Total	Rank	Volume	% of Total	No. of Issues	% of Total	Rank	Volume	% of Total	No. of Issues	% of Total	Rank	Volume	% of Total	No. of Issues	% of Total
Drexel Burnham Lambert	1	$1,544	55%	28	58%	1	$4,346	58%	46	54%	1	$10,358	69%	67	54%	1	$7,239	50%	83	44%
First Boston	—	—	—	—	—	5	325	4	3	3	6	390	3	5	4	6	640	4	9	5
Morgan Stanley	—	—	—	—	—	10	80	1	1	1	8	319	2	5	4	3	1,050	7	13	6
Merrill Lynch	2	699	25	7	15	2	427	6	5	6	5	530	3	4	3	5	666	5	9	7
Salomon Brothers	—	—	—	—	—	3	423	6	4	5	3	865	6	9	7	2	1,464	10	13	6
Prudential-Bache	4	40	2	1	2	6	275	4	6	7	2	950	6	13	11	9	435	3	8	4
Goldman, Sachs	—	—	—	—	—	9	125	2	1	1	10	100	1	1	1	7	615	4	5	3
Donaldson Lufkin & Jenrette	—	—	—	—	—	—	—	—	—	—	—	—	—	—	—	—	—	—	—	—
Smith Barney	—	—	—	—	—	—	—	—	—	—	—	—	—	—	—	—	—	—	—	—
Kidder, Peabody	—	—	—	—	—	—	—	—	—	—	—	—	—	—	—	—	—	—	—	—
PaineWebber	3	225	8	1	2	7	235	3	3	4	11	65	1	1	1	11	206	1	2	1
Shearson Lehman Hutton	6	25	1	1	2	8	230	3	1	1	4	718	5	8	7	4	708	5	8	4
Bear, Stearns	5	35	1	1	2	4	380	5	5	6	7	360	2	4	3	8	456	3	7	4
R.G. Dickinson	—	—	—	—	—	—	—	—	—	—	—	—	—	—	—	—	—	—	—	—
All Others	—	230	8	9	19	—	571	8	11	13	—	297	2	7	5	—	1,084	8	31	16
Total		2,798	100	48	100		7,417	100	86	100		14,952	100	124	100		14,562	100	188	100

TableB-3
(Continued)

	1986					1987*			1988				
	Rank	Volume	% of Total	No. of Issues	% of Total	Rank	Volume	% of Total	Rank	Volume	% of Total	No. of Issues	% of Total
Drexel Burnham Lambert	1	$15,775	46%	82	35%	1	$11,623	40%	1	$11,907	43%	76	48%
First Boston	6	1,650	5	11	5	3	4,031	14	2	3,908	14	16	10
Morgan Stanley	3	2,817	8	15	6	2	4,353	15	3	3,132	11	11	7
Merrill Lynch	2	3,782	11	25	11	4	3,536	12	4	2,098	8	11	7
Salomon Brothers	4	2,814	8	16	6	6	1,153	4	5	1,751	6	9	6
Prudential-Bache	12	357	1	4	2	15	49	—	6	1,182	4	7	4
Goldman, Sachs	7	1,228	4	9	4	5	1,975	7	7	805	3	6	4
Donaldson Lufkin & Jenrette	13	338	1	7	3	8	493	2	8	776	3	5	3
Smith Barney	—	—	—	—	—	11	249	1	9	696	3	5	3
Kidder, Peabody	9	880	3	7	3	7	504	2	10	551	2	5	3
PaineWebber	10	545	2	4	3	13	100	—	11	360	1	3	2
Shearson Lehman Hutton	5	1,903	5	11	5	9	349	1	12	350	1	2	1
Bear, Stearns	8	1,145	3	14	6	12	105	1	13	280	1	2	1
R.G. Dickinson	—	—	—	—	—	—	—	—	14	16	—	1	1
All Others	—	1,234	3	29	11	—	506	1	—	—	—	—	—
Total		34,117	100	234	100		29,026	100		27,812	100	159	100

* Data on number of issues and percentage of total not available.
Sources: *Institutional Investor*, various issues; IDD Information Services, Inc.

Table B-4

Market Standings of Fifteen Current Volume Leaders
Mortgage-Backed Securities Offerings, 1984–1988
Full Credit to Lead Manager
($ millions)

	1984		1985		1986		1987		1988	
	Rank	Volume	Rank	Volume	Rank	Volume	Rank	Volume	Rank	Volume
Goldman, Sachs	8	$252	10	$299	7	$2,608	4	$9,609	1	$17,167
Salomon Hutton	1	4,484	1	7,250	1	16,911	1	18,697	2	12,965
Merrill Lynch	4	805	4	1,194	3	7,642	3	9,346	3	9,444
First Boston	2	3,127	2	5,960	2	12,141	2	17,003	4	9,435
Shearson Lehman Hutton	3	1,542	3	1,561	4	4,099	5	6,073	5	8,405
Morgan Stanley	—	—	9	323	5	3,805	6	6,461	6	7,699
Bear, Stearns	6	265	—	—	11	1,192	9	3,679	7	7,569
Prudential-Bache	—	—	15	91	9	1,396	10	2,442	8	6,206
Drexel Burnham Lambert	—	—	5	870	8	1,550	8	4,438	9	4,486
Kidder, Peabody	—	—	8	370	6	3,003	7	4,762	10	2,943
PaineWebber	—	—	7	544	10	1,209	12	1,100	11	2,606
Citicorp	—	—	14	100	13	507	11	2,004	12	1,550
Donaldson Lufkin & Jenrette	—	—	—	—	—	—	—	180	13	1,241
Smith Barney	12	75	—	—	—	—	—	349	14	858
UBS Securities	—	—	—	—	—	—	—	—	15	738
Total		12,009		19,803		57,532		88,679		93,318

Sources: Corporate Financing Week, a publication of *Institutional Investor*, various issues.

Table B-5
Market Standings of Fifteen Current Volume Leaders
Municipal Debt Offerings
Bonus Credit to Lead Manager, Except Full Credit in 1987 and 1988
($ millions)

	1980			1981			1982			1983			1984		
	Rank	Volume	No. of Issues	Rank	Volume	No. of Issues	Rank	Volume	No. of Issues	Rank	Volume	No. of Issues	Rank	Volume	No. of Issues
Merrill Lynch	4	$1,427	105	1	$2,580	155	1	$1,471	273	1	$5,736	276	1	$5,981	293
Goldman, Sachs	1	2,265	109	4	1,897	150	3	3,616	207	4	3,530	177	6	4,225	196
Shearson Lehman[a,c] Hutton	—	—	—	—	—	—	—	—	—	—	—	—	7	3,500	166
First Boston	8	960	51	8	1,188	48	7	2,040	75	10	1,809	69	9	2,411	86
Smith Barney[b]	7	1,008	46	6	1,524	80	6	2,666	106	7	2,480	92	4	4,998	134
PaineWebber	3	1,810	129	2	1,955	129	4	2,855	190	8	—	—	8	3,157	164
Prudential-Bache	—	—	—	—	—	—	14	675	47	11	1,487	79	10	1,926	101
Morgan Stanley	15	—	—	15	368	13	—	—	—	—	—	—	13	1,139	43
Bear, Stearns	—	—	—	—	—	—	—	—	—	—	—	—	12	1,320	71
Drexel Burnham Lambert	—	—	—	—	—	—	—	—	—	—	—	—	—	—	—
Rauscher Pierce Refnes	—	—	—	—	—	—	—	—	—	—	—	—	—	—	—
Donaldson Lufkin & Jenrette	—	—	—	—	—	—	—	—	—	—	—	—	—	—	—
Lazard Frères	—	—	—	—	—	—	—	—	—	—	—	—	—	—	—
Chase Manhattan	—	—	—	—	—	—	—	—	—	—	—	—	—	—	—
Citicorp	—	—	—	14	370	29	—	—	—	—	—	—	—	—	—
Salomon Brothers	6	1,347	83	5	1,759	97	5	2,837	159	3	3,843	167	3	5,108	191

Table B-5
(Continued)

	1985			1986			1987			1988		
	Rank	Volume	No. of Issues	Rank	Volume	No. of Issues	Rank	Volume	No. of Issues	Rank	Volume	No. of Issues
Merrill Lynch	1	$13,554	610	1	$7,148	270	1	$6,891	98	1	$12,532	221
Goldman, Sachs	2	10,234	331	2	7,010	202	2	6,625	78	2	12,468	161
Shearson Lehman[a,c] Hutton	7	7,927	349	4	6,005	175	7	2,194	48	3	9,153	248
First Boston	3	8,354	229	6	5,160	129	5	5,287	57	4	7,491	116
Smith Barney[b]	8	7,476	285	5	5,542	212	3	6,201	88	5	6,634	165
PaineWebber	9	7,453	363	8	3,655	140	6	4,420	66	6	4,225	72
Prudential-Bache	13	3,320	199	11	2,801	127	13	1,447	28	7	3,673	161
Morgan Stanley	10	4,089	131	—	—	—	11	1,612	21	8	3,420	37
Bear, Stearns	12	3,532	175	12	2,588	92	12	1,597	35	9	2,801	56
Drexel Burnham Lambert	11	3,874	210	9	3,279	122	10	1,943	48	10	2,800	84
Rauscher Pierce Refnes	14	2,315	118	—	—	—	—	—	—	11	1,919	43
Donaldson Lufkin & Jenrette	—	—	—	15	1,690	58	9	2,010	19	12	1,592	35
Lazard Frères	—	—	—	—	—	—	14	1,409	4	13	1,515	17
Chase Manhattan	—	—	—	—	—	—	—	—	—	14	1,493	23
Citicorp	—	—	—	—	—	—	—	—	—	15	1,306	19
Salomon Brothers	6	8,155	345	3	6,427	212	4	6,007	43	—	—	—

a. Reported under title *Shearson Lehman Brothers* in 1985, 1986, and 1987.
b. Reported under title *Smith Barney Harris Upham* in 1980 through 1987.
c. Reported under title *Shearson Lehman/American Express* in 1984.

Table B-5
(Continued)

Historical Rankings of Predecessor and Other Firms

1980	1981	1982	1983	1984	1985	1986	1987
2 E.F. Hutton	3 E.F. Hutton	2 E.F. Hutton	2 E.F. Hutton	2 E.F. Hutton	4 Kidder, Peabody	7 E.F. Hutton	8 E.F. Hutton
5 Kidder, Peabody	7 Kidder, Peabody	8 Kidder, Peabody	5 Blyth Eastman PaineWebber	5 Kidder, Peabody	5 E.F. Hutton	10 Kidder, Peabody	14 Lazard Frères
6 Salomon Brothers	9 Lehman Brothers Kuhn Loeb	9 Shearson/ American Express	6 Kidder, Peabody	11 Dean Witter Reynolds	15 Matthews & Wright	13 Rothschild Unterberg Towbin	15 L.F. Rothschild
9 Shearson Loeb Rhoades	10 Shearson/ American Express	10 Dean Witter Reynolds	8 Shearson/ American Express & Affiliates	14 Rothschild Unterberg Towbin		14 Dillon, Read	
10 Lehman Brothers Kuhn Loeb	11 Dean Witter Reynolds	11 Lehman Brothers Kuhn Loeb	9 Dean Witter Reynolds	15 Dillon, Read			
11 Dean Witter Reynolds	12 Bache Halsey Stuart Shields	12 Dillon, Read	12 Lehman Brothers Kuhn Loeb				
12 Bache Halsey Stuart Shields	13 Dillon, Read	13 Boettcher	13 A.G. Becker Paribas				
13 Rothschild Unterberg Towbin		15 John Nuveen	14 Boettcher				
14 Dillon, Read			15 Rothschild Unterberg Towbin				
15 Boettcher							

Sources: Institutional Investor, various issues; IDD Information Services/PSA municipal database.

Table B-6
Market Standings of Fifteen Current Volume Leaders
Negotiated Corporate Equity Offerings, 1982–1988
Full Credit to Lead Manager
($ millions)

	1982[d]			1983[c]			1984			1985			1986			1987			1988		
	Rank	Volume	No. of Issues	Rank	Volume	No. of Issues	Rank	Volume	No. of Issues	Rank	Volume	No. of Issues	Rank	Volume	No. of Issues	Rank	Volume	No. of Issues	Rank	Volume	No. of Issues
Merrill Lynch	2	$3,616	68	2	$5,237	109	3	$1,189	33	2	$4,361	70	4	$5,320	103	2	$5,850	71	1	$7,377	81
Shearson Lehman Hutton[a]	11	413	19	9	1,708	64	5	925	18	4	3,794	55	6	4,342	83	5	3,823	55	2	5,565	36
Prudential-Bache	14	291	7	12	1,096	40	9	535	20	12	493	25	9	1,990	28	13	1,155	15	3	3,325	14
Goldman, Sachs	3	1,819	27	3	5,022	81	1	2,097	36	3	4,246	42	1	6,530	72	1	8,598	58	4	3,077	39
PaineWebber	—	—	—	—	—	—	—	—	—	9	942	32	11	1,507	46	12	1,169	23	5	2,856	20
Wheat, First Securities	—	—	—	—	—	—	—	—	—	—	—	—	—	—	—	9	2,535	4	6	2,150	2
Drexel Burnham Lambert	13	366	13	10	1,691	50	8	575	24	7	2,012	46	3	5,589	84	6	3,265	55	7	2,037	26
First Boston	6	955	19	6	2,173	49	6	919	17	6	2,520	32	7	3,814	32	4	3,940	44	8	1,636	22
Salomon Brothers	5	1,064	15	4	4,521	58	4	1,068	21	1	4,961	54	2	6,497	73	7	2,856	41	9	1,551	24
Alex. Brown	—	—	—	—	—	—	11	323	12	15	319	17	12	1,225	44	8	2,748	40	10	1,243	22
Kidder, Peabody	4	1,173	33	5	2,249	69	7	713	27	8	1,438	31	8	2,681	61	10	2,183	32	11	1,039	21
Morgan Stanley	1	4,014	43	1	5,382	70	2	1,600	25	5	2,875	37	5	4,419	61	3	4,101	48	12	987	16
Smith Barney	—	—	—	13	1,026	30	10	328	9	11	515	17	14	1,011	26	14	1,011	26	13	897	14
Dean Witter[b]	—	—	—	—	—	—	13	204	17	10	682	19	—	—	—	11	1,405	20	14	583	7
Donaldson Lufkin & Jenrette	—	—	—	—	—	—	—	—	—	—	—	—	—	—	—	—	—	—	15	464	9

Table B-6
(Continued)

Historical Rankings of Predecessor and Other Firms

1982	1983	1984	1985	1986	1987
7 Blyth Eastman Paine Webber	7 Rothschild Unterberg Towbin	12 Lazard Frères	13 Bear, Stearns	10 Lazard Frères	14 Oppenheimer
8 Dean Witter Reynolds	8 Lehman Brothers	14 Bear, Stearns	14 E.F. Hutton	13 Allen & Co.	15 Dillon, Read
9 Rothschild Unterberg Towbin	11 E.F. Hutton	15 Becker Paribas		15 Bear, Stearns	
10 Lehman Brothers Kuhn Loeb	14 Blyth Eastman				
12 E.F. Hutton	15 Lazard Frères				
15 Warburg Paribas Becker-A.G. Becker					

a. Reported under title *Shearson/American Express* in 1982.
   Shearson/Amex and Affiliates in 1983.
   Lehman Brothers (Shearson Lehman) in 1984.
   Shearson Lehman Brothers in 1985 through 1987.
b. Reported under title *Dean Witter Reynolds* in 1984, 1985, and 1987.
c. *Lehman Brothers* as #8 reported volume of $1,759 and number of issues of 42.
d. *Lehman Brothers Kuhn Loeb* as #10 reported volume of $417 and number of issues of 7.
Sources: *Institutional Investor*, various issues; IDD Information Services, Inc.

Table B-7

Market Standings of Fifteen Current Volume Leaders
Initial Public Offerings
Full Credit to Lead Manager
($ millions)

	1983[d]			1984[c]			1985			1986			1987			1988		
	Rank	Volume	No. of Issues	Rank	Volume	No. of Issues	Rank	Volume	No. of Issues	Rank	Volume	No. of Issues	Rank	Volume	No. of Issues	Rank	Volume	No. of Issues
Merrill Lynch	4	$782	23	2	$499	13	3	$1,074	20	1	$2,411	46	2	$2,537	26	1	$4,348	28
Shearson Lehman Hutton[a]	—	—	—	—	—	—	2	1,098	7	6	1,429	22	5	1,557	26	2	4,044	16
Prudential-Bache	6	757	28	—	—	—	11	178	10	3	1,556	10	8	959	10	3	3,194	12
PaineWebber	—	—	—	10	109	9	10	194	8	9	965	23	9	847	13	4	2,789	16
Wheat, First Securities	—	—	—	—	—	—	—	—	—	—	—	—	4	2,035	3	5	2,150	2
Goldman, Sachs	9	418	10	4	192	8	1	1,706	13	4	1,462	15	1	5,714	16	6	1,726	15
Alex. Brown	10	409	19	8	127	5	—	—	—	14	514	26	3	2,370	26	7	1,062	15
Drexel Burnham Lambert	11	350	13	5	176	16	7	271	14	2	1,716	39	7	989	28	8	668	11
First Boston	15	222	6	3	274	6	13	169	3	5	1,431	13	11	650	6	9	585	9
Salomon Brothers	1	1,196	18	—	—	—	5	375	5	11	828	12	6	1,062	11	10	517	7
Smith Barney	—	—	—	—	—	—	15	126	7	13	627	18	—	—	—	11	513	3
Dean Witter[b]	—	—	—	11	100	7	6	273	7	15	498	10	10	797	6	12	500	4
Piper Jeffrey & Hopwood	—	—	—	—	—	—	—	—	—	—	—	—	345	4	—	13	345	4
Donaldson Lufkin & Jenrette	—	—	—	—	—	—	—	—	—	—	—	—	—	—	—	14	216	4
Kidder, Peabody	8	419	11	14	79	8	4	550	12	12	663	20	12	642	16	15	126	5

Table B-7
(Continued)

Historical Rankings of Predecessor and Other Firms

1983	1984	1985	1986	1987
2 Rothschild Unterberg Towbin	1 Morgan Stanley	8 Bear, Stearns	7 Lazard Frères	13 Oppenheimer
3 E.F. Hutton	6 Lehman Brothers (Shearson Lehman)	9 Lazard Frères	8 Allen & Co.	14 Morgan Stanley
5 Shearson/Amex and Affiliates	7 Shearson/Amex	12 E.F. Hutton	10 Morgan Stanley	15 Dillon, Read
7 Morgan Stanley	9 Becker Paribas	14 Morgan Stanley		
12 Lehman Brothers	11 Dean Witter Reynolds			
13 Bear, Stearns	12 Bear, Stearns			
14 Lazard Frères	13 Rothschild Unterberg Towbin			
	15 Lehman Brothers			

a. Reported under title *Shearson Lehman Brothers* in 1985 through 1987.
b. Reported under title *Dean Witter Reynolds* in 1984 through 1987.
c. *Lehman Brothers (Shearson Lehman)* #6, *Shearson/Amex* #7, and *Lehman Brothers* #15 had total volume of $364 and number of issues of 12.
d. *Shearson/Amex and Affiliates* #5 and *Lehman Brothers* #12 had total volume of $1,050 and number of issues of 34.
Sources: *Institutional Investor*, various issues; IDD Information Services, Inc.

Table B-8
Total Commissions of Large Investment Banks, 1976–1988
($ millions)

	Large Investment Banks	Total Industry	Percentage of Total
1976	$393	$3,156	12.5%
1977	369	2,809	13.1
1978	478	3,778	12.7
1979	419	4,022	10.4
1980	652	5,682	11.5
1981	662	5,340	12.4
1982	803	6,012	13.4
1983	1,216	8,350	14.6
1984	1,068	7,095	15.1
1985	1,127	8,238	13.7
1986	1,439	10,473	13.7
1987	1,816	12,646	14.4
1988	1,160	8,784	13.2

Source: Securities Industry Association.

Table B-9
Balance Sheet Assets of NYSE Member Firms, 1975–1988

	1975		1976		1977		1978		1979	
	Amount ($ millions)	Percentage of Total	Amount ($ millions)	Percentage of Total	Amount ($ millions)	Percentage of Total	Amount ($ millions)	Percentage of Total	Amount ($ millions)	Percentage of Total
Cash	$833	3.3%	$761	2.0%	$797	1.8%	$984	1.8%	$1,763	2.4%
Accounts receivable: brokers	3,171	12.7	3,955	10.4	4,982	11.4	5,109	9.5	7,304	9.7
Accounts receivable: customers/partners	8,230	32.9	11,611	30.4	13,768	31.6	16,070	29.8	18,383	24.5
Long position in securities	9,867	39.4	20,029	50.8	22,106	50.8	29,410	54.5	44,542	59.4
Other	2,950	11.7	1,825	4.7	1,968	4.4	2,329	4.4	3,012	4.0
Total assets	25,051	100	38,181	100	43,621	100	53,902	100	75,004	100
Balance Sheet Liabilities of NYSE Member Firms										
Money borrowed	7,224	28.8	20,605	54.0	21,879	50.2	25,766	47.8	32,410	43.2
Payable to other brokers and dealers	3,019	12.4	3,554	9.3	4,891	11.2	4,676	8.7	6,806	9.1
Payable to customers and partners	4,512	18.0	4,911	12.9	5,216	12.0	7,321	13.6	11,309	15.1
Short-position in securities and commodities	1,002	4.0	2,129	5.6	3,980	9.1	6,601	12.3	13,706	18.2
Other accruals and accounts payable	5,634	22.5	3,069	8.0	3,722	8.5	5,139	9.5	5,774	7.7
Total liabilities	21,331	85.4	34,268	89.8	39,688	91.0	49,512	91.9	70,005	93.3
Total capital	3,660	14.6	3,913	10.2	3,933	9.0	4,390	8.1	4,999	6.7
Total liabilities and capital	25,051	100	38,181	100	43,621	100	53,902	100	75,004	100

	1980		1981		1982		1983		1984	
	Amount ($ millions)	Percentage of Total	Amount ($ millions)	Percentage of Total	Amount ($ millions)	Percentage of Total	Amount ($ millions)	Percentage of Total	Amount ($ millions)	Percentage of Total
Cash	2,339	2.3	2,307	1.9	3,947	2.3	3,034	1.4	3,454	1.3
Accounts receivable: brokers	11,617	11.4	11,977	9.9	20,255	11.8	24,491	11.4	25,731	9.3
Accounts receivable: customers	23,727	23.2	21,764	18.0	24,503	14.2	33,017	15.4	30,234	11.0
Long position in securities	60,573	59.1	79,698	65.9	116,647	67.8	145,134	67.6	204,616	74.3
Other	3,986	4.0	5,214	4.3	6,789	3.9	9,108	4.2	11,428	4.1
Total assets	102,242	100	120,960	100	172,141	100	214,784	100	275,463	100
Balance Sheet Liabilities of NYSE Member Firms										
Money borrowed	40,694	39.8	61,862	51.1	84,350	49.0	104,593	48.7	155,132	56.3
Payable to other brokers and dealers	10,882	10.6	11,141	9.2	19,028	11.1	20,451	9.5	20,944	7.6
Payable to customers and partners	15,067	14.7	13,340	11.0	16,593	9.6	19,771	9.2	20,443	7.4
Short-position in securities and commodities	20,532	20.1	17,302	14.3	28,771	16.7	38,622	18.0	44,028	16.0
Other accruals and accounts payable	8,232	8.1	9,147	7.6	12,620	7.3	17,140	8.0	18,068	6.6
Total liabilities	95,407	93.3	112,192	93.2	161,362	93.7	200,577	93.4	258,615	93.9
Total capital	6,835	6.7	8,168	6.8	10,779	6.3	14,207	6.6	16,848	6.1
Total liabilities and capital	102,242	100	120,960	100	172,141	100	214,784	100	275,463	100

Table B-9

Balance Sheet Assets of NYSE Member Firms, 1975–1988 (Continued)

	1985		1986		September 30 1987		December 31 1987		September 30 1988*	
	Amount ($ millions)	Percentage of Total	Amount ($ millions)	Percentage of Total	Amount ($ millions)	Percentage of Total	Amount ($ millions)	Percentage of Total	Amount ($ millions)	Percentage of Total
Cash	$5,378	1.4%	$7,482	1.7%	$5,039	1.0%	$5,990	1.5%	$8,472	1.8%
Accounts receivable: brokers	50,174	12.8	54,941	12.1	74,920	15.0	51,312	12.6	57,261	12.3
Accounts receivable: customers/partners	47,462	12.1	55,035	12.2	56,930	11.4	38,998	9.6	39,657	8.5
Long position in securities	275,633	70.0	351,065	70.0	342,249	68.7	291,735	71.7	339,388	73.0
Other	14,431	3.7	18,018	4.0	18,706	3.8	18,809	4.6	20,288	4.4
Total assets	393,205	100	452,541	100	497,844	100	406,844	100	465,066	100
Balance Sheet Liabilities of NYSE Member Firms										
Money borrowed	196,302	49.9	239,504	52.9	261,481	52.5	209,981	51.6	248,198	53.4
Payable to other brokers and dealers	44,266	11.3	42,824	9.5	56,135	11.3	36,191	8.9	40,428	8.7
Payable to customers and partners	33,203	8.4	41,994	9.3	39,149	7.9	35,561	8.7	35,090	7.5
Short-position in securities and commodities	71,184	18.1	66,997	14.8	73,864	14.8	60,163	14.8	72,731	15.6
Other accruals and accounts payable	26,211	6.7	31,112	6.9	32,223	6.5	29,402	7.2	30,462	6.6
Total liabilities	371,166	94.4	422,431	93.3	462,852	93.0	371,298	91.3	426,909	91.8
Total capital	22,039	5.6	30,110	6.7	34,992	7.0	35,546	8.7	38,157	8.2
Total liabilities and capital	393,205	100	452,541	100	497,844	100	406,844	100	465,066	100

* Latest data available.

Sources: NYSE Fact Books.

Table B-10
Combined Profit and Loss Statements
All NYSE Member Firms, 1980–1988
($ millions)

	1980	1981	1982	1983	1984	1985	1986	1987	1988
Revenue									
Commissions	$5,682	$5,340	$6,012	$8,350	$7,095	$8,238	$10,473	$12,646	$8,784
Listed equities, on an exchange	4,238	3,955	4,484	6,132	5,233	6,070	7,562	9,225	6,514
Listed equities, OTC	45	73	61	112	75	92	116	89	48
Options	715	608	737	798	822	881	1,159	1,323	687
All other	585	704	729	1,309	965	1,205	1,637	2,013	1,535
Gains/Losses from Trading Accounts	3,138	4,238	5,952	6,839	7,564	9,944	12,561	9,973	11,293
Market-making OTC equities	564	607	656	1,381	863	1,230	1,762	1,838	1,231
OTC market-making listed equities	60	38	38	52	46	53	73	75	52
Trading debt securities	1,894	3,081	4,455	4,418	3,525	7,207	9,240	6,766	8,208
Market-making options	2	–1	11	64	31	159	99	70	–12
All other trading	577	550	828	983	1,148	1,349	1,462	1,303	1,866
Gains/Losses from Investment Accounts									
Realized gains/losses	560	574	607	738	714	1,089	1,143	68	1,392
Unrealized gains/losses	456	570	380	496	698	838	1,244	80	1,192
Profits/Losses from Underwriting	104	–24	160	166	–10	187	–162	–40	155
from Equities	1,328	1,568	2,316	3,541	2,706	4,250	5,939	5,157	5,158
Margin Interest	403	424	328	755	248	748	1,372	1,248	1,218
Revenue from Sale of Investment Company Shares	2,089	2,890	2,011	2,130	2,868	2,578	2,920	3,352	3,029
Fees: Supervisory, Advisory, Administrative	105	122	288	952	751	1,643	2,801	2,209	1,414
Revenue from Research Services	175	275	356	570	694	947	1,467	1,812	1,889
Commodities Revenue	14	16	8	19	11	18	46	24	23
Securities-Related Other Revenue	625	581	663	826	739	983	1,065	1,093	1,379
Other Revenue	1,728	2,965	3,942	4,385	6,283	7,176	9,552	11,680	14,703
Total Revenue	586	1,229	1,056	1,217	1,792	1,758	2,117	2,799	2,762
	16,030	19,796	23,210	29,566	31,216	38,621	50,082	50,811	51,825

Table B-10
(Continued)

	1980	1981	1982	1983	1984	1985	1986	1987	1988
Expenses									
Brokers' Compensation	$3,050	$3,334	$4,104	$5,750	$5,249	$6,904	$9,184	$9,335	$7,582
Clerical and Administrative Employee Expense	2,548	3,086	3,703	4,890	5,148	6,219	8,423	9,080	9,283
Partners and Officers Employment Expense	568	648	754	982	934	1,120	1,358	1,508	1,338
Other Employee Compensation	170	191	258	448	396	331	440	631	528
Floor Expenses	754	725	864	1,143	1,163	1,310	1,698	2,188	1,754
Brokerage paid to brokers	263	265	317	390	399	442	557	764	666
Commissions and clearance	283	247	276	390	395	460	644	833	562
Clearance paid to nonbrokers	162	156	208	247	258	285	357	426	402
Commissions paid to others	45	57	64	116	110	124	140	166	124
Communications	838	1,103	1,270	1,538	1,766	1,922	2,288	2,556	2,550
Occupancy and Equipment	514	678	853	1,138	1,504	1,831	2,179	2,729	3,053
Promotional Costs	347	457	530	735	769	842	1,036	1,203	1,003
Interest Expense	3,445	5,685	5,481	6,058	9,505	10,128	12,425	14,271	16,311
Losses—Errors and Bad Debts	205	154	193	233	212	266	432	1,143	438
Data-Processing Costs	156	217	273	343	420	478	632	760	737
Nonrecurring Charges	31	17	7	99	26	99	71	100	56
Regulatory Fees and Expenses	66	79	101	134	145	245	310	328	372
Other Expenses	1,077	1,281	1,784	2,251	2,372	2,797	4,096	3,806	4,331
Total Expenses	13,767	17,652	20,175	25,743	29,608	34,481	44,571	49,639	49,335
Net Income	2,263	2,144	3,035	3,824	1,608	4,140	5,512	1,172	2,490
Net Income after Tax	1,222	1,158	1,639	2,065	868	2,236	N/A	N/A	N/A

Source: Securities Industry Association.

Table B-11
Combined Profit and Loss Statements
Large Investment Banks, 1980–1988
($ millions)

	1980	1981	1982	1983	1984	1985	1986	1987	1988
Revenue									
Commissions									
Listed equities, on an exchange	$652	$662	$803	$1,216	$1,068	$1,127	$1,439	$1,816	$1,160
Listed equities, OTC	563	566	702	1,049	915	967	1,185	1,467	945
Options	3	20	8	19	2	5	30	14	7
Debt securities	48	38	57	67	70	74	84	104	62
All other	37	37	35	82	81	81	140	232	145
Gains/Losses from Trading Accounts	1,273	2,042	2,675	2,708	3,397	3,876	5,152	3,831	3,871
Market-making OTC equities	91	70	87	244	119	188	263	346	148
OTC market-making listed equities	0	0	0	0	2	0	0	0	0
Trading debt securities	1,004	1,673	2,095	2,013	2,702	3,021	4,198	2,869	3,313
Market-making options	6	-11	-9	42	-3	103	72	46	-30
All other trading	173	310	503	409	580	565	620	569	440
Gains/Losses from Investment Accounts	277	318	217	365	364	409	523	95	288
Realized gains/losses	218	339	196	282	343	472	627	-10	345
Unrealized gains/losses	60	-21	21	84	22	-64	-101	105	-58
Profits/Losses from Underwriting	332	369	560	1,051	734	1,377	1,968	1,814	1,864
from Equities	121	120	99	230	98	223	354	231	218
Margin Interest	217	232	188	269	385	374	483	610	486
Revenue from Sale of Investment Company Shares	1	2	3	10	11	29	51	40	18
Fees: Supervisory, Advisory, Administrative	15	51	57	85	111	175	308	353	399
Revenue from Research Services	1	0	1	0	0	0	22	1	0
Commodities Revenue	14	15	20	62	65	290	236	197	432
Other Securities-Related Revenue	663	1,328	2,061	1,984	3,327	3,490	3,883	4,728	7,516
Other Revenue	230	627	361	458	640	952	1,195	1,289	1,014
Total Revenue	3,674	5,646	6,944	8,209	10,103	12,098	15,261	14,774	17,049

Table B-11
(Continued)

	1980	1981	1982	1983	1984	1985	1986	1987	1988
Expenses									
Brokers' Compensation	$334	$441	$604	$857	$786	$1,123	$1,533	$1,438	$1,111
Clerical and Administrative Employee Expense	464	595	794	1,048	1,140	1,302	1,919	2,172	2,357
Partners and Officers Employment Expense	122	143	193	289	301	401	523	600	637
Other Employee Compensation	0	0	0	0	0	0	0	0	0
Floor Expenses	95	98	143	203	216	219	327	479	465
Brokerage paid to brokers	49	54	77	106	121	131	185	292	290
Commission and clearance	31	28	39	65	60	50	84	115	82
Clearance paid to nonbrokers	16	17	28	32	35	39	58	72	94
Commissions paid to others	0	0	0	0	0	0	0	0	0
Communications	109	141	172	231	261	287	394	445	410
Occupancy and Equipment	77	101	134	206	259	317	416	555	656
Promotional Costs	55	69	79	110	140	149	205	241	194
Interest Expense	1,510	2,859	3,157	3,358	5,318	5,722	6,435	6,736	8,655
Losses—Errors and Bad Debts	12	14	22	29	21	24	43	169	19
Data-Processing Costs	26	38	45	68	85	141	201	254	268
Nonrecurring Charges	0	1	0	0	0	7	19	59	12
Regulatory Fees and Expenses	5	8	10	23	28	34	50	41	38
Other Expenses	217	269	385	415	394	615	1,130	895	796
Total Expenses	3,025	4,775	5,739	6,836	8,948	10,332	13,193	14,082	15,616
Net Income	649	871	1,205	1,373	1,155	1,766	2,067	693	1,433
Net Income after Tax	351	470	651	742	624	953	N/A	N/A	N/A

Source: Securities Industry Association.

Table B-12
Staffing Analysis of Large Investment Banks

	1980	1982	1984	1986	1987	1988
Total Compensation ($ millions)	$920	$1,592	$2,228	$3,975	$4,209	$4,105
Pretax Profits ($ millions)	$649	$1,205	$1,155	$2,067	$693	$1,433
Total Number of Employees	15,773	19,922	25,124	38,223	36,201	34,729
Per Employee Compensation ($ thousands)	$58	$80	$89	$104	$116	$118
Pretax Profits ($ thousands)	$41	$60	$46	$54	$19	$41
Ratio of Profits to Compensation	0.71	0.75	0.52	0.52	0.16	0.35

Source: Securities Industry Association.

Table B-13
All-American Investment Research Team
(Team Count on Both an Unweighted* and a Weighted** Basis)

| | Unweighted Rankings | | | | | | | | Weighted Rankings | | | | | | | |
| | 1985 | | 1986 | | 1987 | | 1988 | | 1988 | | 1987 | | 1986 | | 1985 | |
	Count	Rank	Count	Rank	Count	Rank	Count	Rank	Count	Rank	Count	Rank	Count	Rank	Count	Rank
Goldman, Sachs	34	3	37	3	32	3	42	1	102	1	81	3	83	3	83	2
Drexel Burnham Lambert	24	10	27	6	32	3	41	2	88	3	72	4	58	5	48	8
First Boston	35	2	39	2	44	2	40	3	98	2	95	1	87	2	83	2
Merrill Lynch	46	1	46	1	45	1	39	4	84	4	105	2	114	1	101	1
Prudential-Bache	—	—	17	12	29	6	34	5	55	7	48	8	31	11	—	—
PaineWebber	27	6	31	4	29	6	33	6	65	5	55	5	68	4	51	5
Shearson Lehman	12	14	11	15	13	15	32	7	50	9	21	15	—	—	18	15
Donaldson Lufkin & Jenrette	25	9	28	5	28	8	29	8	59	6	52	6	53	6	49	7
Smith Barney Harris Upham	24	10	25	10	31	5	29	8	52	8	49	7	40	9	39	11
Salomon Brothers	26	7	26	8	27	9	25	10	48	10	48	8	49	7	50	6
Kidder, Peabody	30	4	27	6	24	11	19	11	37	11	46	10	45	8	53	4
Dean Witter Reynolds	26	7	15	13	17	12	18	12	35	12	34	12	30	12	48	8
Morgan Stanley	29	5	26	8	27	9	17	13	26	14	38	11	36	10	42	10
Wertheim Schroder	22	12	18	11	15	14	15	14	25	15	25	13	30	12	33	12
Cowen & Co.	10	15	13	14	—	16	13	15	29	13	—	—	23	14	24	13
C.J. Lawrence, Morgan Grenfell	—	—	—	—	—	—	—	15	—	—	—	—	—	—	—	—
E.F. Hutton	15	13	—	16	—	12	—	—	—	—	23	14	17	15	—	—
Oppenheimer	—	—	—	—	—	—	—	—	—	—	—	—	—	—	20	14
Sanford C. Bernstein	—	—	—	—	—	—	—	—	15	16	—	—	—	—	—	—
C.J. Lawrence	—	—	—	—	—	—	—	—	15	16	—	—	—	—	—	—
Montgomery Securities	—	—	—	—	—	—	—	—	13	18	—	—	—	—	—	—
Bear, Stearns	—	—	—	—	—	—	—	—	9	19	—	—	—	—	—	—

* Unweighted count: Total of individual counts of first, second, and third team selections plus runners-up.
** Weighted count: Total as before but with 4 rating assigned to a first-teamer down to 1 assigned to runner-up.
Sources: Wall Street Letter, Institutional Investor, various issues.

Table B-14
U.S. Merger Volume, 1966–1988

	Value of Merger Transactions ($ billions)	As Percentage of Market Value of Outstanding Equities
1966	$13.6E	2.0%
1967	27.8E	3.2
1968	43.6	4.2
1969	23.7	2.6
1970	16.4	1.8
1971	12.6	1.2
1972	16.7	1.4
1973	16.7	1.8
1974	12.5	1.8
1975	11.8	1.3
1976	20.0	1.9
1977	21.9	2.2
1978	34.2	3.3
1979	43.5	3.5
1980	44.3	2.7
1981	82.6	5.3
1982	53.7	3.0
1983	73.1	3.4
1984	122.2	5.6
1985	179.8	7.0
1986	173.1	5.1
1987	163.7	5.0
1988	247.6	9.9

Source: W T Grimm, Federal Reserve Board.

APPENDIX C

JAPANESE FINANCIAL SERVICES STATISTICS

Table C-1
Consolidated Income Statements of All Japanese Security Firms, 1983–1987
(¥ billions)

			Years Ending September		
	1983	1984	1985	1986	1987
Operating Revenues					
Brokerage	¥9,011	¥10,869	¥14,082	¥24,387	¥32,033
Commission, other	3,420	4,428	5,416	6,910	10,343
Financial income	3,205	3,876	4,711	5,280	5,625
Trading income	1,657	2,098	3,482	4,576	4,669
Variance	—	2	1	2	2
Total Operating Revenues	17,293	21,273	27,692	41,155	52,672
Operating Expenses	13,091	15,665	19,056	25,163	30,534
Less financial expenses	1,661	2,084	2,537	2,829	2,362
Adjusted operating expenses	11,430	13,581	16,519	22,334	28,172

Gross Profit (before corporate overhead)	5,863	7,692	11,173	18,821	24,500
Adjustments to Gross Profit					
Corporate overhead (including financial expenses)	1,661	2,084	2,537	2,829	2,363
Extraordinary items	174	249	407	575	36
Undetailed variance	−17	−14	−8	58	577
Total Adjustments	1,818	2,319	2,936	3,462	2,976
Net Income before Taxes	4,045	5,373	8,237	15,359	21,524
Less reserve for taxes	2,414	2,900	4,803	8,958	11,388
Net Income	1,631	2,473	3,434	6,401	10,136

Source: Japanese Securities Dealers Association.

Table C-2
Growth Statistics of Tokyo Stock Exchange and All Stock Exchanges in Japan, 1949–1988

End of Year	No. of Companies Listed		No. Shares Listed (billions)		Shareholders' Equity (¥ billions)		Market Value (¥ billions)	
	Tokyo	Japan	Tokyo	Japan	Tokyo	Japan	Tokyo	Japan
1949	529	681	2	2	—	—	¥122	¥129
1950	583	764	2	3	—	—	169	179
1951	554	729	3	3	—	—	257	273
1952	575	758	5	5	—	—	641	675
1953	587	784	7	7	—	—	847	894
1954	599	782	9	9	—	—	743	782
1955	596	783	10	11	—	—	1,058	1,102
1956	596	786	15	15	—	—	1,640	1,705
1957	602	789	19	19	—	—	1,675	1,746
1958	601	786	21	22	—	—	2,323	2,409
1959	603	792	26	26	—	—	3,777	3,929
1960	599	785	33	34	—	—	5,411	5,644
1961	1,007	1,265	50	50	—	—	6,140	6,430
1962	1,183	1,455	60	62	—	—	7,661	8,003
1963	1,258	1,574	69	72	—	—	7,428	7,718
1964	1,270	1,591	79	82	—	—	7,425	7,694
1965	1,255	1,577	80	83	—	—	8,511	8,805

Year								
1966	1,246	1,562	83	86	—	—	9,390	9,737
1967	1,248	1,561	88	92	—	—	9,271	9,639
1968	1,242	1,552	94	98	—	—	12,665	13,134
1969	1,250	1,556	103	107	—	—	18,353	19,030
1970	1,280	1,580	114	119	—	11,075	16,236	16,825
1971	1,303	1,606	122	127	—	13,018	22,715	23,520
1972	1,323	1,627	132	137	—	15,575	48,055	49,548
1973	1,372	1,680	144	150	14,104	18,116	38,556	40,034
1974	1,390	1,709	152	159	16,226	21,429	36,042	37,469
1975	1,398	1,713	166	173	17,122	23,413	43,245	44,780
1976	1,401	1,716	175	182	18,960	23,590	52,994	54,923
1977	1,407	1,724	186	193	20,463	27,694	51,574	53,638
1978	1,389	1,709	192	200	29,045	30,356	66,342	69,065
1979	1,398	1,723	199	207	32,380	33,783	69,303	72,024
1980	1,402	1,729	208	216	36,121	37,575	77,075	79,952
1981	1,412	1,745	222	231	41,138	42,794	91,906	94,862
1982	1,427	1,769	231	240	46,484	48,335	98,090	101,242
1983	1,441	1,789	240	249	51,287	53,304	126,746	131,231
1984	1,444	1,802	249	259	56,654	58,935	161,812	167,496
1985	1,476	1,829	259	268	62,496	65,082	190,127	196,222
1986	1,499	1,866	268	278	69,368	71,711	285,471	293,028
1987	1,532	1,912	281	291	79,817	79,879	336,707	345,604
1988	1,571	1,967	295	306	90,701	92,825	476,850	488,065

Source: Japanese Securities Dealers Association.

Table C-3
A. *TSE Stock Trading Volume and Value (First and Second Sections), 1980–1988*

Calendar Year	No. of Trading Days	Volume (billions of shares)		Value (¥ billions)	
		Total	Daily Average	Total	Daily Average
1980	285	102.2	0.36	¥36,490	¥128.0
1981	285	107.5	0.38	49,365	173.2
1982	285	78.5	0.28	36,572	128.3
1983	286	104.3	0.36	54,845	191.8
1984	287	103.7	0.36	67,974	236.8
1985	285	121.9	0.43	78,711	276.2
1986	279	197.7	0.71	159,836	572.8
1987	274	263.6	0.96	250,737	915.1
1988	273	282.6	1.04	285,521	1,045.9

Source: Tokyo Stock Exchange.

B. *Stock Transactions by Investment Sectors, Percentage, 1982–1988*
(Based on Value)

Calendar Year	Corporations	Individuals	Foreigners	Total
1982	48.4%	40.7%	10.9%	100%
1983	42.4	43.7	13.9	100
1984	43.1	42.8	14.1	100
1985	50.6	36.9	12.5	100
1986	59.9	29.2	10.9	100
1987	62.0	27.7	10.4	100
1988	67.9	25.0	7.2	100

Note: "Corporations" include securities companies, insurance companies, banks, investment trusts, business corporations, and others.
Source: Tokyo Stock Exchange.

Table C-4
Big Four Market Share of Trading Volume, 1982–1987

A. OTC Bond Trading

	Fiscal Year*						
	1982	1983	1984	1985	1986	1987	1988**
Transactions (¥trillions)	¥319	¥360	¥564	¥1,742	¥2,567	¥5,416	¥3,967
Market share (%)							
Nomura	27.4%	25.0%	22.3%	13.2%	10.6%	14.2%	12.6%
Daiwa	18.0	17.1	17.1	9.5	8.0	6.5	9.0
Nikko	14.5	15.2	14.3	8.0	6.6	5.5	7.2
Yamaichi	15.1	15.4	13.9	8.4	8.4	5.3	6.6

B. Stock Transaction Volume

	Fiscal Year						
	1982	1983	1984	1985	1986	1987	1988**
On the 8 stock exchanges (billions of shares)	88.7	123.5	116.2	151.5	225.2	304.6	307.1
Market share (%)							
Nomura	15.1%	14.8%	14.5%	15.1%	7.7%	18.7%	15.0%
Daiwa	11.1	11.4	11.8	10.9	10.7	10.3	9.4
Nikko	11.8	10.9	10.4	10.2	10.6	9.7	8.7
Yamaichi	10.6	10.6	10.9	10.5	10.3	11.5	9.3

*Ending in September.
**1988 numbers are for 1988 only.
Source: Daiwa Securities.

Table C-5
Japanese Bond Market Volume, 1980–1987
(¥ billions)

| Calendar Year | No. of Listed Issues[a] | Government Bonds | | Convertible Bonds[b] | Yen-Based Foreign Bonds | Others[c] | Total | Tokyo OTC Markets[d] | |
		Block Trades	Total					"Repos"	Total
1980	527	¥1,432	¥1,601	¥2,178	¥14.7	¥81.4	¥3,874	¥156,007	¥272,503
1981	572	2,236	2,387	3,102	14.8	74.4	5,578	141,531	288,429
1982	641	3,983	4,172	2,383	13.9	71.6	6,641	135,274	327,108
1983	659	8,573	8,792	6,592	12.7	51.9	15,448	137,205	385,097
1984	736	22,337	22,601	11,713	12.7	32.6	34,359	148,703	692,470
1985	854	39,152	39,428	22,165	20.2	29.2	61,642	251,557	2,164,669
1986	973	49,648	49,917	53,078	37.4	26.0	103,059	590,803	2,619,876
1987	1,192	56,358	56,918	50,869	88.4	24.0	107,899	1,216,891	5,544,390
1988	1,360	34,474	34,842	43,513	21.0	21.4	78,398	1,314,326	4,175,170

Notes: a. As of the end of each year.
  b. Includes bonds with stock subscription warrants.
  c. Includes municipal, government-guaranteed, and industrial bonds and bank debentures.
  d. Volume is total of sales and purchases in all sorts of bonds, including convertibles.
     1. Trading volume is counted on par-value basis.

Source: Japanese Securities Dealers Association.

Table C-6
New Japanese Bond Issues via Public Offerings, 1982–1988
(¥ *billions*)

| Calendar Year | Interest-Bearing Government Bonds | | Discount Government Notes | Municipal Bonds | Government-Guaranteed Bonds | Corporate Bonds | | | Yen-Based Foreign Bonds | Total |
	Long-Term	Medium-Term				Electric Power	NTT	Others		
1982	¥11,937	¥3,849	¥469	¥669	¥2,218	¥841	¥120	¥306	¥663	¥21,071
1983	14,869	5,045	492	699	2,619	439	105	209	720	25,197
1984	13,640	3,913	658	794	2,634	727	185	85	915	23,552
1985	16,699	3,762	682	766	2,455	538	235	112	1,115	26,364
1986	16,219	3,322	779	903	2,907	490	300	186	637	25,753
1987	17,986	3,027	622	846	2,202	530	385	28	448	26,074
1988	17,557	2,505	628	1,101	2,513	688	150	72	635	25,849

Notes: 1. Bonds issued in foreign countries are excluded.
2. Convertible bonds and bonds with stock subscription warrants are excluded.
Source: The Bond Underwriters Association of Japan.

Table C-7
Underwriting Volumes by Big Four Japanese Securities Firms, 1973–1987
Total of Bonds and Stocks
(¥ millions)

Fiscal Year Ending in September	Nomura	Yamaichi	Nikko	Daiwa
1973	¥684,356	¥536,174	¥491,989	¥442,257
1974	476,530	373,002	357,736	320,070
1975	545,851	446,668	432,452	419,286
1976	779,904	490,876	487,536	477,427
1977	1,150,409	592,650	631,008	585,601
1978	1,717,175	1,012,532	1,000,491	929,283
1979	1,266,911	743,393	707,548	707,575
1980	1,436,228	755,285	776,389	686,301
1981	1,469,067	818,347	821,683	742,396
1982	1,660,468	1,001,356	952,365	948,270
1983	1,330,701	753,589	701,063	691,349
1984	1,501,803	982,048	920,531	1,014,845
1985	2,052,991	1,240,087	1,238,422	1,213,508
1986	1,917,581	1,224,709	1,140,101	1,184,148
1987	2,885,846	1,692,114	1,672,755	1,644,793

Source: Daiwa Securities.

Table C-8
Ranking of Japanese Financial Organizations by Number of Owned
Stocks of Customer Companies

Rank	Financial Organization	No. of Shares (millions)	No. of Companies
1	Nippon Life Insurance	10,814	1,064
2	Daiichi Life Insurance	5,725	655
3	Mitsubishi Trust	5,579	759
4	IBJ	5,106	606
5	Sumitomo Trust	4,577	815
6	Meiji Life Insurance	4,538	492
7	Nihon Shoken Kessai	4,500	247
8	Sumitomo Life Insurance	4,340	600
9	DKB	3,798	670
10	Mitsui Trust	3,315	613
11	Fuji Bank	3,258	648
12	Yasuda Trust	3,220	669
13	Asahi Life Insurance	3,212	364
14	LTCB	3,150	409
15	Mitsubishi Bank	2,982	579
16	Sanwa Bank	2,909	605
17	Sumitomo Bank	2,855	459
18	Toyo Trust	2,828	608
19	Mitsui Bank	2,386	386
20	Tokio Marine & Fire	2,265	481
21	Daiwa Bank	1,897	426
22	Tokai Bank	1,811	504
23	Mitsui Life Insurance	1,678	235
24	Taiyo Life Insurance	1,617	87
25	Taiyo Kobe Bank	1,454	552
32	Kyowa Bank	933	278
35	Bank of Tokyo	816	160
46	Nomura Securities	349	130

Note: For each customer company, only the twenty largest stock owners are counted.
Source: Toyo-Keizai, "Kigyo Keiretsu Soran 1989," Triangle Research.

Table C-9
Ranking in Number of Customer Companies, 1988[a]
(National)

Rank	Banks	No. of Companies	Share (%)
1	DKB	8,113	12.0%
2	Mitsubishi	6,278	9.3
3	Sanwa	5,585	8.2
4	Sumitomo	5,315	7.8
5	Fuji	5,235	7.7
6	Tokai	4,223	6.2
7	Mitsui	3,805	5.6
8	Taiyo Kobe	3,392	5.0
9	Kyowa	2,503	3.7
10	Daiwa	2,174	3.2
11	Takugin	2,007	3.0
12	Hokuriku	1,582	2.3
13	Saitama	1,465	2.2
14	Shizuoka	1,402	2.1
15	Shoko Chukin	1,249	1.8
16	Yokohama	1,129	1.7
17	Hiroshima	1,074	1.6
18	Fukuoka	1,072	1.6
19	Hachijuni	1,016	1.5
20	Joyo	958	1.4
21	Daishi	940	1.4
22	Chugoku	939	1.4
23	Ashikaga	925	1.4
24	Shichijushichi	907	1.3
25	Hokkaido	839	1.2
26	Gunma	776	1.1
27	Chiba	773	1.1
28	Juroku	724	1.1
29	Yamaguchi	683	1.0
30	IBJ	639	0.9
	Total	67,722	100.0

a. Number of companies that designated each bank as a main bank.
Source: Diamond Weekly Magazine, December 10, 1988.

Table C-10
Ranking in Number of Customer Companies, 1988[a]
(National)

Rank	Bank	No. of Companies	Share (%)
1	DKB	25,790	11.2
2	Mitsubishi	21,966	9.6
3	Fuji	19,059	8.3
4	Sumitomo	18,703	8.2
5	Sanwa	18,060	7.9
6	Mitsui	13,825	6.0
7	Tokai	13,567	5.9
8	Taiyo Kobe	13,330	5.8
9	Shoko Chukin	10,783	4.7
10	Kyowa	9,981	4.4
11	Daiwa	8,407	3.7
12	Takugin	5,479	2.4
13	Saitama	4,720	2.1
14	Hokuriku	4,146	1.8
15	Yokohama	3,944	1.7
16	IBJ	3,307	1.4
17	Shizuoka	3,150	1.4
18	Fukuoka	2,905	1.3
19	Hokkaido	2,809	1.2
20	Hiroshima	2,581	1.1
21	Norin-Chukin	2,534	1.1
22	Joyo	2,394	1.0
23	Mitsui Trust	2,382	1.0
24	Mitsubishi Trust	2,381	1.0
25	Ashikaga	2,316	1.0
26	LTCB	2,262	1.0
27	Nihinihon	2,212	1.0
28	Sumitomo Trust	2,166	0.9
29	Chiba	2,147	0.9
30	Nagoya Sogo	2,035	0.9
	Total	229,341	100.0

a. Number of companies that do some business with each bank.
Source: Diamond Weekly Magazine, December 10, 1988.

Table C-11
Combinations of Main Banks and Managing Securities Houses
Serving the Same Corporate Clients

	Nomura	Daiwa	Nikko	Yamaichi	Other
Daiichi Kangyo Bank	69	19	38	58	32
Sumitomo	60	74	13	32	3
Fuji	42	19	20	102	16
Mitsubishi	33	14	71	50	11
Sanwa	82	26	13	33	24
Mitsui	84	15	18	19	10
Industrial Bank of Japan	25	12	42	35	14
Long-Term Credit Bank	12	4	5	6	3
Mitsubishi Trust	2	4	10	6	4
Mitsui Trust	9	1	5	8	0
Sumitomo Trust	4	8	9	5	3

Source: Koichi Noda, "Recent Developments and Challenges by the Japanese Banks and Their Strategies for Future Survival," unpublished independent research project, Harvard Business School, May 1988.

Table C-12
Consolidated Balance Sheets of All Japanese Securities Companies
(¥ billions)

	1970	1980	1987/9
Assets			
Bank Balances, Cash and Deposits	¥183	¥581	¥2,705
Securities in Inventory	338	500	2,011
Margin Transactions (Loans)	129	1,252	6,525
Securities Deposited by Others	620	2,139	12,215
Other	124	368	1,076
Total Current Assets	1,394	4,840	24,532
Fixed Assets	154	432	1,540
Total Assets	1,548	5,272	26,072
Liabilities			
Short-Term Borrowings	401	644	2,979
Margin Transactions (Borrowings)	48	506	1,915
Securities Deposited for Short Term	204	351	478
Securities Deposited in Lieu of Cash	410	1,785	11,732
Other	157	760	3,861
Total Current Liabilities	1,220	4,046	20,965
Fixed Liabilities	46	97	679
Specific Reserves	80	91	276
Shareholders' Equity			
Capital Stock	84	263	686
Legal Reserves	10	109	508
Surpluses	108	666	2,958
Total	202	1,038	4,152
Total Liabilities and Equity	1,548	5,272	26,072

Source: Japanese Securities Dealers Association.

Table C-13

Educational Backgrounds of the Big Four Japanese Securities Firms' Leadership Compared to Those of Selective Japanese Commercial Banks

Alma Mater of Executives	Nomura	Daiwa	Nikko	Yamaichi	Fuji Bank	Mitsubishi Bank	Sumitomo Bank	Daiichi Kangyo Bank	Industrial Bank of Japan	Long-Term Credit Bank
University of Tokyo	8	3	5	6	22	23	16	11	30	12
Kyoto University	3	4	1	2	3	0	6	3	2	4
Tohoku University	1	0	0	0	0	1	0	2	1	2
Hokkaido University	1	1	0	0	0	0	0	0	0	1
Kyushu University	0	0	0	0	0	0	0	1	0	1
Osaka University	0	2	0	1	0	0	4	1	0	0
Nagoya University	1	0	1	1	0	0	0	0	0	1
Hitotsubashi University	3	4	2	1	4	5	2	2	5	3
Waseda University	4	3	5	4	1	0	1	1	0	0
Keio University	2	6	4	5	1	5	3	6	2	1
Other Private	4	7	6	12	0	1	4	1	0	0
Other National	9	2	10	1	2	0	5	2	2	0
Municipal	—	3	1	2	1	0	0	4	0	0
Vocational School/ High School	4	2	4	5	1	0	0	0	0	0
Total	40	37	39	40	35	35	41	34	42	25
Youngest Member (Class of)	1965	1961	1961	1961	1959	1959	1962	1957	1959	1960

Source: Koichi Noda, "Recent Developments and Challenges by the Japanese Banks and Their Strategies for Future Survival," unpublished independent research project, Harvard Business School, May 1988.

INDEX

411